# PRINCIPLES

Principles: A Manual For Understanding Human Existence
The Complete Story Of Creation And Evolution

Copyright © 2016 by Frank Knowlton

All rights reserved. No part of this book may be used or reproduced in any form, electronic or mechanical, including photocopying, recording, or scanning into any information storage and retrieval system, without written permission from the author except in the case of brief quotation embodied in critical articles and reviews.

Book design by The Troy Book Makers

Printed in the United States of America

The Troy Book Makers • Troy, New York • thetroybookmakers.com

To order additional copies of this title, contact your favorite local bookstore or visit www.tbmbooks.com

ISBN: 978-1-61468-349-0

# PRINCIPLES

## A Manual For Understanding Human Existence

THE COMPLETE STORY OF
CREATION AND EVOLUTION

Frank Knowlton

# Introduction

Science has always fascinated me, especially the phenomena of electricity and gravity. My interests were further fueled when my good friend and neighbor gave me some of his old textbooks which explained electronics and the fundamentals of electricity. At about the same time, I began working for an electrical contractor and was sponsored in an electrical apprenticeship program. It was while attending classes at the apprenticeship program that my interest in the phenomenon of electricity and the importance of electrical theory became deeper. I learned that phenomena were "things", circumstances, unusual events, and principles, and that many of these events can be detected by the physical senses, yet these events or principles could not be fully explained. Therefore, my studies led me to conclude mankind did not yet have the answers concerning these actions.

This mode of thinking is where I got the idea to focus my own investigation into the old and forgotten sources of scientific knowledge. Those scientific building blocks of knowledge which were the very foundation of modern science. I was thinking that there was the possibility that some bit of knowledge was missed or misinterpreted by researchers, and now should be rediscovered and re-evaluated. I was on my way in search of the source of electricity and the source of gravity, focusing on the oldest sources of scientific knowledge available.

Previously, I had been a student of the mystical "readings" which came from the famous clairvoyant, Edgar Cayce. While living near the Edgar Cayce Library, I became aware that there were other clairvoyants who had existed at one time or another in history. Andrew Jackson Davis, the Poughkeepsie Seer, was one of those mystics from the past. He was a known clairvoyant who had written numerous books, but was not popular. I found a few of Davis' books in the library and attempted to read them, but soon realized why he was not popular. His writings are intricate and complex, resulting in great difficulty reading a few paragraphs, so these books were forgotten. Now, thirty years later, living in the Hudson Valley, I am still doing this scientific research into gravity and electricity and still had not found the answers I was seeking. For some reason I remembered Andrew Jackson Davis and wondered if there was the possibility of hidden and undiscovered knowledge to be found in his writings.

I knew a bit about clairvoyance from studying the insights from beyond man's awake consciousness which were given by Edgar Cayce and so I suppose I had a good understanding of metaphysical language, which gave me the ability to decipher what I was reading in Mr. Davis book.

What I was reading was absolutely astonishing. Davis' book, THE PRINCIPLES OF NATURE, HER DIVINE REVELATION AND A VOICE TO MANKIND published 1847, is divided into three parts, and it is within part two that is buried among the mass of words, the complete story of creation and evolution. It is not the biblical story found in the Judeo-Christian Bible. Davis' version of creation gives so much more detail and goes into great depth. I soon realized, without doubt, that Davis' view of creation had much more scientific depth than the biblical one, almost as if it had come directly from God.

It was disappointing for me to finally realize that probably no one else was aware of the full extent of what Davis had given to mankind. I searched and searched for someone else who may have read Davis, discovering what I had read, but all indications pointed to the obscurity of this book. Yes, some people claimed to have read Davis, but I wondered why they were not jumping up and down with a joyful heart, expressing this "wonder" to the rest of the world. I expressed to all my family and friends my findings and some even attempted to read Davis, but they expressed reading him was difficult, if not impossible, or they were not interested in his peculiar knowledge. I decided to re-tell the story of creation, as derived from Davis' book, putting it in a manner which would be easier to read and understand. In order to preserve Davis' message, I have frequently used his unique words and phrases throughout. And that is how the manuscript, PRINCIPLES, came to be.

One last note on the writing style of Andrew Jackson Davis. The information flowing out of his writings are excessively repetitive in their nature. Mr. Davis' method of relating his story of evolution is by building upon his main theme. The story spirals along, reviewing what was explained previously, then adding new detail. This pattern is repeated throughout his book.

So, may I suggest that the reader follow along with this story as it explains the creation and evolution of man, as it spirals along on its journey, and if you will, please read the whole story before giving judgment.

Dedicated to the advancement of mankind,

*Frank Knowlton*

# Section 1

In the beginning the **Universe** was one boundless, undefinable, and unimaginable, ocean of **liquid fire**!

The Universe was one vast expanse of a liquid substance without bounds. This was the original condition of Matter, it existed without forms, because it was just One Form. It had no motion, yet, it was itself, eternal and unending motion!

The original was a Whole. Parts did not exist and particles did not exist. This boundless liquid fire was one Particle. It had no beginning and has no end.

The Universe had **no disconnected power** because it was One, but realize, the Whole had the **essence** of **omnipotent power**, and its truly inconceivable magnitude and constitution were of such a nature, to have-not yet develop forces.

So then at the very beginning, **Matter** and **Power** were existing as a whole **inseparable**. This is the state of oneness! This is the Vortex.

The **Matter** contained the **Substance** to produce all suns, all worlds, and system of worlds. This sufficient supply of Matter which was contained in the Whole, possessed the "qualities" to **produce** all things that are existing on all worlds throughout the Universe.

The **Power** contained in this Great Vortex was the **Great Positive Mind**! And, the phenomenon and principle this Mind developed was **Eternal Motion**! So, it can be said that God moved and the Universe came into being, and all came into existence. And this Great Positive Power contained **Goodness**, **Justice**, **Mercy**, and **Truth**! It contained the **original** and **essential Principle** that is displayed throughout the immensity of space. This One Power is controlling worlds and systems of worlds.

This One Great **Vortex** and Great **Center** of worlds – this Great Power of Intelligence – The Great **Germ** of existences – was one World! The Intelligence had Wisdom **equal** to Matter, and was able to plan and produce all those system of worlds existing in the Universe and to direct their infinite movements. This Intelligent Power had Goodness to **give** perfect harmony, and was able to supply usefulness to all parts of Space.

The Great Power produced **Motion**, **Life**, **Sensation**, and **Intelligence**, to be dispersed upon the countless worlds in existence. These principles are to be the **ultimates** of Creation. Therefore, **Matter** and **Motion** were the only Principles developed; there were no other celestial bodies or objects in existence. Matter and Motion are **co-eternal princi-**

ples**, capable of producing all other Forms, and realize, these Principles were the Germ of all-else in existence.

So in the beginning the Great Original Mass was a **substance** containing within itself the **embryo** of its own perfection, and it became **activated** because of its own laws, and was controlled, guided, and perfected, as a result of its own omnipotent Power. It had possessed and contained the power of **Progression**, but had not progressed. **Crystallization** and **organic life** would be two general developments.

And so, the Great Mass abounded with **Heat** and immense **Fire**, each **seeming-particle** was in reality non-existent. The Whole was a mass of liquid lava. Then, the **first elements** emanating from the Vortex to be developed were **Light** and **Heat**.

The Power is **God** and is the **First Cause**, is the Divine Mind, is the Creator of All. And at the beginning **Cause** and **Effect** were involved in one Universal undulating Motion. The Whole, was flaming with **internal heat** that now was a Cause, and would **evolve** as an Effect the Principle of Light.

It was Matter, Heat, and Light, which constituted the **primitive condition** of the co-eternal material Substance of the Vortex. And as said, Matter and Motion constituted the original condition of all things, existing as an **unparticled** Substance.

The **Original Form** in existence was an **angular** Form or structure. This original angular Form **contained** the **Principles** and **nature** of all other Forms which will be developed.

The progression of the **angular** form of Matter evolved to the **circular** form. But, this circular form at first **did-not** assume a spherical constitution, but instead, the circular was a **combination** of an angular and rectilinear plane. And so therefore, the **continuance** of the angular to the circular was only a "perpetual progressive Form" ascending in structure towards the **spiral** Form. Then, the spiral developed diameters, axes, and poles, **containing** the perpetual angular; and Matter progressed to a still higher and more perfect form, that of the vortical Form, which properly could be termed the celestial Form of Matter. The celestial form is the Spiritual, containing only what is refined, pure, and everlastingly infinite, and is containing unspeakable and celestial glory, brightness, and grandeur.

The **Vortex**, the inconceivably perfect substance of **The Positive Mind**. This Vortex is a **constant development** of "Inherent Principles and Laws", **progressing**. And each "State" of progression assumed new qualities and involved new developments. Degrees of progression.

An example of degrees of progression: - can be seen occurring as the lowest of particles in existence, evolving and progressing into something like this particular sphere of progression called earth, all occurring because **there-was** a constant development of **Inherent Principles** and **Laws**; the lower and original substance containing the higher substances, only undeveloped; and then finally, the perfected sphere exists and contains and "comprehends" all below it.

The **principle** to understand then, is that "the greatest comprehends the lesser", and the greatest is contained in the lesser. And understand that the lower production, which was first, **contained** the greater; even-though, the greater **is-not** yet developed, except it will be developed by order and by the virtue of **degrees** of **progression**. And so, each "state" **evolved** and assumed new qualities, and it involved new developments, until the highest finally develops and puts-forth its everlasting brightness, and is an **index** of its own origin!

# Section 2

For a period of time unimaginable, Matter and Motion existed and reigned throughout the regions of boundless infinite. There were no-other Forms, and no-other attributes evolved from Power; because, all forms **existed undeveloped** together from the beginning. Those developments of Matter were to be **vehicles** of even more sublime and grand ultimates that are to be eternally developed by the **Design** and **Power** of the great Positive Mind of God which were constantly being sent forth from the Great Vortex of Positive Power.

It was **impossible** for Matter to exist without this principle of, - "inherent and eternal production". And it was just as **impossible** for the internal, invisible, Positive Power to exist without Matter as its **vehicle** and accompaniment.

In order for Matter to assume Forms, the **action** of the Great Positive Power was necessary to **impel** the Matter to **higher states** of progression. So Matter, in this way was acted upon, was developed, until it became a **external Equilibrium**, or the **Negative** of the **Great Positive Power** that was eternally acting upon it. And so, the **positive** and **negative** phenomenon was eternally established in Matter. And Matter was thus **obliged to obey** every impulse or force given it by the **internal Principles** emanating from the Great Positive Mind.

The **Great First Cause** was a cause of Pure Intelligence, it was a **First**, or **Cause Internal**. Matter, with its properties and countless combinations, was an accompaniment or counterpart that may be termed a **Second** or an **Effect**. And then the **external** or countervailing Force **developed-by** the action of the Cause Internal, was a **Third** or **Ultimate**.

God's Creation established - "the Law of Universal and Eternal Motion". In the beginning the Great Positive Mind caused, – the existences of Forms that are now universally manifested in space.

So now, having arrived at this **state** and **order** of material formation of the Universe, and now having learned the true conception of Matter and Motion, and having learned of **their** original combination, and then seeing that there was the **self-establishment** of laws and principles which are **suitable** to develop **ultimate** results, and also, becoming aware of the **adjustment** of laws to enable those results to be produced. This was the condition of these first Elements and Principles in the beginning; and now, they were prepared to develop **Forms**. And these Forms to be produced were **similar** in their character to those qualities and standards of the **internal principles**, involved in the Great Mass, and these Forms to be produced, will be made in the **image** of **God**.

At this very **beginning epoch** and state of infinite original composition within the Vortex, all the laws, the elements, and combinations of elements, were at first, **still involved** and **connected** in the Great Mass, to be later developed, and this is Creation. Then, the continuous development occurred, by order and succession of degrees, and it occurred throughout every avenue of eternal motion, life, and activity, this is evolution.

**Forms** are to be produced and then to be "successively developed" and to be **made visible** simply by consequence of their physical development. But now, before discussing the evolution of the Universe, first it is best to review and contemplate, the **Substances** which the Great Mass contains **undeveloped**.

At first the gross, crude, and lower qualities that are contained in the great Mass, has **particles**, which are almost entirely dissimilar to any particles now known. And so, any attempt at explaining the great quantity and condition of the **original substance**, which was contained in this original mass, would be almost utterly incomprehensible, and would create some obscurity to any of those lower and **more-perfected** particles that compose this mass, this great vehicle of Positive Power. Yet still, a general discussion may be useful in an attempt to express some slight idea or hint of the actual nature and destination of those particles and substances of this Great Mass. What occurred **first**, was that the original great mass **had-contained** the **peculiar combinations** of Matter that would form **a Sun**. This **First-Sun** which had been **repulsed** from the Great Mass, is itself, of so-vast a size, that in time, it is **able** to **form** similar masses of materials which all are similar and which correspond to that original great First Sun which was **first repulsed** and thrown from the great Body, thrown from that Vortex or Infinite Center!

And this First Sun is both the beginning and an **index** – a symbol – a representation - of an eternity of worlds and system of worlds to be developed. So now this First Sun and Index of worlds, is considered and named the **Great Center** of Worlds. And all that follow will be developed in **the same** manner as this First Sun was developed.

The First Sun then **launched** outward to the **extremity** of its own atmospheric circle or atmospheric expanse, **Particles** that would become other suns and worlds. Those Particles would eventually create masses or worlds. And then, each of these now-created similar masses, themselves would all create and have subordinate worlds, and then, those subordinate worlds would have their satellites; **they all**, in order **revolve** around each other, and the whole revolves around the Center or Sun which produced them. And this is the process, the development, and the operation **with all** corresponding suns and constellations, all attended with their many planets and satellites, and **all revolve** around the original Great Center or Sun from which the whole emanated!

And so, here is established the **first motion** of **planetary worlds**! These worlds had developed upon **geometrical principles** the angular, circular, and spiral motions. And this eternal establishment, then becomes **the First System of concentric circles**! And as this **great Fountain** has produced from its inherent substance, an infinite number of worlds; those worlds and their compositions, all continually progress. These planetary worlds of the **first system** would perpetually progress to higher states of development; and realize this has been occurring for an uncountable and unimaginable amount of time.

The **next development** occurring upon these Worlds, would be the **crystallization** of the **internal particles** within these spheres, which produced the various **earthy** and **Mineral substances**. The highest states of mineral productions would eventually, by order of degrees and progression of particles, and after a very long time, bring-forth the great substances of the whole **Plant** kingdom which would evolve upon these worlds. Then, in succession plants and minerals would produce the **Animal** kingdom.

So now in review of the process of development, **remember**, even-though that "thing" which is **first**, **contains** the **ultimate**, also realize that the ultimate contained within the first, then **acts** on all things below it; and those things which are below, which even-though are less perfect, these are still symbols of eternal essences which are to be expanded and developed in the **visible Forms** and spheres or worlds that will be produced to the highest degrees of magnificence.

## Section 3

Gaining an understanding of the **attributes** that are contained in and belonging to **the Great Positive Power**, will possibly lead the mind to an improved understanding of what is contained in the Great Vortex of infinite perfection, **only undeveloped**!

**Power** is seen revealing itself in the actions of **guidance** and **directing** – both the **motion** and **control** of the first **Great World** that was evolved from the original ocean of eternal Matter, the Vortex. This **Power** is itself unlimited and uncontrolled; yet, developing **Wisdom** in the process of universal expansion and extensions of its planetary productions. Power is there in the First system, where there is the perfect and unique **adaptation** of every developing constellation, planet, and satellite, all to **correspond** the great Sun of their central motion, which displays the infinite **Goodness** of Power.

Goodness - is the proper adaptation of things to their ends, and undertaking this goal and doing this process in order to **accomplish** some grand and sublime **Ultimate**.

Then the **strict adherence** and obedience of all these first planetary worlds to the **positive law** of cause and effect, displays infinite and universal **Justice**, with each and every thing obeying the original impetus given it; the impetus given to each in the beginning, when this eternal law was originally established in Matter. And so, **Justice** and **Equity**: consist of an obedience to the Law of cause and effect.

The **accomplishment** of the end desired by the Original Premeditator, God, displays the highest and most perfect attribute of **Mercy**, because, **Light** is evolved from the Great Center; and the first true **Elements** are now developed on these worlds; and, air is universally distributed, sufficient to sustain life and to **equalize** the parts composing the great Whole, - and all to **prepare** suitable habitations for plant and animal existences: and this is the **accomplishment** of the ultimate intended. And in this way is displayed the **exalted** and essential **attributes** of everlasting **Mercy**.

Mercy - consists in adaptation of Parts to the Whole, and in the dissemination and sustaining of Sensitive Beings.

**Power** and its **vehicle** Matter, constituted the **Fountain** from which flow all things, on their journey to their ultimate perfection. And this was the beginning.

Countless amounts of times have passed since the Beginning. A review of the process of Creation will build a deeper understanding, by explaining in greater detail the formation of The First Sun which was developed and also the Circles of Suns that were produced in succession, from the First Sun, including the planets and satellites which are all parts of this First System, and any other heavenly bodies that were in succession produced. So, **first** there was the gradual and progressive development of each Form or Sun, these all originating from the "condition of things" first existing in the great Fiery Mass;  **second**, there was the constant and inevitable actions and manifestations which would occur in every epoch or stage of Motion or development of Motion; - then **third**, there is the mutual adaptation of all things which is plainly visible throughout the Universe, and by the perfect and absolute accomplishment of the end desired.

All the above processes in combination **display** the **perfection** of all those attributes of the Ultimate of the Great Positive Mind, which is Eternal Truth! Because **Truth** is the **inherent principle** of **Divine Law** which determines the absolute, certain, and adequate, accomplishment of any good and glorious end contemplated.

Recall in the beginning events of creation, the inconceivable and original fiery **Mass** of Matter which is inconceivable in its magnitude, and that the substances within its composition are of such "state" of existence, it passes all comprehension. Also in the beginning, **Power** wielding its mighty and energetic influence, being **co-eternal** with the substance of Matter, is also of too great and mighty a nature to be imagined or conceived of. And this was the condition of things in the beginning previously described.

It was explained how **Matter** in **Motion** churning within the great mass, had **interacted** and now reached a state of **material formation**, by the formation of particles. Those **particles** of matter in motion, **contained** self-established laws and principles **suitable** to develop ultimate results, including the adjustment of those laws to produce the ultimate results; these particles **were-now** prepared to develop Forms (spheres). These Forms are to be created and unfolded by a process of **graduated** like-developments. Recall that **undeveloped matter** and motion at first, had an almost entire dissimilarity of particles, all existing in the gross, crude, and lower, qualities of Matter contained in the Great Mass, yet, as will be learned, this Matter also contains the particular combinations of particles that are able to form a Sun, which was first **repulsed** from the Great Body's infinite center. And this First Sun produced others. And as was previously stated, this was the establishment of the **first motion** of planetary worlds.

**First**, what would happen in the infinite mass of Matter or the Fountain, is that there was developed **Heat** and **Light** by virtue of inherent, existing, essential, innate, **Fire**. And Power being **Positive**, developed a **Negative**; or in other words, the eternal **Law** of **Gravitation** was established; and so, in this manner was **Motion** eternally established - occurring in and throughout the vast material composition of the Great Mass.

Now, the extension and outer-limit of the **atmosphere** from the **Great Body** or Fountain, was likewise infinite. And the Great Center constantly gave off Heat and Light, **each** of which was a development of Matter, thrown off by the Fountain's **repelling** power. Flaming with the most inconceivable heat, its **vaporized materials** extended from the nucleus far beyond the extreme bounds of human imagination. This superior combination, as was evolved from the Center, was **suitable** for the formation of immense worlds known as the physical universe.

The **Substance** of heat and light or **anti-particled matter** which has been constantly thrown from the Center since the beginning, **became** at length of time, a **Nebulous Zone** surrounding the immensity of space!

By constant action and development of the **particles** within this nebulous zone, which were subjected to the **motion of attraction, repulsion**, and the **laws of condensation**; including a **repelling** of that Matter which was **averse** and opposed to the process of consolidation, and also a **attracting** of those particles which were of like **affinity** and were suitable to become part of the same Mass; and **this-was** the manner in which the formation of Worlds was first instituted. So, by "the law of progression and development" from the Great Center, until the **material evolved** was "fitted" to produce a World, and then, other worlds, all being similar to the Great Original Source. The similarity of things in the Universe is because, there can only be One Law. There **can-not** be more than one law or else there would be confusion in the Universe.

These first Worlds which were formed would be correctly termed **Suns**, and all were produced from **that** original and inconceivable Mass of unparticled matter which was existing before the process of **consolidation** commenced. There was an incomprehensible and incalculable number of Suns or Centers which were produced by the development of the elements of Heat and Light and their **gradual condensation**. And from these first suns or centers, there were created **systems** of **planets**, each of which revolved around its controlling Center **according** to the development of the **circular** and **spiral** motions, and the influence of attraction and repulsion; this is also known as the laws of **centripetal** and **centrifugal** Forces.

The "first great ring" or "plane" or circle of these condensing and converging formations was in that manner commenced and completed. This took time unimaginable to elapse. And there was the constant evolving and throwing-off from the Great Center - of **Light** still more perfected, and this produced innumerable millions of Suns, which occupied **another** orbit or circle in relation to the Great Parent of their formation! After more time and by a very similar process of **organization** of Parts or particles, these **Suns** of the second circle, by attraction, condensation, repulsion, and the evolution of their own atmospheres, produced planets and satellites, in a manner similar to those infinite formations of the first circle or plane of suns.

The **extreme heat** from the great Center of worlds, whose intensity would transcend any conception of the the hottest artificial fire, was constantly evolving and throwing-off **light** so intense, that the strength of this light would have repelled planets from their orbits near its source, if such were possible, - this radiating light formed another Circle of Suns, the third circle of Suns. Each system constantly develops its laws, forces, and motions, and expands in power and contracts in volume, according to the **law** of **equal magnitudes**. And each of these third circle of Suns possesses matter still **more refined** and unparticled, than those of the former or second system. And because of this refinement the Suns and their planets were formed out of Matter even more refined, as was being evolved from their own Centers. And so, there was an endless circle of suns and formations produced, and each is similar in character to other circles, each circle being a system of eternal systems, and an **index** and symbol of the Great Sun or Focus of undefinable magnitude from which all emanated, from the Great Fountain!

In still more time unimaginable a fourth, a fifth, and a sixth Circle of Suns was established, all in similar fashion.

The **sixth circle** of formations that was produced, these are all **Suns only**. Because these Suns have not yet become properly consolidated and their atmosphere have not yet produced other formations; and so, they are at this time pursuing their undefinable orbits in the form and composition of **blazing comets**.

In a general review, the First Sun or Great Center, flaming with the most inconceivable heat and with its vaporized materials **extending-out** from the nucleus far beyond the utmost bounds of the human imagination. Then, by the results of **chemical association** of **particles** of like-affinity or gravitation (which are synonymous), this vaporized igneous atmospheric substance of the Great Body, over a period of time unimaginable, gradually **divided itself** into six concentric rings, something similar to the condensed rings of Saturn.

If it were possible for the Great Nucleus to remained stationary, it would be the common focal point of all the concentric rings, being equidistant from all parts of their respective circumferences. But, since there is a rapid motion of the Great Body, which it had possessed from the Beginning, this motion would instead, produce an elongation of these rings, being somewhat analogous to the trail of a comet, and so, leaving the Great Mass of Materials in its rear, as the tail. Now, supposing the Motion to be in an elliptic orbit, the sudden re-curve and centrifugal impetus of the projecting trail, occurring at every passage of the Great Body around the **foci** of the ellipse, would finally (when condensation became sufficiently advanced) produce a **detachment** of the great vapory trail, which would subsequently assume a spheroid form and become a Sun, representative and corresponding to its origin. It was in this way the **six nebulous zones** formed a similar number of Central Suns, and from these have produced a similar number of Universes! These we call a "circle of suns", - that is, circular planes of suns.

**Our Sun** and System, and all the innumerable stars which the telescope of the nineteenth century could reveal, belong to the **fifth** great circle, or plane of formation.

The **Nebular Theory** of Creation, as presented on this magnificent scale, does not depend upon any present nebular appearances in the heavens.

The Great Center from which all of these systems and systems of systems emanated, is still an exhaustless Fountain of never-ending materials. It is a **Vortex**, breathing forth **a system** of concentric circles of suns and systems of suns. It is an everlasting and unchangeable **parent of all things**. The Parent is still, an **ocean** of **fire** smoothly **moving** with a **wave-like motion**, this, representing the phenomenon of **God** with holy perfection. Everlasting spontaneousness, co-eternal and powerful. And this Truth, which is displayed throughout the immensity of space, and there is an infinite action, the Whole, not shrinking, but instead becoming larger and more **expansive**. It is a **Germ**, everlasting and infinite, **developing** inexpressible Attributes in the "successive degrees and orders of formation", throughout the vast Universe and for the boundless duration of eternity!

# Section 4

In **review** of the creation of the six circles of suns to further describe their development, - there is the magnificent **Nebulous Zone** which was **thrown-off** by the Original Parent Sun, and this atmospheric Zone was formed by the incessant emanation of Light and Heat from the first and Great Eternal Sun, the Vortex, and it expanded through the regions of infinite space extending out and reaching to a distance **far-beyond** the **sixth** circle of Suns. The great "mass of fiery-matter" produced and contained **Heat**. The heat contained **Light**, which, by orders and degrees spread throughout the expanse of infinity and developing planetary Suns and Forms and Systems like the original. And this wonderful Light was of the peculiar composition adapted to, and assigned for, the production of an infinity of worlds and systems of worlds. All following the same Laws and Principles as is in the first Great Form. **Light** is a **perfection** and development of the original composition. And Light formed the Nebulous Ring or Circle which was surrounding undefinable space.

Positive and Negative constantly acting on and producing eternal motion throughout the mass of nebulous associated particles. The **Positive** or attraction, **called** into a great center, **particles** of like-affinity and "suitable" to enter into combinations. The **Negative** force, or the repulsion, threw off from the great body particles "not suitable" to its interior combinations. And this is the process by which the Suns of the **first circle** of Suns or **plane** of Suns were formed, occurring at equal periods. These Suns of the first circle especially the center of them, were still fire-inconceivable and these also gave off an emanation of Heat and Light. This **Light**, or the particles composing it, "gathered", in the same manner as the Suns themselves were formed, and produced planets and satellites. The Suns being too light-weight and unparticled, **could-not** consolidate in the manner similar to the condensation of their Light in other Centers or Worlds. But, the Light thrown from those Suns, was capable of becoming "less rare" than their own compositions; it was therefore, by the **constant absorption** to those rays of light, that would produce in each of their planets, a **hardened** or consolidated combination of **particles**.

The number of planets and other formations emanating from these Suns of the first circle, is incalculable. Each of these Suns has its own established planetary system, each planet observing the same **lane** and taking the same direction, moves around the Sun or Center which formed it. These planets can not properly be termed planets: because, their compositions are **too-rare** to form mineral substances. These planets are rather an **adhesion** of particles caused by the law of condensation and mutual attraction or gravitation; but these are still bodies almost completely consisting of a fiery interior constitution. These Suns are in reality what would be termed **cometary bodies** each of which pursues the orbit of its first formation according to the bulk and density of its peculiar elements.

Such is the condition of the **first** infinite **circle** or **plane** of Suns and of the Worlds produced by them.

A still greater accumulation of particles sent off from the Original Great Sun, produced another circle, like the First, - with a corresponding number of planets and satellites. The Suns in this **second circle** being still more rare than those in the first. When compared to the first circle of suns, these have "less fire", but contain "more heat"; and they are capable of expanding, and sending forth more unparticled Light relatively to the first circle of suns. The same Laws still work their mighty influence throughout the circle formed by these Suns: and by a constant emanation of nebulous matter, planets are placed at irregular distances, in constant process of formation. By the force of **attraction** that these Suns of the second circle possessed, all particles **negative** to their own composition, gravitated to them: other particles, by virtue of **existing motion** and refinement, were **repulsed** or thrown off these Suns, with a velocity inconceivable, are now seeking substances of like affinity among other formations in the system which the Center Sun had thus yielded forth.

The condensation of materials into planets belonging to this system, was produced by a constant attraction or **absorption of light**, the rare particles composing those gravitating to, or being attracted by, the sun of that system. And these spheres may be truly be called **planets**; this is because they would gradually **condensed** into particles of **earthy composition**. The closest formed planet to that particular sun is harder than the second; and the third is still more dense than the second; and denser and rarer alternately and correspondingly succeeding each other, throughout the worlds composing one of these systems.

The condensed particles and the progression of those particles, forming a substance that could be called "earthy", are totally **unlike** any compositions of a terrestrial nature that are known to be in existence by the human mind. It is impossible to calculate the immensity of the circumferences or diameters; because they are infinitely larger than several millions of the Suns belonging to the fifth circle of suns or our circle.

The Suns of the second circle transcend, mankind's powers of conception and imagination. And then recall, that the suns of the first circle and their planets, are still even more inconceivable – adding to that incalculable thought, is to realize the unimaginable and unchangeable **Sun** that gave them all an existence.

## Section 5

The Suns forming the **third system** of concentric circles or plane of suns, have less heat and more light than the former system, and are **nearer** the state of condensation. Still they are **not-condensed**, because they contain Heat inconceivable. Their **Light**, associating with **atoms** of like nature, has become suitable to produce still denser bodies, more-so than are produced by the Light of those of the former second circle; and so, these Suns were **destined** to produce planets of a still more condensed and consolidated constitution.

In this third system, the **constant interchanging** of particles, the throwing off of the non-associating atoms, and the receiving of others of like affinity, gradually produced its own system of **planets** and satellites, corresponding to other creations of like nature. The particles which have progressed to the **terra-material** formations of these planets, are still of such a peculiar and refined nature that no substance known on earth bears a resemblance to them. The first planets of this **third circle** of suns have assumed a hardened surface having **two strata**; the first of which is an unimaginable formation of particles of sand. And it is this same hardened composition which makes up the first and second planets of the third circle of suns.

The Suns of the **fourth circle** contain still less heat and light than those of the third circle; but still, the intensity of each, is incomprehensible to the mind. They send off **light** still more **unparticled**, such that they become **active agents** of Light.

It was after an inconceivable period of time and from a constant and relentless emanation of this **unparticled matter** from the fourth circle of Suns which this matter composed, this radiation produced corresponding systems of planetary worlds, diminishing in number and magnitude, yet too mighty in expanse to be calculated or comprehended.

In a similar manner as occurred in previous formations, it was by virtue of the **motion** going on throughout this great system of Suns, and by the laws of condensation, absorption, gravitation, repulsion, and association of atoms, the **planets** formed from the matter of this fourth circle of Suns, became still more dense in their constitution than before described in previous circles of suns. And, as the laws and principles pertain, the planets that are nearer these Suns have progressed to "earthy" formations and developments; while those that are further away from the "center Sun", are still more refined and less dense in their particles compared to those particles that compose this "earthy" substance of the nearer planets. Some of these "earthy type" formations nearly resemble the present appearance of this globe our earth, but is not of the same constitution or quality. Though the materials of this fourth system are **more refined** and perfect than the previous planet compositions; not necessarily in quality, but rather in particles. In this fourth system, those planets that are progressed, have three formations or **three strata**.

Likewise as previous the **fifth circle** or plane of Suns was brought into existence, and its laws and principles of formation corresponding to the other circles of suns creations. These fifth suns are composed of less heat and light, relatively than do the fourth circle; but still, their heat and light are immense. And particles which were evolved from these Suns were still more **refined** and **ethereal** than any previous suns. By the virtue of "eternal laws, both inherent and immutable" contained in this composition, the particles of this system, gradually and correspondingly brought into existence an immense number of planets and satellites, the magnitude of which is not yet fully determined or comprehended. And by the operation of these eternal laws and after an inconceivable period of time, the planets were created which belong to **our** own **Solar System**.

Planets that are nearer to these Suns of the fifth circle, are correspondingly denser than those further from them. The **distance** that the **light** of the Suns of the fifth circle passes-off into space, is too vast for ordinary conception, - but still is limited compared to the extension of the Light of the Suns of the previous circles. The same process of planet building occurred within the fifth circle of suns, where a condensation of particles from a fifth Sun, such as, "**o**ur solar system", which stands as a representative of all others in this fifth circle, and it has produced various strata of earthy formations. And there are many Suns contained in the fifth circle of Suns.

Our Solar System as stated is a **representation** of the Suns of the fifth circle; so, as our system is observed, what is seen, is the **first planet** is extremely dense and its surface is composed of a mineral and rocky substance. It has combinations similar to those upon this Globe, but which, are more defined in appearance, though not in quality. This one has been named **Mercury**.

The next planet has strata formations four in number, the last of which has not yet been fully developed; and it is less in density of composition than the former. This has been named **Venus**.

The third planet in this Sun's formation, has combinations of earthy substances still less dense than the former. The number of formations and strata developed is five, the last being **nearly complete**. This is the planet **Earth**.

The next planet from the Sun is **Mars**, which has corresponding formations of strata. This planet is less dense than Earth.

**Jupiter** the next planet in succession out from the Sun, has a greater number of "earthy" formations than the previous planet, which are still more refined in quality and constitution.

**Saturn** has formations **unequaled** by those of any planet between it and the Sun. The composition of this planet is still less dense and less gross, being somewhat more refined. It has formed a **nebulous zone**, and then afterward, formed another zone, - each of these nebula as we know, still surrounds this planet as **rings**, unbroken but slightly condensed; but, this nebulous zone will ultimately condense and compose other nebulous masses, the Whole of which will ultimately **form** a globe which will assume a **track** according to its own specific gravity, as have all others formed and do operate within this system.

There are more planets still further from our Sun and they grow less dense and more refined the further the distance from the Sun. Some pursue their orbits **uncondensed** and **unstratifed**. Their orbits are immense, but are in **proportion** to the refinement of their constituents, which means **not-being** suitable to **associate** with any other compositions from our great Sun which produced them. From **this cause**, those planets are repulsed to the extreme distances from the Sun which each now occupy. And these are **comets** – each of which will assume the constitution of a planet of like nature with all others in the same circle of formation.

A **sixth circle** of Suns was in order of succession produced; and these Suns contain **no fire**, less light, and more **electricity**. And these Suns having **not-yet** become Suns in the proper; and this is because of their inherent qualities and compositions. These future Suns are at this time **traversing** almost the **bounds** of **undefinable space**. The orbit of their revolution surrounds space incalculable.

## Section 6

**C**reation has occurred, back from time unimaginable. The **Universe**, a boundless accumulation of particles which have **assumed**, (by Virtue of Inherent Qualities given to these particles by the Great **Divine Mind** and the First Cause): - **forms, orders, degrees, associations,** and **correspondences**. And realize that **every particle** from the first circle to the last circle, has been **destined** to seek-out and find its particular **association** and gravitate to **that center**. And this, is the process that established **Forms** (spheres), and perpetual **Forms** such as suns, planets, and would produced **Order**. And so, it is by the **association** of each particle, this "Order" spread throughout the vast Universe. And it was, particles of like affinity, from the lowest to the highest, that would by **Degrees** established throughout every department of Creation, these associations.

There is constant gravitation of particles going on throughout the whole mass of material compositions. And Order has now been produced in this vast and universal extension of Worlds and Systems of Worlds, throughout immensity of space; it is God's plan, design, and Creation. It is by the development of "inherent qualities" - to an external manifestation of those qualities, and a progression of all things to the **attainment** of ultimate refinement and purification.

Each mass of particles, successively and without pause, **throws-off** all those **particles** that have become **ultimate particles**. Then, those ultimate particles will proceed on-ward to produce, sustain, and "associate", with **others** of like-affinities and natures. These substances thrown-off have become, **too-pure** and **unparticled** to associate with substances and particles of a grosser and denser quality.

So therefore in review, the **Great Sun** – the unimaginable ocean of liquid material - was a Center from which, "rolled-forth" an **atmosphere** of particles which extended throughout immensity. This atmosphere of particles, at a distance unimaginable from the Great Sun, formed the first circle of suns. The condensation of these particular particles into **masses** of joined particles occurred at the **extreme extent** of those particles **station**, that would produce these Suns. And it is from the production of theses circle of suns that **Order** and **Form** were developed from the successive formation of these heavenly bodies.

And so the Suns of the first circle are an **ultimate-of** the original **Great Sun**; and those of the second circle may be called an **ultimate** of the first circle. They are no-more than accumulations of particles, and because of this these are considered planets. And then the third circle of Suns are an ultimate of the second; and the fourth, an ultimate of the third; and the fifth, of the fourth; and the sixth, of the fifth. Thus there is **no disconnection**; but there is a perfect harmony and unity in all celestial and terra-material productions; and so, each may be considered as a "**part**", which is **necessary** to the completion of the Whole Universe of boundless infinitude!

Time and space**,** height and depth**,** length and breadth are **annihilated** in this vast system of concentric and celestial circles – a perfection and perpetual development of the Great Fountain from which they all successively emanated.

One of the Suns of the second circle is several millions of trillions times larger than the Sun of our Solar System of the fifth circle! And the time elapsed during these formations is incalculable. Millions and millions of millions of Worlds (an infinity of worlds) are traversing the boundless fields of immensity, with these displaying a most perfect order, arrangement, and organization. These Worlds are constantly producing new particles, which gives evidence and an index of new and youthful productions, which are constantly succeeding. An infinity of worlds and formations, and consequently **re-formations** having condensed and consolidated by a gradual association of Inherent Particles, both gross and refined, each of which gravitates to its like, and they **possesses motion** in **proportion** to the **specific density** or rarity of the substances with which it is in combination. So, there is from the Great Fountain, **the Germ**, the parent of all these worlds that were thrown-out into infinity; an everlasting combination of materials, which when completely developed, will extend into infinite space, and will light up every chamber throughout the vast Universe, with Light inaccessible and without compare.

Creation then, has just-commenced! Elements, which by constant flux and reflux are engaged in producing a universe of eminent grandeur and infinitude! The Great Sun which was **pregnated** with the immutable eternal **essence** of the divine Positive Power, is continuously forming particles of Matter. The Great Sun contained particles destined to become infinitely sublimated and modified. And it is the inherent nature of all things, from the beginning, to assume and become "Forms" and develop **characteristics** that correspond with the **interior invisible** qualities **contained** in the particles. Those Forms or spheres which were assumed or conglomerated, then observe perpetual Order, and develop degrees of progression in accordance with the inherent and invisible qualities of their "cause" and actuator. And that is a Law and a constant.

# Section 7

The total amount of **time** elapsed in the **forming** and **evolving** which has taken place on our planet Earth up to present, **would-not** even equal one second when compared to the amount of time elapse in the production of even one of the systems that has been explained and contemplated. And yet Creation, or the existence and production of Worlds, has been but one moment in progress, as compared to the **duration** of the formations that are to go on throughout time and space unimaginable.

All these Systems involved within the six circle or plane of suns, with all their emanations and appendages, are in essence **one** System, one Structure, one Evolution of worlds. One infinite Production from one eternal Origin. All these have arisen from the Great Vortex and are at the same time progressing toward the beginning, by becoming **refined**. All will return to the Vortex of Positive Power, returning to become one with God. And so all the various changes and conditions that the particles of each system have assumed in Form, order, specific gravity, geological developments, undefinable and unimaginable revolutions, these all can be viewed as a **reciprocal** and incessant interchanging and **circulation** of parts and particles. The vast ocean of materials is in ceaseless motion and activity. The Universe, is much larger than has been assumed. So then, when was the **beginning**, and when shall be the **end**, of **eternal time**? The **thought** finds no resting-place, it searches throughout the chambers of the heaven of heavens, and roams through the labyrinths that are continually opening into new fields of celestial beauty, which all utterly transcend **all mind's** thoughts and imaginations, all except "**That Mind**" that produced them.

Thus the **human mind** can not conceive of **eternity** or **infinity**; for the mind is limited in its nature, it belongings to, and was produced by, finite Forms and it is existing among transient things. So, consequently the mind's thoughts must have boundaries; and therefore subject matter of the mind's thoughts must be **limited**, or else the mind could not comprehend them. But sometimes in its sparkling brilliancy the **imagination** will pass off day-dreaming or meditating into infinite space, and then, the mind not being able to perceive limits, becomes confused and bewildered. So now, in an attempt to paint a stronger mental picture of mind's limitation, let it be known, that no human power nor human invention is capable of representing or describing any correct idea, or even any notion, of the actual immensity of these "Sun Systems" which extend and expand throughout **unmeasured space**. No mathematical calculation can be made respecting them; because numbers are lost in worlds whose numbers of measurement transcend the conceptions of the human mind. Mathematical figures may be combined to such an extent they would transcend comprehension. And no matter how extensive the mathematical figure may turn out to be, it still has limits, and is therefore of no comparison.

# Section 8

The **Mind** may be mighty enough to **comprehend** one system and its compositions, forms, movements, and also comprehend all the objects and forms of the perfect and imperfect that are all existing upon its surfaces. And, the mind may-be sufficiently expansive to comprehend the interior, the invisible realities, and external appearance of all things existing there-upon that surface; and the mind may be penetrating enough to understand the "Motive Power", and Energy of all action, motion, and sensation; - and, "these would be mighty conceptions" – and these would constitute the **full range** of human thought! But still, how comparatively **limited** and contracted are these conceptions, compared with what is still developing!

Therefore, the human mind is absolutely **incompetent** to conceive of infinity; and so, to the mind this word vibrates and echoes no corresponding thought. The word infinity, as applied to indefinite space, is one word that is substituted in place of an idea or conception. And there **never** was, and **never** can be an adequate conception of eternity; for the thought of this in-itself is a non-entity, and the word expresses no significance. What the **mind** really and truly is, is a **composition** of the refined and perfected materials of all-else existing, and it-refuses to associate with things of a lower order and less degree of refinement; but instead, has a tendency to pass-off on its way to explore and associate with something of a like and lofty nature. The mind is **heading** to much higher and exalted spheres and aspires to explore more profound Things. Mind is only seeking its equilibrium. The mind is gravitating toward the sphere that is attractive to it. It is **endeavoring** to pass from its present state, to some unknown, yet attractive, habitation among the avenues and chambers of the spiritual and celestial forms.

All of the mighty systems that were evolved from the Great Center, **observe** both a **rotary** and **orbicular motion** according to the density or rarity of each, as they move around the Center from which they emanated. The very **moment** that an association of particles was established, then the action and reaction, condensation, and the rotary and orbicular motions, were produced. And as stated before, the intervening distance between a planet and the Sun each orbits around, is determined by the planets density and rarity. There was **no disconnected force** or impetus applied to the bodies that have been formed, to set them in harmonious motion. No foreign power impulsed and guided them, in their order, or in their respective planes of revolution; but instead, it was **Inherent**

**Laws** which developed and brought them into action, and are capable of **controlling** these manifestations.

It is necessary to contemplate, discuss, and understand more, concerning the nature of the **physical forces** that drive the processes of development of Matter. First to be described, are the great eternal elements that were **successively developed** and evolved from the Great Center that had first contained them, and these were **Heat**, **Light**, and **Electricity**.

**Heat** was an emanation from Fire. And the **Light** produced from Heat - by its **becoming less particled** and more rare and active, was so much **sublimated** and **refined**, so that its **ultimate** development is that all-pervading element existing throughout the Universe, **Electricity**.

Electricity **could-not** have existed in its present condition **primitively**; because, there were no means, and no substances qualified to develop it.

But, as the **First** (heat) existed alone, and then, by its constant progression and development until the element of Electricity was produced as its ultimate, clearly shows that electricity was a progression and **perfection** of that thing which was eternally existing. And the law implies, that the lower contained and developed the highest, while the highest acts on, and pervades, all below its exalted state of perfection. Hence, **electricity pervades all things.** All bodies, all substances, all elements, and it also **passes unrestricted** through every avenue and pore that exists in **every particle** throughout the Universe. It is the **elastic substance** that exists within and surrounds all things. And it is the **powerful agent** of Motion, Life, and Activity.

**Electricity** is constantly and incessantly engaged in rarefying and purifying all things; and is a **medium** to transmit Power and Matter, within particles, from one substance to another, and from one planet to another, and from each planet to its particular Sun.

There is **not-existing** any quantity of electricity in our Sun amounting to a positive or attractive power. And there **is-no** such thing existing as positive repulsion, that could be produced by any element or principles of like nature. And Motion is **neither** produced nor sustained by any such actuating principles. **Nor** is anything formed or organized or existing, as an effect, or produced by positive-opposites. Because if a substances could be produced in this way, it would be existing in a **vacuum**, and between two antagonistic principles; and then it could experience no motion, no action, no exchanging of particles, no increase, and no decrease. It would be an immovable and unchangeable object, destitute of all life and would have no use.

But, **instead** of opposites existing, there is a **harmony** in all the formations, and a **positive** and **absolute necessity** of each production. And these formations then proceed on their journey, according to the forces and elements originally existing in the Vortex of Positive Power and in the Fountain of chaotic materials. And so said once again, all the systems of suns and planets, with all their appendages, and all the vast assemblages of worlds throughout the sidereal regions, **were all** brought into existence by the united and harmonious action of fixed and established **Principles**.

So then, what exactly is meant by **attraction, gravitation,** and **condensation**? Simply it is, **an association of particles**, possessing **mutual affinities**.

Another consideration in reference to an association of particles, or development of a Form or sphere, is that there is constantly "a refinement of inherent particles in all bodies"; so that there is also a constant passing-off of any of **those particles**, which have now become "**too refined**" to continue an association with that same composition any longer. And these refined particles are attracted to and gravitate towards another a new association of particles of like-affinities. And so the constant attraction existing between all bodies in the vast system of the planetary worlds, is due to a mutual gravitation from each of the particles that have become **fitted** to associate with each others composition. And so as a result of this principle of mutual affinities, worlds and worlds of worlds were made, and in this manner they are sustained. And the result is **universal motion**, from the **angular** to the **spiral** it was developed. And in this way does, and shall, the Great Eternal Laboratory unceasingly produce and reproduce, until all things and all substances shall become rarefied, refined, and **perfected**, and that is when all will gravitate to spheres of celestial attraction and **spiritual association**.

## Section 9

Creation is complex, and a review of information already given with the addition of more in-depth descriptions will now be given of **planetary formations** of the Great System and those Inherent Laws by which these formations were produced in Order, Harmony, and Progressive Development, and is **now-presented** to the mind: - so it was in this general manner planets were developed from primeval Matter, - which was originally **Fire**, then matter "being acted upon" by the Great **Positive Power**, the Vortex, which contained this Matter as the only substance. Matter being "throw-out" to become an **atmosphere**. All material substances and compositions originated and were **put-into** action as a progressive sphere or atmosphere, all proceeding from the **Great Internal Actuator**. And then, a **progression** (before described) leading to the organization and establishment of systems of Worlds, which occurred all through-out the Universe. Then, the constant operation of all laws Inherently contained in the Great Mass, **have-sustained** all things that are now in being. The immensity of space is now peopled with worlds, planets, and their appendages, all corresponding with one-another and existing in harmony; also, there exist **finer** and more **remote** assemblages, which are beyond the power of human vision! Creation and Evolution are the same event which is the alpha and omega of Existence.

**Learning** of the **plan** of the Great System, as it has been given, gives order to the thoughts, and assists the mind in its endeavors to comprehend the Universe's vastness, and understanding this **plan** is the only-means the mind can conceive of the countless worlds in existence. If a more specific description were given the mind would not comprehend, and it would be distracted. For instance, as an example: - if the geological formations of these various Worlds were considered, from their **primary condensation** of particles in their **lowest point** of gravitation; and then in addition, if the various **divisions** of those condensation of particles, which are **not** stratified yet, were also presented; and if their present external appearances were also given, together with their diameters and circumferences, - all this description would be revealing something which the mind could neither comprehend nor associate with by any process of analogical reasoning or any power of expansive thought. So, what does a **true conception** of the Universe and of its harmonious formations give to the human mind?

However when the **truth** is known, it should lead the mind to **conceive** of systems that **correspond** to each other, that are in harmony with each other; and the mind would then, be able to-make useful and extensive

**generalizations**, - the result of gaining this knowledge would be to **cause man** to carry-on **more harmoniously** in his own life. Man's mind would know the **teachings** of the beauties that exist in the Universe, and to apply them correctly to his own happiness and usefulness, and to the happiness of his fellow man.

So then, the Great Sun of all Suns, the Vortex of the Great Positive Mind, in the beginning emanated the **Three Principles** and **Elements** that are **mediums** and **connecting links** of universal **motion** and **activity**.

The **Fountain**, the origin from which they all sprang into existence, was an emanation from the **Interior**, and from **qualities** and **essences** which were existing in the Interior. And so, realize, that the Great Body of the Great Mind, - was an **atmosphere** or a halo surrounding the Great Center or Sun internally existing. And these great elements, **Heat, Light,** and **Electricity**, were **successive** developments of this Great Mass. Each element being properly developed, and then the last, Electricity became an **active agent**, a **Negative** to the **internal**, Positive Power. And so Matter, existing in its **unparticled state**, was the **vehicle** and substance through and upon-which the **two great powers** (positive and negative) could-act, to produce all that has been rolled forth into the immensity of space.

**Electricity** therefore **pervades** the infinity of space. It **penetrates** all substances, and exists in and throughout all Worlds, with all their component parts. It exists in everything and everywhere; and truly there is not even one particle in all the realms of infinite space, that has not in its compositions the **unparticled** and **active agent** of electricity. Being the **ultimate** or the progressed and perfected **essence** of the Great Eternal Sun, Electricity pervades all things below its preeminent state of perfection, - and therefore, is a **Negative** to the internal and still more-perfected – the perfection of inconceivable purity – the Great Positive Mind.

These three are the **only Principles** and **Elements** in **existence**: and all other things are mere **modifications** of these Principles. This emanation or radiation from the Great Body may be termed an **atmosphere**, a halo, or **nebulous zone**, that surrounded the immensity of space with brightness and beauty most inconceivable. And thus is the action which **originally established** the eternal **Truth** and real **Reality**, that everything **has** its own peculiar atmosphere, and consequently its specific and necessary association.

An **atmosphere** is a **progression**, or an **ascension**, from the denser mass of particles **seeking association** with those elements of **like-nature**, and this atmosphere **consists** of substances which have become

**too-refined** and **unparticled** to continue to exist in that central mass of a dense quality and composition. An atmosphere is something that is developed.

The **stratified atmosphere** that is formed around **every** body, substance, and globe, in existence, is actually an **emanation** from the body or substance and a **perfection** of the particles composing It. In some cases it is called an aura. Therefore, there is an **atmosphere** belonging to **every particle** in being, the composition of which is much-finer and more perfected than the substance from which it emanated. And, it is according to the **quality** of such an emanation, that its **relative distance** is established, and of the **character** of the **association** - which It seeks.

The sixth circle of suns has become established, - **Creation** is still continuing and is still **evolving**, and this fact can be clearly seen in the process that is occurring yet not compete, as the immutable laws have been brought into being, within this sixth circle or plane of Suns. As stated, these suns are not yet fully condensed and organized into systems like other circles of suns, but are still in a condition much like a **cometic nuclei**.

# Section 10

There may-be to the **observer**, an apparent **confusion** existing among the innumerable **visible bodies** that now inhabit the ocean of space. From mankind's point of view, those objects in space do not appear in perfect order, and they do not assume Forms and become condensed before the human eye to plainly see. And seemingly, there is an **appearance** of **irregularity** throughout the sidereal heavens of space. But these **external appearances** are **deceptive**; because the **whole structure** of the Universe is really only compositions of particles, **sustaining** relative points and locations **given-them** by their own natural compositions and associations.

All Things in the Universe are but **parts** composing the Great Whole. There is **no interference** with each other, **no interruption** of each others movements; but all move onward with inconceivable rapidity and do so in the most calm and peaceful manner that can be imagined. These parts then in truth, not only "answer the purpose" for which they have assumed their present condition, but also are almost **intellectually**, "reciprocating particles and essences with each other", and still more, because they are disseminating **freely** heat, light, and electricity, - which give **new** and living **energies** to particles and substances with which they come in contact. And most important, **all particles** will become a - **Spiritual Essence**, and then all things arrive at an **exalted state** of spiritual and celestial perfection!

Thus **all matter** will pass through the **multifarious forms** and **stages** that are existing, and all will ultimately be **resolved** into the **unparticled state**, and will **ascend** to associate with higher and more glorious spheres – of **spiritual composition**. And when all motion shall have become so perfected as to result in **sensation**; - and all elements shall **equally** and **reciprocally** attract and associate; then, - **Perfection**!

Then with perfection, **when-all** reach the spiritual composition, the **Great Positive Mind** will **be Positive**, to the great **Negative** formed by the perfection of all things else in being. And then **Deity** and **Spirit** will be existing only! Therefore, the **Spiritual Principle**, the destined ultimate of all things in existence, will be **Negative** to the Great **Positive** Mind God.

The human mind has a **tendency** to conceive of, "locality" and with boundaries; and it is impossible for the mind to understand infinity. This is the reason why the **Truths** within this story may, at first, seem obscure and vague. However, if the mind were like Space, then **thought** would have no boundary; and if the mind were like Time, Space would have no distance.

## Section 11

It is made evident to the mind that the great **Internal Invisible**, is the **real reality** of all, and this reality produces **Causes**, which produce **Effects**, and these effects produce other causes and effects, and that is the **eternal truth**! The great eternal **Interior** and the great eternal **Exterior** constituted the only Principle and Form in being, and that is **Oneness**!

And as an **atmosphere** of eternal elements was gradually and perpetually evolved, this constituted the **Great Sun** – which was a **Form** - of the **Interior**. The Great Sun may be called an atmosphere or **Form** which is surrounding the Great Positive Mind of God. And so it is, that **all-things** have an interior, and have a corresponding external Form. And there is also an **aeriform** emanation proceeding from every substance in universal space.

One eternal and immutable **Law** pervades all matter in existence. This Law being immutable it can not react, it can not change, **nor** can there be any retrogression. **Progression** is the main attribute and the specific **effect** of established laws. And the "activity" in all things is an inevitable result of the same principle of successive Progression.

Adjustment and harmony, - refinement and purification, - these are the **necessary effects** of Nature's established laws.

Two Principles – two real realities, **Power** and **Matter**, internal and external, positive and negative, cause and effect, were at the beginning, and are the only coupled existing principles. These existed in the beginning, and there **can-not** now be any more than these two.

Now, there is in existence innumerable kinds of earths and terra-compositions and unnumbered millions of Worlds, with **many** supposed original elements and numerous mineral forms. And finally, there appear to be in the Universe an indefinite number of **directly opposite** and **antagonistic** substances, essences, qualities, and principles. All these are not really antagonistic, but are **peculiar associations** of bodies, of actions, and elements, which are contained in the Great Whole, and are but "**modifications** of the inherent quality" which is contained in the undeveloped Sun of the Universe.

And so, as the **outer** must be and is an **emanation** from the **internal** or Center, so then, that which surrounds, **is-not** an antagonist of – and **is-not** opposed to – instead, it is in perfect **harmony** with the internal; and both **united** by the moral goodness and virtue of their inherent power, and acting together harmoniously and reciprocally they **produce** eternal motion. Therefore there are no opposites – **no antagonistic principles** existing in the realms of infinite space. All things in Nature are incessantly and harmoniously seeking their **equilibrium**. And all throughout the vast system of planetary formations, there is constantly occurring a **universal reciprocation**, so that particles may gravitate to some like substance or principle existing in some part of the remote regions of space . And this is **a constant** of the Universe, where all matter and motion will **finally** become what they originally were and will be **resolved** into **one** grand and glorious Sun, more refined and perfected, more excellent in all its qualities and composition. And at that time it **may-again** bring forth a new system of suns, and an infinite corresponding creation throughout space. This may be termed the Beginning and End of One Time: - this **contracted idea** is the **most extensive** one that the mind can possibly **conceive** upon this subject.

## Section 12

The endless series of interconnected Causes by which infinite space has been filled with systems of unnumbered worlds, was originally established by the **Force** and spontaneous action of the **Will** of the Eternal Mind, God! His **Will** is the executive Power, actuating all things throughout eternity. The Will of God is represented by the immutable and changeless Laws, that He has filled with Motion, Life, and Activity. This Will was and is the **Cause** of all things. And the things God created were **balanced** by proper materials.

Comprehending as best one can the nature, quality, and essences, of the original First Eternal Cause, the Will of the Creator, will provide to the human mind a genuine and indestructible basis on which it may rest a "true understanding" of the workings of the Universe, and all its causes and effects.

Unwarrantable hypotheses concerning the origin of things have arisen, because there **is-not** a correct understanding of the apparently extreme opposites, such as heat and cold, light and darkness, life and death, activity and repose, and all their intermediates. In order from mankind to gain the awareness and knowledge which is **necessary** to give a proper understand these apparent **opposites**, one should view them in the "light" in which they appear, after having the changeless law of the Eternal Positive Mind impressed distinctly upon ones understanding. Then after gaining this awareness, and having for a foundation "**reasoning**", which is everlasting and infinite, the mind would be led to a truthful understanding of all appearances, Forms, and effects, issuing forth from the fountain of God's creation! **God** is the pure intelligence and the omnipotent actuator! All throughout immensity there is perfect harmony, unity, and reciprocation. There is no unjust absorption; no unequal and unnecessary attraction; no destroying or annihilating of one body or particle for the immediate or isolated and selfish supply of another. There is no inequitable drawing from any parts, qualities, or elements, to sustain others. But all give to and take from each other, only that which is necessary and useful to each, **reciprocation**.

It is while existing in **Forms**, as mankind now are existing, that man's purpose is **revealed**, and it is that they should **conform** to the immutable laws of Matter. And as mankind learns and conforms to these harmonious, immovable, and established laws, they **will-progress** and form a perfect and harmonious System. Then mankind would become true correspondents of the vast Universe, and then would be harmony, joy, excitement, equality, glory, perfection, and eternal happiness. And as the Whole existing in harmony and peace, and following a positive progressive ascension; mankind would receive the tranquilizing influence of Divine Law, whose very essence is the perfection of Goodness and Truth. Then, opposites would not be known; for Knowledge and Truth would annihilate their appearance and their seemingly destructive influence from the Universe forever.

Now in review, - up to this place in this story of Creation, - the original state of **Matter** existing in space and its general combinations and characteristics have all **been presented** to the world for their consideration and investigation - together with the general laws and principles which are indivisibly connected with the Great Mass. And also given, is the general mode of operation of the Universe; the formation and constitution of worlds; and the **relations** that they sustain to each other, have also been presented for contemplation. The mind has been led to consider the "successive formations" of innumerable suns and worlds.

However currently, **mankind** should feel ashamed and depressed; because they are the **only-beings** who have pursued a path and course of **isolation** and **selfish action** and have allowed themselves to be governed by laws which **never-did** and **never-can** exist in Nature, **nor** can they exist in the plans and institutions of the Great Mind.

## Section 13

When contemplating the original cause and beginning of all things and contemplating the workings of the entire Universe, the **mind** becomes lost in the immensity of the subject. It therefore **requires** nearer and more tangible subjects of thought and deeper explanation than those facts which have been so-far given in this general manner, and previously considered. The mind is **incompetent** to grasp the mighty Universe. **Therefore** the magnificent **Solar System** with which our own planet is immediately connected, shall **next** be the **subject** of a expanded **investigation**. And as stated, by understanding one particle of the great Universe, will eventually lead to the correct knowledge of the Universe itself.

In the process of studying **our solar system**, which includes following the process from its creation to its present state of evolution, we will conduct this study by considering both the **scientific** and **philosophical** views. This study is done this way specifically for the purpose of carrying a deeper conviction of truths here proclaimed! This investigation will pay special attention to information relating to this globe earth. So in a course of mathematical calculations, astronomical, geological, and physiological explanations, there will be **revealed** the order and condition of those creations in our own **solar system**. The terms World, Universe, and Nature, will be used and applied as are significant and necessary to the present Solar System and of all the globes existing in it.

# Section 14

The Wonderful Sun or the **Center** to which our **Solar System** belongs, is only a **remote planet** of another system, which was existing prior to our Suns formation; and it was **Russian** astronomer, **Maedler** who discovered that our system is moving towards **Pleiades** and requires many millions of years to complete a single revolution!

The Center, our **Sun**, is an **accumulation** and agglomeration of particles **thrown** from other spheres; and these became united **according** to the "law of mutual and inherent attraction" or gravity. The Sun's igneous composition contains heat, light, and electricity, which are the **successive developments** of all primeval matter existing in an agglomerated condition; and, this accumulation of Matter also being subject to general and universal laws governing all Matter.

Our Sun's materials were **thrown** from other bodies during their **revolutions** around their common center, propelled by a force termed the **centrifugal force**, or the tendency that a revolving body has to throw particles from its surface. Then, these particles **congregated** by **mutual** gravitation, to form the Sun as we know it. And, our Sun is being governed by the **same** laws that govern other spheres. It has the same motions as do all other celestial spheres, and revolves on its axis with wonderful velocity, and in an elliptic orbit around the **Center** which it belongs.

The great internal portion of the **Sun** is an immense mass of **liquid fire** and the **evolved-atmosphere** may be considered as being a part of the great body of our Sun. This **atmosphere** or "nebulous zone" of our Sun, is composed of accumulated particles **and** at one time in the distant past, this atmospheric body **extended** to the orbit that the planet **Pluto** now occupies, and now **traverses** as a **cometary body**. As our Sun began to agglomerate, heavy or **dense particles** which are now part of the components composing the whole mass of the Sun, took the **lowest point** in the center of the great body and the more refined particles assumed and sustained **different distances** and "stations" at their lowest position inside the great body, **in-accordance** with the density or rarity of each particle. The Sun has two original motions: one upon its axis and the other is its orbit around its own Center Pleiades.

So our Sun has now come into being, as just described; **and-now** it is to be the **source** that will **produce** our solar system; and the Sun performs this task of **planet-making**, in the same manner, following the same laws and principles, as did occur with our Sun's own formation, and as did all other heavenly bodies. So now to begin with: all **emissions** of **particles** which were **thrown-from** the Sun, are **governed** by the law of centrifugal force, and by the natural tendency of each particle to **seek** its own congenial association and establishment of the equilibrium of its dense or rare composition. Those emitted particles are to gravitate to a "station" or position in space depending upon their density and types of associations. Our Sun's **elliptical orbit** is **rendered** that way by the benefit of the **original** primary force **given each atom** of the Great Body of the Universe by God.

The **throwing-off** or centrifugal force which the Sun **generates** in its motion, produces the force needed so that atoms will pass **outward** from the center of the mass, in the **direction** of the **plane** that the sun's body is observing in its own motion. Also, the **accumulation** of particles at the extremes of the Sun's elliptic orbit **is-greater** there, than at any other point or locality around or within the Sun's central body. And **according** to the **law** of "eternal reciprocation and gravitation of particles", there **would-not** have been an accumulation at these localities, had not the particles that were thrown off previously, "become suitable" to associate and conjoin with particles that were already existing.

Therefore, no law of positive attraction actuated them, or withdrew them from particles to which they previously adhered, - nor did any law of positive repulsion repel them from their original station. Neither repulsion nor attraction as a law, as these laws are generally understood, produced any effect upon these **foreign particles**. But, there was a **mutual** gravitation or association of **suitable materials** and atoms to assume such a Form.

The **quantity** and **quality** of Matter **contained** in our **Sun**, was enough, that it subsequently formed all the planets, satellites and appendages, as well as, all the **Forms** possessing motion, life, and activity in this particular solar system. To produce the planets, there was involved the continuous process by which particles and substances **passed** from the great center, outward; and this process was aided by the Suns **motions** and a **internal process** where particles, atoms, and substances, that had **become sufficiently refined** to "assume" higher **areas** of activity **within** the original great mass the Sun.

Now in **reviewing** these great developments concerning our Sun, a **generalized** description follows: - from the **igneous** and unformed center of our newly forming Sun was developed **heat**, which was the first formation of this mass of particles. The extreme of this heat was the commencement of **light**, and this was the second formation. **Electricity** followed next as a **consequent development** of light. And it was this third **active fluid**, electricity, that extended to the utmost extreme of the whole mass of the Sun, including its successive radiations of atmosphere which would eventually transform into planets.

And it was from successive development of fire, heat, light, and electricity, that the general elements composing the Sun were produced. Without these elements it would not have been a sun.

Next, there is placed before the mind the **proposition** that the circumference of the Sun's atmosphere **had-extended** to the orbit that is now occupied by the ninth planet of our Solar System, Pluto. Next, it is necessary to understand the operation of the two great motions of the Sun, especially that of its elliptic orbit **around** a more inconceivable Center. And then it will come to mind that by the result of the throwing-off or centrifugal force which the great Body generates in its motion, atoms will **pass outward** from the center, in the direction of the plane that the body is observing in its motion. And then also, realize that the **accumulation** of particles at the extremes of its elliptic orbit is greater than at any other point or locality around the great central body.

## Section 15

Knowing exactly how **electricity** relates to our solar system should surely yield a greater understanding of the activity of Creation and evolution around us. In the development process of the great Center **our Sun** now has successfully developed **strata** or atmospheres of **elements**. These strata of elements extending-out from the densest particles composing the Center, outward to the final, ultimate, and last element, the development of electricity. Electricity is the highest of all material refinements and pervaded the lower substances, entering into every particle where it had been originally contained, but undeveloped. And this **electric fluid** is the **subtle**, powerful, and **active agent** contained in every particle, it penetrated to the lowest depths of the Sun, existing there, and also extended to an undefinable expanse throughout space. The particles that accumulated and agglomerated at the extreme point of the elliptic orbit of the Sun's revolution, were inherently associated and "joined together" by virtue and action of this **electric fluid**, and by the specific **density** or rarity of the particles that were thrown to **that** station by the centrifugal action which the immense Sun had in both of its motions. Electricity was the **medium** and active agent to transmit and transfer every molecular substance to new stations. Electricity may be considered a mediator, or an "associating principle", that **unites** antagonistic particles. And it is the **all-pervading** influence, acting upon the highest and lowest particles of every state of material association. And it **gyrates** from the lowest particle to the highest, **uniting** and associating all particles according to the density or rarity of such, until it reaches the highest point, or "forms an association" with principles of its own affinity.

Electricity is the invisible controlling element, "whose results are known laws". This energetic principle is the motivator which **actuates** all ultimate **motion** of all material constitution. And it was this subtle fluid, combined with our Sun's originally motion, gained during its formation, that the ninth planet Pluto was formed. Pluto was formed at the Sun's farthest point during its elliptic orbit; and now Pluto orbits as a cometary body at the outer-most circle of the Sun's atmosphere.

What is the nature and cause of motion? Motion has been previously described, and whether this description was adequate will not be debated, however by knowing a planets motions, give insight into the forces and processes which formed a particular planet and continue to operate upon any developed planets. Most human minds may not possess an adequate understanding of the laws that produce Motion, even though they depend upon this universal and constant occurring phenomenon.

First know, that the **principles** of Motion are **existing-in** Matter, and which are **coeval** with Matter, as was previously spoken. Once it is realized that Matter and Motion are united, then, **general cause** will be expected to produce invariable corresponding effects, and cause and effect will be perceived to exist as one general principle. Still, there is not just one motion, there are thousands of **intermediate motions** produced by **incidental** and subordinate **causes**. But, even though they exist, they are incidental and they **do-not** undermine nor do they interrupt the action of the general and established principles of motion in Nature.

Modern science is completely **correct** with its knowledge that Motion is the effect that one body produces upon another. And so if a **substance** or a body **be dense**, then its **pressure** or **action** upon another substance will be in proportion to its density, and will produce proportionate effects, because every action requires an equal and opposite reaction. And all particles **act-on** each other in this way, both separately and in combination.

Therefore, a universal motion **exists**: because, the **action** of one particle will set in motion every other particle, whether single or compound, existing in the Universe! The **movements** of all things therefore are **graduated** in accordance with the "station" or position of the substance, and its crudeness or refinement, being dense or refine. The very **moment** the "original impetus" was given to Matter, the never ending and ceaseless motion of **all bodies** throughout space was **eternally** established! And motion can not be understood or adequately accounted for on any other principle known to characterize any form of combined elements: and on this ground only may be rested an understanding if motions cause and manifestations.

So then, motion should be understood and regarded as existing in primeval matter, and that motion **constitutes** the general Principle of Matter, and it also is the highest and most perfect attribute of "Interior Development". The **original force** and energy given to the first particle, **caused** all other motions. So therefore, Motion is an "eternal-principle" existing in Matter originally established by Infinite Power.

So when considering the numerous movements and manifestations of Nature, the basis of the investigation should consist in understanding this originally-established principle; then from this one principle, there should be **expected** general developments of motion, which will correspond to, and then following the universal law. And with this information, now the mind should be able to understand the formation of the Sun and the law that controls its mighty movements.

The grand and most important motion belonging to the Sun is the one it performs in its **orbit** around its center Pleiades. The **cause** of this established motion was the initial-force given to the **arriving** particles of the Sun by the action of the powerful throwing-off of those speeding particles coming from that Center (Pleiades) to which it belongs, and the incessant and **violent force** that accompanied the **reception** of those particles and the impetus originally given to the formation causing rotary motion, also-produced a corresponding motion in an elliptic orbit, at a distance from our Sun's original Center, in proportion to the Suns density.

And the motion our Sun has developed upon its own **axis**, is that still more **violent** motion that was given it by the **reception** of particles which came with such a **velocity** as to **cause** it almost **instantly** to revolve. The motion given to the Sun was the result of the impulse of **moving particles**, the tendency of which was to produce like motion. And why did particles stop there at that particular area in space? Because of the density and refinement of those particles. This Motion therefore was a **natural** consequence of a kindly **reciprocation** of atoms. This action would be the **beginning** process of **condensation** and accumulation of the moving particles, and was an **inevitable** result **caused** by both the **accumulation** at the center of dense particles that associated more closely with each other, and by the **escape** of more **refined** parts which assumed **higher stations** in the vast body. This was a mighty and extensive accumulation of particles that had constantly occurred over the course of countless ages, and one which produced the Sun into the great dimensions that are now known

# Section 16

Its a fact that Andrew J Davis was the **first** person to **discover** both the planets Pluto and Neptune and to name them, and Davis did this by making note of them in his first book, published in 1846. Another fact concerning Davis's foresight was, that electricity and batteries were not yet known, or at least not well known, and science lacked knowledge of this phenomena. Anyhow, the **first planet** formed was the ninth planet **Pluto** a cometary body, being composed of particles that had been **destined** to accumulate at that distance from our Sun. These particles which had originally been throw-off by the motion of this great Sun, and obeying the law of reciprocal gravitation.

The eighth planet – **Neptune** evolved second, following the same principles of formation and following the same general laws of Motion of any planet; it is situated within the orbit of Pluto merely because Neptune's composition was **more dense** than the first one evolved. Neptune's density is four fifths that of water, and its atmosphere is exceedingly rare, containing little oxygen, but being mostly composed of fluorine and nitrogen. No organic beings from earth could exist there alive, even for one moment.

Neptune has six satellites orbiting around it; and this whole system began forming after the original particles were throw-off from our Sun, and would finally reach their "station" or destination in space, where they would then require an unimaginable amount of years to pass, as the formation of this planet and its satellites **evolved-into** spheres. Recall, that particles of Matter, especially in large portions, would agglomerate and gravitate together, the particles taking either a lower or higher **station** according to the specific gravity or levity or those agglomerates, - and this is the accumulation and formation of Matter into planets, satellites, and asteroids. This knowledge is useful and necessary as a basis on which the mind may rest its geological researches when they arise, and also may rest a proper conception of all **ulterior effects** and developments.

There have been some scientific minds whom believed erroneously, that there are in existence elements which are apparently **not controlled** by the same general law; their thoughts and opinions concerning the subjects of heat, light, and electricity, with reference to their character, attributes and governing principle, saying that each of these elements have a separate law governing them. However, in this story, as has been shown, the Great Center or First Sun, as one original substance, **develops** heat, light, and electricity **successively** as atmospheric elements, and all **according** to the law of refinement and progression. All of Matter and all the elements are fundamentally and essentially the **same**; and a different law **can-not** govern any particle or element in the Universe; there is no law except from that Inherent Law that has been eternally established. Simply understand, that all Matter in its primeval state was of an igneous constitution, it then follows as a consequence that all things existing, must be composed of materials from the Great Mass. Everything and everybody came out of the same boiling pot. Therefore heat, light, and electricity **are-still** all Matter, but each occupies a **different station** lower or higher, according to its respective degree of **refinement**. And the constant emanations of each element are governed by the original attributes established in the eternal law of motion, as producing **progressive development** in all things. This, therefore, constitutes the **grand general law** that governs all elements in space.

# Section 17

The Seventh planet **Uranus** or Herschel, was the next sphere in order that was produced from our great Sun. And during its first stages of formation it would have been seen as an accumulation of inter-associated, **igneous**, ratified particles, whose rarity **unfitted** them for any other sphere of association. The **diameter** of this planet during its formation, and **previous** to any other formations of moons and satellites that now belonging to its system, was then nearly three million of miles. However the diameter of Uranus **after** the six satellites were formed is now thirty-five thousand one hundred and twelve miles stated in the year 1846; and in contrast, the measured diameter using modern twenty-first century instruments is stated to be approximately thirty-two thousand miles.

It was by virtue of the planet's inherent motion, six satellites were **successively** developed. The most rarified accumulation was the sixth satellite which is farthest from the main planet, and the unrefined, crude and more dense satellite is nearest to the planet. Each of the satellites gradually and steadily was produced by the general laws of association and condensation.

While Uranus **revolves obliquely** on its axis, its satellites observe an angular inclined rotation, - this apparent dissimilarity of general and rotary motions certainly created wonder and astonishment in the minds of astronomers from the 1800's. Uranus's closest satellite is not much further than the moon is from the earth. At times Uranus is apparently eclipsed by her extremely eccentric satellites, seen as blue and dark spots which from earth, appear to cross Uranus's surface. It will yet be discovered that these satellites are really in unison and harmony with those satellites of Uranus's kindred planets. Further, this planet orbits around the Sun once every eighty-four years. And its distance from the Sun is greater than 1,800,000,000 miles. This large planet moves at the rate of fifteen thousand miles an hour.

The real density of this planet is little more than water. No Life of any kind exists here. The planet's atmosp**here** has a light reddish appearance, and its own body appears extremely opaque. It is of an igneous and carbonaceous constitution, having one three hundred and sixtieth part carbon to one part of oxygen. This is not-carbon of the nature that is developed in the primary layer of earth, nor is it like any elements or gases that have been development here on earth. And in this planet there is no geological developments further than the igneous primary coating or crust that now envelops it.

## Section 18

As stated, the satellites of Uranus apparently observe a different direction in their orbicular revolutions compared to what is observed from any other spherical body, including the planet's attached system of spheres, and these observations have led to varying opinions and theories, many which have attempted to nullify and dispute the uniformity and progressive developments that took place in the formations of our planetary system. And some opinions have found fault with this **Nebular Theory** of Creation. However this Nebular theory of Creation which is being given in this story, will in time, along with the use of more advanced equipment and instruments, show that these contradictions and particulars of Nature will be rectified. **Generally**, the variations in the densities of planets receding from the Sun are uniform; and also, **generally** the planets orbicular velocities are in harmony and coincide with the order and distance of each planet from the great Center, our Sun. Therefore, Matter and Motion being **generally uniform** and **progressive** in their manifestations; and so then, any "particulars" **can-not** deny or alter the truthfulness of the Nebular theory. By realizing that within the universal plan of planetary formations, **there-are** these **particulars** and apparent contradictions; however, they will be ultimately found to be **intermediate** and subordinate manifestations of the grand general law, and hence perfectly conformable as incidental effects.

# Section 19

**S**aturn the sixth planet from the Sun, was the fourth planet produced by the Sun. The particles initially thrown into the Sun's atmosphere, **destined** for the particular position or "station" in space of Saturn's orbit, and these thrown particles would condensate and form a congregation; and again, there was a further accumulation of atoms and particles from our Sun's atmosphere, by the action of "inherent motion" already existing in those atoms, and those congregating particles also **supplied** the rotary and orbicular motions as they came rushing into the accumulating mass.

Of course this planet was at first in an extremely igneous state, yet this state would adjust and cool somewhat as more and more particles emanating from the Sun ultimately organized the planet with Matter. Numerous ages elapsed before this planetary body would become internally and externally condensed by processes of chemical action and the necessary action of the evolution of elements.

In the earlier stages of this planet's development there were **constant emanations** being radiated from this body that were excessive – but the causes of these discharges is obvious. Saturn being composed of much denser materials than the former planet Uranus, and because Saturn is possessing a greater magnitude, its **power** of action and its capacity to **receive** particles was much greater than those same forces, of any other planet **yet-existing** at that time period. Matter is generally **more active** in its primeval condition and that shows with the process of this planet's formation. Saturn's igneous composition, being very active in receiving particles suitable for its association and its ability in **disengaging** the **non–essential** parts, elements, and atoms. These emitted and thrown particles produced the **nebulous zones** or belts that now surround the primary planet, and which we now know as Saturn's rings.

These nebula zones existed for many ages in the form of an igneous atmosphere, their distances from the main planetary body are naturally dictated and formed according to the law of association and centrifugal force, and by the density and rarity of its chemical composition. The evolution of the nebulous atmosphere from Saturn was **incidentally influenced** by the **existing forces** of the previously formed planets Pluto, Neptune, Uranus, all these forces then combined with that of the Sun. This action produced an active agglomerated atmospheric zone, according to the laws of mutual association and condensation. And this was the process for the formation of the first zone or ring.

The formation of Saturn's second ring was an **emanation** from the first ring. The nebulous rings of Saturn, like the planet itself, have become condensed near their surface, assuming forms oblately spheroidal. The **reflections** of Saturn's **satellites** onto the various parts of the **rings** and by frequent eclipses, give the surfaces of these rings an appearance of roughness and brightness. Saturn's rings will eventually and ultimately form globes.

The center of Saturn is still an igneous, unstratified substance, the surface having become chemically condensed by the **escape** of internal heat and by the **production** of organizing and animated gases. The diameter of Saturn is about seventy-nine thousand miles. Its distance from our Sun is more than nine-hundred million miles. It revolves in ten and one half hours. And this planet's great orbit around the Sun, takes thirty years. The inclination of its orbit to the ecliptic is about two and one half degrees, and this sphere revolves with the enormous velocity of twenty–two thousand miles miles per hour.

The inclination of this planet causes the light of the Sun to strike it vertically for a distance of several degrees on either side of it's equator, where there are twenty-five thousand days and nights in one of its years, while at the same time there is only one night and day at the poles. This planet, being situated and organized differently from the other planets, having zones which others do not, and possessing a greater number of satellites that any other planet belonging to our solar system, has long been the cause of wonder and admiration among mankind.

The distance the first ring is from the main planet is twenty thousand miles. Space between the rings is three thousand miles. The distance of outer ring is seven thousand miles; and its diameter is two-hundred thousand miles. The rings have nearly the same density as Saturn, and so, the rings revolve as quickly as the planet and also require about ten and a-half hours. The space existing between the outer ring and the first satellite, is twenty-nine thousand miles. The distance from the primary planet to the first satellite, is over one hundred-seventy miles. The mean distance form the outer satellite to the primary, is over two million miles. The other five satellites hang-in-there depending on densities and diameters, and are situated in-order of their development.

The current computations made in reference to Saturn and its satellites, add stronger proof that the law of uniformity and progressive development exists in all bodies belonging to the solar system. First, the planets diameter, velocity of motion, and period of revolution, are in exact accordance with this law, as might be expected from its density and comparative distance from the Sun. And, secondly, the first of Saturn's rings sustains a distance from the primary planet in a manner that corresponds to its magnitude and density; and these are two of many indications of the unity and harmony. Therefore Saturn, its rings and satellites, **present** to the man's view one system of progressive development as this is considered in a general point of view.

## Section 20

The geography of the planet Saturn has great beauty and is divided into two thirds water and one third earthen material. It is entirely free from all volcanic and catastrophic activity and so the planet's surface being even and undisturbed. There are only a few "earthy" prominence projecting out from the surface, and these are found near the poles; but none are found at the equator except a few higher regions of land which connect themselves with some other higher lands that form the borders of a chasm which contains a large body of water.

The surface of Saturn has developed a crust. The planet has become **suspect** of supporting life and the question arises, does or did life exist on these planets? The human minds on earth being limited as they are, can not answer this in a truthfully manner. The human mind can only be expected to know that if life does exist on another planet, it will resemble the living things known to exist on earth. However, the human mind should-not speculate on this topic, because it **has-not** had any experiences which allow the mind to form a comparison with. Yet, suppose life exists in another dimension or realm, or maybe the densities or components of any life-forms are less, so that a body or form is invisible to man's senses? Clairvoyants, prophets, seers, mediums, and many people in general, believe that there is life after death, and this notion extends further with some minds claiming that they are able to see life-forms. Nearly the whole race of mankind existing on earth believe in the existence of life after death, and believe that some-type of an essence lives on. So then, if there is life after death, then, where do all these "souls" go to when the body dies on earth? It is common to hear of stories of living people claiming to see spirits, ghosts, apparitions, and the likes. And these notions are expanded even further by the particular modern day **prophet** and clairvoyant Edgar Cayce, the well documented "seer", claims that after a person dies on earth their souls or spirits **sojourn** to other planets within this solar system to gain knowledge and experience of other houses in God's Universe, souls doing this sojourn action in-between earthly incarnations of that soul.

The mysterious topic, "the **possibility** of organic plant and animal life existing on some other planets in this or some-other solar system besides earth", was openly discussed by at least two modern day prophets, Edgar Cayce and Andrew J Davis. Both of these fascinating minds were able to perceive the existence of life-forms whom had died. Davis claims that the Universe is full of organic life, existing on millions and millions of planets. From their altered state of consciousness or clairvoyant state, Mr. Davis and Mr. Cayce both discuss the organic kingdoms that they are able to see existing on some of the planets in our solar system. So with two very interesting and accurate prophets, separately, and in different centuries giving similar observations, certainly gives an interesting twist into **other-realities** of the Universe. Davis claims that the inhabitants of other planets in this solar system **represent** either higher or lower forms of the same species within this system. So, a man on Mars represents the man of earth just existing as some more perfected forms and some higher stages of human organization, and man on Venus represents less perfected forms and lower stages of human organization. Quite a theory.

The information on extra terrestrial life-forms from Davis's writings are **not-included** in this story. If someone is interested in these topics, they would be found in parts of Sections 20, 21, 23, 24, 26, 27, in *The Principles of Nature, Her Divine Revelation*.

# Section 21

In this section, the information on extra terrestrial life-forms from Davis's writings are not included. If someone is interested in these topics, they would be found in Sections 20. 21, 23, 24, 26, 27 in THE PRINCIPLES OF NATURE, HER DIVINE REVELATION, A VOICE TO MANKIND by Andrew Jackson Davis.

# Section 22

The fifth planet from the Sun is **Jupiter**. It is also the fifth planet in succession to be developed by the Sun. And just like the formations of the previous planets, Jupiter is another accumulation of our Sun's atmospheric particles, that were "**drawn**" to this region of space, where the conglomeration named Jupiter, now orbits. Recall that the Sun's atmosphere had previously extended to this station in space. Jupiter's development as a planet followed the same laws of association and condensation and it was particles repulsed from the Sun, that were "seeking" association among the combinations that had been forming in space. After a long period of time this accumulation **became-qualified** to assume specific motions, and would also develop a spherical form. And in the beginning period of this planets condensation of material, the primary sphere and atmospheric emanations of this newly forming planetary system extended outward in space to the orbit of Jupiter farthest satellite.

Our Sun **becomes** more **dense** by throwing-off refined particles. As the Sun's density increases, then correspondingly, the particles being emitted also have become denser. In-turn, the planets that the Sun produces, are also becoming more dense. And this is evident in Jupiter's density because it is more dense than any previously developed planets. The present density of this planet is one and a quarter the density of water.

Jupiter orbits the Sun with a distance of four-hundred and ninety million miles between them. Its diameter is eighty-nine thousand miles and it evolves on its axis every ten hours. It orbits around the Sun which takes nearly twelve years.

There is an almost imperceptible inclination of Jupiter's orbit, such that, our Sun rays strikes the planets surface vertically at the equator, unceasingly. And it is by the consequence of Jupiter's great velocity of rotary motion, that this planet has somewhat flatten poles and is bulky and full at the equator.

Four satellites orbit within Jupiter's system which is three fewer than Saturn, and because of this, it is easy to relate, that Jupiter has more bulk and size that Saturn. Jupiter is fourteen hundred times the bulk of earth and contains nearly three hundred times the amount of Matter as does earth.

This planet being the largest in our solar system, would seem at a superficial view, to refute the **doctrine** of "uniformity and progression". However, the **causes** which were brought into operation upon the accumulation of particles composing this planet, were very **dissimilar** to those that acted upon Saturn. And the cause of this anomaly, was the **tendency** of "associated particles" to **adhere** more closely in this planet than they had done in Saturn; this occurred because the particles which were accumulating to ultimately construct Jupiter, possessed **greater density** and **stronger** mutual affinities; and if this had not been so, then particles would have been thrown-off from the primary mass and would have produce another satellite. But the ejection of those particles **did-not** occur. It was because the greater density and stronger affinities between particles, together with the combined forces existing in the Sun and the other planets, **prevented** any farther development of Jupiter's particles. These were **incidental causes** and acted upon the body **merely** because, during its development it was placed under **different circumstances** than those that were in operation with any other planet in this solar system, before or since Jupiter's creation.

In all its general conditions though Jupiter exhibits a **general uniformity** similar with all other planetary developments, - but in **this situation** of planetary formation and in one **other** particular, it apparently seems to contradict the Great Law established, **yet understanding** that any and all such discrepancies owe their existence to **foreign** and **incidental causes** will show that the formation of this planet is not refuting the great general and eternal law, but instead are absolutely confirming the original and universal principles and forces which had in the beginning, emanated from the great Vortex of infinite Power.

Each particular particle in a planets formation sustains a position according to its specific quality and magnitude, and a particles mutual association is called **gravitation**.

Jupiter's first satellite is two hundred and sixty-six thousand miles away from the main mass, and its revolution is one day and eighteen hours. The second satellite is four hundred and twenty thousand miles from its primary, and its period of revolution is three and a half days. The third satellite is supposed to be the largest one of this planet, but is **not-correct**. This satellite's mean distance from Jupiter is six hundred and seventy thousand miles, and has a period of revolution being seven days. The fourth satellite is over one million miles from Jupiter, and revolves in sixteen and a half days.

# Section 23

In this section Mr. Davis gives information concerning the organic substances of Jupiter. He describes them and uses the descriptions to form an analogy between life existing on earth and life existing on other planets, and Davis claims these are given by the clairvoyant for the purpose of "giving mankind living on earth lessons to improve humanity".

# Section 24

In this particular section the inhabitants supposedly existing on Jupiter are discussed.

## Section 25

The four **Spheroidal Bodies**. Approaching nearer the Sun from Jupiter are located these four **Spheroids**, happily existing between Jupiter and Mars. These four spheres have similar orbits and revolutions around the Sun. The names of these are **Ceres**, **Pallas**, **Juno**, and **Vesta**. The appearance of these planet-like orbs may at first cause confusion with the plan of "progressive development" of a solar systems planetary arrangement. But instead, these spheroids sustain an interesting relationship.

At first it was **believed** that these four spheres were some remains of a comet that appeared in the year 1770. The comet was sighted but then it mysteriously disappeared. So when these spheres were discovered the hypothesis of being remains of a comet had its origin, and to add to this mystery, there is the fact that the orbits of these spheres are extremely elliptic and are constantly intersecting the planes of each other, which had falsely led to astronomers of that earlier period to make this speculation about their origin being a comet.

Another fact is that two of these four spheroids seem to have a luminous atmosphere, rather dense and changing, and it was supposed by some to be the remnant of the luminous trail of the cometary body. However these spheres were not produced from comets. Because, **comets** exist as an **ultimate** of a solar system and they maintain their orbits with a **perfect precision** as do the planets. And comets holding a **position** in space in accordance with their bulk and density, they travel in their own paths **undisturbed** and **beyond** the possibility of disturbing any other body in the Universe. It is known that comets take anywhere from forty months to five hundred years to accomplish their revolutions around the Sun. It is known that a comets velocity increases as it approaches its own particular solar system's center.

**Comets** are composed of unstratified particles, an **ultimate** of the solar system, and they are **governed** by the same unchanging laws of gravitation or association that control every atom in space.

So in contemplating the **origin** of the four **Asteroids**, know that they **conformed** to established laws of development and follow these laws as do every-other sphere. Then, as one is considering the magnitude of Jupiter and Mars and then comparing these two planets to the **combined magnitudes** of these four asteroids, there will be seen that there is a relationship existing between those planets and these smaller bodies that are between them: because, the **diameters** of these bodies **united**, would **conform** to the law of "successive development", situated between Jupiter and Mars.

These four spheroids have a density greater than Jupiter, as they should from following the law of positive progression. Their density being more than two times that of water. If these four bodies were combined and condensed properly like other planets had formed, they would have a diameter less than Jupiter, but exceeding that of Mars. The first spheroid Pallas exists two hundred and twenty-five million miles from the Sun, and the last sphere is two hundred and sixty-six million miles, the other two are in-between.

After the development of Jupiter , our Suns atmosphere had technically decreased and now only **extended** to a position beyond that of Mars to where the orbit plane now occupied by **Pallas**. And so according to principles previously established, the gathering of particles or the "association of particles", would **produce** an agglomerated igneous mass of matter. The **density** of this composition, being greater than any other body in our solar system, at that time-period, **prevented** this igneous mass from ascending to any higher station or orbit from the Sun.

However, there **was-not** a perfect association of interior materials. Great **convulsions** were constantly occurring, all-throughout the interior of the sphere's composition. The interior heat being so excessive, that evaporation **could-not** take place with sufficient rapidity to give perfect relief to the great expanding-force of the interior elements. Nor could elements "chemically associate", nor could a unity exist in the partly stratified exterior. This accumulation of materials then being internally disunited, and then also, because the whole mass had **not-yet** become situated perfectly under the influence of attraction and repulsion, - so, the whole mass was **shattered** by an **incomprehensible expansion** of interior elements, and was blown apart. The action of this catastrophic event split the one mass into four major pieces, causing the spontaneous formation of four masses of **associated** particles and they soon transformed to **became** what they now are, **Four Asteroids**. These four spheres were almost instantly brought under the direct influence of Jupiter and Mars, which resulted in a uniformity of motion.

The only thought concerning these asteroids useful to man is that they had shown the natural result of what occurs when the interior elements within a planetary sphere are **discordant** and **opposed** to each other. Order and harmony are the natural results of perfect principles – and so are disorder and confusion the natural results of blending together and commingling of opposite and antagonistic principles and elements!

# Section 26

    The fourth planet from the Sun is **Mars**, yet Mars was the sixth planetary formation of our Sun, and this is depending upon whether the four Asteroids are counted. Mars was produced following the same laws and procedures as occurred previously with the other planets. Formed by the actions and results of **principles** previously explained.

    The density of Mars is three times that of water. The principle of progressive and "successive development" continues and its unwavering process reveals, as it should reveal, a **decrease** in magnitude and an **increase** in density as compared with previous planetary productions from our Sun.

    The mean distance of Mars from the Sun is one hundred and forty-four million miles. And its diameter is about four thousand two hundred and twenty miles. Because this planet is beyond the orbit of Earth, it is naturally a **superior** planet and is composed of a superior quality and constitution of materials. It rotates upon its axis in twenty-four and a half hours, and obits the Sun in six hundred and eighty-six days. Mars's extremely dense atmosphere presents to the human eye, an illumination of a red appearance. The cause of this is that the materials composing the stratified parts of this planet are greatly attractive to the particles of light thrown form the Sun. The atmosphere of Mars, extends upward twenty-five miles higher than earth's. The surface of Mars presents a great deal of unevenness, and has an rough appearance being from the many catastrophic events which have occurred. There are several parts of this planet with an abundance of extreme elevations, including many projections of rocks jutting up from its interior; these elevated areas are mostly existing at the poles, but not the equator. Also at the poles there are peculiar changes and radiations of light – which give an indication of diversity of seasons.

# Section 27

In this section, the information on extra terrestrial life-forms from Davis's writings are not included. If someone is interested in these topics, they would be found in Sections 20. 21, 23, 24, 26, 27 in THE PRINCIPLES OF NATURE, HER DIVINE REVELATION, A VOICE TO MANKIND by Andrew Jackson Davis.

# Section 28

The second closest planet to the Sun is **Venus**, and it is the eight planetary development of our Sun. Earth, as everyone knows is the next planet in succession after Mars to be developed by the Sun however a description of Earth will be delayed so that Venus can be described first, then Mercury and lastly will be Earth.

Venus presents herself as evolved from the great central mass of the Sun. It had developed and evolved as a planetary body by the same unchanging laws of the Universe. Her density is greater than earth's, as it should be, which is six times (6x) that of water. Its diameter is nearly eight thousand miles. This planet exists and orbits sixty eight million miles from the Sun. Venus's period of revolution around the Sun is two hundred and twenty-four days. And it has an axial rotation of twenty-three and a half hours.

Its the planet known as both the **morning** and **evening Star**. There are high mountains and ejected rocks, that disturb the otherwise smoothness of her appearance. Some of these tall mountains are several miles higher than are the highest mountains on Earth. Especially on the **polar side** facing earth, whereas the **other side** has more smoothness. A great portion of this planet is covered with water. The atmosphere surrounding Venus is somewhat like earth's, but is composed of **less rare** particles than that of earth. The atmosphere of Venus allows more sun-light to enter.

# Section 29

The first planet and nearest to the Sun, **Mercury** is the ninth planetary sphere formed from the Sun's original atmosphere. Mercury is the ninth planet formed from the Sun excluding the four spheroidal Asteroids. Mercury was also created by those unwavering laws of **successive development** of planetary systems, as all previous spheres were created.

Mercury takes the bottom rung closest to Sun as it should, being the **densest** of planets in this solar system. Its orbit is more elliptical than Earth or Venus. Mercury's diameter is three thousand two hundred miles, and its distance from the Sun is thirty seven million miles. This planet takes a period of eighty eight days to make a revolutionary orbit around its center, our Sun. The velocity which this planet moves through space is one hundred thousand miles hour. Mercury rotates on its axis twenty four hours. The density of Mercury is nearly nine times that of water. And because of its orbit and placement near the Sun, it receives about seven times more light than does Earth.

Presenting both an increase of density and also a increase of motion, Mercury **confirms** the truth that was intended to be expressed, that **all materials** in the Universe **seek association** according to their specific gravity and quality. Mercury is so near the Sun the planet is not always visible. There is an intersecting of orbits, which causes it to pass over the disk of the Sun only about thirteen times in a century.

The **atmosphere** surrounding this planet is extremely luminous, and because of the planets proximity to the Sun, one would assume that there would be excessive light and heat; but, the heat and light that are received on this planet are not so excessive as might be supposed. The **materials** of this planet do not have much affinity for either light or heat. Therefore the planet's materials **rejects** (reflects) any light or heat that is excessive and **retains** only the quantity suitable for the planets necessary actions.

Some portions of this planet's surface are very uneven while other parts are extremely smooth. Also, there are two great barren deserts covering almost one third of this planet. One item is that there is excessive **subterranean heat** which exist, and this produces great internal commotion and excitement "watery" elements near the borders of these deserts, some of the vents ejecting boiling "water". In a similar fashion, there is great commotion and excitement occurring within the atmospheric elements. Great and fierce winds are sometimes produced on this planet and these are in response to those elements that are seeking an equilibrium. These winds generally occur near the region of those deserts and these great winds carry with them the excessive heat.

# Section 30

Following a **review** of our Solar System which will lead finally to a description of the evolution of the planet Earth. But first it is necessary to described in more detail the luminous **Center** of this solar system, our Sun. The Sun is a ball of fire, and has been spoken of many times during the descriptions of the planets as each one came into being. And all planets in this solar system have their **origin** from this Sun. The Sun's diameter is more than eight hundred and eighty-six thousand miles.

The Sun is a **never-failing** symbol and is the embryo of all material formations in this solar system. It is the Vortex of this solar system, the great Center, and it had previously contained all that has been "breathed" into existence and is connected to our planetary system. The **reason** why our Sun originally came into being is because all materials composing this sphere were motivated, activated, and sent in motion, on their way to their **destiny** by Inherent Forces which were impressed on them by the Creator.

The remaining particles still contained in the Sun and not used in planet building are particles of a crude and unrefined nature and are mostly existing in some interior portions of this sphere, while materials near the surface are constantly evolving refined elements in the form of heat, light, and electricity.

The **Sun** is the central body from which all the planets and satellites within the extreme circumference of this great mass's influence have been formed. It is still incessantly giving off particles that have become rarefied and refined. And this Sun, of the fifth circle of Suns, continues to **exert** an **orderly influence** upon all Forms and particles in the planetary system. It **can-not** decrease in magnitude because it has "become a planet of the **requisite** degree of density"; and it has formed all the planets that it can produce. The whole solar system is now **counterbalanced** by the Sun's own magnitude, and with the **whole** planetary system **united**. There is **co-joined harmony** because all are following the general and established law of gravitation or association.

It is now necessary to give deep reflected thought and analysis to all the creations within this solar system, doing this in order that the mind may become aware of the original Design.

There is no dispute that **order** and **uniformity** are existing in the formation of our solar system, beginning from the first body evolved, and continuing to the last. Mercury the last planet produced being more crude and dense, then proceeding outward, the planets and satellites become more **refined** and less dense. It was revealed that the planets further away from the Sun **evolved satellites**, while those which were nearer to the Sun **did-not**; these results occurred because "refinement and activity" are the **consequent results** of each other; while on the other hand crudeness, imperfection, and comparative rest, are the **results** of those sluggish materials which compose the nearer planets. There is perfect order, perfect uniformity, and perfect harmony, in this process.

The idea of oneness is a difficult concept or law to express; in basic terms, it is "the law of ceaseless progression" occurring in the Universe and everything is progressing towards its ultimate. That same law is established and at work here in our solar system, just the same as is everywhere. The lowest **contains** the highest, **undeveloped**, and then, the highest **pervades** the lower and **extracts** from the lower all particles **fitted** for higher degrees of association. This law occurs throughout everything and our system is merely a **representative** of the action of the whole Universe.

# Section 31

The formation of each planetary sphere existing in our solar system has been discussed, except the description of Earth's formation which has been left for last. Therefore a description of Earth's formation will **soon** be given.

Motion, Life, and Sensation, are **essential developments** which **must-occur** upon any planet that will develop plants and animals. First, plants develop from the minerals contained in that planet, and **Life** occurs when those mineral particles form combinations, which then develop **Motion** or movement, and this process **is-how** and when plants truly come into being. **Any planet** in the Universe whose minerals form into combinations, and then, those mineral combinations move-about, then a living plant has been formed and there is Life on that planet. And there are a lot of planets existing in the Universe that possess life. So it can be seen, there is this wonderful "**connection**" between things; minerals that develop motion become living plants; and plants that develop Sensation, are animals.

The mineral Forms created on a particular planet are **dependent upon** the original materials and atoms composing that planet under review; next to occur, depending upon the particular minerals of a planet, is the criteria which depends the **plants** that are formed. And then, the **animals** of that planet are dependent on both mineral and plant Forms of that particular planet's developments.

It is the existence and evolution of plants which bring into creation the principles of **Motion** and **Life**. And then the animal kingdom is only "**one degree**" more perfect than the plant, and this higher development is characterized by **Sensation** - which is a result of Motion and Life. So therefore, it is only when these three principles Motion, Life, and Sensation, have been developed and **combined** into one Form which bring into creation the animal. And then, it is **only** when a correct conception of Sensation is understood, that we can know of **Instinct**. Then with the development of instincts the animal Forms **represent** higher stages of refinement of an organism, and this development shows that there is a "unbroken" **connection** between animal and man. This connection confirms and reveals that Man stands as an **ultimate** of all the materials and Forms on the planet's surface; because, Man is only one more degree of development or just one more step above the animal which exists below them. Man then is the ultimate; and man becomes the ultimate by adding one more degree of refinement to the existing three original principles. So within Man there exists the **four principles**, that of Motion, Life, Sensation, and **Intelligence**.

Motion symbolizes Life, and is representative of Life. Life then symbolizes and is representative of Sensation. And Sensation then symbolizes and represents the beginnings of Intelligence. There is an **unbroken chain** in all of existence. And there are **successive links** of connection that are part of this chain, which are all parts of Creation. These connecting links are observed between the mineral, the plant, animal, and man. The same laws and the same unbroken chain with its successive links, holds true with all the various productions of mineral, plant, animal, and "mankind" which are existing on other **inhabitable planets**.

However sometimes man is **not-able** to understand or see the connected chain which exists, nor see the interconnection between things. Sometimes there are **extreme differences** between the things man sees, and this event rightly clouds his mind and so the connection is **not apparent**. The mind tends to sees things as being apparently separate and disconnected, - then the mind immediately, but incorrectly conceives of this strange idea of positive-opposites and separatism, the mind in error develops the conceptions of positive-opposites such as death and life, good and evil, and light and darkness.

Man's confusion is from **ignorance** and the failure of their undeveloped minds to understand the necessary inter-connectiveness of things and developments. All **discord** is cause by man and his undeveloped mind. It is only necessary to realize that higher Forms **evolve** from lower Forms. So, the lower contains the higher. One is connected to another and each is necessary for the other. The higher existed in the lower, **undeveloped**.

**However**, in order to have a proper conception of light, life, and spiritual intelligence, we **must-first** see that which is apparently the opposite. And then the very moment that we see the lower conditions, we form a conception of the higher conditions; but this we do not do until the lower conditions are made visible and known. This process at this present time, is a necessary part of man's development, so that spiritual growth can occur. It appears that in-order for mankind to grow, they must first conceive of opposite and extremes such as life and death, good and evil, and a separation from oneness, and **experience** the ramifications of our separation, and then gaining a correct understanding of the inter-connections which exist we begin to develop spiritual awareness.

So by showing that the lowest **typifies** the highest; and the very moment you conceive and understand such a possibility, such a relationship, and representation, then all ideas of opposites are **annihilated**, and there will be an awareness that everything is connected. Realize that the First must exist before the Ultimate, the Alpha before Omega; and all things

**must** harmonize perfectly and all conform to the established "law of universal and eternal progression". The Yin and Yang of things. Therefore opposites do not exist. And so, what is gross, crude and imperfect, and apparently opposed to higher developments, **merely** has not progressed to the standard of perfection that we have erected in our minds.

The concept of Oneness can be stated as a general law, "that the lowest not only typifies and represents the highest, but one is absolutely-necessary for the existence of the other". And believe, that without general principles, putting out general uses, to produce general ends, none of these Forms would have existed. Truth is **cause** and **effect** are inseparable. And so within this **Truth** it not only establishes an unbroken connection between every particle in the Universe, but presents to our minds, and especially to every inductive mind, that this is the highest representation of the **original design** conceived by the Great Positive Mind!

So it can be stated again and again, that within our solar system all things in the Universe are represented. Our Sun was represented as originally extending Its substance and Its atmosphere to the orbit of the outermost planet Pluto; and it was shown that by a process of shrinking and condensation, and an evolution of particles, the Sun and the planets have assumed their present form and condition.

## Section 32

Our planet **Earth**, is the third rock from the Sun. Earth is the seventh planetary system which was developed in succession from the particles thrown-out from our Sun. And that is the **origin** and beginning of **the World**!

Philosophical **science** studying Nature, reality, and existence, has attempted with great effort to discover and **account** for the origin and formation of this globe; and have been doing so on principles of Nature and Reason; while, **theology** has put forward a great effort to **sustain** forever the **opinions** that were **imagined** and entertained by the primitive generations of mankind. And then these mythological opinions have been sanctioned by theological authority; however this authority itself is also based upon imaginary beliefs and mythology.

Over the course of time, our great system of science has arrive at some general truths concerning Earths origin and evolution, but these discoveries have been obtained with great difficulty. The majority of mankind existing on earth have obtain their beliefs and truths in error, by pursuing curved lines through the labyrinths of **mythology** and various **superstitions** beliefs, all which have been sustained in **every age** and in **every nation** of man. These realms of darkness and ignorance are still in the present day **concealing** the real truth under a veil of **mythological opinions**.

Thankfully, Scientific philosophy has demonstrated that there are immutable natural laws, and have revealed that there is a Truth which is immortal and which is found in the **unchanging** nature of all **principles** governing the Universe.

Mythology and countless superstitions **persist** though, and are still a strong force into the twenty-first century; because as some influential minds have **ignorantly supposed**, - that the world **assumed** its present form and condition "in an instant of time". And others, have **supposed** that from an incomprehensible nothing, a tangible something was created.

Another important item to impress upon the reader's mind, is that these mythological opinions of early primitive nations have been **manipulated**, and over time, were gradually and almost imperceptibly **modified** as new thoughts and knowledge came into man's awareness and unfolded within the developing minds of mankind in general. It was by a **gradual modification** of early mythological opinions, that "a duration of time" was **devised** and concluded to be the beginning – to be the period of the creation of the world as some people know and believe still today. However the duration of time for the beginning of earth **varied** from six thousand to forty thousand years depending upon whose mythology was reviewed. And **those** early records and separate mythologies of ancient nations, have been brought forward by **tradition** and actually **revered**, and continue and are further used and **sustained** in-order to confirm these **opinions** from mythology as being the truth.

These mythological beliefs prevailed **universally** without relief until a mind (? Galileo) **became** enlightened through the activity of mental **reason**, which allowed the discovery of the true position and place of the **Earth** among the other planetary bodies. However, this man was almost crucified, and had to relent upon his revelations. His "lighted-mind" was nearly extinguished. And man's path of advancement again became a slow and treacherous course.

Theology and philosophy have been apparently opposed to each other. While one is **endeavoring** with all its energies to discover an indestructible basis upon which a **true theory** of the origin could rest, the other is putting forth any and all the deplorable **obstructions** that naturally arise from ignorance and fanaticism. Our World, has given birth to all the **thoughts** that have been conceived by mankind ever since their minds became capable of thought. Earth is the **theater** of human action; it is the **habitation** of pain and pleasure, of life and death, of knowledge and ignorance.

The Earth and Nature's laws have given existence to Man, who is the ultimate of material perfection. Nature has endowed mankind with faculties and powers and sensibilities. And Nature has **stamped** into every particle of mankind's constitution the **original imprint** of eternal Design. Nature openly display's God's eternal design by Her immutable and unchanging laws, which in a glorious display have produced this organism and organization of Man.

But man is a mess, and instead of cherishing the spontaneous flow of positive and progressive thoughts coming from Nature, especially those thoughts respecting the foundation and magnificent structure of the Universe, instead, the mind of man has forgotten or eliminated any hint of Nature and Reason in his thinking, and has gone in search of things that are **destructive** to the happiness of the world. And because of this, **man** has **lost sight** of the **true relationship** existing between Nature and Science.

The whole world has been in such a depressed and degraded condition for so-long a period, no words can be found to describe the **misery**. And it has been the fault of mankind **solely**, which has brought this profound misery into existence. There is a **raging battle** between man's developing intellect and their developed ignorance. The intellect constantly yearning for freedom and truth; while the constant yearning of a narrow and undeveloped mind is to **conceal** the light and truths which Nature sets out for mankind.

Plenty of facts have been obtained by the minds of man, seeking to answer all the important questions that need answering; yet, important questions remains unanswered; "just **how**" were the materials and essences that compose this world, produced in the first place? And how, were they formed into their present condition? These are very important questions, yet, even though these questions are intimately connected to the **aspirations** of every inquiring mind, there still has been no answer to them.

It is for this reason, "because man needs to know it", that it is **necessary** to obtain and adequate answer to these unanswered questions. Besides, what could be of more value and of more importance to man then to have a knowledge of our world's original condition, and of its ultimate termination?

So with all those questions in mind, here and now in entering into the subject of Earth's origin; giving generalizations that are so immense and so wonderful, it is **necessary** then, to **pursue** every particular and nuance that is connected with this vast undertaking, and doing this investigation so that nothing may be misconceived or misinterpreted.

## Section 33

At a period of time too remote for computation, but at least several billions of years ago, there was an **accumulation** which was composed of an inconceivable and incalculable magnitude of atoms and particles which had previously constituted the atmosphere of the Sun, that would begin to condense into this **conjunction** of particles called **Earth**. These substances following their original impetus, became **condensed** by the **action** of perpetual **inherent** energies which had **existed** in the original accumulation; and these were able to **produce** the oblate spheroidal Form of the Earth, and also there was plenty of the needed materials to form its inspiring satellite, the **Moon**.

The whole massive body of Earth's atoms was **sustained** in the appropriate position in space by the **mutual relations** existing between Earth and the Sun. Those particles thrown from the Sun, became associated by the **natural affinity** which they had for each other as a result of the **refined condition** in-which those particles had chemically progressed, **before-leaving** the great central mass of our Sun.

The **Force** by which those particles and substances left the Sun is termed **repulsion** and their association together is called **attraction**; and the position of the earth in reference to the Sun is the result of what is supposed to be the "laws of attraction and repulsion", however the terms attraction and repulsion **are-not** use correctly in that phrase, but are only used by necessity. Realize that particles are continuously emanating from our Sun out into space; but only those particles that **were-suitable** to enter into the composition of earth's young igneous mass **gravitated** to it, and **immediately** established an **association** with it. The whole mass of earth was in a state of **igneous-fluidity**. For a long period of time the diameter of spherical Form of earth was of such a immense magnitude; because the particles had not yet condensed completely. **Heat** of great magnitude kept the youthful sphere in an igneous liquid form; the interior of the whole **rugged sphere** being **agitated** from the center to the surface with great wavelike motions. And for reference, the type of undulations which were occurring, would be those motions which naturally occur in such a great a mass of uncondensed and molten lava spinning and moving through space.

The whole earth mass had developed a motion that **complied** with the impulse of **Force** originally given to earth by the particles thrown-out by the Sun; those particles traveling at an unbelievable velocity, came **slamming** into the existing massive accumulation of atoms, causing the mass to spinning faster now; and as a consequence of the spin, the rugged and **angular** shapes and masses of materials rapidly began assumed shapes and Forms which progressed to the **spherical** Form, and this sphere gradually develops diameters, axes, and poles. Over time as the materials of earth became more development and they became more perfect, earths rotary motion became improved and firmly established. From the **improved** rotary motions and revolutions, the forming planet **assumed** the correct bulk and Form, and **position**, to "obey its original impetus" as part of Creation.

The Rotary Motion is an **effect produced by** the impetus of particles and atoms **rushing** to the great body's position in space. The Revolutionary Motion in an elliptical orbit, having an aphelion and perihelion in contra-position to the Sun, is **an-effect** produced by the general energy force given it, by a perpetual application of those same Forces which are producing the rotary motion. The elliptical orbit of earth gives **evidence** that the whole body was **thrown** from another body more immense, and earth having the same motions as that larger body. The primal condition of earth was that of a kind of fire-matter in a state of "active fluidity"; this fact which is very evident, because if primal earth were originally of a solid or elastic state, it would-not have been able to assume a spheroidal form. Also, the fullness and bulge at the equator represents another indication that the earth was originally fluid-like.

# Section 34

As stated previous, the atmospheric reach of the original mass of substance from the Sun, which now composes the Earth, also originally included particles in the vicinity of the orbit now observed by earth's satellite the **Moon**. And the satellite (moon) shows in its motion, precisely the effect of what has been asserted were the forces acting upon it.

The accumulation of atoms and particles comprising the earth and moon, occurred in a succession of events; and during the early stages of development there was **constantly** an interchanging of particles going on between the earth and moon, with each accumulation of atoms and particles and chunks **slamming** with great velocity into the accumulating masses.

How is it that these atoms and particles composing the earth and moon **reached** and then **sustain** their relative positions to the Sun? How could the particular distance be obtained, the density, the motions and velocity have occurred, except by the result of the primitive law and condition of Matter; which is the **relative affinities of particles**, and this is a general truth. As stated, the original **Form** of the earth and moon, were angular, meaning not-spherical. Then the large particles and Forms ascending and changing rapidly to the circular Form, and this is also a general truth.

It is **impossible** for any substance of Matter to **assume** - any Form, above the angular, as the first stage of that Form. First is the angular. It matters-not, how rapidly this Form is modified to the circular, or spiral; but the **first** must exist before the second or before any other can. And although that change from one form to another may be imperceptive to the senses, that change **must occur** in all the lower states of material composition.

The **Trap** and **Basalt** that have been **thrown** from the interior of the earth by internal heat are existing **indications** of the first angular Forms which were produced, especially as these are the most prominent and rugged manifestations in Nature.

The Earth displays rugged and uneven portions such as mountains, valleys; and these structures were **formed** when the Whole was in a state of undulating (wave-like) **agitation**. And it was **only-when** the fluid Mass became gradually **transformed** near its surface into an elastic state, that this roughness of hills and valleys was produced as a **solid** and definite Form of landscape.

There is an item which needs contemplation and to keep in mind, is that from the very beginning the elements and constituents that were involved in the great earthy Mass, were **adequate** in their **properties** and qualities. This is stated because, when the particles of this great mass, were

**subjected** to **favorable conditions**, they "inherently" and "successively", **produced** all Forms that have been constructed; not only in the mineral, but in the vegetable and animal kingdoms as well.

Deep beneath the **crust** of this great mass, there are existing undeveloped beauties and magnificence not comparable with anything which has been developed on this planet so far. Several thousand miles of molten lava and unimaginable fire rolls through the subterranean abodes of the Earth.

The story now proceeds with a description of the formation of the **early casting** of this igneous center, or in other words the formation of earth's primary crust. Geological research has done much to bring the principles of Nature to the mind of man. And they have been extremely helpful in dispersing the darkness that has so long concealed the origin and primitive history of our earth. Geology has led to many useful classifications, both in the mineralogical and zoological developments of this globe, and in many cases, their true "basis" appear to have been discovered and have been of great use as man has investigated their origin. However it is impossible for the mind to observe the adaptation of one composition to another, nor can it easily-see the relations that are harmoniously existing between the elements of all sciences and of the world. This simply means there is much more to learn.

# Section 35

As stated, the whole fiery fluid mass was in a state of motion and agitation. Then gradually over a very long period of time the surface started to cool, becoming **relieved** of its heat. The consequence of this heat loss led to a **shrinking** and **condensation** of particles, and in time, the whole surface became **united-together** by an elastic **coating**.

After another very long time period, this elastic surface became sufficiently consolidated and cooled to produce the **primary granite** rock. And as more heat escaped from the internal fiery interior, so did particles **ascend** from the molten mass and **unite** with the consolidated parts of the coating. And it was by a process of constant accumulation and dispersion of molecular substances, that the original primary rock or granite was developed.

The earth's surface was extremely uneven, and would became more so by the **increase** of catastrophic convolutions and volcanic operations. Those tremendous upheavals of the crust and molten matter had followed this **closing-up** of the interior heat, by the newly forming crust.

There was inconceivable **agitation** of the internal portion of earth, with the **mighty conflict** of the roaring elements. The expansion of heat and particles, and their constant struggling to obtain relief, **produced** some of the most terrific explosions imaginable. And rock materials were thrust upward through the crust. These mountains of rock are still standing as good evidence of the **original** internal excitement reigning throughout the bowels of the earth. These rock ejections which had reached the surface crust, caused immense valleys in which were contained seas of almost bottomless depth and in some cases had depths of 400 miles from highest point of land to bottom of that sea of liquid material.

At this time-period in the course of earth's evolution, a "**watery solution**" covered nearly the whole face of the this planet; and it was by this watery element's incessant and powerful actions, that gradually wore-away at those towering rocky portions that had been previously ejected. This "watery" **solution** was an "active agent" and was an element of action causing erosion. Know that the element which was in this period known as "water", does not exist now nor did it have the same constituents as the water now known on earth. Because in the first place, it was **impossible** for **oxygen** and **hydrogen** to have been developed in that age, especially in any sufficient quantities to produce the oceans of the size that were then existing. Nevertheless, other types of chemical processes continued, and it is known to almost all researchers of the twenty-first century , that **oxy-**

gen composes a great part of the **whole** crust of the earth; and **nitrogen** greatly pervades Nature; and that **hydrogen**, is intermediately active in many substances, and hydrogen also enters into the composition of the watery substance. Also **fluorine** has also been lately discovered, which is rather an ultimate of nitrogen and hydrogen in the combined states in which they are often found. And **carbon** at the beginning was existing in some forms, **though-not** so extensively as the other elements, carbon being seldom found in a pure state, though it sometimes occurs in fine, pure forms, as those of diamond. To make a clear point concerning the abundance of these early formed elements, know that, there is **not existing** in Nature any combination of particles that does not contain some or all of these elements just mentioned; and, it is impossible to find them totally disconnected from other substances.

However-inconsistent the above proposition may appear, it is nevertheless true, - and for the obvious reason; that, at this stage of earth's formation, oxygen and hydrogen **could-not** have composed water; because in this stage of development, those elements had no attraction-forces yet, so they could not have been developed. Those elements, therefore remained in their gross form; and the **decomposition** of which, produced a very dense watery liquid of a nature and density, one fourth the specific gravity of quicksilver or liquid mercury.

It is **only-by** having the correct knowledge and understanding of the physical laws governing Matter, (or of the tendency that matter constantly indicates), that a true conception can be formed of qualities contained in any composition, whether simple or compound. Many Chemists know these exciting facts to be true. And with a **standard** of **density**, which science has founded, it is then, that the **densities** of all other bodies are able to be expressed according to their **relations** to this **Standard**.

The properties of Matter have been one of the leading subjects of investigation by the entire scientific community, and there has been much discussion among scientific minds, whether Matter is ultimately **indivisible**, or whether it is infinitely **divisible**. First know that the whole Mass of Matter, including all elements and principles, is **Conjoined** by **Association**; and this Fact, whether it is relating to substances gross or refined, defies all power to reduce particles composing any form of matter to their ultimate state of disconnection. So then, it is upon this **foundation** that rests principally the **proposition**, that the **original fluid** contained in "watery" element existing upon the face of the world at that age, **could-not** have been as **rarefied** as the water formed from the combination of oxygen and hydrogen as we know it today.

The substance known as granite, is of itself a chemical **combination** of other substances in-which one or more of the following may be found. **Mica**, but this is not generally very prominent; but **feldspar**, **quartz**, and **horn-blended**, are more conspicuous. Also keep in mind, that these minerals themselves are composed of an indefinite number of elements and particles. Realize, that it is by an infinity of minute particles, which themselves have a far-more interior composition, in which the prominent substances, or rocks, or the elements contained in them, are chemically organized and established upon this planet as well as others.

Hopefully it will now be easier to see that the **density** of the "watery element" covering the earth's surface was in **proportion** to the **density** of the composition of the granite, whose interior components bore a similar relation to the substances entering into its own composition.

## Section 36

**M**atter is a word used throughout the world as **equivalent** and equal to the substance of **everything** in the Universe. But then, as matter **evolves** and new elements and substances are formed, of course then new names and phrases are then needed to describe them. So as **substances change** and **e**volve, the names by which they are designated, change and develop, but matter is always matter.

So then beginning at **granite**, with this crystalline igneous rock being **originally** of the proximate density of one-quarter quicksilver, then next, we come to an element of the density of **sulfuric acid**; then to the density of **water**; then to the density of **sulfuric ether**; then to the **atmosphere**; then to its ultimate **fluorine**; and then to the imponderable **elements** known as **magnetism** and **electricity**.

There is a range and a diversity in Nature's **elements** and they have qualities and motions that are of both a simple and compound nature. And in addition, there are some attributes of Matter that **are-not** as yet in the least bit understood or imagined. Because it must be remembered, that it was **only after** there was discovered the principles of the **diamagnetic** which had already been seen and were already being utilized, that the evidence of phenomenon of the compass needle deflection was discovered and explained by Mr. Micheal Faraday. (note: during the original "clairvoyant episode" from where this material originates; which was delivered by Davis on April 29, 1846, in which Davis made reference to Faraday's recent discovery of the dielectric or intersecting principle, even though Davis had no knowledge of Faraday) ......."*an imponderable element (magnetic) had recently been discovered,* **this element** *whose* **motion, intersected** *the current contained in a wire, producing the direction of the magnetic needle*". Mr. Davis discussing Mr. Faraday.

So in review of the formation of **elements**, there was occurring at the time-period discussed prior, when the crust was just formed, and when the **whole-face** of Nature experienced the most inconceivable and devastating **convulsions**, and this event causing the ejection of rocks and mountain prominence. Well, also at that time-period, there was existing between these rocky protrusions, narrow spaces or valley's, which were **filled** by a **fluid element** that had a density of one fourth the density of quicksilver, or somewhat exceeding the density of sulfuric acid, or about twice the density of today's water. This **fluid** was originally produced by a development of the **grosser forms** of oxygen, of sulfurous acid, of alumina, and of carbon. And this "watery" substance was active in the process of erosion.

The crude and **unrefined forms** of these elements, as they were first existing, actually are the only forms that could possibly have been first developed. These elements were unfolded and **developed** by the "action" of the **envelope** or crust of the whole Mass, and by the **affinity** which the new and lighter particles had for the atmosphere, which had began to be formed and was now beginning to surround the world. These separate elements of a crude nature, when conjoined, **produced** the "watery element" which had a specific gravity that was similar to and also conforming with, the substances that are found in granite.

The granite, as it became more developed and refined, and also because of the fact of its high density, the coating **was-able** to sustain a joined and interlocking **association** and relation to and with the interior igneous elements below it. Visually it could have been imagined as the granite and everything else as **floating** on a big fireball.

In speaking of the **atmosphere** that had begun to develop and which surrounded the whole Mass, was altogether **unlike** that atmosphere which now encompasses the earth. The earths fiery internal elements had produced a dense atmospheric composition whose specific gravity was **almost** as dense as today's-water is dense. These new elements chemically "ascended" into earth's envelope, becoming a comparatively dense atmosphere, by the **action** of refinement and affinity. No Form possessing Life could have existed upon the earth's surface while the elements of water and atmosphere were in this state. And this was and remained the state and conditions of the earth, for countless ages.

The **atmosphere** was composed of a very small portion of nitrogen, one-sixth portion of carbon, and the remainder consisted of the imperfect developments of hydrogen, sulfur, and fluorine. The **peculiar** affinities which these elements chemically sustained to each other have since changed and evolve and have become greatly **modified**. Because at that period of evolution, all elements of earth were imperfectly developed. Certain ones though have progressed up to our present day, and have by now **ascended** to the perfected Form of elements of our present atmosphere; whereas, carbon and other simple elements have gradually become **sequestered** among the mineral and plant compositions, both on and beneath the earth's surface.

Giving a brief review of planet earth's evolution during this epoch, shows the chemical development of some **refined particles** which were previously components of the original "watery" substance and these have since, by chemical processes, evolved and have **ascended** and **assumed** the progressed chemical **Forms** of the simple and compound substances of the **atmosphere**, all of-which surrounds the world and pervades into the immense space surrounding us; while at the same time **other** particles, elements, and compounds, coming from inside the earth, have also gradually chemically **ascended** to take their place and to "fill the deserted stations" of the elements rising into the atmosphere, and to now **become** the "new watery element". And still, **others** again have **descended** to enter into the mineral substances which they chemically have had an affinity for.

Here is the whole process of the formation of the primary layer of crust stated again in a shorter manner: - it was during this early epoch in earths evolution, and after the granite had been formed. And this first layer of granite then being a composition of mica, feldspar, quartz, and hornblende, which, when the process of the **condensation** of the primary coatings chemically **ultimate** particles occurred, would **produce** the watery element; then, the chemical **ultimate** of the watery element, in turn would **produce** the atmospheric envelope. These chemical processes were simply the **successive developments** of substances and solutions from one composition to another; and this transpired, as one substance **became able** to produce and sustain those new element productions above it. And of interest is that those particular chemical productions and developments were the **only** elements that could-have existed at this epoch of earth's formation.

Other evidence to confirm the density of this "watery" element during this epoch, consists in the **fact**, that all the original rock protrusions and prominence were acted on and **worn away** by the watery solution then surrounding them. Our present water is a great force in erosion, however today's water could not have produced the same effects as the "watery" element now spoken of. And so the elements of the water were chemically connected with other substances, and the action of those elements in combination, **accelerated** the disintegration and erosion processes. And if it were possible to have a telescopic view of the earth made at this period, say from Mars or Venus, the earth would have exhibited a deep red appearance, and the sphere would have been encircled by a very dark ring of atmosphere, nearly the same as we would naturally expect if a planet were in a state of fusion, or in a burning condition.

As this watery element exerted a **constant action** of erosion with ceaseless waves and currents grinding upon those early rocks and particles, caused a great deal of this eroded material to became debris. All this **debris** then was gradually carried and **precipitated** to the bottom of the sea in the form of **sediment**. Deposits of sediment were in this manner formed and built-up in every chink and crevice or any other vacated portions of the sea-bottom, and this occurred all throughout the earth. And then, as the **accumulations** increased, so that the **heat** existing beneath the whole incrustation, **rose-up** through the deposits and cause those particles to chemically interact and **became united**. This process, is how the primary stratified rocks known as **gneiss** and **mica-slate** interspersed with **mica-schist** and some others were formed so long ago.

So then as the very first formation - **granite** was an **index** of the watery and atmospheric developments at the very beginning of that earlier time-period, by revealing the **relationship** involved in the **refinement** of those first water and air elements which had become developed from that first mineral laden primary coating; and so, the **second** crust formation is an **index** of those new elements existing within this new time-period, where by these new elements **must**, out **of-necessity**, become purified and comparatively refined as a continuing process into this new era. And this **same action** of development would occur in every **succeeding stratum**, unfolding new elements and **new principles**, and the **ultimate** of these processes tended to be, the continual refinement of the watery and atmospheric compositions.

# Section 37

The science of Chemistry has investigated and compiled plenty of valuable information in connection with the solids, fluids, and gases, in existence and being developed in all the various periods of earths progression. Science has not however, been able to discover all the elements that are existing in the composition of the earth. So there's plenty of investigation ahead. The **primitive elements** are supposed to be fifty-five in number, about forty of which are **metallic** and the rest are **non-metallic**. These, in various modifications, are supposed to not only "form" the substances of the whole earth, but also produces its gaseous elements.

Of the primitive elements, there is one very important fact in relation to **oxygen** and **carbon** existing on earth, which is that these two elements, in great quantity, pervade the substances of the crust and on the surface of the earth. Carbon and carbonic acid gas (carbon dioxide) are the ones that had prevailed more extensively during the period of **early stratification** much more than at any time since that period. **Lime**, contains in every cubic yard, ten thousand cubic feet of carbon dioxide. And not only with lime, but also it is known, that the carbon element also enters into the composition of **coal**, to the amount of from sixty to seventy-five per cent. This in a way proves that these substances existed in the period in very large quantities.

So then, the **condensation** and **sequestration** of carbon into the substance of lime and coal, gives clear understanding of its original state of development. And the fact that it **descended** into such states of **consolidation**, shows plainly, that the carbon element was "taking the place" on earth, of other chemically refined substances that had **ascended** into, either the watery element, or the atmosphere. And if all these processes are viewed with the theory of "successive development" kept in mind, it then can be clearly seen, that carbon was **superseded** by a more rare, refined and perfected substance which has chemically ascended.

Another interesting issue is the **accumulation** and **stratification** of substances which were originally contained in the composition of the weathered granite or the "watery" **granite solution.** It also can plainly be seen, (and it also proves), that each of the **four substances** mica, hornblende, quartz, and feldspar, were composed of particles that still could be further subdivided. Many **portions** of the primary rocks are characterized by one or more of these compounds and this fact helps in distinguishing them from the neighboring portions. And such are, the quartz rock, mica, schist, and others each having sometimes the **same position** in the order of formation with strata composed of other substances.

In this discussion, there is an attempt to impress upon the mind, that **no substance** has as yet been formed, which does not **at-least** contain some small portion of the properties and elements that were existing in the primitive formation. And, that the first sedimentary strata followed the granite formation as a **sole-consequence** of the watery elements **action** of erosion against the ejected rocks and mountains previously spoken of. And, **neither** this first sedimentary formation **nor** the previous primary granite formation has any infusoria or marine polypi fossils. So, no signs of life yet.

The granite and sedimentary rocks may therefore be considered as constituting the **first coating** or covering of the igneous mass of the world.

Now, before proceeding further in our researches, which will go deep into the geological developments that are taking place at this new and succeeding events; it is important to first, understand the **laws** of **crystallization**. And thanks to discoveries in chemistry, it is a well-established truth, that every substance in a state of crystallization **possesses** Forms, that it **never again** assumes in subsequent condensation. This occurs before its coherent elements are reduced to a fluid or gaseous state. Crystals may be produced by the **compression** of substances before they enter into any higher state than that of fluidity. And crystallization may be produced by other processes, the most perfect of which is the **sublimation** of particles by reducing them to an ultimate or gaseous condition.

Corrosive sublimate (mercuric chloride), phosphorous, platinum, and diamond, all display **Forms** produced by the condensation of sublimated and gaseous particles. And this phenomenon has been so uniform, that it is now exciting the attention of philosophic minds, the result of which will be a **new theory** concerning "the atomic structure of the Universe" (stated-1846).

The **first** stages of crystallization in any substance demonstrate the **angular** Form of each and every particle engaged in the process. The **first congregation** of particles produces the least perfect form of crystallization. And by **dissolving** this crystal, and causing its particles to **ascend** into the fluid or gaseous condition, and to become again **condensed**, there is produced a finer and **more perfect** form of the crystal. This therefore **proves** that as **atoms ascend** from the lowest state toward the highest, they assume more perfect forms. They become, in passing from the angular toward the circular then to other forms so **perfected**, that when condensed, they compose the most perfect state of crystallization.

Those grand observations made by the science of chemistry, therefore, have led to this far reaching discovery into the processes of structure and form of the Universe, and in addition there are other improvements, which is to establish their understanding of the "progression and perfection of forms" such as are seen in the examples of all crystalline bodies.

The element of **silicon** combined with oxygen forms the substance known as silica, which is found in granite. And how easy it is to discover the reason why a formation like that of granite should have been the first produced! It is because the **original atoms** were **angular**. These Forms, being the lowest and most imperfect, take the first point in the formation. And recall, "the first contains the highest undeveloped".

Therefore, more recent Formations display new compounds, new conditions, and new appearances; but they contain **no-new** substances that granite had already contained. No elements have been brought into being during the successive stages of formation which did not already exist in the beginning. And the only-difference between the higher and lower substances is due to the change in the Forms and in the composition of particles.

And now, to give a quick review concerning this latest chapter in earths evolution. The earth primitively, was in an undeveloped condition. The very **first** condensation produced the **granite**; the **second** development was that of the **fluid-mass** referred to as the "watery element"; and the **third**, being the **ultimate** of the last two, which was the development of an **atmosphere**.

The granite, the fluid, and the atmosphere, all continued to progress and they became essentially **changed** as circumstances had changed. All by the action of a **constant sublimation** which was going on then, and is still going on.

This period, when all chemical and mechanical causes were in full operation, and the primary rock formation was being developed by subterranean **agitation** and **fusion**, these rock formations were forced into strange positions.

The **circumference** of the earth at that period was a little more than thirty thousand (30,000) miles around.

For a period of many ages the **coating** of granite had continued to form and eventually reached a thickness of nearly one hundred miles; and this formation event was **before** the **gneiss** and **mica-slate systems** started to make their appearances and started to added their own layers. These sedimentary systems formed layers which assumed a thickness according to their position and relation to the granite.

The action of erosion by the "watery-element", is also a major **component** of the changes in the rock formations themselves, because the elements contained in the water-solution would enter into the compositions of these new formations by condensation. And it was because of **constant** chemical "workings" of the interior and external elements of earth's crust, that eventually would cause the lower strata of this thick granite coating to became modified, and the highest portion of the strata became partially disintegrated or eroded; then, by constant accumulation of sediment, would eventually form the **clay-slate** and **grauwacke slate** system. And this formation may properly be termed the **transition** from the **primary formation** to the **fossiliferous formation**.

## Section 38

Transitioning from the primary formation into the **fossiliferous formation**, there is the discovery of many **fossil** remains which give a clear and positive indication that plant **Life** had begun. In this succeeding formation, are found the series of fossils known as crinoides, conchiferae, poliparia, crustacea, and indistinct traces of marine polpi. It is evident that at this early time-period, **imperfect plants** must have had been in existence, because there are many of these early fossilized flowerless plants, crinoidians. Geologists then, had adopted the conclusion that a modification of the atmosphere and of the earth led the way for Life!

So what was occurring then, was some of the original primary coating of earth's igneous Mass, had by the chemical action "ascended" and transformed this granite into the formation of the **grauwacke** slate system. And also at this present time, by chemical action, the water and atmosphere have become one more degree refined. And also now, **Motion** is in a sense, ascending, meaning that movement is occurring within these chemical compositions and are starting to be a part of, "Forms **possessing** Life".

A great question arises that needs a solution; does Motion produce the phenomenon of Life?

Searching for the first indication of the origin of Life, has been a subject of much speculation. The question has been subjected to deep investigation, and yet no powers of scientific analysis, nor that of human speculation, have been able to solve this great mystery.

But, the subject of **Life** can be easily demonstrated when the situation is correctly considered, which includes the understanding, that the first of all things, is an **embryo** of all other existences; and that, the first is a **Germ** or seed, - containing the essential qualities which are necessary to produce higher states of refinement. And that, when subjected to favorable conditions, "It", that Germ, will unfold and develop its real nature, and it will **expand** into new forms, new substances, new elements and organizations. And, it was the great positive mind of God, which created the embryo, the first and the ultimate, as one; and this is a most important realization.

**Motion** is the first of all living Principles contained in living Matter, - and then, the ultimate of this combination of motion and matter, together with its proper vehicle – a Form or body, **Matter** then "produces" **Spirit**.

And therefore, it should be easy to understand that **one-more** step in the order of this step-by-step ascension, rising from the original condition of matter which had first given meaning to the word Motion and what the word indicates, and that one more step would produce the phenomenon of Life. This should be clearly understood, because then, it will be clearly seen, that there was a **similar ascension** of materials which occurred just to form a proper vehicle for the Spirit in the first place.

**Life** occurred because it was **designed** to do so. And the ultimate purpose of Life, anywhere, is to produce man! And the "Man Being", is the **vehicle** for the Soul, which is a part of Spirit, to allow Spirit to come into **material** existence; to experience; to develop Spirit, even though Spirit existed in the beginning, Spirit is the **companion** of God which will **unfold** and develop by dwelling in **both** the physical and spiritual bodies of man. **Motion** is the first of all **living Principles** contained in living matter to develop.

No imaginary forces were needed to cause and bring about Life. No outer-space microbes were required, and no magic wand, nor did God breath literal divine breaths into the nostrils of man. Nature contains all the forces necessary to institute all the conditions, and is able to produce all things and developments that occur in this planet earth and on its surface. And it is by having a **correct** understanding of the **uniformity** in **Nature's** laws, one will be able **to-begin** to form an adequate conception of the successive developments leading to the **conclusion**, that "Motion Becomes Life"!

And so now, in this present period, is the **first-era** in which Motion becomes Life, and in which, materials enter into **combinations** suitable for life's development, - and of these various combinations of mineral particles, it is - **Plants** which are the types and indications of that **first-unfolding** of the **first-principle** of Life.

Exactly by **what process** was it that Life could have been first developed? This is a question of the utmost magnitude. Because philosophically, understanding how Life developed involves a mind which understands that the outcome of that all important **first development** of Life, will eventually **lead** to the development of **Man**. And the reason for stating this is because, the development of Life was set-up as part of the original Plan, and so, at the **very moment** that **one particle** attained Life upon this earth, then this action would automatically **determined** as an **inevitable progression**, the process in which life, sensation, and intelligence **would-begin** and continually occur with endless results.

Recall then, that in the very beginning of the Universe, the premise that if **Motion** were **given** to one particle in the great Original Mass, this action **would establish** Motion in **every atom** in existence, and this Motion would be Eternal. Well then, how inconceivably important is our earlier question of "did motion produce life"? The answer is yes, **Life** is a "progressive development" of the principle of Motion, and how gracious is it that **marine plants** were the **first forms** suited for such a glorious development and the **first** to possess Life.

Animals **could-not** have existed before plants, because the first principle Motion, **will-need** to develop into an **ultimate**; and so, in the **second** succession, just **containing** one more principle, - Motion, which only the plant typifies one step **above** the mineral kingdom.

# Section 39

What is required now, is to give a **definite explanation** of the origin and character of the **first Forms** which Nature breathed into existence, they came into "being" at a time previous to the end of the carboniferous formation and continued to the time of the fossils which give those first indications of Life beginning. The most useful resources for this task are the sciences of Chemistry, Anatomy, and Physiology. And with these wondrous branches of knowledge we **learn** of Nature and how she unfolds her worthy creations. It is an exciting time of evolution, within the event of Creation.

It has been theorized that at some point in the future of research, **chemistry** will **unfold** the fact, that **Light** when confined in a-certain condition, and condensed, **will produce water**, and then, when the water just formed is subjected to the vertical influence of Light, will produce by its internal motion and its further condensation, a gelatinous substance of the composition of the spirifer is produced, and it is this motion which would indicate animal Life. And then by continuing with the experiment, by taking that same "gelatin mass" and decompose it and subjected it to evaporation, the **precipitated particles** which still remain, will **produce** putrefied matter similar to Earth, which will produce the plant known as the fucoides.

In the results of the above experiment, **rests** the "probability", (though not the absolute certainty), of the truth of the description to be given next, which will **be-about** the first Form possessing Life.

It was previously remarked, that all the elements of earth had undergone a substantial material **modification**, and this process had occurred at the close of the **transition rock** formation or grauwacke system. At this time, many portions of the sea-beds were **susceptible** of giving birth to new Forms, because of the chemical changes which had occurred. The **change** in the "watery element" had been just a general change; because carbon had-become more universally **scattered**, while oxygen at this time, had only been produced in relatively small portions and was **just-now** beginning to develop into its present gaseous state, but still, only imperfectly.

There is more to state, because it was at this time period, the substance found in granite known as **quartz**, which is the most perfect combination of oxygen and silicon, was **combined** with the **limestone** in-which the carbon portion it contained was extremely condensed. This whole combination of substances, chemically, generated warmth. The warmth, plus the combined elements, and plus the already favorable chemical **affinities**, which the water and atmosphere had **created** in some portions of the seabeds and also portions of partially protruding rocks, **formed** a **composition** which **seemingly did-not** move and assuming **apparently**, the state of rest and repose. **However**, it **was-not** at rest though, but in-reality and without notice, there was the **imperceptible motion** existing within it. It was **decomposing** and **uniting particles**, and chemically creating "a principle of internal vitality".

So it was **Here** in this decomposing clump, which manifested and brought into action the "generating power of motion", and produced the phenomenon of Life, of Death, and of Reorganization. See, that it is because of this fact, that, - the action of the **decomposition** of any one atom in these giant gelatinous masses, would **represent** the disorganization of all-bodies, or **death**; while the **recombination represents** the principle whose "impregnation" results in bringing into existence **new Forms** and organizations, and new **Life**.

The constant activity existing in the whole mass, united by those chemical forces previously explained as association or affinity; not only shows the unchangeable Laws of Motion; but, clearly represents all phenomenon that are presented in the process of **gestation**.

**Masses** of this **now-living** plant species just described, were **existing** in various locations of the earth, mostly upon the segregated beds that had been previously formed by the **action** of the "watery" elements grinding upon that first stratification on the earth's crust, the erosion. These masses, **breathed** into existence, the Forms termed **flowerless** and **marine plants**, the highest type at this time is the fucoides, which is another term for brown seaweed.

There is a need for the reader to realize, that the actual base **support** and **foundation** of these Formations of plants, **consisted** principally of the conglomerated substances of mica, quartz, and hornblende, these elements **modified** by "the connected and associated particles of lime" – which would then, in decomposition produced from their inherent elements, those new Forms described above. And let it be further impressed, that granite and limestone, including the mica-slate, **had-not** previously entered, as part of its makeup into any particular **organic** composition. So here came into existence new compositions.

Plants of this period **did-not** have perfect form, they were simple and lacking in the development of their ultimate portions which would later develop, such as seeds, flowers, and foliage; and these first plants were unsuited for any other purpose, other than for **that-purpose** of producing a higher order of Forms. But here, it was in these simple structured plants the first time motion and life acting together became **visible**. Motion recall, was originally and eternally established in the beginning of Creation; while Life, which is Motion's first ascending development was **first** brought into **being** in the imperfect forms of marine plants, **because** "all conditions agreed for this development". No **artificial** energies were required to bring them into being. No new force, quality, or principle, was necessary for the successful development of Life. These plants were the **representation** of the highest process of **gestation** and reproduction at that period.

# Section 40

Life has begun; and now, it continues; and **ascending** in the scale of being, the radiata and polyparia stand next in order of production into Life. These plants came into being as the results of the **decomposition** of the former substances (fucoides). And it was these **combinations** of substances, combining with other elements, the whole mass **assuming** as a **consequent**, the next-development, the next step, (which we will entail the improper use the term "radiata" when discussing them), but there were no radiata in existence yet. But for now these radiata types existed both upon the **inland** portions in abundance, and these Life Forms could also be found extensively swarming, through the "watery waste".

The tiny **polypi** were active in **forming** from the solution of lime and other chemical compositions of a similar nature, the formations of imperfect **coral reefs** which now stand as evidence of the ingenious work of these life forms. The **radiata** were lower orders, and assumed the form of **suspended moss**. These types of radiata, having **developed** an interwoven and complex membrane, which, became the **vehicle** of **transmitting** imperfect **sensation**, the next principle of life. This first membranous development, was first-exhibited in the **radiating feelers** that were thrown-out from every portion of the united substance of this organism.

The **feelers** became so perfected, that any molecule or substance passing near them would be suddenly caught; and then by the process of active decomposition, the radiata would play a great role in **combining** and **uniting** these substances with their own substances; and it was from this, which would **cause** their "nature" to be subjected to constant change. Through "successive modifications" of these radiata over time, the **articulata** were developed as the next Order. This Class which may at this time still be termed plants, were formed and constructed with innumerable chambers and multi-valved portions. The whole mass being entirely ventral. Species of these are the annelidans and serpula.

The species of annelidans and serpula were of a peculiar characteristic, where they **sustained** their existence by "successive re-assumptions", which is the process where these great masses of plants would actually "grow upon themselves". Then **uniting** with these "constantly changing radiata", were the **univalve** and **multivalve** shells which included the **crustacea** (trilobites), and the radiated spirifer which is now extinct.

As a **link** in the **transition** from radiata to the articulata, the **productus** and **terebratula** occur. This mass of organisms were chiefly formed of the **particles** that were **floating** in the solution of lime, mica slate, and gneiss, but this was after these had been modified from the first forms. The productus modified and became another type, and was an **active agent** of constant **transmutation**, this activity of the productus is known because fossil Forms which were **found-above** their fossils show a connection to them, and the only the big difference being the fact that, it was only a plant **more perfected** and was now constructed of more complicated in its parts.

In this present **class** of plant formations (because, in reality no other species were yet existing), numerous **shells** were formed; and these were ventral valved, and chambered, and also were interlined with a soft **gelatinous** moving living **membrane**, located near the osseous portion of the animal. Many of the above Species became extinct a long period before the completion of the carboniferous strata. But no sensation is motivating this organism.

The whole earth globe was in a transition. This was a very active period with constant development and which the activity lasted a very long time, almost inconceivable to the mind. What is interesting about the action of Nature at this period, is that She shows no events of upheaval, no catastrophic occurrences or sudden eruptions, no earthquakes. But instead, it was calm and quiet, so calm that if the earth were viewed by a bystander, it would have appeared that the surface of the world was entirely **desolate**; because there were **no objects** in sight nor even in existence, **except** those very small marine plants. But, as minute as these plants were, **they-do** stand in **analogy** to the mighty developments that have occurred in the earth, in the water, and the air of the earth. And it is these very same Forms that represent the "**progressive development**" of Motion to Life, and importantly is shows a progression within and organism of the **lower** to **higher** species. There was a constant ascension of each type and species to "higher stations". And recall the procedure, that, as these species progressed higher, the **vacuum** caused by their ascension, **were** immediately **filled** by particles that were ascending themselves, up from their previously lower stations of development.

The Whole system of evolution was gradually and truly **unfolding** the **correct conditions** for the introduction of a **new Era** which must occur. And when the **termination** of the present Era is distinctly proclaimed complete, then soon, in the succeeding new era there **will-be** the production of more-exalted and refined organizations; and it will be these new Forms coming into existence, whom are **destined** to become developed as those **changes** in the elements, conditions, and forces, continues to take place and evolve.

Now though, all the **plant** developments of the grauwacke and clayslate system will be grouped together into one general class, as that class of the **invertebrate**; and the reason for this classification is that of all the living developments of this period, Sensation still **has-not** as yet developed and become a distinct principle; though there are traces of its beginnings.

Animals **could-not** have existed previously to plants, simply because the **conditions** of the earth and its elements were not adequate to sustain animal life. It is at this period, the conditions of **carbon** and other kindred elements were **more-suited** to sustain the minute creations and developments of the plant kingdom. And the elements of earth were in the proper proportions and had sustained the proper combinations for these organic structures to form.

When the word Sensation is used to applied to life, vitality, or minute motion, is when the word is **used-improperly**. The reason for this error is because in reality **Sensation** is-as distinct from life, as Life is from Motion. Because Sensation is the Principle that **connects** the inner life or Spirit, with the external body. And it must be kept in mind that Life **may exist** where Sensation **does not**.

So, just what is **Sensation**? It is a physical feeling or perception transmitted within an organism, which is a result from something internal or external that happens-to or comes in contact with the particular body, and then, a **reaction** is "**noticed**" by that body.

From Matter in Motion, which leads to Life, then Living organisms develop the Principle of Sensation; from Sensation develops Instincts; and Instincts lead to Knowledge; and Knowledge leads to Intelligence. This description of Sensation is an **attempt** to explain the phenomenon of Life as a mere "ascension of the Principle of Motion". Motion, is simply further developing its Inherent energies, and by Motion evolving it is **causing** a very small, almost imperceptible **transmutation** and **reproduction** of the substance in which the principle exists.

Animals are **characterize** as having Sensation. A positive distinction between the plant and animal creations does not appear before the carboniferous stratification, when the disintegration, decomposition, and segregation, of the primary formations had become much more extensive.

Before describing the next formation which is the carboniferous formation, it is necessary to overview the subdivisions which occurred, and these are made of ascending layers of **strata**. The **first** of these layers or strata has been termed the **silurian**, owing its name to the people who lived above this land portion in the country where these rocks are discovered. The **next** layer in order above the silurian is termed the **old red**

**sandstone system**; and an important fact is that crystallization is **not-visible** to any great extent in the composition of this massive layer of old red sandstone. It is very **evident** that this Formation was produced by the **congregation** of **ultimate particles** of mica-slate, gneiss, limestone, and shale. These particles had become so modified that **only** sandstone could be produced by them.

In this present period there were some **trap** and **basalt** formations existing as **projected** rock, and these can be found in various parts of dry portions of the crust, but, these rock formations existed much more extensively **under** the surface of the water-element. These dense rocks contained great quantities of crystalline matter; however, as stated, this crystalline rock **was prevented** by circumstances, from forming in the sandstone system. The Sandstone Formation is in some parts of the globe varying in thickness from three thousand up to ten thousand feet.

**Animals** have now already arrived, and within this period and they continued to progress in species and even developed a still higher Order of animals, which the Silurian system is ultimately **known-by** and typified by which are fishes. **Fishes** now became extensively distributed throughout the water. And **corals** were existing in abundance. The **terebratula** continues but has not been modified very much within this particular era. The **spirifer** and the ortho-spirifer have this time became **extinct**, and only a few traces of them continue to exist, their remains are found in the upper strata; however, those ones found in the upper strata are modified. The productus **ascends** in genera in this era.

Developing upward in evolution from lower mollusk the **gastropod** becomes developed, and then this organism by still developing further, progresses to a still higher species which is the **cephalopod**. The radiata and articulata also still in their stages of development and progression, now begin to assume the Form of the **scorpion** and **insect** and between these the **fuci** sustains an intermediate position.

The seas at this time were inhabited by annelidans and scorpion fishes, and as these progressed the **ultimate** development of these fishes, nearly represents the shark and sturgeon. The annelidans were a species of sea-worm,which can still to be found upon many coasts and coves, mostly where stones and other bodies of concealment exist. Of this Class there are two kinds, the white and red, the first of which is **hermaphrodite**, sustaining an intermediate position between the lower type and the higher, of which the serpula becomes visible.

## Section 41

Plants of this Red Sandstone period have ascended to the **sigillaria**, but this progression has occurred with little or no true modification from the previous organism, although this **same** plant will subsequently develop further and **ascend** to the class **coniferce**; this plant which-will exist and thrive in the carboniferous formation and be seen in the slender beautiful pines of which fossilized remains are found.

This period also represents a more **distinct separation** between the plant and animal kingdoms; because now there exist a much more definite line of demarcation which can be boldly and correctly drawn between them. And as this era progresses these distinct representations will become more clear, and this demarcation will be further discussed when a description is given of the crust of the earth as it was existing **prior** to the **change** of the dense element which resulted in the formation of the limestone.

This particular era shows an further development and ascension of animals **one degree** above the basic avertebrated organisms. And if any of these successive animal developments were to be correctly arranged in order, the highest species would show great dissimilarity and a superiority over the very first species of the same classes. It is these particular higher ascended animal species which-will be designated as the beginning of the **osseous fish** development. Bone formation processes are just beginning and are starting to show in these animals; this fact is know because fossil remains show that even higher and more complex and more muscular organizations, of the sandstone period of which fish is a type, **have-not** as yet assumed the development of the **posterior portions** of their spine, which of course would characterize the proper vertebrates. Animals are **not-yet** a complex organism, because **none** of the species of fish then existing would evolve in their organization much beyond the gelatinous composition of the annelidans, except some slight yet noticeable developments in form and texture.

**Limestone** is formed in this time-period; so a short explanation of the processes involved in the formation of limestone is warranted, which follows: - there were various particles suspended in the "watery solution" which were still being acted-upon chemically, and these were in a state of change; at the same time this watery solution was also being actively carried by the tides. These tides were excessive in both force and magnitude. And these powerful tides almost covered the entire face of the earth. So, it was by the action of the powerful tides carrying this limey chemical solution, and then **depositing** those **particles** which were still in various chemical processes, including various other local causes occurring. This is the method how, the extensive solutions of **lime** then existing, **became**, when **conjoined** with other substances, **deposited** to form the great series of strata known as the **carboniferous limestone.**

Dry **land** would appeared during this time-period and from this creation there soon **began** a process where **soil** was developed or formed from the action of decomposition of the masses of gelatinous substances which previously existed upon those same portions of dry rock. Then it would be from this newly forming soil, which would sprang up living minute plant Forms. Many marine-animals and various land-plants all came to life in this period. Then after a time the land plants would begin to grow in places which before, were covered by the "watery waste". Some of these land plants grew in such a manner that they began to **shade** a small portion of the earths surface for the first time.

There has been a constant process of **crust** formation occurring from the igneous mass below; but lately there would be **noticed** that the existing mountains were becoming bigger and higher, and also other new mountains were starting to be ejected from the crust; these events were the result of increased subterranean pressures within earth's interior, which was now progressing into a much more lively and reactive state of turmoil.

The specific **cause** of the increased interior forces **had to happen**; the increased forces and pressure were solely the result of chemical process and developments which had been occurring within the "watery element", in the atmosphere, and within the igneous mass; so this expansion of earth's crust was part of that process and was a necessary event or result of the processes. There were constant developments and **constant changes** occurring with those **Elements** composing both the interior and the exterior components of earth. The growth of the mountains were a **signal** that changes in the atmosphere and watery element had occurred, and it was also a **signal** that the molten interior elements were in a state of action and agitation. There was both an increase in the interior forces, and a decrease in density of the "water-element".

Earth's elements have been chemically **evolving** forming new elements, new compounds, new mixtures and chemical solutions. Significant chemical changes would occur in the **main elements** of the atmosphere, the watery element, and molten mass, **until** the distribution of opposing pressures became **unbalanced**; it was the progression and ascension of materials which **had-placed** the external and internal equilibrium of earth's crust in this unbalanced condition. The equilibrium was gradually

**destroyed** and it was by **transitioning elements** in constant recombination processes, whose previous **density** had been sufficient to **balanced** the expansive force of earth's interior. However now, because of the decrease in density of the atmosphere and "watery' element there developed this imbalance between opposing pressures upon earth's crust. The only possible remedy for this situation and only means for the planet to **restore equilibrium**, is for the internal pressures to be relieved, and so the forces **must-have** a means to **vent** the increased turmoil.

The internal pressures need a method to redistribute the sphere's opposing crustal pressures. There are various manners of venting. Sometimes volcanoes are able to relieve those forces; sometimes earthquakes do the trick; and sometimes, if the action of imbalance is excessive, there has to be a major inundation. **But**, in this present situation, the opposing forces were unbalanced to an **extreme**, so much so, that in order to restore the equilibrium, earth needed an **extensive upheaval**; and it was a joyfully occasion for earth, because the necessary action which finally **provided relief** in this situation, was the upheaval of the **mountains** now known as the **Apennines** and the **Andes**.

Any further description of the mountain upheavals **should-not** be continued here though, or at least not until some **preliminary** geological **observations** can first be given, to paint a clear picture of this major event in earth's evolution. These generalize observations concern the **concepts** of not only inequalities and catastrophes which concern previously occurring mountain building, but also to reveal thoughts and concepts which concern these new mountains productions which are ejected during this pending upheaval. The reasons for all this hoop-la and clarification, is because sometimes these catastrophes **may-seem** out of order with the laws of nature; and some observers may believe that these events are absolutely destructive events initiated by God, yet they are not!

The most-significant change the earth would experience in this particular catastrophic event would be the **sudden** action of the **condensation** of the earth sphere, a compaction of the whole mass of the planet, causing the planet to **become** two thousand miles **diminished** in circumference; and so now in a comparison, earths previously stated magnitude of thirty thousand miles, which it had sustained during the elastic state of the primary coating of granite, and now decreasing in size to a circumference of twenty-eight thousand miles around.

Also the Seas were not so deep as before the catastrophe; however the actual surface area of the Seas has now greatly **increased** and became more extensive. This radical increase in volume of the Seas was caused by the **expansion** of previously condensed particles which were composing the water element. It is a well-known law in chemistry that as particles become sublimated they naturally expand and so will consequently occupy a greater space than before. This post-catastrophic time-period would represent the condition of the "improved watery element" in a much more chemically **progressed** state.

The water had expanded in volume so much its water level rose higher up the mountains, now reaching nearly to the tops of those great mountains, so that now, only the higher peaks were noticed poking up from the depths. Interestingly, the watery element contain an enormous amount of debris, and contained shells, plant material, and animal remains, all of which had then existed during this era. This debris was **transported** by the tides to the higher regions of those mountain peaks. Sometimes the discovery of this debris high-up on these mountains can still be a bit confusing; mostly because, in addition to the water and tides placing this debris high-up, there **was-also** the situation of rock-masses having been thrust-up and become ejected above the crust, and some of those ejected mountain had **previously** been sea-beds. Yet, these incidental and local occurrences should not cause any confusion with geologist and naturalist, nor should these destroy the order of creation in the minds of these scientists; because local events are particulars and incidental, and where it is by **coincidence** that these previous formations and succeeding formation are **found together**. Beware of particulars, when looking for general truths.

There is another item to make conscious note of, which is to realize that the tides **were-greater** at that period than they are now know to operate. Because the waters at that particular time-period were gathered up and accumulated as great tides, reaching to immense heights every fourteen hours, this tidal action being **twice elevated** during the period of the earth's revolution upon its axis, which required twenty-eight hours when the circumference was twenty-eight thousand miles.

The **theories** which have been presented to the world concerning the phenomenon of tides generally have been **incorrect**. It has been **supposed** by a conspicuous astronomer (Galileo), that tides were produced by "the law of attraction" - and stated, that by the action of the Moon upon the Earth the tides are produced. However this **can-not** be true; because attraction **is-not** an established principle, **especially beyond** the atmo**sphere** of any body or substance. To show plainly the **impossibility** of this being the **cause** of tides, here is presented some of the chief considerations which have an important bearing upon the subject.

If the Moon has any attractive influence upon the Earth, at least more than what consists in the natural relationship existing between the two spheroid bodies, why then, when the Moon is in conjunction with the Sun, does not the water become more elevated on the side of the Earth next to these bodies, as might naturally be expected if such attraction existed? And also would not, the substances upon the opposite side of earth weight less? Also when the Moon is on the opposite side of the Earth, and the Earth sustains a position between the Moon and the Sun, why is not the elevation of water occurring at all portions of the Earth? Because if the Moon and Sun exert an equal influence, the result should be equal heights of water all over Earth, such as large lakes.

# Section 42

The **falling** to earth of some substance previously suspended in the air, has been termed **gravitation**. The **tides** have been considered as a result of the same principle of gravitation. And all things have been represented as **possessing**, to a greater or less extent, the principles of attraction and repulsion – a perfect and established **antagonism**. And sadly because of the fact that, to the vast extent which this belief is now entrenched and extensively prevailing in the hardened minds of mankind, it is not possible that a different theory or hypothesis can be given or received **unless** the new theory it is **able** to addresses and explain, to man's full understanding and satisfaction, **with-more** plainness and **logic** then the already existing theory.

It is a well known truth in the science of astronomy, and in the principles of mechanics, that a body **rotating** on its axis, like the earth does, has the greatest tendency to **throw-off** substances in the direction in which it revolves. And as the Earth revolves from west to east, and at the present time once in twenty-four hours, **it-must** of-necessity, produce two elevations of water, **especially** the way the water surrounds this whole globe. So, every twelve hours, the water would be elevated at the extreme east and extreme west, or in other words, at given opposites of the Earth or antipodes. The elevation of water once in twelve hours, is a result of the **centrifugal tendency** that the globe creates in one half of its period of rotation, - and then corresponding rising tides, being in this way produce on the opposite sides of the Earth.

There are many things operating **incidentally** upon the water which will **produce** variations in the periods and elevations of the tides in different places upon each portion of the Earth. Though a correct knowledge of the law of fluids will demonstrate the cause of the whole phenomenon. To know about the action of tides, is to understand the natural tendency of fluids and any other substances that respond in this way, when subjected to a **centrifugal force**.

Now continuing with and investigation of this passing epoch by giving a review: this period - which is the **termination** of the Red Sandstone System, there was the **modification** of the elements of the water. Also, the water was **agitated** by wonderful tides, which caused the depositing of fossils almost to the peaks of the high mountain chains. And now the equilibrium was mostly entirely destroyed; which occurred by **sublimation** of particles composing the elements, and also by the operation of the exterior weight of the crust becoming unequal and **unbalanced** in pressure, compared with the **expansive force** of the turbulent internal molten composition. The result of this imbalance, was some of the most mighty and unbelievable agitations of the interior molten mass, which caused tremendous **quaking** of the whole earth. Just the **noise** alone would have shattered into atoms the structure of man's body. The **convolutions** that occurred with this **catastrophe** were so immense, they would-have presented the appearance of utter-destruction; and it would have seemed that the materials of the whole Earth had experienced one universal clash in an instant of time.

It was by these **sudden** and **violent earthquakes**, that would cause the crust of the Earth to be **broken** apart. Almost instantaneously, unbelievable masses of stone and molten mineral substances, together with the **remains** of organic beings previously upon the surface, were **thrown-upward** to an immense height. The sudden up-heaving **broke** apart stratum after stratum of rock formations into great and small masses, while other strata were **bent** and **twisted** into every possible position. The whole action of the upheaval exposed many previously hidden rock formation such as, trap, basalt, granite, sandstone, shale, and doing it in such a manner that these broken layers of strata seemed confused and deranged.

It was at the very moment that this terrific occurrence took-place that a process commenced in which the great mass of **lava** thrown from the interior, **combined** with the previous solution of **lime** and **coral** reefs, they soon **divided-part** becoming separate and **condensed**, then this combination became chemically **attractive** to the element **carbon** which was generally pervading the earth at this time; the **result** of this whole combination, was a **condensation** of a great portion of the whole-mass **into** the **carboniferous limestone** and **coal formations**.

And so the element **carbon**, which had been **previously** and extensively associated with atmospheric elements, had now by this process **became disunited** from other particles within the atmosphere. And in a chain reaction effect this major change in the elements resulted in another important change and **modification** of the composition of the "watery" element; and the exciting result of this action, caused again, another chemical ascension of the primary elements into the atmospheric envelope and this action would form the new and more **congenial** atmosphere for earth.

The **new mountains** developed and formed from this catastrophic event are: the Altay, Ural, and Himalayas (in Asia); the Alps (Switzerland); the Apennines (Italy), and Pyrenees (between France, Spain). Also, the mountain chain bordering the Euphrates River, and others in Asia. In other portions the Grampians (Scotland); and a small line of mountains which extends almost to the border of today's Russia. And, the Andes (of South America), which now, still today, answer as vents to relieve internal heat, liquid. The Rocky mountains had-already been in existence, as were also the Alleghenies but, they became enlarged.

There was a **Great Division** of the earth, **into** what are now known as the beginning of the **Eastern** and **Western Hemispheres**.

A **quarter** of the entire land-mass of earth made its appearance at this epoch – a much greater quantity of visible land was added than has ever been gained in such a short time-span. Much of this new land was the result of the "watery element" having now **increased** in bulk and **decreased** in density. Each chemical change in this liquid ocean of earth, brought that "watery element" another-step closer to the water developing the necessary composition of elements to become like our water known in the twenty-first century, which is water of perfection and an ultimate production.

Now was the commencement of a **New Era**. The whole face of the earth had changed. The entire landscape was transformed by the catastrophic events which had established continental divisions, two separate hemispheres, and other major features such as mountains and valleys; and earth **has-not** as yet experienced a similar significant catastrophic material changed like this past one; and our planet earth has stayed **relatively** in the same shape and condition.

Within this present New Era which is beginning, the water-element **will-continue** to modified and improved, chemical changes continue to change this group of liquid elements, the water **will-begin** to become **suitable** to give birth to more perfect organizations. And the present atmosphere encompassing the whole globe is improving similar to the water. The relationship between the atmosphere and water is critical in sustaining new Orders of terrestrial and marine plants and animals. Seas, lakes, and rivers, **now-became** the primary **circulating media** through various parts of the world, **transporting** particles and substances from place to place. The earth, water, and atmosphere became **correspondingly perfected**.

## Section 43

In this new period, after the **lapse** of seemingly countless ages since the upheaval, more dry land had become visible. Earth was smaller and more compact, the water, the mountains, and atmosphere finally counter-balance the molten interior and **re-established** the **equilibrium**.

The water continues as a powerful force in the action of erosion. The water acting upon various substances is also the active agent of transporting and depositing those particles of debris. The constituents of the watery solution are able to **generate** Motion and Life within all the gelatinous compositions that were able to receive this Life force. The water **gave fertility** to the inland portions of dry land, which had previously been concealed beneath over-flowing waves. And all these life giving processes **could-not** have happen without the earth changes. With the equilibrium now re-established, all was again rendered calm and quiet. Great chemical changes occurred, and continue, so that the atmosphere was becoming **fitted** for the further chemical ascension and refinement and further producing ultimate particles.

Yet **carbon** was still existing to a great extent in the atmosphere, while at the same time **oxygen** was still almost entirely undeveloped; and it was **nitrogen** which formed a great portion of the air, **neutralizing** the action of the other elements; because, if the chemical compositions of carbon and oxygen had not been **counteracted** by an associated element like nitrogen, all things would have instantly become **inflamed** and the combination would-have dissolved everything on earth quite rapidly. But because of the **method-how** those particular elements of the atmosphere interacted chemically they were not volatile and instead assisted in renewing the equilibrium, and from this there **was-created**, congenial and suitable combinations that could be **useful**.

This is the era when Motion **transcends** Life and becomes **Sensation**! And also, this is the era in-which **Forms** will fully **transcend** being plants and become substantial species of **animals**. Geologist have given a term for this era and called it the Carboniferous Formation. It was in this era that the avertebrated and osseous fish species now **had-begun** progressing to higher degrees and stages of perfection. This period of stratification is considered by geologists as the **third general subdivision** including the primary. And said again, Sensation **had-not yet** become a true unfolded **principle** of the original law it was apart of, before this period, but in this formation **it-will** become so.

And just to verify the significance of the theory of progressive development, recall that with the last upheaval, all things had been thrown into chaotic conditions; and sometimes, the sublime workings of Nature are seemingly destructive; yet out of chaos continues the orderly and "positive progression" of Life. And what has now been developed as new, is really only the **perfect** mutual **adaptations** of all things to each other. And each is produced as a connecting link, leading to a further progressive unfolding of higher forms. And this is the epoch when "**Types**" of species were ushered into being.

According to an appropriate declaration made in other writings; which were implying, that a almost inconceivable period of time had elapsed since; with Nature and her world of Forms and beings which She had developed, including all those living Forms which had existed before this era. All **could-be** combined into one unimaginable night or "evening". And so now, it is a "morning" of a **new day**, of a new existence. Therefore it is said, "**the evening and the morning were the first day**".

This is a truly remarkable era in the geological history of the earth's formation. Before this period, the Earth was apparently "**without Form and void, and darkness was upon the face of the deep**".

The darkness hinted at, was from a dense atmosphere. And then as the atmosphere changed and became more refined, then **more light** from the Sun was able to **penetrate**. And so now it would be seen that there was more beauty; and the more the Sun's rays penetrated, then the more darkness was dispersed. And here in existence is the **first time** that **animated Forms** lived upon dry land.

Geologists have developed **theories** as to the exact conditions and circumstances under which the **coal formation** was produced but these are not entirely correct (circa 1846). In many portions of the world, **coal** is found to be resting upon the primary coating, while in other places it lies upon the various strata of the transition rocks, such as quartz, and slate, and is especially found on the limestone strata.

In addition these transition rock formations also had develop ironstone, limestone, sandstone, and various other kinds of deposits. Some of these **enter-into** the composition of coal itself, while others merely formed intervening strata between the layers of coal. It is evident from this, that the substance of the **ironstone** and other compositions, had a **peculiar affinity for** the "carbon of the atmosphere"; and this being so, those rock compositions attracted and became chemical associated with carbon. And the whole as a consequence, became **condensed** into the formation which coal is a prominent part.

An important item to keep in mind, is that **various parts** of the sea-beds **had-not** been subjected to the same amount of abrasion as others;

and they **became** proper receptacles for the formation of the coal, and that is **including** the stratifications that are associated with the coal.

As stated, dry land became visible as a **result** of an active **gelatinous development** which had occurred as huge masses of plant material assimilated great amounts of light and heat, and so, these masses also **combined** with the previously decomposed vegetation substances. This combination **possessed** the principle of vitality and activity. The substances in the decomposing plant material had became **reorganized** into different components. Then, it was by the activity of the new plant growth, which had becoming saturated with this decayed material; then next, the light and heat activated and caused chemically processes to begin that transformed the decaying material into new substances.

# Section 44

**I**mmense and lush masses of **plant formations** became thickly dispersed upon those land areas which had been raised from the depths by the great catastrophic upheaval. **Trees** growing in this period, towered to a great height, however these plant species are now entirely extinct. In some places **moisture** was a driving force, promoting a great lushness to all the plants. There was an **abundant** supply of required elements adding to a plant's richness. So exceedingly fertile were these vegetable portions, that plants, in their rapid growth, **extracted** the strength of each other, with many plants falling down and decomposing on top of each other.

The decomposing plant matter began to formed heavy beds of **moss**, and in a beneficial manner, these mosses had a capability of **collecting** the important nutrient substances they required. And then the huge masses were gently **washed** from their locations by excessive **tides**. These huge masses continued to float and increase in size, then, these gradually **sank** below the surface and settled upon the shale and limestone substances, which as it turn out, were quite suitable **foundations** for this great mass of material to decompose. Then, interestingly, lime and shale in **solution**, along with more and other disintegrated and floating **particles** of the watery solution, now began to **cover** the sunken mass of decomposing Matter. And next, over a long process of **time**, this same watery solution full of debris would finally **settled** upon the same Mass and formed an overlaying stratum of **shale**.

Plants of the twenty-first century as we know, emit oxygen, and plants also attract and assimilate into their composition nitrogen, carbon, and other useful minerals, and these substances **become** a part of the plant's organized forms, part of their constitution. **But** the plants that existed during the carboniferous formation were quite different. Of course, they still took in minerals and such, and were adapted and "able mechanisms", for the transformation of inherent elements into the atmosphere by **reflux**. But what made those plants of the carboniferous different, was that the plants were more perfectly **adapted** to assimilate a very large amount of **carbon**, - which in reality entered **almost purely** into their forms and became an **ingredient** which was dissimilar to any known upon the face of the earth. Their **food** was carbon! And their **Soil** was the progressed, gelatinous, vegetable decomposition of primitive ages. Then the next step in the process was when these masses of plant material were decayed and condensed and were finally **transformed** by the action of elements, they would eventually **constitute** the carboniferous or coal Formations.

Conditions **were perfect** for the production of stratum after stratum of coal and other deposits. And this process would have continued, possibly even to this very day, **except** that the substances which had been in solution and which were abundant throughout the waters became exhausted.

Another interesting fact to keep in mind, is the **importance** of the intermediate strata in the process of coal development. The **intermediate stratum** became adapted and almost "designed" as a **base** upon which other strata of coal might be deposited and **perfected** by action of chemical processes. It is important to know that if these intervening strata of shale, limestone, ironstone, and sandstone, had not settled upon each succeeding stratum of carbonaceous matter, then the substance of coal certainly would **not-have** been in existence, especially in its present Form. It was absolutely and positively **necessary** that these watery chemical solutions were available first-off, and were also able to form the intervening strata; and that the water should perform its circulating functions and depositing of material; and that the general surrounding elements and conditions would be as favorable as they were; because when all conditions are conjoined, these might produce and condense both the plant mass and its concealing stratum that has settled on top.

Coal, will be considered **the first** of the secondary Formations. The coal era presents very important pieces of information which give leads into the proper understanding of geology, and gives **hints** regarding the process of Creation and its evolution. The importance of this era is understood when it is realized that the **withdrawing** from the atmosphere of carbon, which then entered into the compositions of both coal, and into the carbonate of lime, **must** of necessity **produce** a great change in the atmosphere and also the earth and water.

And as **carbon** had **before** composed a great portion of the **atmosphere**, the absence of this element from the atmosphere created a void, which must now of necessity, be replaced and re-supplied by other chemically ascending gaseous particles of a different nature. What happens is that the combined changes of the earth, water, and atmosphere, sets-up the "ripple effect" and causes a **great change**. The change was gradual at first and would be almost **imperceptible**. This change **started** at the end of the coal era but when this period came finally to a close, the whole combined **change** was comparatively **great**. Because now the elements were **fitted** to give new Life, form, and texture, to the inhabitants of the sea and land. These new Forms had an altogether **different** character from any existing creatures and structures before.

"The chain cannot be broken", and this chain now extends from the original primary formation, to the coal era.

## Section 45

It is **not-proper** that anything should be considered sacred and holy, **merely** because we have lost the time period of its origin, and its possibly being lost among the revolutions of numerous ages. **Nor** should an enthusiastic veneration be held and cherished for the **idea** of the creation of anything. This form of reasoning is not reality because the term creation has no meaning. The origin of every Form, Principle, and Substance, in being, owes its existence to some **prior cause**. And it should be remembered that Cause and Effect are eternally inseparable. These have been inseparable from the commencement of all Causes – and this law will continue until the accomplishment of all Effects. One Eternal Cause, and One Eternal Effect.

With all the facts that have been shown, how could there possibly be an argument against the truthful and magnificent doctrine of "Progressive Development", which we also call evolution. The transformation of elements into new Forms and combinations which occurs during this carboniferous period , becomes a matter of **necessity** that started-off from the **sequestration** of that almost all-pervading element **carbon** into other substances. And this action is therefore, a conspicuous and decided change, and therefore a **new era**.

How did this **New Era** come about? It was during the process of this present formation and also the previous formation various **metallic** substances whose distinct characteristics designate them as minerals, became deposited in areas where a **constant action** of segregation and separation was taking place. The first of these deposits that became separated is **Tin** which lies nearer to the primary coating than most of the other deposits. Then in sequence following tin, there are deposits of **Lead**, **Zinc**, and **Copper**, which were finally segregated and deposited. Theses deposits are interspersed in various strata bearing a close relation to the coal, mountain limestone, and new red sandstone deposits; while the deposits of **Silver** and **Gold** are found among the accompaniments of ironstone, which is found more in the carboniferous and many other subdivisions of the Secondary Formation.

Chemists have supposed that the atmosphere is composed of elementary substances, and this is true; but, gaseous elements **could-only** have **originated** from the minerals of the earth. So these particles of the atmosphere are therefore chemically ascended molecules, which may be considered as the **perfection** of mineral bodies previously existing within the earth, like those elements which still remain concealed in the crust of the earth for future discovery. The substances known as carbonate of lime and coal, **must have received** their main component ingredients from the particular atmosphere that then enveloped the earth. It is known that **carbonic acid** was extremely abundant and provided the necessary chemical composition to produce the lush plant vegetation in great abundance. Plants of that period were somewhat similar in nature with the **equisetaceae** plants, which were easily decayed and decomposed, and this is the reason why **no-remains** of these plants will be found.

Vegetable productions that were established and developed in this period varied from **Moss** to the **coniferae-trees** which at this period existed extensively in marshes; these types of plants would also be found existing on dry land, but only where there was sufficient **moisture** existing; most of these moisture loving plants were sigillaria and monocotyledons organisms.

The plants of the **first species** were composed of a gelatinous cellular tissue whose fibers and complex membrane constituted the **medium** of Life, and this is where the **power** of assimilation and reproduction was seated. From those plants came the mosses, then from mosses came the **ferns**, and from these fern came the coniferse. These coniferse are considered an imperfect type of pine tree, yet some of these tree types were extremely large, their height was from twenty to sixty feet. Their limbs were straight and fern-like, their leaves somewhat like those of a palm. The early-existing flowering plants of this era **developed** a **seed-vessel** containing seeds, but there were few plants existing that had seeds with two lobes; this fact is because the **exogenous** species were **not fully** developed until the close of the carboniferous era.

Many of the various kinds of **animal Forms** that had **previously** existed, now became entirely **extinct**; while the mollusks, cephalopods, and others, were still being reproduced in abundance. The spirifer is entirely extinct; while the terebratula, productus, and others of like nature continued in great abundance through all the ages of this present carboniferous era.

The seas were extensively inhabited by species of **scorpion** and **saurian** fishes which were slightly like a sturgeon fish now existing. These creatures thriving in this era were still existing in their rudimentary state, and almost could be considered embryonic, plus they had no vertebral portions, rather, they had developed a **gelatinous cord**, that will in later and subsequent species develop into vertebrae. These creatures in many ways characterize all the species of fish that were then traversing the chemical solution known as the "watery"domain.

As this present era progress further, it was easy to notice, plants and animals now **differed** from those of previous ages; animals had **developed vascular tissue**, which is seen by the conjoined boxed scales and the interwoven network existing upon the class of **sauroid** fishes which existed now. Plants also **exhibited** the same step of progression or increase of development, by exhibiting an **exogenous** nature, - which was distinguished by concentric or spiral arrangement of particles from their outward coating.

Cotyledons **were-not** existing, except the monocotyledons which sustained an intermediate position between the cryptogamis and the dicotyledons which are the highest type of the vegetable kingdom.

## Section 46

Fishes continue progressing in this era, unfolding various species which at first consisted of organisms being entirely cellular, - to now in this era these new creatures have developed to a level where one creature **finally** possesses **both** cellular and vascular tissues. This is a development of great importance because in this period it will be **first-observed**, the **establishment** of the imperfect **serous** and **mucous surfaces**. The importance of this development can-not be over emphasized because it is upon these two organ-like surfaces, Sensation **must** inevitably **exist**. It was through the development of these **two-opposing** surfaces that Sensation would **become** an **established** Principle. And even though at the beginning of this era these surfaces were still yet, imperfectly developed from Motion and Life; it would not be too long before improvements transpired; and as this era progressed, so did the development of Sensation.

Not only did the principle of Sensation become established, but consequently, **inclinations** must have been the result of this development; because, it is from these three principles motion, life, and sensation, when they are **finally** brought **together** in one animal organism is when **instincts** or a **living desire** has been developed. And this is the **first principle** that corresponds to **thought**! Therefore it was the principles of motion, life, and sensation, that these **sauroid fishes** had developed and possessed that represent those very same principles, but now in a far **more perfected** form. It will be the animals which-will develop these combined principles to the highest degree, which then corresponds to the principle of **Intelligence**. And so finally, the **inhabitants** of the **seas** would manifested for the **first time** the complete process which unfolds the original principle the law of Motion.

A similar process unfolded with the evolution of land plants: **first** the cellular plants were flowerless, consisting of mosses, ferns, fungi, and others, which corresponded to one-membrane and radiating nature of the first animal species. **Then**, as these plants progressed they developed the exogenous form, and went further with the development of flowers which with animals **corresponds** to Sensation. Plants were first to bring Life to the planet and the fishes brought about Sensation.

In many instances Nature's developments are sometimes seen as being dissimilar, and sometimes so dissimilar that it is almost impossible to arrange the developments of Nature into a perfect order; the time and circumstances are beyond the ability of natural calculations.

The organisms that are existing during this present **new era** are unlike and seemingly disconnected from the original organisms of the same types. But to see the order and connection, it is only necessary to know that the things Nature develops are **constantly** assuming new Forms, and these new productions are **in-accordance** with existing causes and existing laws. As the **conditions** in the environment changed there also can be observed corresponding changes or developments in the Forms, essence, and quality of each of the two kingdoms, plant and animal.

By the **close** of the carboniferous era it appears **evident** that all Forms of earthy, mineral, plant, and animal were **modified** and advanced **one** more **degree** of development **superior** to what had existed in any prior age. And it can be observed that this period is one of the most perfect and decided **links** in the general chain of progression.

As this era was nearing completion there had been both extensive changes in the atmosphere and in the water. These chemical changes were mostly **occurring** from the **depletion** of **carbonic acid gas** and from recombination of the main external elements. The previous **equilibrium** of the interior and exterior of the earth is somewhat **disturbed again**. External pressure was **diminished** becoming too weak and inadequate to counterbalance the expansion of the igneous mass within. The atmosphere and water were now too light to balance the molten interior. Consequently, Nature was in danger of an instantaneous convulsion. If a view of earth were possible now, the **face** of the earth would have appeared as if Nature were clothed in a dark cloak and had sunken into a death-like sleep. There are no busy insects, no birds singing, and the forests and marshes looked desolate and forgotten. Nature's **previous** living active energies, had now sunk into **repose**. All conditions were seemingly immobile and were **in-need** of some more active energies to renew and to again, set in motion those now paralyzed substances, plants, and animal Forms that had spread over the earth.

**Darkness** was again upon the face of the deep, and the waters were **moved** with ceaseless **agitation**; and there were frightful uncontrolled waves that again almost lashed the mountain-tops.

It should be **now-evident** that **inherent forces** were moving upon the face of the waters, causing inconceivable excitement and agitation; because **now**, the **equilibrium** had been **destroyed**. It was the **expanding** particles of the earths interior pushing upward. The water and atmosphere together were unequal in pressure to balance the expanding interior; so, a **change must** inevitably follow.

As a consequence of the disturbance and imbalance in equilibrium the molten **igneous fluid** exhibited very forceful and rapid motions at **vari-**

**ous parts** of the interior of the earth's crust. Violent trembling occurred, followed by volcanic explosions and lava flows, these mostly occurring in the Andes and some other mountains; but the **venting** action of the volcanoes was just **not-enough** to restore the equilibrium. So, the rapidly **expanding** molten interior caused great **earthquakes** that shook the earth; and in some portions shaking earth to the **Core**. There was upheaving of portions of earth's crust, even the primary rocks together with trap, slate, shale, sandstone, and various strata of the carboniferous formation were affected. These strata were turned and twisted from their original beds, sometimes into perpendicular and inclined positions, with several miles thickness of previously-formed strata being broken and contorted.

There were great **earth changes** and catastrophic events; some land portions which had previously existed below the surface of water, now were raised up to a great height, and then in other portions, land was pushed downward becoming lower than its previous position. New mountains being raised, and previous mountains broken down. New valleys and coves were formed which would now constitute the **beds** and **borders** of large Seas.

The chains of mountains in regions of Asia, Scotland, and Switzerland **had-now** became permanently established. Among those mountains of Asia was **Mount Ararat**, which before could only be seen a little above the surface of the water. This great **convulsion** of Nature was **universal** throughout earth; though it affected some parts more than others, the reason for this, was because some of the existing mountains had volcanic vents that had been effective in relieving the internal pressures surrounding those portions.

## Section 47

After a period of time the **evolving** of the internal elements soon **quieted** the agitation of the water and atmosphere. And this was because the **density** of the environment had become greatly changed. Now both the water and atmosphere in combination again, had became equal to and able to counterbalance the expansive tendency of the interior elements. And here again, the equilibrium was restored. There was another great change which might have been noticeable in the aftermath of the convolution, because it resulted in **another shrinking** of the **crust** of the earth and compaction toward the center. And in conjunction with that compaction was another **reorganization** of the "watery element".

With this particular earth change and compaction, there was a **dissipation** of still more of the carbon element that was in the air, and it would now be **replaced** by **oxygen**. So then, oxygen, nitrogen, and a small portion of carbon, together with other particles composing the water, now composed the atmospheric envelope of the globe.

The earth soon generated new chemical compositions upon its surface; these being a result of the **emissions** of volcanic ash, lava, and the likes, spewing from the interior **substances** that were released by the action of the venting volcanoes and earthquakes. It was from these volcanic particles that a **new stratification** was formed, and this geologist have subdivided into three distinct substances. These substances were all existing and apparent in some portions of the previous stratifications.

It's known, that limestone contains a great amount of carbon as explained, and this fact **reveals** limestone's **true-affinity** for the carboniferous formation. Also **quartz**, along with other substances combining with the metal **Iron** and then this compound combining with oxygen; the whole united substance **produced** a new combination which is termed the Ironstone (oxycle of Iron), and Magnesian limestone, - all of which is covered by heavy beds of **Marl.**

There is a well known fact derived from chemistry, that each of the original elements contained in the composition of the earth, supposedly fifty-five, combines in various ways with other elements by chemical affinity. And so, compounds change, and then the new compounds will also show a similar change in form, appearance, and properties. And this whole process takes place **solely** by the chemical processes of combination and recombination of elements, so what is noticed is that all Forms, from the angular to the circular, during their processes of **crystallization**, are constantly revealing the same general law of "progressive ascension". And this law is then **revealed** by the presence of these new and higher mineral, plant, and animal, Forms and various compositions which are constantly being produced; and these changes are in reality **merely** a progression, even though the elements and essential qualities are the same and remain unchanged. So then, the present formation which is the **New Red Sandstone** only unfolds a new earthy substance which was a result from the previous upheaval and the entire change of the water and atmosphere which are now surrounding and acting upon the earth at this new time-period in evolution.

The earth again has compacted and shrunk, becoming less in diameter; the water has also become less in density and bulk; and the atmosphere became lighter and **more-refined**. And the newly combined and recombined **elements** were now **prepared** to bring forth new substances and new plant and animal Forms, both in the sea and on the land. Realize that Earth and her productions have only been resting for awhile. Yet now, Nature was **revived** from a long sleep, now with new laws, new principles, and new elements, She puts out Her energies to use, creating new life and new beauties, and there is new **light** from the Sun because the atmosphere is lighter in density. This renewed living energy will now be **breathed** into existence. And, *"the firmament was above, and divided the waters, and the comparative darkness was dissipated"*. Everything about earth has now become a **different** character and condition from those things what had existed in any other eras before this sandstone era, - so far in the process of creation and evolution of our earth.

Therefore the expression is rendered clear and forcible, that "**the evening and the morning were the second day**".

Geologists have named and classified many of the species of plants and animals of this era, obtaining information from the fossils that have been **discovered** relating to this period, but have not succeeded in discovering any of the species intermediate between one class and another, nor any cause why new forms should now be created. And from these investigations geologists have formed assumptions or deductions based upon the lack of finding fossil remains during the end of the carboniferous formation. They had supposed that the original Forms and species of land-plants were entirely destroyed at the close of the carboniferous.

Ferns, mosses, and fucoides, had found a foothold and flourished during this new red sandstone era, though not very extensively. The marl-beds were a formation developed as the result off a **great-collection** of the lower orders of the mollusks: - this is known because those beds are apparently masses of shells, each bed-mass **represents** slightly all the types of the mollusks which are formed from the **crystallized carbonate** of **lime**. And in addition these beds have yielded a great variety of the lower species of mosses, but these plant masses never developed further or ascended to the higher ferns or the coniferas which represent the pine-tree of present day.

At the **beginning** of this new era the only progress which can be noticed in the plant kingdom, consists in the development of a more substantial class of plants; and this class of plants is represented for comparison by the pine, oak, birch, maple, trees known today. Plants species in general within this new period were neither efficient nor abundant; there were very few flowering plants among those that did exist. Of the **ammonites** and **calamites** existing in this period there was a small almost imperceptible change that had occurred in their forms, habits and compositions. Also geologists have made wonderful discoveries, finding the tracks of huge lizards, birds, and tortoises, that had been existing in this era.

Yet all things are connected, and even though a great change had occurred and had rippled all through-out Nature on earth, including the new plants and animals, the order of progression **was-not** interfered with, not even by that sudden transition and recent upheaval. And because there has been no-interference, the **chain** of progression continues **unbroken**. And although Nature at times exhibits moments of violent activity, this does-not disturb the order of existence nor change the law of progression. The catastrophic events which occur are a **part** of evolution and not only do they occur, but they need to occur. These frightful events are just as much a part of evolution, as is fish climbing onto land, because living on planet earth involves this mechanism of re-energizing Nature. These events are **affirmative indications** of Nature's workings on our earth and confirm that Nature's **intentions** are to **produce** mankind as the ultimate progression.

So here is the scenario and process of earth's recharging mechanism in review: - which is, that in the evolutionary process of Nature on earth, a time comes when all things within an era have ascended one more step in their evolution and have become more perfected; and then, when living energies are depleted and Elements have chemically changed, well then, as the "point of no-return" approaches, when the equilibrium of earth has become unstable and the balancing mechanism has become totally destroyed **between** the interior and exterior forces of the whole mass, then without doubt, a universal convulsion **must-result** as part of the process.

But balance is soon restored between the external and internal portions of the crust, and these peculiar earth changing events are only a **static condition** and they **do-not** change the order and harmony of Nature's established laws. And even though the event does modify greatly many things such as the atmosphere and water which had acted upon the previously existing Forms, - understand that those newly modified conditions will in-turn interact, modify, and combine with, the new species of plants and animals in a display to reveal and develop new energies and new principles.

# Section 48

It should be of interest to have a description of some of the animal Forms living during this new red sandstone formation, given to the reader which may help create a mental-image of some of those varied animal Forms, telling some facts in relation to some of the most prominent species. And in addition, fossilized evidences of these Forms can be found among the classifications already made by scientists; and in regards to adding information to those preexisting classifications in this review, there will only be given a general view of the **new energies** which **must** have resulted in the creation of these new Forms.

But before giving that overview, it is **important** to first give a few preliminary **facts**. The intention is for this information to create an adequate mental image **of-why** those particular kinds of animals existed during this period.

To understand the situation of all living Forms of this period, it is necessary to know the important fact that the **density** of the gaseous **atmosphere** was **greater** than what we experience in the twenty-first century. The weight of the atmosphere combined with the weight the "watery fluid" together, balanced and **equaled** the expansive force of the interior of the earth. At this particular period the weight of the atmosphere created a pressure of thirty-seven quadrillion, four hundred and six trillion, three hundred and seventy billion tons; or a little more than thirty-seven pounds to the square inch (37 psi). Therefore, from the extreme density of the atmosphere it should be understood that the comparative pressure of the air weighing upon and pushing down upon those land animals was great. It makes perfect sense then, why the animals of this era would have required big bones and muscles. And the same can be said of the plants needing sturdy stalks and stems.

The **ichthyosaurus** is among the first Forms of this period that have attracted attention, especially because its spinal column represents the partial **ossification** of the previous gelatinous substance of the spine, even though it is not altogether vertebrated, only near the neck and extremities; and then, the center of the back being entirely ossified. It **resembles** a **saurian** or lizard, but also is slightly represented in the shark, and also it had characteristics which can be seen in the modern crocodile. Its nature was totally **carnivorous**. It could live either in or out of the water; and this arrangement can be deduced from the shape of its thorax and posterior sternum. This animals structure indicates that it possessed **adipose branches** which served as a **respiratory organ**. Therefore, it could remain under water, or it could **inhale** the existing elements of-which constituted the atmosphere of that time-period, which was carbon nearly-counterbalanced by oxygen. This animal sustains a position between the previous saurian and the true lizard. The **color** of this animal is dark with an inter-mixture of red and green colors, and the exterior coating being hard and turtle-like.

The true lizard is represented in the Order of animal which the **plesiorsaurus** is ascended from. This is a higher class than the previous reptile, though it was similar in many ways, but this animal existed in the water only. Being extremely carnivorous, feeding on lower order of fishes and any other infusorial productions. It's **color** was entirely black, with it's surface being a little more elastic.

Another Order of animal is represented in the **megalosaurus**. This is **considered** an animal and is very different in its form and disposition which represented the lower orders that preceded it. This animal represents a **fully vertebrated** animal. It has a very long and large body, with peculiarly formed ribs. The ribs indicate how the motion of the creature is generally connected with the locomotion of the whole body. Two of its legs have been termed **wings** which could be seen from the wing's spread and complex form. It also had two sets of **fins**, constructed to give great force and velocity of motion thru the water. This animal possessed "great power of muscle **contraction**" because it could **raise** itself up nearly perpendicular from ten to fifteen feet. This animal has been termed a lizard and would still have been considered such, if it did not have a tortoise-shell-like coating. The coating of this animal was very rough and complex, hard and shark-like.

The megalosaurus is seen modified in the next animal, that of the **pleitheosaurus**, which is a higher class. The pleitheosaurus differs in habits and it is **herbivorous**. Its form is very long, and for comparison it can be seen represented in the young whale of today's era. It traveled extensively on dry land and the **ferns** growing freely, are what constituted its peculiar food. Its body surface is more ordinary rather elastic and whale-like.

**Maslodonsaurus** is similar to pleitheosaurus. This new species possessed similar habits and even a similar disposition except this animal had progressed with its form of locomotion and had evolved **nearly** to the **digitgaded** form of mobility, and moved by walking on its toes, but not its heels. This animal's body was in some ways nearly like that of an elephant, except that it was dark and hairy, plus its length varied in the various species of this animal, from five to sixty-six feet. The highest of this Class was termed the **iguanodon**, - which had enormous **organization**. The iguanodon Class was the highest organism on earth during the deposits of the New Red Sandstone, and it also was superior to all others in its size and power.

Plants and animals of this period represent Forms which have developed a "progressed condition" and one more step evolved over previous sea animals and plant productions. Each new species coming into existence had a **slight variation** and often differed from the previous specie. All these progressive changes in the plants and animals could only have occurred as a result of the **changes** that had previously occurred in the chemical components of earth's mass, the water, and atmosphere. Many lower species continue to swarmed the seas in great abundance; and over the countless age of that period those gigantic animal Forms just described became developed and existed.

It would be by the **close** of the carboniferous era many plant species had already became extinct; but, the chemical and mineral **substances** those plants had taken into their systems and utilized, **remained** as organic and inorganic elements which would soon **become** part of the new compositions and new Forms that were evolving and these new creations will **utilize** these elements for their existence.

It may tax the mind to realize how the **iguanodon**, which is the highest Form existing in this era, is directly connected to the very first Form to have develop, which is the **radiata** organization, the animal which had originated at the very beginning of **this plan** of "successive development" of all Things and Forms. Sometimes the analogy between the two is so completely lost in change, that the human mind can not imagine that **there-is** the most distant **relation** existing between them. But the fact remains, it was simply successive developments of things, - from the lowest to the highest. So, no matter how disconnected the order of creation appears, this can-not alter the general truth; that the whole displays a "harmonious adaptation of parts". The succession of this **adaptation** represents, the **orders** and **degrees** of creation.  And the lesson that needs to be learned from this, is **not-to** always depend-on appearances or only to just understand the particulars of a situation or organization; but instead, realize that it is by having knowledge of the **general truths** of a matter and understanding the interconnections between things, that the plan of Nature is known. And general truths **will-lead** to a understanding of how universal laws, principles, and developments, are all evolving as they follow the original Impetus of the Creator!

## Section 49

By the **close** of the carboniferous formation the fish had became abundant throughout the waters as was stated. And then, at the **opening** of the present new red sandstone formation, there is evidence of the development of the **turtle** and then the **bird**.

The class of animals known as iguanodon had several species that were existing at the present sandstone formation and the highest development of these is represented in the **rhinocerosaurus** and also the hippopotamus of present. And as stated previously some of these were digitigrade and being whale-like in its habit and elephant-like in its disposition.

On the tree of life above the lizard-like Class there is a **winged ornithosaurus** called pterodactyl, it has two legs which had wide-spread and complex feet; it had a large low body, and this animal was very ferocious.

**Turtle-birds** existed in this period and apparently were frequently around water, and some of these animals had left tracks along the shoreline. There were also existing an **inferior** species of an animal which had a peculiar appearance which was somewhere **between** a turtle and a bird, and this animal had a bat-like Form, and some of these somewhat strange looking creatures are found in fossil remains upon the higher strata.

The **marl-beds** seem to represent the previously described animals more than any prior formation. The cause of this peculiar connection, is because those animals previously described, had existed a long time before the formation of the marl-beds, but the animals became changed and partly extinct at the **close** of the marl-beds and spilling into the **commencement** of the **Oolite Period**. Geologists have discovered the fossil remains of these animals where they were left at the end of their period of existence. Another interesting creature found from this period and is also the largest animal, was represented as a enormous snake-lizard. The largest birds had the appearance that would represent the ostrich of today, this animal of-course was an imperfect type of the bird creation, and these bird-like creatures had evolved and ascended from the iguana to the ornithosaurus. These were amazingly enormous animals.

The **whole** animal creation of this period can be placed into two distinct Classes – the **lizard-turtle**, and the **turtle-bird** and neither of them have visible characteristics to any extent which would show them as being similar to any of the animal creations of our present day. The lower Classes were extremely carnivorous, while the higher Class were herbivorous. All these classes of animals living in this period were fully or partially vertebrated, and the main bones of these creatures contain marrow and periosteum.

The extreme density of both the atmosphere and "watery solutions", had continued into this new period and the extreme density and the **peculiar** chemical compositions of these environments **prevented** the development of any light-weight bone or fast acting muscles and nerves. And furthermore because of this 37-psi density, all animals of this period were extremely large and heavy, making them sluggish, yet powerful. The dispositions of these animals were ferocious and carnivorous; however, these were necessary characteristics and are the **result** of the lowest **development** of the principle of **Sensation**.

Although some animals of this period had developed what were apparently **wings**, these appendages were used only as implements to give aid in the animal's movements thru the watery deep, or could also be used to raise themselves a few feet up from the surface of the earth. In a way, the use of the wings to raise-up could actually be viewed as being one of the first examples of **flying**. There is another interesting anatomical structure which had improved within the whole animal creation, which was the respiratory organs; these were developed to correspond with the dense and peculiar atmosphere of that period.

The Earth at this period has plant and animal developments that **represent** the lowest and the highest, and all the intermediates, of all previous periods, and this is an important item to reason upon. Sensation had become imperfectly developed in the last era, and in this present period, Life and Sensation have unfolded new principles, new Forms, and new dispositions. Because the animals of each class are more perfectly organized, and each class unfolds new attributes of Life and Sensation. And when all of these things are joined together as "the glorious productions" of one of Nature's days of creation, then these will give insight into Nature's succeeding creations.

**But**, Nature has now become **modified**. All Nature's previous essences and principles have been "used-up" and are spent. The previous equilibrium **has-now** again become **nearly destroyed**. Energies that had been renewed after the previous upheaval, are now again exhausted and **no-new** exertions can be made. The whole of earth is in a state of paralysis.

**Darkness** is beginning gradually to cover and hide the features of many things. The fertility of the earth has become partly destroyed and the Forms that had re-clothed the face of Nature on the previous morning of the second day, - have now sunk into another deep repose; and know that every morning becomes an evening. So life, beauty, and youthfulness, become aged, tired, and death has occurred! One must realize that every substance in being, no matter how great, is really just the lowest symbol of some still higher Forms that will be successively developed. It is an event that must occur, because things change and die, in-order to bring-about the new.

In the scheme of things Nature's beauties and elaborations will now **yield** to a final point of completion. Now as the living energies are spent, all things show outward signs of **retrogression**; yet, internally and invisibly, these seemingly destructive developments give evidence of the **unfolding** of "interior beauties", to produce a more exalted state of physical and mental organizations.

All the many positive developments and progressive **modifications** which have occurred within the period of this red sandstone formation, including the internal particles of the earth, in all plant and animal Forms on the earth, and in those particles of the water and atmosphere, **had-become** so vigorous and wide-spread; that the energies used to facilitate those modifications had almost become depleted, and with that, a **change must occur**; this present depleted situation was similar to all other earth changes that had occurred at the close of those previous ages. So at **this moment**, was when the whole earth is **clothed** in the evening-quiet of a long-enduring day. And the fiery-element of the earth's interior became **agitated**. The earth's rumbling was not because of sulfur, or electricity, or water; but instead it was by the **insufficient** stabilizing pressures of the external-elements; because the water and the atmosphere, both in their processes of chemically evolving, had significantly **decreased** in density by this time. The result of this imbalance of pressures, was the **upheaval** of many-more portions of the earth. This present convulsion **was-not** as violent as the previous catastrophe, nor was this event as generalized, nor as wide-spread. The hills that had been formed by the previous undulations of the interior mass were pushed upward and now became much **more elevated**. And all the different strata were again, broken and contorted in various places of the earth's crust. Many beautiful **caves** and subterranean passages were formed in the interior of these convoluted portions.

This **explosion** was rather **gentle** in comparison with the former catastrophic event, and this event was felt generally south of the equator but was also noticeable at the poles. The earth **diminished-instantly** in bulk, and this action was accompanied by the thrusting and projection of various islands and island chains, these new land-portions mostly made their appearance in the South Seas. Some of these islands were previously sea-bottoms that had been covered with immense productions of **animalcules** (coral reefs). These coral reefs were so immense they extended in length, from twenty to sixty miles, and had obtained a thickness anywhere between three to eight miles. And the sight of this is truly amazing, and then to realize, that two hundred of those animalcules could dwell in a drop of water. Coal reefs **confirm** the statement, "that the parts create the Whole; and the Whole **must-have** first consisted of parts, or else the Whole could-not have existed".

## Section 50

The sudden upheaval has now finished rumbling and the Earth's trembling has now subsided, and all of Nature's various departments have now begun to assume a whole different-aspect of existence. What would now stand-out and be noticed, was that it appears like Nature is resting. Many plants and animals which previously existed in plenty, were now **scarcely visible**. Many of those Forms and Beings whom had rummaged-about during this passing day of evolution are nowhere to be found; the only evidence of their existence are their fossil remains. The earth, the water, and the atmospheric Elements have again endure multiple chemical changes and processes, all instigating further developments, growth spurts, new creations, all whose efforts show that things in general were altogether differently combined and very much **refined**. The previous dense **atmosphere** surrounding the globe, now had developed a condition **suitable** for the transmission of more light from the Sun, and this opening will be beneficial to nearly all things. It was **not-until** this period of earth's development could the Sun's energy generate so much **light** and **heat** among the associated particles of the atmosphere. More light entered because the Elements composing the atmosphere were now **chemically changed**, and were now formulated with lighter and less dense molecules. This was the **dawn** of another **New Era**, and many positive **indications** of this new era could be noticed in the new substances, new conditions, and different circumstances.

These new environmental conditions are becoming **active agents** that will "breathing into existence" new plant and animal productions. And as this ushering-in of new combinations will constitute the **beginning** of a new era, then, without doubt it becomes nearly impossible not to admire the forcible passage in the "primitive history" of the earth, which declares, "**the evening and the morning were the third day**".

In this new morning, on the third day of creation following the latest upheaval, the **first** geological development which follows the **completion** of the New Red Sandstone is the chemical **Oolite Beds**.

The **first** of these Oolite beds are formed by the **aggregation** of the calcareous substances formed into great masses of materials, and this would constituted one stratum or layer. And within this first compacted stratum, are found the substances of alumina-shale, magnesian limestone, coral-reefs, and various species of the lower Orders of infusoria and mollusks.

In our modern times, there can be found mysterious places where some of this oolite material are found united and this material is sometimes even found **below** the level of the previously created new red sandstone, or sometimes oolite is found even **below** the carboniferous formations; and then, in other places this aggregated-material lies directly upon the new red sandstone. First of all, **calcareous** substances took the **lowest point** in all of these lower strata and lays near the bottom of the layer. But in the higher strata and higher layers, it is found that these calcareous combinations of substances are composed of much **finer** materials. So to give the answer to this **dilemma** of multiple discoveries and describe the **cause** of it is as follows: - recall that at the prior upheaval and latest agitation of the earth, the seas, and the air; well, it should be realize that all-sorts of **debris**, practically anything which could be imagined, was tossed-about and **stirred-up**. Then next, when the agitation had finally calmed and ended, and when the equilibrium was finally restored, this calm was the opportunity for the water and earth to finally **settle**. And it was during this settling of previously agitated particles which produced the first strata above the sandstone. The heavier and more course calcareous materials resettled first, and then finer materials took longer.

The whole Oolite **process** was strictly a **chemical** one, and was formed by processes and conditions that had not before existed. And it is this particular stratification which has attracted a great deal of attention among geologists. The focus on the oolite strata is because this layer represents a complex formation of materials which was the **result** from the decomposition of previously-existing plants, animals, and mollusks, together with the deposition of solutions of existing substances upon the land and in the water; and the whole process tends to make the formation of this stratification mysterious.

Massive amounts of these decaying organisms were all intermixed and combined with the debris suspended within the watery-solutions, including any existing **substances** that were plentiful in the water and on the land formed the oolite deposits. And if this formation is view without much thought or awareness, the whole stratification appears very mysterious.

One thing known in geology, is that lime in various proportions enters into the oolite formation; but the cause of this mystery has not been completely discovered or the process well understood, which would possibly unite the substances of previous formations with the living substances of the earth and this would present the whole formation as a aggregated stratification. Yet by performing various chemical processes on the substances of various oolite beds, **alumina** and other substances will be revealed; yet these substances are not naturally occurring ingredients, but as a condensation of the dissolved particles of previous formations

Another item is that this oolite formation has also been a source of extensive **speculation** in an attempt to explain how all the numerous plants and animals which existed and reproduced in the previous era, could have become **entirely annihilated**; all vanished with the exception of a few fossils which escaped unharmed, these fossils were preserved by being shielded from the corrosive natures and decomposing conditions that followed the end of the previous period.

Some geological investigators have speculated and have theorized that a meteor or asteroid caused the dinosaurs to become extinct. But from here, the answer is no! To obtain the true answer, it is necessary to know that organic and inorganic Forms are constantly changing, and all the **particles** composing those extinct Forms **change**, decompose, and then finally they all progress into new things, and these new Forms or things are changed again, and then again the particles will compose some new Form or new substance. And it is by this **unchanging law** that the whole animal creation which had previously existed at the **close** of the third day of creation, **had entered** by a "chemical combination process", into the Formation of oolite stratification.

The dinosaurs and other plant and animal Forms which became extinct **had-contained** within their bodies all the necessary Qualities and Elements that would be **required** for the next species of plant and animal productions. And that includes all the new substances and atmosphere which will be needed for the development of new and more **perfected** specimens. So the extinction of all the gigantic, gross, and crude types of animals and plants was caused **solely** by the death of the organisms and then, were completely **decomposed** into mush and eventually **absorbed** into oolite Deposits. This new aggregated oolite formation then **resulted** in the production of new energies and elements, and soon the produced new **Forms** which possessed more refined and improved characteristics.

The sea in this new period was abundantly filled by fishes, these varying from the lowest and smallest types, and progressing up to the most gigantic swimming saurians; many of these new creatures were very similar to those creatures existing in the previous red sandstone era. Keep in mind that within the early stages of the oolite period **no-new** plants and animals were produced which would solely exist on dry land. But as this period progressed this fact would change, because as the productions of this era unfolded further, and **after** all the necessary chemical processes had transpired and **now** the elements of the atmosphere also were chemically change and was now better suited to **usher-in** those new land dwelling plant and animal Forms.

It has been explained, that during the transition process between two separate eras, there occurs the **destruction** of nearly all the living plant and animal species of the passing era, and this action usually happens at the close or transition of **each** new day. Well, the best way to view this transition event, is to not be fearful, and instead, understand that the process is really no more mysterious, or complex, or dramatic, than the action of **depositing** a new **living germ**, which will in time, by processes of growth and development, bring into existence many new and far more magnificent productions of plants and animals. So it can be said in a grand manner, that every new condition is a **cause** to unfold higher developments – whereas, each new-day of creation constitutes a great Cause, and also it is a great **effect** and perfect **use**; and these are all united in one principle, and this is one of Nature's most refined principles, the **oneness** of **purpose**.

There is a wonderful inter-relationship existing within all things in Nature, and that interrelationship can be noticed with regards to this present oolite formation; as the mind becomes aware of this friendly connection between all the general **processes** that were occurring **to-form** these oolite deposits, then a **deeper knowledge** concerning the specific events which had enabled the development of this formations will be known. And then with this new and guiding awareness, a researcher may find an avenue for discovery and be able to expose a place where they may find these connections existing as an **unbroken chain** of development and discover the **causes** of the **new effects** which are presented in this period of earth's history.

What else may be revealed by understanding the oolite deposits, is why fossils are discovered in some portions of the earth that were formed-after the species to which they belong were entirely annihilated. And also in a general sense to be able to determine how such a stratification occurred in the first place, because, somewhere lurking in the knowledge of these geological things, consists the answer to the **great mystery** of universal **death** and universal **resurrection**, a phenomena which the whole earth exhibits.

## Section 51

Now as time passed, and the oolite formations progressed-on, and all those **new chemical** compositions were produced, these, leading to the production of some new plants which had now become visible. Of these various new plants were included the Classes sigillaria and coniferae. Plus, there was also a higher class of ferns, and the lowest species of the Iceland-moss.

Previously during the sandstone period there was rain, and in this later oolite period it also rained; but now these **rains** became more frequent; increasing mostly because the process of evaporation had increased. Stemming from the increased moisture, the earth became very fertile in many areas. Trees of the types coniferae, oak, and birch, in this period known to flourish. These growths were extensive especially near the equator where the temperatures were more constant. The rains soaking into the soil was beneficial to the growth of extensive fields full **grasses**, almost similar to the rye grasses of today. But the grass and grain were not considered refined and would be seen as imperfect.

This truly would be considered a productive period in earths development, because now with earth in a more refined condition there has developed many **new energy** sources; there were different and **more-refined** chemical reactions, all forming new chemical solutions and combinations; all these processes are very **intimately connected** with the **unfolding**, evolving, and development of higher species of animals. One important development in particular may **be-perceived**, which is the **development** of a **species** of animal that **man's branch** of evolution is derived from. The Branches sprouting from the Tree of Life are bi-fabricating and sub-branching much more.

Earth's new living energies have now **spontaneously** produced **new types** of Forms in the animal kingdom. The **lowest** type of these new animal creations is the mollusk; and progressing up to **highest** animal production of this period, being that **special** animal production, which are the beginnings of the imperfect Forms of the **Marsupial** animals. And as these imperfect marsupials began to developed and evolved further, there would be some which will **became** an altogether **differently organized** animal production and will be very **differently formed**, so much more different than any other animal that ever existed on earth any time before this period.

It surely would be impossible to name or to list every distinct type, of every class of terrestrial animals that existed on earth's surface **prior** to the production of the species of the **marsupial** class which has here- now been mentioned. It is however, **this class** of the **imperfect marsupial**, which is soon **to-become** developed into a whole new, and altogether-differently constituted form of animal.

These very special marsupial animals constituted the lower Class of the **Mammalia**, this is a class of **oviparous** animals that have branched-out from the tree of life to become very different in many ways, not only in their form, habits, and disposition; but also in their **manner of reproduction**, which had somehow developed unlike any other oviparous or egg laying animals.

And in discussing a new manner of reproduction and interesting item comes to mind, - other than it being explained here, just **how-would** it be possible **to-know** the type of animal leading to man? Well, the answer to that, - it **is-by** an animals nature and constitution that a determination can be made. And in tracing man's branch on the tree of life, - the nature and constitution that is sought-after, - concerns finding-out the first animal where there is **first-displayed**, the principle of **gelatinous utero-gestation**.

Other oviparous types including birds, fish, reptile, and also including many subdivisions of the saurian, all possessed very different powers and abilities, - especially with respect to their process of **reproduction.** And in some-cases, the **off-spring** of these animals were **very-unlike** their parents, especially if the parents were of mixed types.

So now, just beginning to evolve on planet earth in the oolite period is this new Class of animal, this new Type of animal is so **unlike** any previous productions. Some researchers in their attempts to trace the special evolutionary branch that marsupials are derived, - are also trying to determine at which specific period the **mammifers** were first developed; and they may find the investigation of that particular topic of research to be a difficult task, simply because, **not-every** distinct Type and Class of terrestrial animals which had existed on earth, have as-yet been discovered, and so, there are no complete fossil records existing of this and previous periods.

In this period three distinct Classes of plant **Forms** had their existence. These plants gave earth the appearance of lushness, and was mainly a result from the fertility of the **calcareous composition** of the oolite layers and formations which turned out to be very important to the promotion of plant growth. All three of these Classes of plants have similarities with the plant Classes of the previous formation, and this connection can be seen in the **fucoides** and in the **endogenous** and **exogenous** plants which existed in the oolite period. The one plant receives its substances from the inward, and the other receiving them from the outside.

Along with the three classes of plants, there are also two distinct Classes of animals existing now: the **Saurian Oviparous** and the **Marsupial Mammiferous** – each of these animal Classes possessing different habits and dispositions, and each Class observing very different processes of reproduction.  Within the marsupial mammiferous Class there exists the **rodentia** animal, the ruminating or cud chewing animal, and the digitigrade animal with toe-walking characteristics. In this oolite period, the highest of the rodentia Class of animal developments is the **creature** which **possesses** the **three** natures combined, (even-thought these three natures are imperfectly developed). These three distinct characteristics represent the different **conditions** these animals were subjected to and experienced all during the development and unfolding of this species; and what occurred, was one Type of this creature was rendered **more-perfect** than the other, and the most perfect being illustrated in the lower mammifers of earth.

The **mode** in which **gestation** of progeny takes place in animals is about to **change**! The change does involve both plant and animal life as will be explained; but first, it is important to understand how this mayor change unfolds and also how the change in a animals organs, becomes **utero-gestation**. This **requires** an understanding of the chemical processes and combinations of the oolite stratification; and even though understanding the chemical processes occurring may seem like an odd place to begin, it is not. There is an intimate connection - from the chemical processes within the oolite - effecting plant Life - which in-turn **has effects** within the animal kingdom.

There were several geologists who had formulated **opinions** concerned the **oolite** formation, and in particular had opinions concerning those parts of these formations which are termed the "dirt-beds". Their thoughts and opinions on this matter, was they **assumed** the dirt beds to be collections or "beds" of materials which must have been formed as a result of the agitation of the seas, which then, they assumed caused the action of separation of materials and particles. And **assuming** further, that this action, in turn caused the currents of the seas to change. And then **assuming** that, at the termination and whirlpools of these newly formed currents, the debris of plant material along with any other inorganic and organic materials, all became collected together and was transformed into a stratum of **coal**. These assumptions which were made, were all **base-upon** the observations of those researchers who noticed that an oolite layer is found collected under this stratum of coal.

Coal, however, **was-not** formed after the completion of the general carboniferous era, except by some incidental circumstances that occurred in various regions of earth.

The **real reason** for this strata of oolite, discovered under a formation of coal by geologists, **are-only** the **associated particles** which have a geological connection with each-other, and these, being of marl-stone, iron-stone, and sandstone-shale. These materials are the **same-materials** that are also represented in **lower-strata** of the deposit **made-after** the new red sandstone. In various places this has been termed the **lias** and marl-stone formations.

As was previously discussed, **the-remains** of all organic beings became chemically **dissolved**; and this occurred from the general chemical changes of the earth, water, and atmosphere. And then this dissolved material **entered**, by **chemical affinity** - into the oolite formation. Therefore the oolite deposits - **contains** - in its substance the Germ of "higher existences" of both plants and animals that will form. So what that means, is, it will be the dissolved deposits of those **previously existing** plants and animals whose elements of a **germinating tendency**, - was then assisted by the congenial existing elements of the environment, these together, would **insured** the unfolding of new Forms of life, almost all displaying youth and beauty.

An important feature of the present oolite era is that it can be viewed as the collection, combination, and then the condensation, of the **ultimate substances** of the previous ages; and it was these substances in the air and in the water which combined with the decaying organic substances. **These substances**, by **becoming associated** with higher developed particles, (such as ones that are being chemically developed); and then all this has produced the fertile and productive **soil** that exists upon the earth's surface in this period. The more perfected soil, plants, and animals, which would be found in this era simply **could-not** have been produced **before** this particular period.

## Section 52

When studying geological formations to obtain data, there may be the tendency of the research to look under a microscope, and from there, only be able to notice the incidental changes that had occurred; and by doing this, the mind loses sight of that universal order which is taking place. Because, it can only be from having a clear understanding of the physical changes which occurred, such as changes in the appearances and characteristics of those plant, animal, and mineral, of previous ages, that someone could really be able to correlate how the **conditions**, which have become generally **changed**, actually occurred within the Whole. And as each **ascending-law** of development was evolved, and then it assumed new modes of action within those Forms and creatures, can in the general view see, the whole is perfectly connected.

The present oolite period is no different in its general view than from previous developments. Because the present plant and animal Forms continue to show the same corresponding connection and successive development which had occurred in all previous ages. The pattern of development by plants and animals of the oolite era as they should, follow the same pattern of consistency in the methods in which all things develop.

Now, to describe the **processes** by which that significant **change** of **Form** occurred, one which brought about **utero-gestation** which would become established in the **marsupial mammifers**. It is very **difficult** to describe or even to give an answer in a manner which would give facts as evidence, the reason being, is because of the lack of hard evidence. And so with no evidence to make comparisons, it must be **impressed** upon the mind, that the animal **species** of that oolite era now under review, presents an **ascending type** of animal, one that will be physically advanced. And these new developments and advancements in the animals Form will be a result which **originated** from the new chemical compounds and energies which were deposited in the whole oolite formation. A change had taken place in plants and animals because the change was **necessary** to these life Forms for **survival** and a continued existence. So as stated, the plants and animals of the oolite formation where like a seed germ, an embryo, or some initial setting or stage, from which to advance.

These **new chemical conditions** appearing in this oolite formation are the necessary and important ingredients that were needed to unfold a **new type** of Form. And it is this marsupial Form that will continue to unfold the ascending law of development, and a development that is **to-become** a type of organization that finally **produces indications** and hints of a **new** branch of animal, and the marsupial animal is a **representation** of higher Orders to come. And most importantly, this is the beginning of the strong branch that leads to the production of **Man**.

There are now in this oolite period, **three** different animals that have all developed new physical advancements within their reproductive organs and methods of producing progeny. It is the **oviparous**, the lower **viviparous**, and the higher order of **mammiferous**, that represent the three general processes of **utero-development**.

The **first**, represent the rudimentary process by which the **deposited ultimate** substance of the body, **unites** with **particles** of **like-affinity** and assumes the **globular form** or an embryo. And then by a process of constant activity of the portions surrounding the globule, an incrustation or shell is formed. The whole process is what constitutes an **egg**. And this egg, by processes varying according to the immediately surrounding conditions, unfolds and **displays** the type and character of its parent.

The **next** mode ascends and develops to a higher level of the previous egg forming process, and this presents a **different mode** of how the **combination** of elements and substances occurs, because it was by developing new organs for reproduction and unfolding a higher order of interior qualities in which this process transpired. And this ascension would **established** the **ovary-globules** – which are now represented in the lower classes of the viviparous animals, but still undeveloped; and this particular mode is visibly developed and refined, existing mostly in the higher orders of that animal, and this new mode will continue to develop in time.

And the **third** representation or mode becomes revealed and is found in the order of animal which is immediately **above** the first viviparous developments, which are **the marsupials** – whose habits, nature, and dispositions, present an entire change: and their organization presents a **further unfolding** of many of the undeveloped compounds, which were contained in all the lower types then in existence.

Geologist in their research have discovered in the first and second divisions of this oolite formation, some distinct species of the mammifer, but **have-not** discovered any connecting links between these earlier existing species, at least not by the 1840's when these discoveries were made. Anyhow the species that have been discovered, somewhat have a relation to the lower marsupial animals of our present day. But those earlier ones had a character which was very different, and their organization much more crude.

It should be known that it was the surrounding **environmental conditions** which those animals had existed in, which made the difference in their development; and because they had existed in more favorable conditions this led to the evolving of the higher orders, and this process would occur in this oolite period more-so than of any previous ages. And the **connection** existing between each class, can not properly be seen until the **discoveries** which **will-be** made in the future, to be found in other strata to be investigated, this future discovery will aid in fully determining the whole class of animals pervading the early and lower secondary formations.

In review, the hospitable conditions which have been discussed had helped to advance the animal kingdom at this time, earth being far more **superior** in its conditions than in previous ages; and remember, that these facts can be generally understood just by considering the **modifications** that occurred in the **elements** at the close of each epoch of development.

The principles that were **required** for a change in the process of reproduction were at first, mostly involved in the lower classes, because at that initial period those principles were undeveloped. And those principles would only become unfolded and be **revealed** in the higher classes of animals, in time. **Therefore** the marsupial animals were the only animals which – possessed the three principles, motion, life, and sensation, in a much **more perfect** state, more-so than any animal that had existed before. And the instrument, the vehicle, the animal, with which these three principles were **finally** shown to be more fully active, - **must have been** an animal that was in a similar way perfected.

This whole process just described in the animal, is **similar** with that more advanced process of reproduction occurring in the dicotyledonous forms and functions of the **plant kingdom**. This marsupial animal possessed as it did, those all important **serous** and **mucous surfaces** which exist within animal creatures. These surfaces in their early stages, were very imperfect, and were especially **weak** in generating the required living and active energies of the body. But even in their early development they were able, and did perform the function in the lower and higher species which was **necessity** for the development of the **seminal secretions** which were **induced** by the sensation of coitus.

As an example of these two surfaces (serous and mucous) is seen in the heart and lungs, these two surfaces perform the action of **systolic** and **diastolic** motions, they likewise generate, (when in equal activity), the **chemically-combining sensation** whereby the whole process of utero-development becomes permanently established. And at each stage of the **unfolding** and developing of these special biological qualities, then, new adaptations **were necessary**, so that the species might live after being brought forth and then be able to survive to reproduce.

The marsupial animals **displayed** the **principles** involved in the **positive** and **negative surfaces** or mucous and serous, in a manner **more perfect** than any other animal had done. For this reason they **could not continue** the oviparous process of reproduction. And the fact-being that these animals were entirely viviparous and mammiferous, they are those creatures that **displayed the law** of "progressive development" and would advance and ascend to higher species.

It should not be necessary here and now, to give a minute description of the process involved in all the many steps and stages of development, from the time when the animal creation assumes the character of the marsupial. This will be reviewed later; and the reason for this postponement is because the **principles** which are involved in the process of **transmutation**, are not altogether understood by most. The view-points and conclusions that are held and cherished by many, **prevent** an open mind. And furthermore these close-minded **opinions** have erroneously concluded that the animals of every class, are apparently distinct and disconnected productions from each-other, and that, every class sustains it own types. These speculators have in error drawn conclusions and adopted the notion that each separate class is the result of an immediate creative power. And probably the reason for this gross error in judgment is that **none** are known by man to **change** the character of species in particular before their eyes.

No discovery has yet been made which seems to give a good indication or is able to describe distinctly the process of **transmutation**. However transmutation means development, and it does not imply divine intervention. Transmutation is a **constant** manifestation in Nature and is strictly a development within Nature; this development process is revealed by the fact that nothing exists in Nature **except** what involves, "the principle of ascension and progression".

Now looking at the **elements** which **surround** the **earth** during this period, it is now known these elements owe their existence to an aboriginal condition of the whole mass of the earth starting from a primordial condition. And by now it should be clear to the reader, that the **stability** of the inner mass of earth is dependent upon the stability of these surrounding elements. And it has been shown that plants **require** for their production a proper condition of the earth, **including** those existing elements of the atmosphere. Plants could not exist without these elements. The animals **require** the plants, and the highest of the plants require the lower species of plants. And even all the gigantic carnivorous saurians sustain that same relation to the lower species of the same class. So, all those that were first and herbivorous, became adapted to the requirements of the higher orders, some of which are carnivores. Therefore realize that each kingdom, mineral, plant, and animal, presents a **series** of corresponding steps and **degrees** of development side-by-side with each-other, because they all depend upon each other. And so with the marsupial which the oolite period has presented, these are those animals whom constitute an ascending step or degree above previous species, - at the same time they are still connected with all previous organizations below them on the scale of evolution.

There is no violation of law or order in this higher development; but sometimes there is an apparent disconnection between the very first Forms developed on the earth and with the marsupials, especially when the two separate species are compared with each other. Also, recall, that errors can occur in the process of making this type of comparison, and a researcher may lose sight of the **slow processes** of change which all Forms passed through from the lowest, then ascending to the highest type in the animal kingdom. And this similar process also takes place in the plant and mineral kingdoms as well.

Soon to be described will be the development of a whole class of animals whom present themselves to Nature, as these animals **ascend** in their evolution to be the **first type** of creature developed to where we **may-recognize** the undeveloped principles composing the physical and mental constitution of **mankind**, and this event occurs during the **Secondary Formation**. At present there is no more to be given concerning the **gestating principles** involved in the marsupial animals.

## Section 53

Next is the description of the gradual processes occurring as the many **successive** and similar looking Forms of **animals** (which follow those first animals) and are now beginning the process of the **change** in reproduction. And it will be noticed that many of the orders, series, and degrees, of animals that were existing during the **oolite, cretaceous**, and **tertiary** eras, were actually of a higher nature and more developed than they are designated by geologists.

The remains of those **plesiosaurus, iguana,** and **sauridon**, which have been found among the **upper strata** of the oolite, and also were found at the commencement of the **cretaceous Period**, in reality merely show the **continuations** of the similar reptiles which existed before the completion of the new red-sandstone system. The **majority** of the earth's land portions during these periods, including the general elements, **were not** very favorable for the production of the marsupial animals; while in other land portions, these marsupial animals had found a home and they thrived. One item which may cause confusion is that there are some marsupial animals that had been existing, sometime before the commencement of the oolite period, and their fossils may be discovered there among the components of the oolite formations.

Stated previously, the general law of reproduction had greatly changed, and the **result** of the change was the **decline** of some of these lower species of animals which did not evolve; and so, it would be only the **higher orders** of all species that would **carry-on** and be perpetuated, simply because these higher species were able to adapt. These higher animals **had-develop** the necessary means of reproduction that **had-corresponded** to the chemical changes that had occurred on earth and this helped these animals to adapt.

Geologist have distinguished the main classes of animals of this period, but have not discovered all of their varieties and **modifications**. For example, the **Sauracephalus** is among the lower order of the species that existed during this transition period between the oolite and cretaceous timelines. This organism is remarkable and stands-out in evolution because his particular creature is the **first** animal that possessed the true **division** of the larger and smaller **brains**, whereby **systolic** and **diastolic action** was firmly established as **governing** the whole vital motion of the body.

Then, from Sauracephalus, there is a **connecting link** and a somewhat similar species of which the **Steptospondylis** is and example – this creature has the nature and habits **both** of the carnivore and herbivorous, and in some-ways it slightly represents those natures of the water-bird. This animal has been discovered in the strata of the **miocene** and has **been-supposed** to be a sauridon which was related to the monitor and iguana. Then there is a higher order of the megalosaurus, which is also existing in this period; and with this animal there is formed a connecting link between the lower order and the higher classes of animals: - and from this proceeds many species of the Class **mammalia**.

The whole animal kingdom at this period is **divided** into three degrees: the **saurian**, the **tortoise**, and the **mammalia**. The mammalia are comprised of the **rodentia**, the **ruminantia**, and the **digitigrade**.

The **highest** of the mammalia **unfolds** new principles and new forces; and as a whole, these developing energies appear to **indicate** an **ascension** and further development of the laws and principles of motion, life, and sensation. The highly carnivorous nature of this creature existed as a **prerequisite**, enabling the **unfolding** of the higher class. In this animal the **two-surfaces** - the serous and the mucous, are distinctly developed; and then, as a **consequence** of the mucous and serous surfaces, there is the important **development** of the **contracting** and **expanding forces**. These forces are so important in the development toward man. And the attributes of these forces, are **Sensation** and **Inclinations**, along with the **Passions**, which all **result** from these two surfaces; and these will become the important indications by-which the characters and dispositions of animals are truly known. And what will be discovered is that they are complex.

The unfolding developments in these higher classes of animals has reached a level of progression that is extraordinary; because now in this period, it **maybe** considered that **Sensation** has truly become an **established law**. Know that sensation existed in previous lower animals, and in other periods, but this attribute was **not-perfectly** unfolded in the constitution and development of those lower animals. It is by **the perfection** of this law and principle, which the **two-surfaces** and **two-forces** required to reach that needed perfection. And **now**, for the **first time** many new acting, living energies, were produced. It was by the availability of these energies that the marsupial species was able to develop the process of utero-gestation, and is how it became established.

Giving an overview of the vegetation existing now, it is noted that the number of plant species existing during this period were not very many, and the ones which were existing, are in most instances basically of the **same degree** and **type** of plants as those which had existed in the previous geological formations. And most of these species of plants which had continued to exist were sparse in numbers. Plants of this period are represented by the ferns and coniferae.

To reiterate a point made earlier, consider this fact, - that there is no law more-certain than "the law of constant progression and progressive development of all rudimentary substances". And, there is no period in the geological history of the earth, that manifests this principle more thoroughly than this passing period.

From a geological perspective it appears evident that a change was taking place in the manner of evolution of plants and animals, and this change was in effect near the **close** of the **secondary period** and this change would include all the degrees, classes, and developments of both the animal and vegetable kingdoms. Geologists have not fully discovered this change: because, the **tertiary period** appears to many of them as only being a very slight progression from that of the oolite and cretaceous.

But by performing chemical analysis of the higher earthy compounds created just before the commencement of the tertiary period they will discover this **great division**.

Scientist by the 1850's had formed theories and had **supposed** that the **cretaceous formation** was the result of the liquid solutions of the "watery" element being combined with floating and suspended debris contained in the seas; and they theorized that the motions of the seas was the mechanism, where-by various deposits of this combination occurred. However, it is evident that this formation **could-not** have been accomplished with that method of depositing material, because, these same ingredients had been available previous and did-not form these deposits then. First of all, chalk is known to be the carbonate of lime, crystallized and sublimated, and intermixed with various silicious substances existing in the coatings of mollusks and can also be found in estuaries – if this stratification was formed by these existing solutions, why, was not the same formations produced before?

And so, because it has been known by scientists that the same materials existed during all of the prior formations; then, from these considerations it becomes plain, that the particular formation of this strata, and also continuing into the upper and kindred strata, all **must-have** resulted from some-other cause.

What is known is that the substance directly over the oolite is a kind of sand and clay shale. Then above this, is a bluish and clayey stratum. These plainly represent **the-evolved** and **the-ultimate substances** of the strata laying beneath these layers.

The substance of **lime** transformed into corals by the **infusoria**, and re-decomposed, would form, by condensation processes, the beds of

**chalk**. And within these chalk deposits, and in the deposits above them, is frequently found the silicious flint-stone. This flint is a substance composed of the **ultimate particles** of silica or quartz. These substances have **not been** found below this formation, although in some instances they are existing in the lower strata of the oolite, mostly where the **subdividing** strata are minimal or lacking. This fact does not confuse nor interrupt the order of geological development; for it agrees with all the discoveries of fossils in each department of the animal kingdom.

So sometimes these **irregularities** that may-be seen within each formation of plant, animal, and earth, were **most-likely** the result of some **peculiar** circumstances or some **local causes** that can be shown as being a primary event or mechanism creating or developing that irregularity.

We know that the **weight** of the water and atmosphere **determines** in part the strength and character of the two living kingdoms. Therefore, it is easy to understand why the gigantic dino-saurian herds, that inhabited the earth in previous ages, all had similar large bodies, which were necessary and they show a correspondence to the **enormous density** of the existing fluid and gaseous elements surrounding them; and the reason for this is because these elements were very different in quality and composition from what they have become. Each period of evolution always follows the **same pattern** which occurred in prior formations, and the same pattern is seen in the **characters** of the organic productions of each period, because these were always **in-accordance** with the laws and **forces** that were in action at the time of their development. And it has already been stated, that, this pattern applies to all the changes and re-compositions of the watery and atmospheric elements: because as the elements changed, the kingdoms of the living species **became changed**.

So in review of evolution, sometimes the modifications and changes in appearance within the Orders of plants and animals, changes which required ages to be accomplished, look totally different when compared over time, and the sometimes the connection becomes clouded, especially when comparing a species from the beginning and end of a branch of the tree of life. The first Forms produced on the branch are seen as a completely **different species** from the later Forms of the same class. And when a great dissimilarity like that is observed, the mind loses the connection between the lowest and the highest. But this would not be the case if the mind could comprehend the eternal truth, which will be reiterated: - that all higher things, are **contained** in the lowest undeveloped. And the first and lowest being the **Germ**, all others that follow will (if subjected to proper conditions), **ascend** through the evolution of all the progressive forms, until it becomes a **perfected compound** of the whole previously-existing mass. And the **Cretaceous Formation** exhibits an obvious "ascension of particles" which had previously existed in a much more crude form.

## Section 54

   Recall, the catastrophic events which had occurred during the previous "earth changes". There occurred many devastating volcanic eruptions, which were deemed as "necessary" events which in-turn were the mechanism which changed many land features dramatically, and also is how many of the rivers, seas, and oceans were either formed or re-formed. And, it was these same molten and fiery disturbances, which as a result or effect also created extreme winds and gigantic waves, and then these were accompanied by the production of very heavy rains. The actual **cause** of these waves and fierce wind disturbances originated **near** these eruptions; great portions of the atmosphere were violently and **suddenly displaced** by the vapor **rising** up into the atmosphere, and a vast amount of rising vapor rushed to **filled** the huge vacated space, according to its volume. And when this displacement occurred, some portions of the atmosphere became dense and others rare, the result, were these very strong and enduring winds; one helpful result was these winds actually helped to restored the equilibrium that had been lost prior because of the chemical processes of that time-period.

   It would be the bodies of water which were thrown into agitation by these fierce windy forces, which in-turn **caused** the uncondensed sea-beds to become **disturbed**, stirring up the loose sediment. In this activity much of the of low laying land would become flooded extensively.

   Prior to and at the time of the volcanic activity, the seas still had great abundances of **infusoria** and in addition these waters still had the activity of the **polyparia**; these organisms, together with the **aggregation** of those **substances** that had been transformed by other classes of animalcules had over long periods of time **created** immense coral-reefs. However, it is those same coral-reefs that were **destroyed** and reduced completely into a "watery" solution by the **constant agitation** taking place in the seas and oceans. The entire mass of all uncongenial particles were floating in solution all throughout the watery waste.

   The action of one event, was a cause of similar action in another event. And then it would be by a **constant friction** and **agitation** that a substance **was-formed** which when it finished **depositing** and condensing, produced as was described, the **upper cretaceous strata**.

   The general process just described in the preceding paragraphs represents how all later and succeeding sedimentary rock Formations occurred. But still, this present layer of strata being deposited **indicates** a decided **adaptation** of certain animal species to the necessary development of new animals Forms, and some of these animals are **approaching** the appearance in Form and similarity to that of the **human** type organization. This process will be **discovered** by close chemical analysis of those strata, focusing on where iron-stone, tin, copper, with the iron being above them in sequence – and which is also the same composition that is contained in the solids and osseous substances of the human system. And what will be discovered, is that the **caulk** is precisely the substance which enters into the formation of all the bones, both of the bird and the saurian species of that era. So **now** in evolution, there exists a **more perfect** Form of **particles** that can be utilize in new organic plant and animal Forms that will enable them to become lighter in mass and weight.

It is the chemical **compound** that is combined in the higher and more advanced organism that in reality is just a **unity**-of the lower and more basic substances. And it is the **inherent properties** of these substances, that **govern** the higher substances; and so those properties and compositions of rudimentary substances, formations, or stratifications, should be viewed as beginnings or principles, out of which flow the higher creations. And then it is by letting this fact "become a standard", governing all our investigation of the sciences of things, the mind would naturally become enlarged, just by the act of understanding cause and effect. A cause has an effect, which causes an effect, which effects a cause that will effect the next cause to cause the next effect.

In some of the fossils which have been discovered arising from this present **Cretaceous Formation**, will be found species of animals whose types are still existing. There are parts of this formation that **have-not** been investigated, this is known because there are species of animals from this period which have **not-yet** been discovered. Some fossils of this period, when found, will-bear a closer relation to the **feline tribe** of animals existing, and these are more nearly allied to man than one would surmise, more than has been supposed by geologists.

**Chalk** from this point onward will be found in almost every Form upon the earth in subsequent periods.

Marsupial mammifers, are animals of which **pleilocotherium** and **phascolotherium** are examples, and these have been discovered in some parts of the upper cretaceous strata. But these **do-not** represent the character of the animal kingdom during this period, at least not to its fullest extent.

The commencement of the **Tertiary Formation** almost imperceptibly follows the chalk-beds. And in many portions of earth this Formation is composed of disintegrated limestone and marine lime-solutions, interspersed with decomposed marly-substances. When looking at the strata of this period, it becomes apparent that many species which had existed in those prior periods and had inhabited both the sea and land, **have-now** become **extinct**. What stands-out as remarkable about this period in relationship to that extinction, is that there was a **partial change** of **temperature**, with the ambient temperature becoming **cooler**; and there was the falling of snow followed by the formation of large **mountains of ice**. And in general there was a lighter and more pleasant **atmosphere** encompassing earth.

The **lines** of variation and lines of no variation, which govern our arctic and torrid temperature, were constantly changed during this period; and then, these temperature changes produced corresponding changes it the atmosphere, and consequently changes in the atmospheric temperature resulted in the frequent **melting** of these massive mountains of ice. And of-course it then makes sense that this ice melting was **always** followed-by an increase in the volume of the great body of water situated on the face of the earth, and this caused extreme flooding of land.

It was this period when the **seasons** became established as a pattern; but in the beginning of this period, those seasons were irregular, and the reason for this seasoning, was dependent upon the **condition** of the **elements** of the atmosphere and water. The fact that **more light** from the Sun was able to enter through the lighter, less dense atmosphere was beneficial; this not only yielded more light, but also created more **warmth**, and consequently more fertility. And from all these conditions it is evident that Nature had undergone **another day** of evolution; and now the period had-arrived that now **gives meaning** concerning the original statement *"the greater light ruled the day, and the lesser the night"*.

There is an expression given in a previous writing found in a **historical account** of the termination and **closing** of this period that states: "**the evening and the morning were the fourth day**".

## Section 55

It is the beginning of the **tertiary period**, and as it comes into existence along with it all of its **productions**, it truly is "the morning of a new day" of our Earth's creations. The tertiary formation, was produced from the **deposits** of lime, shale, clayey-lime, marl, and sand, along with the various chemical **solutions** which were then existing in the seas. There was a **constant** action where there was the **collecting** and **aggregation** of those various substances; and together, it was these substances that **over-time** would **produce** both the lower and intermediate strata contained in the Eocene and Miocene deposits; after which, by similar means, the Pliocene with its upper division was formed.

The brief description of the tertiary deposits is given as a lead-in to a description of some of the interesting plant and animal remains which are contained within those deposits as fossils; along with descriptions of events and physical phenomenon which had occurred just before and during this particular period; and then, give insight into the ascension and development of the mineral, plant and animal kingdoms.

There are **wear marks** found on rocks that were left by previous **flowing** of bodies of water in an **oblique** direction from the northwest to the southeast; and clearly these marks show that this action had occurred over a very long period of time. And in addition, there are also **marks** and gouges upon the earthy terrain, which appear to have taken **other directions**. But these **later** marks had been instigated and had occurred **during** the great agitations which were part of the fifth day of Creation.

There were enormous mountains of ice formed by the change of seasons including a general change in the ambient temperature. And because these ice mountains were affected by the temperature change, they fluctuated in size greatly. As temperatures warmed, the ice mountains melted, and **frequently** even becoming entirely **reduced** to a **fluid state**. And what is so interesting about this event, was that at each and every season in which this phenomenon occurred, **great tides** were also produced, which in turn, carried ice and the various substances embedded in the ice to many different parts of the earth.

This is a period of very **extensive erosion**, especially wearing upon the mountains and prominence, which-now the rising waves and tides could easily reach; and those incision marks spoken-of, appear as evidence. Keep in mind that the **position** of the oceans were not exactly in the same position as they are in modern times. During those colder seasons when the **water** was **congealed** into **ice**, the great body of water was much more calm. However when the change in temperature from cold to warm took-place, well, this was the time, the heavy fierce winds would **cause** the **great agitations** upon the waters of oceans and seas and causing their contents to be riled.

During the tertiary formation some portions of the **dry land** became fertile, and grew quite lush with abundant vegetation. There were lower and higher species of plants existing, including sea-weed and cryptoga-mis, and would also include in that list dicotyledonous. All the Classes of palm and coniferae were prevalent, including both the lower and higher species. There was a species of tree, somewhat like the rock-oak we know today, and these were abundant in the forests of this tertiary period. These trees are now extinct, but petrified portions still remain in the upper strata of the pliocene.

The lower class of plant formations in this period, are **grains**. The higher class plants are those of the developing forest, and these are the oak, the birch, and maple types, though these are bulky, gross, and crude in their form, being mostly undeveloped and unrefined Forms of vegeta-tion. And all throughout the animal kingdom there can be recognized, if looked for, a close **relationship** to any of the new developments within the mineral and plant kingdoms, which in many aspects, **corresponds** with the "successive ascension" that had elevated the plant kingdom, by having characteristics that are strong, gross, and imperfect.

Evolved species of megalosaurus and plesiosaurus are still existing in the tertiary, for these **have ascended** and progressed from the **saurian** species, now evolving-into the animal Forms of the semi-elephant and the mastodon, and not to ignore, that there were also intermediate species of the hippopotamus, rhinoceros, **unicorn,** walrus, plus the several species of the huge sloth.

Some early geologists **supposed** that the tertiary period presents the **first distinction** between the lower Orders and the **ruminantia** and **quadrupeds**; these two higher orders, along with the **edentata**, give a good over-view of the general appearance and characteristics which form the distinctive features of the animal kingdom in this time-period. Each of these classes of animals, **represents** the higher order of **utero-devel-opment**. The lower marsupials that were spoken of earlier, had by now become almost entirely **extinct**. So the whole animal kingdom is now rep-resented by an entirely new creation.

So in this fourth day of creation, the **quadrumana** stands as the ex-ample of the highest and most perfect Form of the whole creation, its form slightly resembles the monkey. Geologists have had no means to arrive at an absolute knowledge of this particular species's form, nor its order, nor its character, mostly because this animal existed many many thousands of years before the primitive history of man was even written in its earliest of writings.

# Section 56

The tertiary formation is greatly distinguished from other time periods which have been discussed, and the progressive changes which have taken-place in this period are best represented by giving due recognition to the remarkable animal developments which continually show the **positive progression** of **things**, and show the **unbroken chain** which connects all things is still relevant. So in review of this particular period, - the climate has changed and there was the establishment of seasons. Nature has become more refined and has develop a more formal condition, somewhat sophisticated comes to mind.

It is a **fact** sometimes overlooked, but now needs to be recognized, which is, that the condition of the higher elements, are the **mechanism** so to speak, which **determines** entirely the temperature of the atmosphere. Cold is merely the absence of heat, and heat is the **ultimate condition** of its negative or its "unascended" temperature.

It is nearly impossible to correctly explain, and ultimately solve the phenomenon of the **variation** of the temperature on earth, especially when using available terminology. There are not available terms which give a precise explanation of weather patterns, nor are they expressive of the true conditions causing these temperature changes. Yet, all that is need, is to know that Nature, is still incessantly producing, and is constantly developing in stages, the lower and higher or cause and effect. Nature's intended direction of travel, is strictly in **positive succession**.

As the tertiary formation progressed during this period, the **arctic regions** have become much **colder** than any previous time in earth's history. This **cold trend** which included both polar regions, actually started its trend near the close of the new red sandstone period and has continued during all the subsequent ages, and will continue up until the close of the tertiary. Heavy hard frosts and long periods of snow, leading to the building-up of enormous mountains of ice. At this icy stage of geological progression, it is the arctic which has the coldest period. However, at frequent occasions all this frozen substance would **become-melted** into the waters; then, aided by ocean and sea currents this melt water **flowed** towards the warmer parts of the globe.

The variations in temperatures gave strength to **extreme rain** and fierce wind storms which were also occurring during the tertiary. The true mechanism of rain was caused by the particles of water being **attracted** to the heat, the water would constantly evaporated and then ascended towards the heat, this action causing a denser atmosphere. When these evaporated particles condensed, they form the rain cloud formations. Clouds are the result of the grouping-together of particles of **equal density**; then, they become too dense and fall as rain. This action requires temperature changes and disturbances in the atmosphere. The mechanism of rain (of this type) **could-not** have **occurred previous** to this period, because it was not until the fourth day of creation that the seasons were even established, and that **only-occurred** when there was a proper development of all the requisite conditions within the earth and within the water and atmosphere.

All these events the rain, ice, snow melting, sometimes resulted in **frequent** and almost-entire **submersion** or inundation of the whole face of Nature. Some evidence of these events can be seen in the **Diluvial Deposits**.

Other evidences of the extreme cold toward the poles along with the intense heat toward the equator, consists in the abundant **remains** of calcareous and minute infusory shells, which in many places pervade the southern seas and beaches. And evidence where the chalk beds **are greater** in size as they approach to torrid regions, these beds being in some places nearly joined to the succeeding strata of the carboniferous era. And then, approaching the north, including what was the upper part of both continents, the marl, shale, and limestone formations are all much **more-conspicuous** in both the cretaceous and tertiary, much more than is the chalk or its other kindred substances. This whole process being produced by the revolutions of the **lines** of **no-variation**, and the **radiation** from the poles of the earth.

In the portions of the earth that have been searched, it has been discovered that the calcareous fossils prevailed more in and around the tropics than they did in the northern portions of earth. It was concluded that **frosts** which occurred during the red sandstone period, actually had taken-place during the entire absence of the birds that had inhabited parts of the western continent. Their **tracks** have been discovered in divisions of the strata where **no frost-marks** are seen; which implies that they migrated at the change of the seasons. Plus their fossils **have-not** been found where their tracks were found.

From the red sandstone period to the present tertiary period is when the **seasons** have gradually become established. However, when **comparing** the extreme change that has occurred from that earlier time to the present period, it is **difficult** to determine the cause of the frequent variations of the seasons, and this vagueness is especially the true between the inundations of the tertiary and the start of the "historical period". The cause has not been completely explained; yet an explanation is necessary.

## Section 57

In explaining the seasons, it is not the intention of this story to relieve researchers from the efforts of their minds, as they, in their joy, inquire and attempt to determine the causes of the frequent variations of the seasons. But it is necessary to make known what should be the foundation on which to enable one to determine these fluctuations of temperatures and give focus on what is occurring at the polar regions at different times.

These varying **polar** temperatures occurring at various times, **was-due** to the **changing conditions** of an **existing element** (?-carbon), in its lower and higher degrees of development; and which, (though it is not generated by foreign bodies), this element is **assisted** by them to **sustain** a connection with the whole envelope of the earth, from the lower to the higher strata of the atmosphere.

And another item is that the north has been for a lone time considered as the location of the magnetic pole, this place is evolving incessantly an attractive **electric fluid** which determines the direction of the magnetic needle. And in the torrid portions of the earth, the **particles thrown** from the **Sun**, which when **decomposed**, produce **light** and **act** upon the water and atmosphere. And then this action **results** in a constant sublimation and development of heat or the **magnetic medium**. It is here termed magnetic for distinction; but properly stated, it is the **unfolded heat** contained in the previously-cold medium. The imperceptible rushing of this current toward the north determines the direction of the magnetic needle. Heat is the Magnetic Medium.

There are **three** distinct **currents** related to the **rays** coming from the Sun. The **first** of these rays, is light without heat: this ray produces color. The **second** is light without color or heat: this current of light produces chemical action; such as, the white muriate of silver will be turned instantly black. And all kindred bodies undergoing the same chemical action, are in the same way, rendered susceptible to the same reaction, by this particular ray of light. The **third** ray or current of light neither produces color nor chemical action, but produces warmth by causing friction between all particles on which it acts. And this particular ray of light **acts upon** all similar particles whereby the whole are transmitted to the particles composing the envelope of the earth, and these are suitably digested by plants and animals.

The first of these rays is the cause of all color. The second it the ray that has been lately supposed to be magnetized. It produces the chemical action whereby color and other properties become durable. And the third comprehends these both – and is the active, communicative substance, that generates heat by friction upon the particles of the atmosphere.

**Light particles** are modified, as they pass thru the great atomic envelope of the earth and this is why color is seen, and it is by action of refraction.

There are also **three distinct fluids** crossing the earth from south to the north, and from the north to the south; and this is accomplished by a mutual exchange of elements from the poles.

There is also an **intersecting fluid** that crosses each of the others, and this has been termed the dia-magnetic fluid.

Those fluids are in relations of equality to each other; and where they terminate at the north is the nucleus of the magnetic pole; and, it is the **direction** of these fluids which are what establishes "the **lines** of no-variation".

It is the **motion** created by their **attending fluids** which determines "the **lines** of variation". These lines revolve from east to west half way around the earth while the Sun is passing through one of the signs of the zodiac or by the apparent motion called the procession of the equinoxes. And wherever is the meridian of these lines, there is the **greatest** degree of **cold**.

And furthermore, as these lines come-close to any particular longitude, then, the climate of that portion of the earth becomes gradually changed; and it is in this way, that some portions of the earth which were formerly characterized by blooming fertility and a congenial atmosphere, have since been utterly changed to barrenness, and are now **concealed** from the light of the Sun by a mantle of heavy snow and mountains of ice.

In **proportion** to the predominance of these substances, whose motion constitutes these lines, is the portion of earth where the temperature is rendered cold. And so, every portion of earth that is subjected to extreme and severe winters, is affected by these lines; and places where winter are most severe are directly under their influence.

So, it is by the constant evolving of the cold at the north, that the heat near the equator is caused to be more intense; and these combined, is how there was established the two counter balancing conditions, or a positive and negative – or the lower (or first) circulating **electric substances**, and the higher or **magnetic medium**.

And so in review, it was during the tertiary period that severe **storms** occurred, and also, there were the **flowing** of great bodies of water, debris, and ice. These all are the actions that were **caused-by** the establishment of the seasons of summer and winter, and the variations of temperature, - cause by the revolutions of these **lines** of **no-variation**. It was a series of winters that were extremely severe that ultimately formed those large mountains of ice in the polar regions. And these extreme winters also had resulted from the presence of those lines of no-variation. The **Diluvial strata** were formed by the deposits of the debris and various dissolved substances being carried by these great currents of water. These currents had distributed huge **icebergs** to various locations of the earth, as they moved all this material across the surface of the whole earth, traveling in the same directions as just described.

The finer material of debris which settles and forms layers of strata are termed **Alluvial**, and it is these silty formations that were deposited in many portions of earth, and are especially found along marine coastlines.

During the time-period of the alluvial deposits, there were many occasions of almost universal **submersion** of land areas, occurring mostly in the summer season during the melting action; and then, these melts were followed by the **formations** of ice during the frigid season, causing a **great decrease** in the whole body of water. These extreme events were **frequent**; and after this process had cycled for **many ages**, the combination of water and atmosphere began to **lose** their **required density**, mostly because so much water was being frozen, and it was the loss of density that tips the scales, and would cause the equilibrium between the exterior of earth and interior to again be lost; and then as an effect of this imbalance **must-result** in a **catastrophic event**. This upheaval would be somewhat similar to the previous upheavals of earths interior and exterior.

It is this present time-period, which is **just-before** the beginnings of earth's final geological Formation commonly known as the Historical Formation, that the pending catastrophic event is about to occur. It will be during this time-period when **almost-all** the land plants and animals would be **entirely destroyed**, and the main cause of this destruction of living things was from those frequent and severe **general submersion** of the whole face of Nature by the rising and receding watery element. It had been noted previous, that many **caves** had been formed during a time-period previous this period, and in those caves can still be found the **remains** of several extinct species of animals, whom became extinct due to these floods.

Evolution is a constant process with many series of events. Everything that is in and part of Nature is **successively developing** – always. And now, as it was in previous earth changes, some environmental changes **must-occur**. It was a result from the great **modifications** and upward chemical progression of all organic and inorganic materials, a process which is always occurring in every department of Nature, and here and now the time was right for this major change; plus, the **conditions** that are required for the **unfolding** of the new and subsequent plant and animal production were in place; and change **must-soon** occur; **because**, "unfolding" is a requirement of Nature, so that She may **fulfill** her mission, which is to ultimately produce and develop **Man**. And be assured, that Nature is intent on producing them.

And so, there is a **pending** catastrophe about to occur, which is needed, because in its aftermath, after all the dust has settled Nature will **establish** - a superior geological and chemical condition of the earth, that may be termed *"very good"*; and this change will be beneficial for the requirements of the next kingdoms of plant and animals to develop and unfold, and this includes the development of **Man**.

This is to be the **great transition** of the earth from a state of comparative barrenness and inactivity, to a substantial and long-enduring condition **adapted** to the existence of new Forms, with more perfect and exalted compounds.

This planet has taken billions of years to reach this period in its evolution and now nearly all of the geological Formations that are part of earth's development, are now nearly completed – with the exception of any **artificial formations** that are still in progress even in modern times. Soon, new energies **will-be** revealed that will establish new species upon the face of the earth; and many of these species have types are still in existence even into the present day. When these **new energies** come-into action following this next upheaval, there will be a great **abundance** of the inhabitants of the sea and of the creeping things of the earth. All these creatures have evolved over long periods of time, and are now situated, to produce and *"to bring forth species after their kind, and to multiply exceedingly"*.

However right now, it is at this particular point in geological history where there was a *"coldness"* to the earth, the water, and atmosphere, all-of which **hindered** plant and animal developments so much, that it was only the lower Orders of creation, which could exist and could multiply; which gives an interesting twist, to **the command** given in the "primitive history" saying, *"to all these creeping things to bring forth plentifully their like"*, because this action was a reality and it truly did occur. Therefore the original history of the **steps** and **degrees** of **creation** are verified.

So to give an appropriate expression that would describe this point in the evolution of earth would be to chose the meaningful statement, saying that, "**the evening and the morning were the fifth day**".

## Section 58

The story has now come to the particular period of creation of the earth and its kingdoms which is so intimately connected with the scientifics of the world; this is a period which abounds with distinct representations of all things now existing. This is the "**historical formation**" and this is the moment in time of the creation of **mankind**.

Nature, together with her laws, appear as one vast chemical laboratory, a place where the lowest and most basic elements comprising the whole composition of earth are constantly being purified and developed. And the whole environment of earth is a compound of **poly-gastric globules**, whose power of chemical action and principles of progression, unfold all the Forms that are developed from the original great mass.

The **first** plant and animal types that are presented upon the face of earth at the commencement of the **sixth day** are of an inferior organization and not progressed, yet, when compared with the higher forms of the previous era, they surely would be seen as more advanced and are the superiors of all previous Forms existing before these.

In the world of opinions, there persists thoughts within **some minds** which continue in their thinking processes to prematurely draw conclusions; these minds are **saying**, that every plant and animal species **has-had** a specific origin and each live in an exclusive existence. **However**, this thought process is a **deviation** from any truth and merely stands as an opinion. Instead of an opinion, the study of anatomy is a useful tool to be employed as a basis of finding the truth of evolution and finding the process of "positive progression of Life" from one species to another; however beware, because even many experts of anatomy have also in-error, made conclusions and consider as fact, that every anatomical Form in being somehow (magically) shows substantial evidence that these Forms are specific productions of some power above on high, or by some bolt of lightening, all believing that these life-form productions of earth, are independent of the power that Nature possesses.

But any honest and truthful researcher knows the fact that it is very evident in chemistry that an organic structure of any type or species, **must have been** previously existing in a different-state of composition, prior to the present one that particular Being is now existing in. For example: the minerals within your body at one time was food you had eaten. A building could not exist without first having the materials to build it.

If mankind is to advance as a Race of Man, then one of the first criteria is a necessity for its individuals to have an **open mind**. As our world becomes more united, it certainly cannot be limited by false impressions, opinions, or superstitions. An open mind does not imply giving up freedom nor imply that one's present beliefs must change, **unless** those beliefs are in error and from ignorance. An open mind basically implies that the mind is placed into a **balanced position** of reasoning whereby it can make correct decisions. So in order to make a decision there first has to be a choice between something. Then the decisions made will then be dependent upon choice, and that is real freedom. An **open mind** allows an individual to see different view-points before a choice is made. Nature is so advanced and complex that it is only by the science of **mathematical relationships** or mathematical correspondence, that a knowledge can be had of anything in Nature, and this includes knowing any of Her motives and living energies, and includes any of their effects. It is necessary to know of the **progressive tendency** of all particles in being which are **destined** to obtain higher levels of substances, higher qualities, and more **perfect interiors**.

Beware of a mind that is closed and that **only-sees** externals, seeing only those things which are visible and this action shuts-off the ability to see the whole; and therefore **cannot** understand the complexity of Nature nor gain knowledge of God's Divine Plan. But it will be learned that in an **expansive mind** is prepared; and any time questions may arise, their minds are drawn by an **interior affection** to the Cause of all causes, and that mind analyzes general causes and effects, seeing both the visible and invisible, and this expanded mind **observes** the **perfect adaptation** and arrangement of all things. Realize there exist, interiorly - a grandeur in the visible Forms of Nature exists, which **can-only** be seen by a mind that has first opened their inner eye with their **interior qualities**.

## Section 59

On the **first-day** of creation there was a process of unfolded one of the laws or attributes connected with the Great Whole, and that law is **Power** - and this Power was displayed in **ceaseless motion**.

The developments of the **second-day** of creation, unfolded the attribute of **Wisdom**.

The **third-day**, **Goodness** was manifested in the arrangement and adaptation of all things.

The peculiar conditions and circumstances existing on the **fourth-day**, and the results of them which were "very good", also showed **wisdom**; and there was also developed **Justice** and **Reciprocation**.

The **fifth-day** unfolded a **new order of Beings** – such Beings, that now possessed powers and faculties, and a degree of **sensibility** that was not existing before; and therefore, these Beings were capable of **feeling** the **difference** between the lower and higher Forms. Hence these new Beings could feel a **forbearance**, which meant they were developing self-control, patience, and tolerance.

When a higher and more advanced creature has gained a knowledge of **self** and now has an **awareness** of one's own power and pre-eminence, there is always a **regard** shown by the more perfect Forms, for the lower orders. And this is where a **spirit of mercy** and forbearance was established among the animated tribes of animals existing in this present era.

And now, the great productions of Nature which were unfolded and began evolving on the **sixth day**, had a direct connection with all previous Forms, of all previous ages. And, it was a development of their **interior qualities** which shows a **connection** to the **ultimate ascension** of all Forms, all particles, and principles; and also the **unfolding** of all the attributes which were originally involved in the first type, or the Germ of all developments that followed after it. And while this "sixth attribute" which is being unfolded now, does correspond and connect to all others, and its absolute grandeur rises above the highest conceptions of the minds of the world.

This **principle** of "interior qualities", is an attribute that comprehends all things below its degree of refinement, and it contains qualities that will continue unfolding eternally beyond. This principle is the **medium** of association between all spiritually-expanded minds. It encompasses and pervades all Nature – the whole world – the Universe. It is the **essential** Germ of more perfect beauties – and is the highest attribute of the present sphere of existence. It is **that** "quality", which is to be admired and adored above every other thing. It **should** illuminate the interior constitution of every Being, and should give character to every thought. And while it gradually becomes more and more **unfolded**, it will establish in the mind, an affection for an "interior knowledge" not only of present, but also of ultimate things. This principle therefore, is the **highest** and most perfect principle that has been unfolded from the original germ consisting of power.

This principle is an **index** – and it is the beginning and introduction to what will be revealed through-out the whole of creation of this sixth day.

In general, science is limited and has been used mostly as a **mode** by-which the world has made attempts to investigate external forms. And science **barely** looks-inward and conceives of the deeper and more **interior qualities**. Therefore, that which has been termed "science", is neither knowledge nor is it understanding; because, it **does-not** know the "beginning principles" of Nature, nor does it know Her "universally pervading qualities". For the majority of things in existence, science only sees shadows or sheathings of truth. And if science only sees the exterior, this means that the **interior** cause of every external form has been often obscured and **neglected**.

Yet knowledge of Nature becomes righteousness if we use its power to unfold wisdom, beauty, and the spirit of goodness and benevolences, and unfold universal justice and reciprocation. This special knowledge of things, can generate a dignified forbearance, and it allows for a pure and solemn respect for any and all truths; and importantly, it establishes a well-organized mind. Therefore having true **knowledge** consists in having a true conception of the stupendous operations of the immortal principles originating in the fountain of the **Omnipotent Mind**.

Now, at this point in the story we have ascended the ladder of earth's evolution to the formation of the **alluvial deposits**. These deposits are the **most-evolved geological formation** of the earth. And it is only proper to acknowledge that the **conditions** existing previously and during this period of earthy formation, were essentially a different and separate formation from what is seen and known today; Yet any differences which arise, should correctly be labeled as superficial, even-though that since the time of the alluvial period there have been **incidental** and particular formations which have occurred. These incidental formations and deposits are the result of debris and various chemical solutions that were spread throughout the watery element.

During the alluvial formation it is seen that **coral-reefs** have continued to be produced by the constant work of the infusoria and polyparia organisms; and within their compositions of coral there could now be noticed an improvement and the corals were more perfect, presenting a neatness of texture.

## Section 60

In review, the condition of the earth during the alluvial deposits was very different from the conditions of earth in previous periods; now, with the extreme and constant changes of weather patterns rendered into seasons by the **influence** of the **lines** of variation and no-variation upon the fluid and ethereal elements. Excessive floods and inundations repeatedly overwhelmed the face of earth, setting up a pattern of freezing and dissolving huge mountains of ice. This action continued up to the time of the commencement of the alluvial deposits.

But then, as the alluvial formation progressed many of those high mountains previously existing, had eroded greatly, decreasing in size. The **landscape** had been altered so much by the erosion, that even the location of those mountains were completely changed. The **water** was becoming different too, but this change was only in its chemical combination. The water's change was the result of refinement and ascension of its ultimate particles. And the action of this chemical change caused the **weight** of the whole mass of the atmosphere to be **decreased**. Interestingly the **atmosphere** had **given-up** a great portion of its **carbon** to the various strata and formations of the earth. This chemical ascension of particles of the atmosphere **resulted** in the perfect development of oxygen and nitrogen, and the relative **proportions** of these gaseous Elements developed during the alluvial resulted in them being nearly the same as they are in our present time.

The particles of the atmosphere that are found in the envelope of the earth at any given time, are atoms which have ascended from lower conditions and lower chemical states. And the condition of every earthy Formation is also represented in the strata of the atmosphere. And, each of the earthy **strata** has an ethereal or atmospheric **stratum** which is in direct equivalence to each other. The atmosphere **is composed** of as many strata, in relation with both its general divisions and its subdivisions as are found in the earth's crust.

What is evident from this awareness, is that from the very **first** condensation of the **granite coating**, then, continuing up to the period when a new substance and the next formation was produced; well, the water and atmosphere **must-have** been correspondingly dense and crude in their compositions. And then with the addition of every new stratum and Formation, these new ones **must-have** resulted in a **corresponding** chemical **ascension** of the grosser and more crude particles of the atmosphere that had themselves evolved and developed from the interior elements of the earth. The superficial Formations which have occurred after the alluvial and during the **historical period** of the earth, yes, do have that same process, and they also correspond precisely with the upper stratum of the atmosphere. So, even to the present day, the water, atmosphere, and the continents of the surface, hold a balance with the interior of the earth. So, **beware**.

In an overall review it can be stated, that during **every epoch** or day of creation, all things **became** essentially changed and **adapted** to the needs and requirements of those particular Forms and Beings of that particular day of creation. And each new day **built-upon** the previous days. In a sense it could be said "the earth and atmosphere unfolded their interior qualities", and new laws, energies, and circumstances, were the end results of the development and unfolding during each and every period.

And now with new living energies many new species of **birds** and saurians, and other kindred species are now existing and developing as the alluvial Formation continues; and, although the plants and animals have changed in their Form and their organization, they **continue** to **occupy** the **same strata** of atmosphere that their lowest types originally occupied upon the earth's surface. And it is on this same principle, is involved, the extinction of many gigantic animals that dwelt in the water and upon the earth during the secondary formation.

Develop, progress, evolve, ascend, develop, change, develop, progress, evolve, ascend, progress, evolve; ascending from the void (lowest), to Spirit (ultimate). "positive progression" towards perfection and ultimate **companionship** with God! The whole, therefore, forms a perfect system, a unity, that has a destiny.

The **whole** constitutes an active, living, energetic Form. And the whole is a source, yielding forth minute productions, and these productions gyrate into the most complicated organizations. And the whole also gives energy to the **individualization** of the **interior principles** of man, which is the **Spirit**.

Both the **earth** and the **atmosphere** in the time of the alluvial deposits "are in the proper relations", so to now "join each other" and produce chemical actions, that will **produce** new Beings and new organizations. The atmosphere had reached an excellence, and had become "so far perfected", that it now was able to **join** the **element** of **electricity** which pervades space – pervades the whole Universe.

In chemistry it is known that water is a condensation of the same elements that compose a great part of the atmosphere (which would be very flammable, were they not combined properly). Thus water, is but a **lower**

**degree** of the atmosphere, and the earth is but a **lower condition** of the atmosphere and water, and the "whole" is but a imperfection of that thing, of which **electricity** is the perfection.

The alluvial is the dawn of a new era. For, it is from this period that the birth of more important organizations, leading-on to more important results which are to occur. And the importance of the Forms, Beings, and essences that were developed at this special period, are of such a grand character, that it is difficult to comprehended, even by the most enlarged understanding. First of all it is only by knowing the **Form** of things, that we know of order, and then, by knowing the **order** we learn of degrees, and then it is by knowing **degrees** that **correspondences** and relationships between things are understood. What can be seen from viewing the coating of things, or seeing the external visible form – the quality and **essence** of something may be inferred and understood when viewed properly.

It is by the **essence** which is contained in the **interior** real reality – that all things assume Forms, orders, and degrees, of tangible reality. So go ahead and let the mind draw a conclusion, as long as the mind is using reason to view the interior essence and quality, by seeing the external and visible Form; but, **do-not** let the mind judge that **grand essence** which is in the interior and undeveloped, entirely by the sheath or the external outer coat - either. But instead, the mind should rest upon the **inward conviction** received, both from the internal and the external. And this is **justice** and **righteousness**.

It is evident that if essence did not exist, Form could not: and so, if Form exists, then out-of necessity, that Form's **essence** must be the real cause of its existence. **Essence** therefore **produces Form** by an association and collection of its own qualities. So then, **correspondence** (at least as relating to these and similar subjects), now becomes an **established science,** and the truthfulness of this is perceived from its being founded upon the nature of things.

# Section 61

During the alluvial period nearly all the chemical processes which transform minerals and organic substances and transition them into organic Forms would still continue as has been, but clearly this the most grand of all previous periods. And, it is now known, these new organic Forms contain all the properties and principles of the highest and most advanced productions of the previous period, but now advanced one more degree of refinement. The first Classes of these new Forms consists of the lower marine and land plants. A higher class of **dicotyledons** were abundantly produced in places where dry land could sustain them, in other environments and other portions of earth, there was the class **cryptogamia** developing, and then some lower Forms beneath these, descending to the lowest **lichen**.

Various species of the **exogenous** plants and some higher classes of fern, palm, and other similar orders, have reached a peak; so, at various periods during this last-day of geological formations, many have become extinct – and then others have been more fully developed and have assumed or developed into higher Forms, all being **modified** by the conditions of their environment. Changes to the **germinating properties** of grains and barley shows them evolving from their previous crude state, and now new energies have provided them with the ability and conditions to be more prolific.

It may be said, that "in the morning of the present era", the plants of earth **have progressed** a step in evolution and are flourishing, yet they still are very **different** from how they appear in our modern era. The land portion of earth where these new crops **grew best** was in the southern and eastern parts of the earth, this is where the conditions were more favorable for plant life to unfold. Within the period of the alluvial formation there were over two hundred species's of distinct vegetation in existence.

As has been previously described, there is a **direct connection** between minerals and animal. And in order to give a general view of this **plant kingdom** which stands as a **connecting link** between the inorganic minerals and animal kingdoms, it is necessary to speak of the **general ascension** of **plant** Forms. The purpose of this review is not to describe every plant in existence, but instead,to only describe those particular plant Forms which have **progressed** in their evolution in a manner where this plant now has a uses, or a distinct bearing, or some effect, upon the **corresponding** Forms to be found in the animal creation. And so, it is by the **action** that each of these progressed plant Forms **becoming adapted** to the **wants** and **needs** of the higher and more perfected animal organizations, that these plants will be discussed. Described, so that the requirements and advancement of each species may be properly understood, and also, so that their mutual relations and **dependence** on each other can be known.

There is one common fact that applies with all plant development in general; which is, they all **ascended** and evolved from the **endogenous** plants which were developed as the first and lowest plant.

At the very-beginning of Life, the lowest plant Forms **began Life** with just **one surface** - and this is the method which the plant would **receive** all the required external elemental particles **into** the internal part of the plant; receiving in those particles from both the atmosphere and by general assimilation. This type of plant exemplifies the **one surface**; and it also characterizes the **first stage** of actual vegetation. And it also **answers** to its connected-relationship, and it **corresponds** with the development of the **first animal** Forms, a process, where the crude and simple plant Form **which-only** possessed a cellular tissue, is **similar** and corresponding to a **mucous membrane** of the animal.

The **next progression** of the ascension of Life was the ultimate of this first class of plants, and in this evolutionary step it **unfolds** a new and distinct **coating**; and it is with this next development the plant ascends and **becomes** the highest Form in the vegetable kingdom during the early period of Life. This new plant now develops the **exogenous nature** with an external coating – a **chemical relation existing** between this new outer coating and the inner coating, **whereby** the inner essences are **transferred**, to the external and then the work of **regeneration** is performed.

There is **a coating** that is **only found** in the higher orders of the animal creation, and was especially developed in the most perfect of the mammiferae. This is the surface, **corresponding** to the beginnings and development of the **vascular tissue** of animals.

Nothing happened spontaneously or even over-night; these developments, in respect to these surfaces, took ages to evolve and were subject to many subdivisions over this time, and in each division there is represented a new type, and then it is apparent a new class of plants is developed in each situation.

It is **Nature** in action, She is using the earth to progressively unfold and modify the primitive Forms, and then She has perfectly **adapted** the essence and qualities of one plant, to meet and fulfill the requirements of others - that will be created in succession.

The **flower** is the ultimate and a perfection of the **interior** substances of the plant kingdom; the flower is also the **medium** through which these inner substances are modified; so as to construct and assume new and

**successively-ascending** Forms; and all that are joining in one **unbroken chain**, from the simple and rudimentary, to the higher and more perfect types. And these **plants** possess suitable qualities to **join**, when they are properly developed, the lowest of the **animal** creation. And so, the **present epoch** gives birth to many new animal Forms. And these new Forms are more perfected. The lower orders are not necessarily more complicated or perfect, but the higher orders are, and it is these higher ones that are the ones progressing.

## Section 62

If it were stated then, it would be a correct assessment, to perceive that the Order of creation which is **now presented** for inquiry, is an **ultimate** and a **full development** of all the lower Forms.

And in the present alluvial period, there also continued that same **close relationship** which exists between land and water; because, it was from the **fish** organisms that would evolve into the various **reptiles**, and these would joined the **bird-creation**; and then, it was by the eventual evolution of these bird-like creations, - **and-by changes** in their Form and constitution, **caused-only** by the ushering-in of a new era of existence, that these creatures are what paved the way, leading to "**the change**" and finally establish the **utero-gestation** in the marsupial mammifers.

It is well to mention and worthwhile to remember the fact, that **all Forms** had their beginnings by first appearing as imperfect productions, which were in a primitive state of development. But know, that those crude and earliest of Life Forms would afterwards **progress** and evolve to the perfection of the species which they belong, which is the **male**. This is only because the male of the higher Orders of animals, displays the **most-perfect** degree of development within a Form. This perfection occurs when **conditions** have changed in the surrounding **encasement** of the embryo. And so it is seen that the highest perfection of fetal development is characterized by the nature and constitution of the male; while the unascended or **slightly-arrested** utero-development establishes the **female**. This particular law of development occurs in both the plant and animal kingdoms. And it is during the process of development of both plants and animals, each have a slight arrest of the process and this is what determines the male or female Form of those plants and animals.

In a plant, **pollen** is the ultimate particles of the flower, and we know that pollen is spread by the surrounding elements, being transported to other plants of similar species. These particles are received into the composition of those other plants through the medium of the **two surfaces**, and by this process pollination occurs. There is an almost imperceptible and mutual, **joining** of particles; and in this way, plants are able to reproduce and multiply. This process, occurs only in the **higher degrees** of plants. And then in the **animal**, a very similar and comparable process occurs; and being similar to the plant, this process only occurs in the **higher stages** of animal development.

The **same law** of reproduction influences all the earthy and mineral, the plant, and the animal creations, and even occurs with the elements surrounding the earth; this law is merely a process of production and development which is involved as a component of all things. And this law is **exemplified** through all-these seemingly different process, which only has been given a different name in the arbitrary and conventional language of chemists, but the process and law is really only a grand **chemical action** that all things are a part of, whether in the earthy, mineral, or organic kingdoms, as they **pass-through** along their various stages of formation and reproduction.

The developments of the sixth day of creation clearly give proof that the evolutionary process of **perpetual ascension** has occurred in all previous Forms, types, degrees, series, and developments, of **each kingdom** which had all come into being and existed upon the earth at different periods, during the lapse of numerous ages. It is also evident in the span of the sixth day, that those evolving conditions are not changed suddenly, nor even impulsively; but instead, they are gradually and sometime almost imperceptibly modified, so that finally, a very apparent change or difference is noticed between the first condition and ultimate condition.

There is no newly-created law bringing about those changes that occur, it is still the same laws which are in effect; but, there is merely an almost unnoticeable decrease of some species, and a **change** in the nature and constitution of some others. And so, during this alluvial period the bird-creation, the marsupial, the quadrumana, and even all species that are above these including the development of man, all, apparently **sustain** their distinct characteristics and types **without** any change throughout the entire alluvial deposits. **Then**, as the alluvial formations were near completion, a **general change** had occurred and was apparent. The animal forms of every species had **decreased** in their size, strength, and in their beauty. This major change in their stature appeared as though there was a **general retrogression** occurring. However what had really occurred was the continual **decrease** in the **density** of the atmosphere. The decrease in density had **affected** the development of the structure of bones, plant stems, muscle mass, etc. The bone structure could be lighter, and the size and structure decreased.

An example of this decrease can be seen in the **mammoth**, an animal existing in the alluvial period; this creature is beginning to diminish in size from the **mastodon** which it succeeded, and as this general decrease continues, the change will eventually be seen in the present day as the **elephant**. And the unicorn, the camel, and similar Forms, are merely progressions of animals which were evolved from larger and more gigantic animals of similar species which existed prior. And as the alluvial period progresses further the lion, the tiger, the hyena, and similar species, are developing and coming into being, and all have some slightly different forms and compositions - than those animals of the same species that were existing at the beginning of the alluvial. So all-in-all there is a general weakness in those species.

The **quadrumana**, including all the species of them the monkey, ape, and orangutan, are **ascending** to that special degree of development in which the "type of anatomy" of the first man is represented; but, these have actually **degenerated** in their habits, characters, and in their nature and qualities; especially when these animals are compared to those that had existed much earlier and more so at the beginnings of this alluvial period.

As all the things and Forms existing during the alluvial period progressed, there was also an overall **decline** of all those things and a lessening of form, along with a deterioration of the constitution of things, and this decline rendered all of the varied inhabitants of the earth comparatively weak and diminished. If it were possible, there would have been an awareness noticed by the senses, noticing that the evening of this period was approaching. This particular decline gives insight into the comparative **exhaustion** of those previous energies which had been so prominent at the start of this period. And if it was possible to view the earth from a distance at this time-period, the world would have been observed as a world of **disorganized** and dis-united Forms, as they ultimately sink into **repose**.

And even-though this is only part of the cycle of development where the present and changing Forms and Beings of the passing-day, **must** give-way and give-place to the more-perfect developments of a coming new day. And this action, absolutely indicates and proves the approach of evening!

In the realm of **Nature** there is a universal Law and principles governing development, reproduction, and of progression – and that mighty Law has been established, by the high morality, of **Divine beginnings** or principles known as **God's** will. The Law of Nature whose Principles are **governing** the material world, and in its glory the world is composed of Forms; and these Forms are evolving; and these Forms are the consequence and **inevitable** productions of **interior** and **perfect qualities** of those Principles.

Nature **reveals** interior truths; and it is from the "interior of things" that Nature operates from. These hidden and inward truths of Nature are represented in every **motion**, in every form of **life** on a particular planet, and also, by the development of **sensation**. These three great-truths - are the external **indications** of the **interior** reality of being; then, as these interior **causes** show their external **effects**, then that is when these effects are seen **manifested** by their exterior Forms, and this occurs throughout all of Nature; and it is only after proper development, that these universal Laws **will-be** recognized as being bound-together, in a inseparable relation which these two truths sustain, one to the other.

## Section 63

In the previous section the main focus of discussion was an attempt to firmly established and make-plain, the universal **Law** that controls and unfolds the plant and animal developments. And now, the story will continue towards the advent of **mankind**. So, **starting again** from the beginning of the present sixth day or alluvial formation, and continuing with the various developments and changes which occur within the animal kingdom to facilitate the on-set of mankind, and eventually reach the **Historical Era**, which is the time-period when the sensory **observations** of mankind **began** to be noted.

These **first thoughts** and actions as man was **becoming-aware** of themselves and their surroundings **were-made** by ignorant minds; and these first observations were **interpreted** with the **undeveloped** and ignorant **minds** of those first human beings; then in error these thoughts were passed-on from generation to generation. Earliest man's impressions of their environment could be both actual truths and false mythologies, intermixed. And then later, when writing was established, these ancient imaginary and mythological stories were finally put into **written** forms.

Again Starting with the plant kingdom evolving during in the alluvial period, a **general review** will be given; and in the narrative of this review there will be **included** the addition of those animal characters that lead to the development of **mankind**. So now, at the beginnings of the alluvial there are found within the **plant kingdom** gigantic trees – coniferae types, oak, maple, and palm. Most of the vegetation of the earth was heavy and imperfect; though, in the **eastern part** of the land-portion of earth which had some of the more-perfected Forms of plants in abundance.

The pine tree was in the form of an exogenous plant when the alluvial period began, then after a long period of time, it began to assume the Form of a more perfect pine and its modifications, of cedar, hemlock, spruce, dogwood, and mountain rock-oak. Trees of our modern era have ascended and evolved from this species. The early oak tree species appeared more like that of a boxwood. But oaks of the **eastern lands** were unlike those of any other portion of land, and these oaks of the east became the black, white, and red, oaks as the climate and conditions changed, with this development taking a period of many ages. The maple tree is a modification of the oak, and this tree type assumed its character about eight hundred years after the red oaks became established. These trees evolve and pass gradually into the higher Forms of the same class such as the birch, the chestnut, the butternut, the hickory, the sassafras – and into the simpler trees, such as the ferns and palms. It was nearly nineteen hundred years after the development of the birch and its associated vegetation that the ferns and palms became perfected as they now are and as they flourished, as the vegetation of these eastern lands.

One third of **Asia**, which at this period joins nearly to the **line** of the Himalaya mountains, and runs in a westerly direction to the Euphrates (which then did not exist then), and further extends correspondingly through into **Africa**, following the same geological formations. In the alluvial it is this area of earth which was the most fertile, ever.

The southern portions of the **western continent** also were very fertile, especially the portions of land that are now known as **Central America**, specifically the land mass near and about the vicinity of present day **Yucatan**.

Many portions of land have since become **dry** which were at that period, completely **hidden** by the watery element of the earth. And some of those lush and **fertile lands** are still very productive agricultural areas of our twenty-first century, and are still flourishing with plants that had developed during the alluvial formation.

After many ages of growth, it will ultimately be those early plants of this period which later in this period had developed into very primitive forms of the **grains** and **grasses** that had been spoken of in a previous section. These crude and primitive plants were the very beginnings of such plants as the clove, maize, rye, oats, wheat barley rice; but in their beginning species and their early modifications, these plants were somewhat deformed and imperfect.

From the grains and grasses, next came the development of the lower forms of the **flower**. These early flowers were of a "radiating class" of plants, and are called this because those crude flowers in their beginning stages would develop from an inferior petal which radiated from the axis of their form, reaching out to the circumference they made.

## Section 64

The first **animal** Forms evolving within the alluvial era to be discussed are the simplest and are very much-like the simpler animal Forms of previous periods. These evolved animal Forms have been classified into various species, the whole forming one group or Order; and these are similar to those types of radiata, articulata, and mollusk, in lower stages of creation, the infusoria, polyparia, crustacea, conchiferae, and cephalopoda.

Various species of these lower animals have been **modified** by their surrounding conditions, and in particular, those animals that are similar in level of development as to the **radiata** plants that are now the flower. But these animals have cellular tissue and sensitive substances, as external parts, which extend out-ward like the flower and these radiating parts and are now "**sensing**" the world around them.

The **articulata**, is a more complex Form of animal than previous lower animals, because it has joints and slightly heavier tissue, and these joints are performing the action of **reciprocal motions**. This class of animal had arisen from the very first order of animals, up to the mollusks, including annelidans and piceosaurians which are the highest of these lower animals. These animals flourished in the land portions of the eastern continent, and throughout the tropical parts of the world.

Other species of animals existing at the same time as the articulata and these would be all the higher order animals that include such creatures as the fish, bird, turtle, rodentia, ruminantia, plantigrade, and digitigrade. In addition there are some animals existing which include the inferior orders of the **marsupialia** and **quadrumana**, most of these animals would be found throughout the **east continent** and particularly in **Asia** and **Africa**. And noteworthy is the face that all of these higher Forms extended their existence toward the **northern regions** - with the exception of the birds and turtles and similar types of species, which were strictly tropical organisms.

Huge animals like the **mammoth** prominently existed early in this period, but as this period of evolution progressed, and as each succession of this species occurred, their kindred species would became smaller in size, yet at the same time were more refined in their physical organization. Within the land-area now known as **Arabia** many large herds of these mammoth-like animals **roamed** and foraged for food. Another region these large elephant-like animals existed is upon the land portion now known as **Greenland**, because during the alluvial period this land area was warm and fertile.

Many types and orders of **saurian** animals still existed in this period. These creatures possessed very disgusting and repulsive habits and natures. Some of these were very **deep red** in color, and were very **poisonous**. These adaptable saurians were able to exist both in the sea and on land; but, they only remained upon the earth a total of about three Hundred and eighty years into the alluvial. The cause of their short span of existence and eventual extinction was because they were being **destroyed** by the formation of new **chemical** associations and combinations of elements, which, as it turns out was **very destructive** to the dinosaurs existing in that period of change. However on the other hand, these new element-combinations were **very useful** to the new Forms developing. Actually these new creatures **were-adapted** to those new element combinations because it was those chemical changes which **stimulated** the development and rise of these new Forms in the first place; and then these new Forms would develop and become the successive and higher Forms, which then continue to represent Nature's unfolding presence.

It was two thousand years into the early alluvial period the mammoth and its related Forms had started to die-out. These large creatures would gradually decreased in number, and finally the whole order became **nearly extinct**. A few of these did survive for a longer period; the **fossils** of some of the survivors have been found in **caves** and **icebergs**.

There was a similar kind of animal nearly representing the elephant in form and disposition, but this creature was a whole lot larger. This creature **formed** a **link** between the mammoth and the elephant. A species of this larger animal has been discovered and has been termed the **mastodon**. These existed for about two thousand and five hundred years into the alluvial, and then like the others, finally became extinct.

## Section 65

There is a very interesting reason why these higher species of animals which had existed in the early alluvial, passed into extinction at successive periods, most being wiped off the face of the earth. These creatures had existed for many ages prior to the formation of these deposits as they developed into their higher degrees of progression. But during the early periods of this sixth day of creation, and after these animals had reached their high state of development, they **migrated** to various parts of the earth. These animals were **wanderers** and at times they would became entirely **separated** from each other. This peculiar activity would be the **tragedy** that followed them until their extinction. It was because of their tendency to separate and wander-off that their chances of **reproduction** became **limited**, and finally reproduction entirely **ceased**. And so, one after another they died and finally the order became extinct. In fact there were many species **not-known** to naturalists, which also were existing upon earth during this period but they likewise became extinct.

It was previously explained that the **opinion** which has been nearly universally received and accepted concerning the **destruction** of these lower animals, is altogether not-justified and this opinion is surely not based on facts. These extinct animals **were-not** swept from the face of the earth by any catastrophic occurrence, **nor** did the extinction occur by any circumstances which have been misinterpreted and misunderstood, originating out of the writings of man's "primitive history". Instead the complete extinction of the giant animals of the earth, along with other species that are now extinct, simply occurred from the causes before explained and no other cause can be demonstrated to produced this effect. As stated it was the complete **dissolving** and decomposing of those animals, and then, the remains became united with the existing elements to produce new substances.

The radiata, articulata, mollusk, and vertebrata, existed upon the earth at the commencement of the present era, just as geologist have determined. These are the four great classes of existing in the animal kingdom – though the radiata and mollusk might be blended together as forming one class.

Advancing many ages into the alluvial time-line, the earliest types of the **elephant** are coming into existence. As one crude Form of this large animal passes-off into extinction it would make-room for new and more refined elephant Forms that followed; until finally there was the production of today's elephant. Whole remains of the mastodon have been discovered, some even standing in an **erect position** in the mouth of a **cave**; and the reason for this is because it was "the-nature" of these and other animals to conceal themselves in such cave-like places during their wanderings; especially when they were **alone** and becoming further diminished in numbers.

During the alluvial time-line there had occurred a **chemical anomaly**, there was a certain chemical condition of the sea at one time, in which, by a **strange** and peculiar **chemical process**, some substances contained in this "sea-water" were **united together** and ultimately became **condensed**, and then these condensed chemicals were **thrown** by the waves upon the shores. These substances are now termed **amber**. Some of these contain many minute insects, being transparent and beautifully crystallized. This substance had existed in great abundance at one time.

About this time there were various animal species of the order **quadrumana** in existence, and these have various subdivisions, with the higher species being nearly like the most perfect orangutan of the present day. The individuals of that whole order, were very **much-larger** than any similar Forms of quadrumana now existing and their stature, **exceeded** that of a large man. These were **very-fond** of the water, even though they were in their natures, equally adapted to the land. These did-not survive very long time before nearly all of these became extinct; and it is remarkable that almost every one of these **died** in the watery element and sadly their **fossils** were **deposited** on the bottom of the sea.

It may be surprising to know that there were many distinct orders of animals which dwelt on earth for a short period of time and then they passed quietly away without even leaving a trace of their existence behind. Each of these became extinct **because** of changes in surrounding conditions. And the most immediate cause of the frequent migrations of animals **away-from** each other was the changing environmental conditions. For instance there were some animals existing now in the alluvial, which in the **most-remote** way, represented creatures **like** the lion, tiger, wolf, and bear, but it would be a later-period when these known Forms truly would come into being.

If Nature were now viewed by the haphazard superficial observer who may only be viewing the exterior things, at this time-period there would have been noticed a **confusion** within creation, the cause of this was in part due to the great **dissimilarity** of all the various creatures and from the great diversity existing, not only in their natures, dispositions, and habits, but also by other peculiarities these animal creations may have possessed in those early periods of the sixth day of Creation.

Some animals were entirely **herbivorous**, others entirely **carnivorous**. This was a world of huge, gigantic animal Forms, devouring each other; and some were devouring the vegetation existing all-about them.

The ruminating or grazing animals were at first not very abundant, at least not in the early alluvial, but their populations started to increase and these types would soon became much more plentiful in the **fourth period**, which was about third thousand years into this period. These peaceful animals mostly existed in **Switzerland** but extended through all the **European** countries to some degree. These early existing grazing animals **did-not** form a progressed type which would be considered as identical in a sense to any ruminating animal Forms of modern times.

## Section 66

Now coming onto the **stage** of creation are **types** of **animals** which are representations of new developments within the **lower** types of the **special branch** containing **mankind**, and a few of these types are distinctly coming into Form and being. But before continuing forward with this particular topic, there is a **need** to deviate back-wards a bit, and **trace** the **origin** of these lower types of man; showing the **links** and connections between these first developing species, **explaining** about them in a more detail manner, at least more-so than in previous discussions, where they were only mentioned in passing. This review is to impress upon the intelligence, the important truth which was displayed in the **first ascension** of the original **Interior Principles** which were set in motion by our Creator, showing those Principles that are **now-contained** in these almost man-like Forms; and also to showcase those Principles that will lead to the **individualization** of the inner man.

In the animated kingdom of Nature there were many species that **developed** very **similar** anatomical structures and compositions; for instance, grazing animals stood on four legs, or an elephant-like creature looked something like an elephant. And because these anatomical similarities do exist, this similarity, especially where mankind is concerned, has caused **opinions** to be formed, opinions which have **supposed** in **error** the notion, which indicates, that only one man-like animal form was created and then, that single animal form was modified into the next new form or successive modifications of the original form. But this **is-not** a **correct** assumption. Nature is like the human brain – and is constantly and incessantly producing Forms, just like the brain is always producing thoughts. And so the true answer to the dilemma is that each Form and peculiar organization which is existing in Nature, is **determined** by the **existing** and **controlling circumstances** which were the original **cause** of such a Form's creation in the first place, those circumstances occurring at the period it was created.

Because circumstances occur, it is then **impossible** for any Order of animal to remain intact for many periods and still appear the same as its original and similar type ancestors were; because these newly developing animals are being anatomically changed in accordance with the existing surrounding **circumstances** of their environments; and, even though these circumstances may-not be visible or even apparent to the awareness of the senses, they nevertheless occurred.

This is given as an example: - the mind is acted on by all the immediate and exciting **causes** surrounding it which then, within the mind produce thoughts as an **effect**. And the effect of these thoughts **always vary** according to the variations of the **cause** of a thought. So then in the same sense, animal Forms, are the thoughts of Nature, just as thoughts are the Forms of the mind. A thought is dependent on a cause, and also Nature's production of a particular animal, is also dependent on a cause; and the causes are dependent on the environment, which is part of Nature also.

Now, what follows, is the description of the animal **progressing** to man; and as stated, - it was in this early alluvial period, within the first part of the sixth day of creation, which is the time when the **quadrumana** that were existing possessed great strength and stature, even exceeding that of man today.

Quadrumana (#1), had a body type that was short and heavy, with limbs that were disproportionately long. Their heads were very wide and low in form. They had wide shoulders, and their spinal column, especially in the early species, **resembled** more nearly a spine of a fish. The neck was very short and full and the whole body was covered with thick heavy hair, like many of the plantigrades of that period.

Some parts of the body of this quadrumana **still resembled** those of the lower animals of this species, such as the front limbs, which were **always-used** in walking. The trunk of Q-1, at first would more closely resemble lower orders of saurian animals. And actually some fossils of these animals have been discovered, and **were-supposed** to be a branch of saurian species. But then again, Q-1 also had an appearance looking somewhat like that of a marsupial mammalia.

Even though it had taken many ages of **regeneration** to even come close to revealing an animal Form which would have a resemblance the particular form of a man,- it was **this animal** though, which is the **first type** which **resembled** in any particular form, **man**. Mostly, the resemblance to man would have been seen in the shoulders, back, and hips, but any other parts such as its extremities and main features, still resembled other animals.

This special quadrumana, Q-1, **had-developed** improved body organs, in a similar fashion as did the class of animals which preceding it. The animals had use of the all important **positive** and **negative forces** of the organs. These forces helped to develop the proper functioning of each organ. And clearly it is in these more advanced animals, that the **internal** and **external surfaces** of every organ, nerve, and muscle, are **lined** by the **mucous** and **serous coatings**, which **generate** the **higher forces** of the whole body. Another item about Q-1 is the lungs were divided into two lobes. The heart contained four chambers, imperfectly. The liver acted somewhat like the spleen of a modern man, and the stomach of this creature acted more like a kidney than a stomach. The brain imperfectly performed a duality of corcular motions, but it consisted of one mass without divisions. The cerebral portions of these animals would be considered as being **similar** to a brain having an undeveloped mental constitution. The cerebral portions of this animal **could-not** develop intelligence. It **did-not** generated any thoughts, except those caused by the **sensations** of the body.

This is an animal, **which-did** unfolded the three principles, motion, life, and sensation, in its peculiar organization, and all-in-all was a very powerful animal, except the bone portions of its body were very crude and unrefined in their compositions.

The animal Q-1 remained upon the earth nearly nine hundred years, and during that time the physical elements and surrounding conditions of earth were **rapidly changing** chemically, this action resulted in the rapid development of this animal, which would experience many changes, all of which would combine after a length of time and **resulted-in** the production of an even higher Form of the same Class.

Now this next new species, quadrumana (#2) Q-2, which is a higher Form of the same Class, and now fills the place of the previous quadrumana species, by **ascending** one degree in the Order of organic development. This animal species had a much larger head than the former species Q-1.

Q-2's shoulders were of a similar construction, and they were sitting high upon the body; there was an elongated spine, with a sacral-bone nearly like that of the **ichthosaurous**. The extremities of this creature resembled **partially** those of a bear, and **partially** of a human being; but, they were used for walking, and at this point of development the action of walking was with all four extremities, in a plantigrade fashion much like a bear does.

This animal **could-not** have existed, except as a progression and a evolutionary-unfolding of the previous man-like animal Form.

As the alluvial formation progressed, many changes occurred in the form and constitution of Q-2, and when this occurred a new Form (Q-3) of the same species unfolded and took the place of this previous Form. The Q-3 animal, like its predecessor, was a very dark, **gigantic**, and powerful Being. The anatomy of Q-3 was less repulsive in appearance and had become somewhat refined and was now becoming differently constructed; and now, Q-3 was **being-adapted** to a new use. Its spine was more perfectly formed and it had become less fish-like than that of the two previous species. The bones of Q-3 now contained marrow, and now the spine was **fully-vertebrated**, and at every intermediate portion of the spine there was a budding and developing **ganglionic nerve** to be used by this animal as receptacles for unexpended fluid; these fluids keep the whole body in an active condition.

The heart of this animal was not-yet fully developed, but it was becoming more improved. The brain was very large in Q-3, but very **inactive**. Yet, it was by this brain's heavy and sluggish action, that **gave beginning** and **birth** to the **nervous-fluid**, and by its contraction, the system was charged with plenty of nervous energy; and by its expansion, imperfect **particles** that were existing in other portions of the system were drawn into the brain to be **modified**, and thereby new life in each portion was constantly generated. The hands and feet of this species are nearly similar.

No "interior qualities" were developed in this animal, mostly they were adapted to just evolving and unfolding themselves and then, were in **lineage** to give birth to a new and higher Form. However before bringing into existence the next higher Form, - there were **forces** at work within this Q-3 animal which were evolving, and these would be those forces which later, in future species, begin developing some of those inner qualities.

# Section 67

The creation of a new species of quadrumana Q-4, soon followed the natural decline and eventual destruction of the previous species.

The anatomy of this animal species continues to improve and more-resembled the lower order of the mankind animal. The head and body of this creature were not quite as large. The spine and appendages were differently constructed, and the extremities became modified so only **two limbs** were used for **walking**. The hands of this animal resembled the marsupials that were existing at that same time, and the feet were still those of the digitigrade or toe walk, with the exception, that these feet now had more complicated parts.

Now in this species of the **quadrumana** overall there has begun a **decrease** in the number of species; and when there is a decrease in the number of Forms, this is a sign which **indicates** a composition of more refined materials has occurred within the evolution progresses.

The present class that has made its appearance is Q-5; this animal has **less hair** upon the the surface of the body, and now, the shoulders are not sitting as high as were in the previous creatures. The spine of this species now has becomes **nearly** of the same-form as a man's, which has now developed even to the os-coccyx which joins more perfectly the sacral-bone, through which run the **posterior nerves** which give strength to the muscles and tendons of the extremities.

The general anatomy and physiology of these man-like creatures continues advancing rapidly with each successive-production. Advancement in the physiology of the organs could have been observed in all the **systolic** and **diastolic** motions involved within the body, if that were possible; because these organs are now much more in harmony, and these help create a healthy constitution. These two motions of the organs are of such great importance, and are **controlled** by the **forces** generated by the **mucous** and **serous surfaces**, which are adapted to the digestion and **generation** of a **positive** and **negative fluid**. This special fluid is what has helped this man-like creature to develop the most **perfect-mode** of **reproduction**.

The decrease of body hair is another good indication of the progression rapidly taking place in these animals; because in general, these animals are more refined both internally and externally. However it had to occur, and ultimately there was a **decline** and depreciation of the Q-5 species, mostly as a result of both environmental changes, and the successive progression of the quadrumana in general. And so finally this species Q-5 gave way to a new species, Q-6. Species Q-6 may still be correctly termed a quadrumana, and is a progressed-succession of the last species. These current species mostly inhabited the fertile areas of the **eastern lands**, especially the parts of **Africa** and **Asia**. Both these areas had similar latitudes and they were only divided by the ocean. These lower types of mankind inhabited in greatest numbers in relatively the same regions as did the marsupials.

The anatomy of these present quadrumana, has now progressed to where the body is visually **different** in many ways compared with that of the first Q-1 species; the Q-6 animal is in many ways a **new plan** or type of organization. The head of Q-6 was not as large as in previous species, but now has taken on a more oblong shape, and now **joins** very closely the medulla oblongata. And further-more, the medulla spinalis now more-distinctly protrudes from the medulla oblongata, forming four cervical nerves which are now starting to extend into dorsal and lumbar regions, and these being indistinctly branched at this time. The jawbones were of great length when compare with a human one; the mouth was large and distended, and the cheek-bones were prominent. The head of this quadrumana greatly represented those features of several feline tribes of animals. The nose was broad and flat, the brows were full, and the eyes were rather inclined to the top of the nose.

The feet of Q-6 were becoming more oblong and the ankle was developing more parts, which better adapted the feet to occasionally perform biped locomotion. This much more advanced quadrumana, was nearly free from heavy hair which had grown upon and nearly covered all the previous classes of this animal, especially in early species of Q-1. The hair on the neck and head was still heavy, but it was now somewhat shorter and dark. The color of quadrumana was generally **black**. Once established, this Class **existed** upon the earth nearly seven hundred years. And it was during this time-period in general, that the **whole** animal kingdom had reached an-almost imperceptible higher degree of **refinement**.

The next following class is Q-7, and this creature had an important degree of organization, having more of the appearance of man. This animal was a very large creature, having a **gigantic** Form. In this particular animal species progressing towards mankind, it had evolved and **ascended** to within **one degree** away from the **first** real **human-like** inhabitants that will in time be established on the earth.

It needs to be stated, that the **land-portions** of the earth where these quadrumana Q-7 existed, were almost **constantly** undergoing some **spe-**

**cific modifications** in the topography. These changes were not universal to the earth, but occurred according to the more local events and changes of the interior of earth, as well as the conditions of the surrounding physical elements.

This next Class is (B-1, or #8). B-1 is the animal that has now **ascended** one more **degree** in the scale of animal formations and this will take the animal kingdom to a new level and fulfill a goal. This is the time-period where a creature of earth will be established, and to where a class of animal has progressed and now becomes a **representation** of all-previous Forms that have been created on earth. This creature B-1 can be properly labeled an **ultimate representation** of all living things. In this particular class of animal Forms, the **bimana** organization becomes more distinctly visible.

The main body portions of B-1 have become well formed throughout; there are much more refined heart and lungs, and these improved organs contribute to make-up a well-formed visceral system. Form B-1 is the new kid on the block and is the creature that has reached a higher degree of development over any previous species, mostly because of this animals ability to **generate** more of those active **living-forces** that were spoken-of prior; and it will be because of this increase in those forces, that these particular animals have **almost** developed the capacity for mental perception and intelligence.

The B-1 animal is becoming more upright in stature and possessed a more perfect form of the human-like spinal column it was developing towards – it now being more vertebrated, and it branches-off many more **motor nerves**, which, by them entering into a portion of the ganglionic system, **contributed** to the perfection of the whole internal apparatus, enabling the body to digest food substances more perfectly.

This is the **first type** from which a true conception is able to be conveyed, concerning the **power** of the **mutual** living-forces. Realize, that these progressing animal Forms were rapidly becoming more man-like with each succession; and as they became more fully developed, they also were able to **combine** more and more forces within their organization. Therefore, each new living Form has a connection to the **interior** power of **motion**, this motion leads to the **nervous life** and this leads to the active and **susceptible sensation** that is crucial in its influences on the serous and cellular tissues of the whole body. Thus, these three forces motion, life, sensation, **become** when properly perfected, the first indication of **intelligence**, - which has been termed by naturalists - the instinct of animals.

The form of the head in this animal B-1, was very similar to previous species, somewhat oblong in shape. The brain was smaller, but it had become more complicated and therefore **more susceptible** to be **influenced**. The color of B-1 is black. It still has the long and ill-shaped limbs of previous orders, and a short yet full body continued. Not only were they of great stature physically, but they also had great power of **will**. Animal (#8) or B-1, possessed strong **passions** that were now developing naturally within them. These passions originated from their highly-susceptible **inclinations**, which this animal had been developing **inherently** within their constitutions.

Now that Sensation has become perfectly established within the animal Forms in general, that action of sensations then allowed the higher developed Forms like the bimana, to begin to experiences passions, and inclinations, and a heightened **susceptibility** to sensory input which mainly involved all those external influences that are in their environment. These **reactions** are considered a physiological response, because it is by the **interior sensibility** arising from the **medium** existing upon the **serous** and **mucous** surfaces that all the **interior characteristics** known as sensations and passions, become strong, and are therefore more extensively developed.

Various species of this B-1 animal had also inhabited land-portions in Asia and Africa like others had. Still being animals, they were highly susceptible to the influences of external circumstances, simply because they **lacked** any true **intelligence**. Instead they were reactionary and mostly using their highly develop instincts for survival. The bimana being spoken about here, was a gigantic man-like creature, and if a comparison of these present human-like Forms were made with the size of today's man, these Forms would appear like **giants** in form and stature, making them the largest of any similar manlike-forms on earth.

As these more advanced bipeds continued to develop, they would become the **first** animals that could be said, had **displayed** any true indication of **mental activity**.

Their anatomy allow them to **make** distinct **sounds**, which were produced in the throat. They did not yet possess a glottis and tongue advanced enough that could serve as vocal organs. The sounds they did make were somewhat like those sounds made by species of feline tribes and would not be considered human-like. However, these sounds were **significant** and had some **meaning** to the minds of those other creatures being addressed with that sound.

The habits and dispositions of these bimana creatures lead to their conceptions of building-up, or **constructing** artificial structures to reside, like stacked brush or such – and they often inhabited caves if they were available; but they generally preferred, much-like the previous lower species of the same order, to dwell upon the earth's surface. This species had **lost** their aquatic or amphibious characteristics, which was so unlike some of their kindred species, so they did not swim nor bath much. They dwelt undisturbed upon the earth nearly one thousand years.

# Section 68

The degree of organization of the next Form (#9) or B-2 as this creature stands in the sequence of development, was the first animal Form that approached and gave indications, slightly of the peculiar **characteristics** of mankind. And these manlike animals existed without any essential modifications for nearly eight hundred years. After this period of time, three successive and distinct orders of man-like animals were produced in sequence and had replaced each other, (#'s 10, 11, 12). The highest of these three (#12), was the animal Form approaching toward the human organization in every particular. Of these three highest orders of animals so-far, it would be #12 which inhabited the Asiatic continent, while the other two species of the same class (#'s10,11), were in the south of these regions. And so these three orders of animals inhabited the **three continents** – the southern, western, and eastern –and so these man-like creatures were existing in **three** distinct **tribes**, the highest of which were the tribe existing in **Asia** as was said; and it **would-be** this more evolved group that-came nearer to the development and unfolding of intellectual endowments.

As these three separately existing tribes had become established, this now brings the time-line of the sixth day of creation to a point three thousand and eight hundred years **before** the commencement of the **race** that had been often referred-to in the primitive written record of man.

The surface of the earth particularly in Asia and Africa has now become much more progressed and refined since the physical condition of the planet was last mentioned. It was becoming progressively more fertile, being much more suitable for the requirements of the animals existing at this time, and because of the favorable conditions many plant and animal species flourished.

The inhabitants of Asia (#12) **began** to **unfold** a distinct **perception** of the world around them, using their very heightened sense organs these creatures were developing a distinct sensuous perception or sensory perception. These highly evolved manlike animals had developed a perception of things and an awareness of other-beings, and they had developed to such a high level where now those **individuals** were actually **able** to **represent** their perceptions to one-another with gestures. **However**, because they **did-not** have the abilities to form a conception (that there existed inner qualities), they **were-not** able to progress any further along those lines of perceptions; and so consequently, they remained in their **unintelligent state** for nearly one thousand years.

During that thousand year period the **earth** underwent a **material change**, which resulted in the **destruction** of **nearly** all the various tribes of the bimana types; and this major change would also altered earth's crust, both the geographical and geological conditions of the whole earth. Old conditions were passing away, which then afterwards allows the new and more perfect conditions to come into existence. And it will be from this present destruction, that a **new-order** of creation is produced. And then, it will be **this** new **species** that will be the type to **ascend** to the **highest type**; which is the type of creature that is now shown in today's mankind, Us.

Prior to the earth changes, the earth was **comparatively** infertile and unproductive. Yes there were fertile regions still existing in Asia, but generally most regions of land were undeveloped. However, soon after the destructive changes and upheaval the whole earth would become very fertile and very productive, especially in the types of vegetation that flowered and showed their **beauty**, some were very delicate and **fragrant**. After the earth catastrophe the **eastern lands** will be even more fertile than they are today, many plants developing into perfection, even without the aid of man's cultivating skills.

It was **during** this period of geological change, that a **new tribe** (#13) or B-3 was introduced upon the earth – and now rising entirely above the undeveloped features of all the lower and previously existing Forms. These are the animals which constituted what may be properly termed a **transition** from the animal to man: and these were the **first Forms** that could be properly termed **Man**.

With only a little stretch of the imagination, one might see the **connection** between the description of the earth now being given, by comparing the description with the **primitive written records** which **reveal** the lushness of earth's then-existing condition, speaking as though the earth was a garden. It can be distinctly **proven** that this particular period of earths evolution is **represented** by the original primitive conception relating to the **garden** of **Eden**. The garden of Eden was one of **earliest** of mankind's first mental impressions and awareness that would be **passed-down** from tribe to tribe as mankind began to progress **towards** gaining intelligence.

One of the main topics being described throughout this story has been an attempted to show the grand process of **successive development** of each age, and by now this **should-be** understood. The reader should have a solid base of knowledge concerning all the vegetation and animal productions which have been brought in existence by Nature; knowing that, those first Forms from the beginning and then continuing to the present era, all had **gradually-unfolded** by following those successive developments of the laws of Nature. The process started from the original gelatinous composition, then, following the **unfolding** of Natures productions all the way to the creation of man. All the numerous living plant and animal Forms had followed that special processes, and each Form which was produced assumed orders, degrees, species, associations, and correspondences, as they all progressed on their journey to develop from nothing, and later reach this pinnacle of the creation of man.

**Man** occupies one degree of organization pre-eminent above all the other departments of creation, and this fact is why man is a **representation** of all living things which had from the beginning, contained the germ of which man unfolds. Man is a combination of all Forms, qualities, and essences, in Nature; and mankind is sustained by all kinds of motion, life, and sensation; these each are characteristic of the successive steps, of what is a natural processes and progression. Man is said to be **residing** over the lower Forms, while man is **actually dependent** upon all that is below and around him in being. So, while man is **proprietor** over his own person, they are still **dependent** upon the whole creation below them for their subsistence and nourishment.

Here and now one can rest satisfied that Man is created and they exert a power over all the other creations living on earth. And what has occurred to bring this power to mankind, is that they **represent** all developments of earth and of the Universe, and show those developments are in accordance with all the laws which had originally come from the fountain of **Divine** and living **Principles**. All of creation are "the breathing's" of the great **Positive Mind**, which are flowing through countless avenues and Forms of animated Nature; **until-finally**, that Divine Mind, breathed into man the breath of life, and man then became a **living** Soul.

## Section 69

If there is a desire to **understand** man, then, there is a need to **look closely** at the whole of Nature and see that She is created of parts; yet, when the parts are able to be combined in their various manners, they produce much more exalted Forms and Beings. And it is this fact then, which is clearly seen in man, where man, is that **combination** of all previous progressions which have taken place in the evolution of Nature and her productions. Man is Gods **ultimate** material **creation**, and man will **develop** the **Spirit** through the Soul which on earth exists in the vehicle of the body. The Soul is the connecting link between man and Spirit.

All the laws and forces of Nature can be plainly understood as **converging** to the formation of man. Man then, **represents** the universal progressive development, which is the inherent and eternal law of Matter. Man represents a **resurrection** of every crude and basic material that has come into existence. And it was *"out of the dirt and dust of the earth, comes man"*. The following short sentence can sum up much: "Nature is the cause; Forms are the effects; and Man is the ultimate production", and taking that same thought to a higher degree, it can also be said, that the great Positive Mind as a **cause**, uses Nature as an **effect** to produce **Spirit** as an ultimate. Every particle in existence follows this command.

When the processes of **Nature** are viewed with a scientific mind, the whole of Nature **presents** a connected plan and a **magnificent work**. From one Order of creation to another, Nature, by following her **sequence** of progress and development to higher attributes, **uses** the various species only as **mediums** of **transferring** inferior qualities to higher states. And importantly, Nature is developing interior qualities. And **nothing** is too low on the scale of being to be of no importance; and nothing in existence is useless. Something that at first may appear crude, gross, and imperfect, is in reality a substantial **link** of **Chain**, that becomes absolutely-necessary as a source of **subsequent** developments. The lowest particle in being, represents an endless array of use and adaptation. The workings of Nature are consistent because there is seen the same united activity, the same potent energies, and the same glorious creation of Forms and Beings all coming into a **confluence**; and when this combination occurs, it then **establishes** the organization of **man** into a specific Form, and then man becomes the perfection and representative of them all. Importantly, this man being is the highest organization existing upon other inhabitable planets in our Universe.

So now as this present pre-upheaval time-period is the **closing** of the present era – the consummation of the creations of the whole period and of the end contemplated. Realize that the **germ** of existence is in Nature and the **fruit** of that germ is man. Forms are only the **temporal** combinations of material substances; but the **cause** of which Forms are the **effects**, - is the **invisible** and therefore is **eternal**. All things which have form and have a distinct existence, also have an "interior independence", but externally they are dependent on all other things, and display a universal use. And from this awareness it should be realized, that man, in a broad sense has Free Will, but in truth man only has choice.

What qualities does a creature need to transition into a man creature? For example: what distinguishes a man creature from another similarly appearing bimana animal? Well, what is truly necessary are **inner qualities**. Wisdom and Love are necessary. And so as the first man-like being is initially developing, the **first** and most comprehensive **attribute** which will first be manifested in these new Forms will be, that they have divine **Wisdom**. These man-like creatures will develop and exhibit among them as a group, a **Unity** and Harmonious Reciprocation between the individuals, and these special actions are proof that Wisdom is the higher attribute originating from the fountain of Divine Love. And so, first Love determines the universal relationship, and Wisdom then is the universal adaptation. These two principles are the highest laws of Nature.

# Section 70

In the beginnings of this story there was explained the great Vortex of Matter and Power, telling how this Vortex is a living exhaustless fountain, wherein dwell infinite love and wisdom, and from the Vortex flowed the undefinable Worlds which pervade the whole Universe. And then, it was explained how these Worlds are formed by succeeding and expanding waves; and it was said, that all of the creations existing upon all those worlds - are following the same established principles that are distinctly exhibited in every department of animated Nature. The Universe, is an ocean of activity and it is filled with boundless Love and infinite Wisdom. **The thoughts** of the Infinite Mind of God, are what constitutes the laws of Nature, and the **results** of these thoughts are the animated Forms in being, which of course includes the ultimate of Nature, that exalted Form of man. And this form of man has a similar principle to exist by, because **they-have** the interior spiritual essence.

The whole united plan of Nature in which nothing is inactive – nothing is useless – nothings is absolutely imperfect; a plan where everything sustains an important position in the great architecture of the Universe, this is truly God's will. And it is evident now, that man is created from the dust of the earth, and also, that man is the receptacle of one of the **breathing's** of the great Positive Mind of God. This action has rendered man a perfect Form – a useful agent – a living and breathing **Soul**. *"And thus were male and female created"*. And they were now **qualified** to exercise control over all the lower orders of Beings.

The grand work of Nature is finished. The great End is accomplished. Nature becomes a harmonious Whole. And so the whole earth at this time represents the **close** of a distinct and pre-eminent creation, man; and **somehow** this particular time-period is known by man, because it is recorded information and is plainly **represented** by the peopling of the **garden** of Eden.

Man, this ultimate development of creation is therefore a mirror which shows the reflection of what is apparent at this time, and this is "**the evening and the morning were the sixth day**".

# Section 71

The **Germ** of man has now been traced throughout all of its progressive stages of development; rising from lower degrees through the great body of the animal creations, with its many diversified branches and their modifications, up the blooming perfection of the living tree, whose fruit is the organization of man.

Man (#13), being the fruit of creation, ascended by the process of "successive progression", exists and they now possesses **undeveloped qualities**. Mankind now **begins** to **civilize** many portions of the **earth**. Starting with this present and **rudimental** man, mankind-group #13, they **established** their present existence within and near the portion of **Asia** now termed **Turkey**, extending to the regions of the future-sites of Euphrates and Tigris Rivers and joining in two distinct lines to the locality where **Jerusalem** was built.

Now **also**, as was stated, a group of the lower type of mankind was existing in some portions of **Africa**, but these were **inferior types** of mankind. And being inferior, they could be compared the the lower feline and general mammalia animals existing in these same regions. But for the most-part, the great body or **extended family** of those of the most **perfect** Form, and those which were **truly man**, originally **dwelt** upon the borders and in the interior of Asia. These mankind, male and female, were very large, strong, and had a peculiar gentleness and humility, resulting from a genetic carry-over of instincts from the lower preceding species #12.

The mental constitution and early development of these **higher Forms** at this time, would be seen as a much more social being than it was intellectual. But these mankind were characterized by a great power of perception and memory. Morality and moral qualities **had-not** develop yet within this first group, but some morals would begin to develop and would be found in later races. The arms and legs of these first mankind were slender and slightly bowed.

This higher race, along with the two lower and kindred races has been designated by the comprehensive term **Adam** (13a)– and their associate tribe, which is a totally **separate** and other extended family tribe, and these will be known as **Eve** (13b) – with these two terms representing the **first** and the basis or **foundation** of the more perfect inhabitants which will soon evolve. Adam and Eve were two separate family groups of mankind existing separately and unknown to each other.

For many continuous ages the manner with which they **communicated** their ideas within their own separate family tribe, was by using **ex-**

**pressions** of **countenance** or facial expressions and also outward physical signs. Their clothing was unsophisticated, and they had no conceptions of art and sciences. They had absolutely no mechanical skills; and for the duration of this beginning period they had remained unsophisticated yet they were free from greed and deception.

Then, after the passing of many time-periods mankind began to advance and unfold in many ways; first was gaining the awareness and **need** to exhibit artful attainments and then they began to **exchange thoughts** with each other through the medium of **vocal** and rudimentary **sounds**, consisting of monosyllables.

Then as time passed by more and mankind advanced a little further in development they began to **learn** about things and they had **partaken** a little of the fruit of the "tree of knowledge"; they began to **conceal** their true emotions and attitudes. And they began to "**cloth**" their sentiments with **random** vocal sounds, using sounds that had no meaning – using sounds which **did-not** communicate the real reality of their ideas and affections toward each-other, but instead only conveyed various **deceptive impressions**.

Man's rudimental sounds, **expressions**, and earliest of language, at first displayed no distinct inflections. There were no nouns, adjectives, nor verbs, to clarify those expressions; instead there were only basic gestures and single syllable words. Though it would be by adding the use of **facial expressions** (physiognomy), that these early mankind were able, in a crude manner, to express the **thoughts** which were arising from either interior or external exciting causes. The sights and sounds around them would cause these humans to react physically; these physical actions would cause a physiological response which naturally illuminate the eyes and their features, and at times their entire body; all these actions would help in giving the exact expression of their meanings.

To understand properly the origin and rudiments of **vocal language** there has to be an understanding of the "action of sound" upon the atmosphere, and also sound's vibrations among the intricate chambers of the ear. Because the first inhabitants did not possess perfect vocal powers. This period was within man's early physical developments and so there was still a remaining physical **deformity** of the trachea, larynx, and glottis. These three organs must act in perfect concert to produce the variations of sound. This anatomical deformity did not correct itself until after some further physical developments, which eliminated the deformity.

So humans make sounds when **the will** excites the vocal organs, and there is a communication of **positive power** to excite more perfect particles, that were previously pervading the same organs. And when the vocal organs are in this way excited, they become mediums of the **descension of the will**. This action then, produces a corresponding action upon the particles of the atmosphere. The first particles excited by the organs of the voice-box they in-turn pass-on the action as **sound waves**.

# Section 72

The inhabitants of earth had come into possession of a **new power**; a power which occurred as a consequence of the development and unfolding of their mental faculties, and then, combining that power together with the rudiments of their primitive vocal communication, and now language was discovered. **Language** therefore is a result of **progressive development**.

Language had already existed in a strict sense of the word, but it was in an imperfect form. The earliest rudiments of language were in existence since the first exposure and development of the law of Sensation which occurred within the animal kingdom. It was from that moment when **instinctive signs** were **employed** by the various animal creations. These **instinctive signals** would continue to grow more perfected and useful; and so all of mankind continued to develop mentally; until this present **prehistoric** time which was the establishment and present condition of the early human inhabitants of earth. And so, vocal and verbal communication, **could-not** have occurred before this time, because in the previous periods the atmosphere was too crudely constituted and the air would not have been able produce those needed sound-waves properly.

Not long after mankind **realized** they could use verbal sounds as signs and as a means of expressing their thoughts and attempting to share their impressions to each-other, that sadly, the inhabitants of earth had become **disunited** and disorganized in social affection. This growing disunity among each-other was a **consequence** of the **misconceptions** being conveyed by those deceptive vocal sounds. What was really occurring was that in one sense, mankind had made some intellectual advancements, and began to **add** vocal sounds to his facial countenances and physical signs and gestures. But on the other hand, because of mankind's ignorance, man's mental advancement had **consequences**.

Mankind eventually becoming frustrated with anguish because of the growing disunity, and then finally there came the time when the families of mankind finally **could-not** enjoy each others society; to each individual it seemed as though every expression, which originally had been a pure and simple gesture, sign, or expression, of their facial countenance, was now clothed in a **false sheath** of false sounds and altered gestures; and so from this erroneous action mankind developed an ignorance of others perceptions and the inability to empathize with another, creating disunity and utter confusion among all the inhabitants of earth.

Earliest of mankind had previously lived innocent and pure and only used their countenances to express themselves. But over the passage of time there was a constant increases of selfishness, greed, and deceit, and all of mankind became disunited and repulsive to each other. This particular period of disunity is **spoken-about** within the original primitive histories, seeing mankind in a state of depravity. And it was in this manner that *"their eyes were opened"* and thus they were enabled to *"see their own deceptions and imperfections"*. Man now having this **new power** and ability to express themselves and converse with one another, **also** had developed the ability to **cloth** and conceal both their real thoughts and also their imaginative and imperfect thoughts, all by using false sheaths and **deceptive** aprons of obscurity in their sounds and expressions.

The whole race of man became dejected and depraved: but **not-because** they had violated any physical or mental faculties; and it was not because they had sinned and needed punishment; but instead, it was because their **mental faculties** were incorrectly and **imperfectly developed**. So any blame lies here with ignorance, and it is here in earliest of mankind's pre-history, - is the **origin** of all **deception** – of all **imperfection**. All of mankind's social difficulties are from **selfish** and undeveloped **impulses**. All discord is simply from mankind's ignorance and from their **lack** of proper early development, all of which **incidentally** occurred within these early beginnings; man **did not** fall from grace nor did man sin. Instead, mankind were ignorant and are ignorant. Man may think of themselves as intellectual, yet their actions show a much different reality. Mankind could-not have sinned because they are too ignorant.

Earliest of man existed in an undeveloped state of being and this state is part of progressive development. Recall, the first contains the ultimate, just in an undeveloped state. This is how Nature operates. And the Principles of Nature are Divine. Everything has a beginning and then it develops. Mankind had their beginnings and over time they progressively had to develop further; man's destiny is to be the Being that possesses Intelligence, but at first, this principle is undeveloped. Earliest man were ignorant and **were-not** "guided" on their developmental journey because they had-not developed their internal qualities. So how could they be guided if they **were-not** yet developed enough nor intelligent enough to be aware of any of those "interior callings".

The situation for earliest man was bleak, and within this moment in time misery and immoral associations had their origin. All the **discord** among the groups, the families, and tribes would **continue** and give power to drive their profound **ignorance**, this allowed **vice** and **misery** to increase.

Earth's grandest creation and her highest developed inhabitants, acted more and more selfish as time passes, they responded with more aggressive towards each other, and they became **completely disorganized**. These related events, all played a role in the specific events that would **create** a situation, where the inhabitants became completely unhappy; there eventually came a time when the utter madness was the worst it had ever been, and the breaking-point had been reached, and now various groups **dispersed** and went wandering to new lands.

**Three** distinct **nations** each living separately, ultimately became established; all three **originating** and flowing from the very **first group** of humans.

One of these nations (#1) settled in the interior of Asia; another group (#2) settled upon the eastern borders Asia, and another (#3) settled in the lower part of Africa.

The inhabitants of Asia, which were then divided into **two nations,** consisting of the Original (#1) and the Branch (#2); and these two sustained a close relation to each other and also to the nation in Africa (#3). They were still brethren and they were all legitimate children of the original inhabitants (#0).

But the individual of these nations were all very different in constitutions and dispositions, being so different that they could not harmonize co-socially with each other.

One of the nations, that of (#1), being more advanced, had thoughts existing in their minds for peace, for unity, and they had intentions to labor in concerted efforts and actions. They existed in harmony together, being both kind and gentle, and these men and women had almost shepherd-like dispositions. These would later in the "primitive history" be a nation termed **Abel** and existed mostly in the interior portions of Asia.

The other nation (#2), existed with an opposite disposition, and these were the ones living on the eastern borders of Asia; these people still possessed the various dispositions of the primary inhabitants (#0), being imperfectly organized in their mental, physical, and social constitutions. They displayed the fierce passions of envy and retaliation. They remained undeveloped and crude, and would continue in a misdirected and ill-developed state of being; causing deception, tyranny, false ambition, and arrogance, not only in their dealings with each other, but also with their dealings with anyone else. The original "primitive history" of man would later name this nation **Cain**.

These two nations Cain and Abel co-existed for a period, and now both existing in the similar region in Asia; then, on one cool spring day, the Cain nation **attacked** the Abel nation. Brothers attacking brothers, the two nations **warring** against each-other, in a manner very much like two prehistoric tribes would war. The result of this combat was almost complete devastation for the Abel nation. The Cain nation being more aggressive, now took control of all there was to control. Here represented in these nations is this first stage of what would be termed an imperfect civilization.

# Section 73

The **Cain** nation (#2), the winner of the first battle, and now the powerful nation, had domination over the whole earth; and these fierce people had begun to develop a sensuous knowledge, which is a natural progression because at this period of human development the five senses of mankind were **more developed** than their intellect. Their mental conceptions had began to flow freely, but they were entirely rooted in their five senses, and they continued to have no internal awareness, nor spiritual calling; the reason for this was only because this particular **inherent principle** was still **undeveloped** in early man. Instead this nation of humans had genetically **retained** all the faults, blemishes and other undesirable characteristics of their forefathers, those very first humans.

As these people continued to exist, it was the five senses of mankind's anatomy, **combined** with their undeveloped minds, which propelled this nation to continue their fall into complete selfishness. This nation actually would develop the imperfect characteristics of their forefathers **further**, becoming quite impure, ferocious, and extremely repulsive in their dispositions. Actually taking the notion of "bad", to a new and higher level. This Cain tribe represented lower human beings that were in **despair**, and then **suffering** as they did, because they were **required** by universal law to **reap** the full consequences of those violations and atrocities. The Cain nation was represented in ancient history as **saying** *"my punishment is greater than I can bear"*. They were so ignorant and undeveloped, that they almost constantly made the wrong choices, choosing selfishness instead of goodness. And as the saying goes *"you reap what you sow"*.

Those statements of sufferings made by the Cain nation, were a humble acknowledgment – and a true confession of depravity. From these crude and unprogressed beginnings of sociability and civilization and continuing into our century, it clearly reveals that mankind **has-built** a monumental demonstration of the inevitable **consequences** of social and national violations. This symbolic monument built upon social madness still stands today, still being known and experienced in the twenty-first century.

And beware, because for every violation that occurs in Nature, that occurrence **will-always** be followed by its corresponding consequence, and this fact is evident in every department of Nature. Whether the Form is organic or inorganic, animate or inanimate, the law of cause and effect and reaping what is sown is always at work.

So the **germ** of our **civilization**, now having been **imperfectly deposited** within the framework of early mankind's mental constitution, this

**error** has placed a large population of early man into a very unfavorably situated and having now become imperfectly developed. Man's true passions, true purpose, and pure associations, have instead, been turned into **unholy** and polluted paths of existence. And here is the **origin** and **cause** of all imperfection. The entire population of the earth since this period and during the many many ages of existence still **have-not** been able to discover the cause of the existing imperfections within themselves. Nor has mankind been able to remove the foundation of this fearful monument, and then replace it with a new temple of universal peace, harmony and reciprocation.

The people of nation #2 (Cain), destroyed the environment around them and conquered all that was good. The entire nation then **moved** to another portion of earth, traveling further to the west, almost upon what is now known as the **European** continent. And there in a new region, they continued their imperfect development and social imperfections. The land portion that they had relocated to they termed **Nod**, for this term corresponds to Barrenness.

In the land of Nod this tribe of miserable humans gradually multiplied and became a large and great Nation. They had made some improvements within themselves somewhat, this progression was only by small increments of development within their "internal condition" or internal awareness, and now were able to develop some natural principles within their minds. But, they also continued their hereditary deceitfulness, and when the two traits developed together, it created a extremely-brilliant, tyrannical nation, possessing only a few good interior qualities, and even less development of the qualities of the mind.

**Now**, the story of early man needs to **restarts** from the original garden time, the objective of this is give a **review** of what has been given, but this time the objective is to describe the early development of humans from a different perspective, doing this so that an understanding of the **other nation** which has been termed **Abel** can be known.

The garden of **Eden** literally corresponds to peace and beauty. The **streams** of water that were described as flowing through the garden, were true and actual rivers; however the courses which those two rivers flowed, have since been **modified** and completely **changed** by earthquakes and volcanic action of the earth. These two rivers correspond to fertility. **Adam** and **Eve** correspond to two distinct nations – which ultimately **became associated**, and would combined forming One nation (#0), which existed in the interior of Asia. The tree of knowledge corresponds to the undeveloped embryo of perfection and intelligence.

The terms **good** and **evil** are used as "expressive" of the legitimate fruits there-of something: such as evil being the gross, imperfect, and undeveloped; and then, good as being evil's **perfection**.

The animal of the saurian species of **serpent** that is represented as *"being more subtle than any other beast of the earth",* well this **allegory**, relates and corresponds to the secret, imperceptible progress of an unfavorable and unhappy mental development of the human race.

And eating of the fruit of the tree of knowledge – of good and evil – represents an experience of the fruits of the good, which immediately brings about a knowledge of evil. To know good is to know evil.

So then, **experience** brings-about knowledge: and if the inhabitants of the earth had not seen the very lowest degrees of evil and wretchedness first and at the beginning, then the subsequent nations would not have known or appreciated that which stands in contrast, which is the knowledge of goodness.

The two nations Adam and Eve, had **combined** as One (#0) and had now **obtained** the knowledge of good and evil; and this knowledge corresponds to - *"having their eyes opened".* And now **becoming aware** of their evil dispositions, they then endeavored to **conceal** their dispositions by making external garments: - thus aprons correspond to a fearful secretiveness, and a dread of having their corrupted characters openly seen. This again corresponds to depravity.

This very first nation of mankind (#0) had lost their high degree of innocence and purity, simply because of their ignorance and selfishness; and these imbeciles had become exceedingly evil; then, even becoming more **developmentally impaired** and confused, and eventually even sank into a lower degree of un-civilization.

From this one nation **sprang** the **two nations** (#'s 1, 2,) designated in the primitive history as Cain and Abel - the Cain being distinguished for their external show and high-mindedness, and the Abel being a somewhat meek and unsophisticated nation, whose principles corresponded to the innocence of sheep.

After a time, they had both become great nations, war and devastation would rise between them. And after the devastating war, the **hierarchy** of the uncivilized earth would be seen as corresponding to the **predominance** of ignorance and folly, all reigning over those who wanted peace and goodness.

The individuals from these two branch nations all came from the same original family but they had continued to exhibit differing dispositions and opinions, and were developing selfishness instead of knowing or even learning that there should be harmony; these self-centered beings formed themselves into two groups, and then, this act would finally leading to their total separation. Each group decided to live as **separate** tribes and families, each with their own interests. However it was not a long time after they became disconnected they then began to developed **mutual hostility** toward each other; then next came the **wars** – but these battles were not carried on by open combat or even be using implements of destruction; but instead, it was by the actions of rather ingenious fanatical acts of cruelty and oppression that they fought each-other. Man still is an animal and seems very capable of horrendous atrocities.

It has already been revealed prior, that within the constitution and genetics of the earliest tribes of mankind, there existed passions and principles which were in themselves good traits, but because of undeveloped inner natures, those good principles unfolded improperly. And so after these two tribes had advanced into much larger nations, one of the nations (Cain), who by **misconceiving** the true elements of their inherent nature, had **created** for themselves unfavorable circumstances. Because of this error, any subsequent development of their passions and principles were also entirely **misguided**; and then **consequently** they became a completely degenerate and wretched race. It is the uncultivated state of both the mental and moral faculties of man that are problematic, then from this arose an almost **universal misunderstanding** and an absolute disorganization of any following developments.

It is the misgivings and ignorance of man's inner inherent qualities, and an ignorance of their destiny which are the **origin** of **evil**; and from evil's origins many **serious consequences** have followed! So it is easy to see that it is by man's own ignorance which separates him from God. And these very-same evils still exist in the world in modern times. And **unknowingly** mankind will add tens of thousands of years of misery and anguish to mankind's predicament, **because** it is at this place in the pre-history of early mankind, which are the **beginnings** and the foundation for any and all **theological speculations** that have lead many noble minded persons on a winding path of folly. Many many men and women have spent countless energies trying to unravel the **unsearchable antiquity** of the primitive doctrines, various transcripts, and mythology, which have entirely **deceived** the foundation upon which rests their "baggage" of ignorance.

## Section 74

**A**frica at the time of Cain and Abel nations, contained **two** distinct **nations** – one of these nations (#3) was one of the original branches of the primitive inhabitants (#0), and the other nation (#3a), were originally a part of (#3) and in reality these two groups were just one nation; however, they became **disconnected** by a dissimilarity of disposition and government. They agreed to disagree. a similar situation has existed ever-since and is still alive and in full operation.

**Asia** at the same time-period, contained **three** distinct **nations** – with the greatest number of these inhabitants being those which existed in the interior of Asia and extending their domain to **Turkey**, this is nation (#2). A second nation of these Asians, existed on the border of the Asian continent, this is nation (#2a). And the third nation existed in the region of **Jerusalem**, this being nation (#2b).

These somewhat separate nations, being five in number, were all **descendant nations** from the original three nations who had itself originally **separated** from the original union of the Adam and Eve tribes, all coming from the **original unfolding** of man, rising from an evolved animal species. It **would-not** be correct to mention these five descendant nations as distinct from the primitive inhabitants, the original inhabitants in a sense, were naturally multiplying and spreading-out to subdue the earth. The path of error which man unknowingly chose, was the action of separating themselves by means of selfishness, cruelty, war, hatred, and ignorance; and all these selfish traits were tied together with man's strong **basic instincts** which originated within the lower level of developments as a part of the animal kingdom. Man is truly from the dust of the earth, and the dust has clouded his vision and sense of direction.

So in reality, Africa contained one general nation (#3), and also, there was really only one nation (#2a) which was existing mostly on the Asian borders, especially after the settlement of the Cain nation (#2) had relocated into the land of **Nod**. But, it was these Nod inhabitants that would soon **divide** into three distinct **branches**, first by retaining the original nation, then one branch relocated in a new portion of the earth now known as **China** (2c), and then after a time, some of these explorers would again form another branch and these eventually emigrated and settled in **Central America** this is nation (2c-a).

Mankind at this period did not till the ground, nor build houses, but rather lived in tents made of foliage. Mankind had a diet containing both vegetable and animal forms, and this **food** is, as it was **given** to mankind

**to-know**, - given to know by "instinctive consciousness". So mankind naturally and instinctively was aware internally of some things, and instinctively knew what was suitable to sustain their physical constitutions.

Many **ages elapsed** before mankind had become intelligent enough, to devise a method to **construct** dwellings, made from very large trees that existed. There were some significant and positive advancements made in social settings also which had help in man's ability of **sharing** each individual's sensory awareness, their investigations, and their experiences. Also it was in this period that man's **intelligence** had developed enough to finally allowed them to begin **arranging** their **vocal signs** into a more orderly and **grammatical** form of verbal communication.

Man, with improved dwellings and a rapidly improving language was also developing a general **tolerance**; this ability to be tolerant stemmed from the fact that their communication was now somewhat **more-truthful**, and to a great relief man's interactions were less deceptive. This positive action in-turn allowed for a continued **increase** in intelligence. From these positive interactions, man conceived of the rudiments of **mechanics** and **arts**, and then even more advancement, because it would be from developing these basic artistic methods, some were able to apply these basics techniques into **useful skills**.

At this time of mechanical learning, the nation (2 c-a) was existing in Central America, these originated from China as a branch of the nation (2c), these early explorers **traveled across** both land and water (mostly land), to finally reach the land region of Central America. As said, much of this journey involve land travel because there was no Pacific Ocean yet. The area of the Pacific was a series of land-valleys and island-chains, allowing a somewhat easy travel from China to Central America. Once this exploring branch nation (2c-a) had reached their destination, they rapidly began to **improve** intellectually much **more** extensively than any other of their kindred nations, advancing more than any of the previous nation of man. And these mankind (2c-a) having **ascended** to a much higher degree of sociability and began to **till** the previously-uncultivated earth and became the **first farmers**.

It was these more intellectual and rapidly developing people of Central America who **could-see** a natural adaptation of materials, this awareness would lead to the unfolding and **understanding** of new principles, which improved their thought patterns. For example: they developed an understanding and skill and applied the skill in the process of using **stone** in **building** projects. Paired with these skills of building was the very significant **development** of **unity** and team work; because their internal thoughts showed them that, if they labored together, guided by their **united interests**, life and sociability became tolerable and maybe more joyful. This **southern nation** existed many centuries and ultimately prospered, and it was there in the regions of Central America they built a beautifully-constructed **stone city**, using their yet undeveloped inner awareness and latent artistic talents along with their conceptions of beauty, as decorations and as designs for their magnificent stone buildings.

The other nations which were existing in Asia and Africa had remained in a degenerate condition. These nations still continued to exist in a disunited fashion; the **profound disunity** led each nations to develop **imperfect** social institutions. Many of their civil situations were so uncivilized, that they eventually had to form governments which were essentially **tyrannical**, because these institutions held despotic control over the people, and the people were **willing idiots**. Over time, these Asian and African inhabitants, who were once a strong, athletic, and domineering race, had all begun to **weakened** in stature and strength. The over-all decline and diminishing power had originated by the onset of environmental causes, namely, **changes** in the surrounding **elements**. And all the inhabitants would eventually became part of a degenerate race of mankind both in their physical being and in their social organization.

Nature operating on earth will soon develop mankind into **varieties** or colors. However as yet, none of the inhabitants of the earth had yet developed or assumed a lighter color than that particular skin-tone which may be observed in the Jalofs and Gaffers, and so the great majority of all mankind were black. The colors of the races of man will be addressed in a later section.

As each generation past-by, the general condition and development of man was proceeding very slow and man was **unguided** in all their essential qualities – theoretically these qualities might have been much improved only if mankind had been properly directed and placed on the path of prosperity and development. And most-likely if man had properly developed it would have rendered them into a brilliant and harmonious brotherhood.

## Section 75

Theology began with primitive man. It was from primitive and uncultivated minds that man's first conceptions and first descriptions of the world around them **originated**. These crude early thoughts and unproven assumptions were **unknowingly** and in error, passed-on to the next generations. And to add to this **error** the primitives used basic and crude gestures and verbal communications to explain these myths. And as tens of thousands of years have passed, still today any moral, social, and intellectual, developments of mankind, are all based upon **opinions** and modifications of these same early beliefs and opinions.

Man's ignorance was so profound that nearly all **impressions** and **opinions** concerning their surrounding environment were based-on **mythological** and **superstitious thoughts**. They had no intelligence, they had no knowledge, they had no wisdom; there was no preexisting awareness of right or wrong to compare one event to another.

So whenever an event or situation would occur, the ignorance of man being so great, would prevent a proper interpretation, and so man would form an impression which could either be correct or in error, such as lightening for example. What would the lightening be compared to? What about a simple breeze blowing in the air, or rainfall, where did they come from? So whatever first impression is given to a particular thing or event, is how it was interpreted by undeveloped minds. It was these types of thoughts and occurrences which are the **beginnings** of all **heathenism** found in all civilizations, all are simply from ignorance. **Yet** on the other hand, this is also the **beginnings** of all the **truly-intellectual** developments of mankind also.

Whether these earliest thoughts of man were truth or myth is a moot point, because many of these early thoughts, impressions, and assumptions, were **eventually altered** or modified by unwitting persons who would **further perpetuate** unholy and false-truths, simply by **continuing** to believe these myths were real. However these modifications **were-not** done with malicious intentions, but instead they were also ignorant of their impact and had no idea of the consequences. Within this sixth day in evolutionary history **originates** all **mythology** and heathenism, both which are still embedded in the minds of the undeveloped masses of man. Amazing is it ?

Mythological conceptions and **imaginary beliefs** are the **source** of all **theology**, but this is mainly because there was no other sources of information other than these **various** primitive histories of man. These traditional stories were the **only-source** for information concerning primitive man. Mythological information **existed** before writing was invented. And all these primitive stories were passed-on from generation to generation **using** crude language or forms of expression. They are the **source** which all the various **systems of theology** have had their beginnings. This is the **origin** of all those conceptions which **have-led** the minds of the world into chaos, and into the dark ages.

So many differing **opinions** have developed concerning theology's place in the world, it is difficult to know where is the truth? Yet the correct answer to this should be evident to a inquiring mind, because an inquiring mind knows well, that any and all opinions, no matter what the subject, **must-have** originated from the surrounding **conditions** and **circumstances** existing at that particular time. This **fact** will one day be understood and the problem rectified, because once everyone knows the truth there will be no differences in opinions. Know well, that everybody has an opinion, but not everyone has the truth. The poor social state of man is proof enough that the many paths already taken and traveled upon by all **theological speculators** have barely advanced the social conditions of mankind even a few degrees of mental growth or development any spiritual growth.

In the real reality of existence, there is no-division between science, philosophy, metaphysics, and religion. And this can be explained by showing that - the first one science, is the first principles of, and also the basis for, the second one. The second one illustrates the first and at the same time is a true representation of the third. The third unites with the second, and it flows spontaneously into the fourth. The fourth is the one that pervades all and comprehends them all, and flows spontaneously to a still higher degree of knowledge and perfection, which is to be mankind's future.

And so it is, that nothing is natural which is not **moral**. Because the natural and the moral are **conjoined** principles. These joined principles dwell in Nature and flow out of truth, not by opinion. What is moral is natural. Nature is moral, and mankind has a tendency to ignore or not to see this truth.

All things therefore are good in themselves, but they consist of different **degrees** of goodness, and **each** thing **is necessary** to make the whole a harmonious unity. Know that at some place-in-time in the future, all minds will finally converge to one center; and when that occurs there will be developed the perfected **knowledge** of psychological and eternal **truth.** This future event will be an establishment of some vast, comprehensive,

**united system** of theology – one that will sustain an inseparable connection with the natural interior elements of man, and with the universal laws of Nature.

There have been many metaphysical minded persons at various times all throughout the many ages of mankind, all which have in their time, made many profound investigations relating to the mental constitution of man. These investigators have endeavored to discover the origin of passions, which make-up the elements of the mind - and its thoughts. Metaphysician's are also searching for the origin of Sensation; the origin of affections, and of love. Also they search for Intelligence. These seekers have arrived at varied and **illegitimate conclusions**. And, because they are **not-able** to discover the origin of these things they seek, nor are they able to find the nature of the spiritual composition, they then instead, have erroneously reasoned entirely from **assumptions**. And because all theology has been based upon these **unfounded conclusions** and assumptions, theology has run into difficult issues, especially as mankind has made many advancements in knowledge, all through the ages. And continuing at the same pace, theology has been **attempting** to legitimize themselves by manipulating the imaginative imperfections and superstitions **which-originated** in this primitive period of the world's history, this sixth day of creation.

Continuing now - some of the groups and tribes of **Asia** had not improved very much in their use and forms of vocal communications. Their verbal **language** consisted merely of incoherent sounds made by the **concussion** of the larynx and glottis. At first they **had-not** developed any reasoning for making those sounds, and because of this, their vocal experimentation led to **confusion**, then, ultimately led to an almost complete **social division** among the tribes. Not knowing how to deal with this confusion, tribes would at first, in frustration, just move away from each-other.

Some of these now separated tribes of Asian inhabitants, move eastward and settled in the east of Asia (#2c) others moved into the interior (#2), and still others existing on the borders joining the African continent (2b). All these tribes exhibited a very uncivilized condition, and generally needed to be governed by harsh methods of discipline, and this of course usually included force and bloodshed. This violence in mankind showed in the color of bloody-red which was the scene after their conflicts, and it showed that the characteristics of mankind at that period were not much higher than the lower animals then existing. These three socially struggling tribes, were completely disconnected from the nations in the European continent of Nod and in Central America. The three Asia tribes showed disunity and confusion not only among the separated tribes and nations, but also within families units. All the conflict among them can easily be traced to their poorly developed mental organization,- plus all the imperfect conditions of the environment that were occurring at this period. The conflict and disunity of feelings was seen in a lack of similar social interest; and intellectually, they were not able to obtain any high and lofty principles that would guide them to a improved life. Fact is, these undeveloped mankind had difficulty obtaining the basic necessities of life.

But, the inhabitants of Central America (2c-a) showed a lot more potential, and as was stated previous, these had **advanced** more in many aspects of improved living conditions, especially in the arts, sciences, and basic mechanical inventions. But still, their minds were uncultivated in the higher branches of knowledge and lacked that glorious refinement which man is destined. These people had **advanced** somewhat in language and **communication** which was a key ingredient in their unity. And as almost every century passed, it would be seen that they had developed a distinct **modification** in their form of vocal communication and much improved over the original forms of expression. They developed and spoke a tongue so primitive that no analogy to it has as-yet been discovered, nor can this language be traced to any of the elements of dialect of the oriental regions they had originated from; nor is it similar to any other and subsequent languages, **except** one thing. There were some inflections in their language that could be linked to the Sandwich-islanders (Hawaii).

Moving-on to the inhabitants of the **European** continent, nation (#2) reveals that these mankind also, had-not ascended to any important degree of refinement in any category. And those who inhabited **Africa** (3, 3a) also remained undeveloped. They however were not as brutish as those undeveloped inhabitants existing on the continent of Asia whose three nations were divided into castes and tribes.

As one views the conditions of those nations it **seems** apparent that mankind has taken a wrong turn and made this mistake very early in this period of human existence. However, if a **celestial view** were somehow possible to anyone, the scene of creation and evolution would show that the inhabitants of the earth **have-begun** to make some small improvements and are now **perceptibly** converging to a **higher** degree of unity of interests as a whole.

This is still the time-period when, but few of mankind lived in structures or houses, except those in the European continent who used **tree** materials; and also those more advance humans of Central America who used **stone** - extensively. Generally speaking, vocal sounds differed among the separate tribes, and they each were unable to communicate with others, this was because the inflections and meanings of each tribe's sounds were as separate and dissimilar as was their separate social and intellectual developments; and in addition, there is the fact they are living separately.

Still in this early period of mankind's development, it is now at a time when some of the inhabitants of earth had become **divided** into every kind and degree of **physical-differences**, as well as the disunity that had been caused by their mental and social disunity; and this unnecessary and cruel type of disunity still remains as the basis of hatred which exists among mankind into the twenty-first century.

Another interesting thing about this period to be mentioned, is that mankind **began** to **recognize** within-themselves the processes of mental **imaginations**, they were becoming more aware of themselves. It must have been strange at first to have this peculiar ability, and it mostly occurs within individuals existing in the more advanced nations. However, there still was-not enough mental development within man for them to be able to make any true interpretations of those thoughts. The development of **imaginative-beliefs** would have serious and profound effects upon mankind's future.

It will be this "imaginative-process" that continues-on to form a conspicuous feature of the inner workings of the human mind in all ages. This particular phenomenon is a **very important** item and should be investigated more; because, this process **reveals** the manner in-which these hallucinations had become **mistakenly established** as true, and mistaken as real events. Many of these silly hallucinations are still believed, and the only way to displace them is by scientific research, and then to explain them in more detail in order to establish a clearer understanding.

And the story goes: Once upon a time, after the early inhabitants of the earth had existed on the planet for a time, had discovered the ability to express their thoughts by using sounds. **S**oon-after this amazing discovery, **social-confusion** began to develop and would become permanently established. Social confusion caused by a deceitfulness and misunderstanding of thoughts and expressions. After this initial confusion of tongues and **babbling**, the inhabitants had became disunited – social strife was the result and consequences of the deceptions man practiced upon each other. The origin of these misunderstandings arose from **misconceptions** of mankind's true **interior relations** toward one another, known as selfishness. The lack of understanding would soon cultivate a great deal of envy, cruelty, and misery, which has not yet ceased.

Mankind had become jealous and envious of each other. They had lost entirely all the peaceful principles that had first united them instinctively together as they were in the very beginning. Continued acts of selfishness were the results of a perversion and **misdirection** of the pure passions of man, and from an unfavorable development of their intellect. As a **consequence** of the social confusion toward each other the inhabitants in **imagined** and **conceived** of the **existence** of an **imperceptible enemy**, which they **supposed** was instilling into their minds "a spirit of vengeance and retaliation", and also, this imaginary enemy was generating absolute **evil**. And this imaginary enemy is still to this day lurking about because these imagined conceptions of the **spirit** of **evil** prevailed among most humans.

The unrestrained imaginations of man had now **placed-blame** on some-other thing, saying that the **workings** of the evil influence was the atmosphere or **winds** that were surrounding the earth, and believe that the **light** which was emitted from the Sun, somehow **possessed** the power to **broadcast** and spread-about these evil and malignant influences through the winds and into their minds and their imaginations. So now these imbeciles had imagined that through the atmospheric winds or the "**breaths**", evil came into their minds. Mankind **did-not** understand the fact that **they** were the **fault** and reason for the disunity among them.

As time passed, the complexity of man's imagined beliefs **intensified** and soon became deeply **entrenched** within their minds. As time passed further, and as man's awareness of their surroundings increased, the began to **notice** that their hatred for each other **only occurred** during the day and would occur **especially** when the **Sun** was in the sky shinning its light on them. This belief soon developed into an intense "fear of the Sun"; this is another item which through ignorance still-continues even to our present century. Many of the ignorant masses of man, have developed a love of night and a fear of day.

Now at this place in the story, in an attempt to consolidate this complex story which concerns the **roots** of **theology** together, another **review** of the combat that occurred between nation (#2) Cain and nation (#1) Cain is needed; the reason for this review is so-that the **manner** in which the development of **theology** began occurring among the original five primitive nations of ignorant and superstitious human inhabitants. Now recall that the two tribes (#'s 1 and 2) or Cain and Abel, had become extremely hostile towards each-other. War occurred, and then more wars occurred. The conquering nation, those of nation (#2) settled in the west of Eden, in the land of Nod.

This conquering nation whom were strong in war, also had retained similar **superstitious views** concerning the environment surrounding them, **much-like** the imagined-beliefs their ancestors had first developed, which were imaginary and mythological, just described as a fear of the Sun, or to be more specific, it was a **fear** of the **light** which was being emitted from the sun which caused the fear and superstition. And as was stated, it was here in this period that arose the **origin** of the fear of light and dread of light.

This fear of light and fear of daytime was the **beginnings** of the dread of discovering the **interior light** of man. Mankind had developed a great fear; the fear **had-caused** imaginary thoughts to arise in man's mind as they made **attempts** to **understand** their surroundings. How else could mankind have thought? There were not any means to differentiate one imaginary belief from the next. No way to understand the difference between what was fact and what was imagination; mankind **could-not** understanding the workings of their imagination and were sometimes even afraid of their own thoughts. Fear had closed these minds so tightly they remained in ignorance, which prevented their proper development.

Written evidence of the of these first mythological developments are in existence written in hieroglyphs which give references to this imagined belief system; these references can be found in a few of man's various early written primitive histories. These hieroglyphs were in regards to this very early time of man's theological beginnings; these written statements referred to these close-minded tendencies and ignorance, stating that *"men love darkness rather than light, because their deeds are evil"*.

And so these early inhabitants literally **did-fear** the **light** of the Sun. After a time, after this original fear had traditionally been passed-on through many generations, this original fear would be **modified** by those succeeding generations. These younger and later inhabitants, especially those of Central America, began to **fear** the **Sun** itself. It was this action which is the original imagined- belief leading to the very basis and beginnings of **mythology**.

It would not be until succeeding branch nations of man had developed a step higher, especially those in existing in Central America, whom had **initially** not-only continued to maintain the original fears originating from their forefathers, **but-now** they were also the first inhabitants who began to **summarize** their observations that the **Sun arose** from an indescribable **abyss** below their sight, and they now believed that the Sun was the abyss's **representative**. They imagined the abyss was clothed with a consuming fire. The Sun appearing clothed with a robe of consuming fire, would seemingly, they imagined, present to them evil thoughts and fearful declarations; then from that peculiar thought the sight of the Sun caused them to shudder even greater at the thought of the **abyss** which they **imagined** the sun represented.

In the simple minds of those unfortunate individuals, they could only believe that the abyss was **filled** with much more fiery substance. Nothing excited such deep and general focus of attention among the first inhabitants of the earth, as did the Sun – appearing as it did, to **rise** perpendicularly over the edge of the ground which they existed on; and more, because the sun would then be **watching** them with an immovable and **fiery eye** for many hours; and then, **sinking** down below the ground, in a similar fashion on the opposite side. They believed firmly that as the Sun sank it had then lost all its fiery garments,and was returning to the fountain of fire to be re-clothed, only to ascend again upon the opposite side. They therefore **believed** in an inconceivable fountain of raging fire. The reader must realize, this belief about the fiery fountain (which was hidden), they considered absolutely true, and the fiery realm of the abyss could be demonstrated by its representative the sun, which itself, had been a dread to all previous generations. It was these early beliefs which **formed** the foundation of the-faith system and beliefs of the nation of Central America.

## Section 76

The time-period which is now approaching is **nearly** to the period of-which **records** exist, and many of these earliest recorded stories are contained in the "primitive history"of the earth and its inhabitants. These records were first kept as oral stories and past-down from generation to generation traditionally until the time in which hieroglyphs were invented and formed as a means of writing, then later these same stories can be found transcribed in other written languages.

Before this period which historical records begin, there was a decided **change** in the physical conditions of this world. This particular **event** was a catastrophe or an inundation. Actually this catastrophe has already been discussed in previous sections of this story; recall that it was during earth's **great change** in geography which had occurred prior to the alluvial formations. So a **review** of the catastrophe is appropriate because the description now **includes** the tragedies which primitive man experienced. In the "primitive history" this event would be term "The Flood" or The Deluge", that terrible occurrence which has been referred to in mankind's written histories.

The results of these pending earth changes will be the several **geological transformations** and volcanic catastrophes which would **alter** the features of may portions of the earth. These events would **change** the courses of many rivers and would actually change the positions of many seas. And so as these decisive geological changes take place, it should be noted, that this change is the **last** major earth change which has occurred in the earth's long geological history up to modern present. It is this particular event which is specifically referred to by geologists as the **alluvial formation**. A more in-depth description of this Formation can now be given, because this event **effects** the early inhabitants of mankind as they, in their ignorance, attempt to cope with such a tragic event.

Here and now the story **returns** to the time-period of the alluvial formation.

It is now known that those earth changes during the alluvial **were** evidently **necessary** for the pending requirements of the next class of higher developed plant and animal Forms existing on land, and this includes mankind. It is the Divine Mind's plan for the development of man which **dictates** this **need** for new energies. These changes will be the final and the **ultimate** chemical developments for both the **water** and for the **atmosphere** in the history of the earth, with the water and air now chemically constructed as they were **destined** to be. These seemingly devastating earth changes should now be viewed with awe, and they should be seen as a necessary and an anticipated part of the eternal **positive progression** of things. The chemical adjustment of the elements of earth's environment were necessary to produce the water and atmosphere that are known to everybody. But this last chemical adjustment of the air and water has **consequences**; because it is now **known** that any change in the atmosphere's constituents or changes in the displacement of earth's large body of water could be catastrophic.

**However**, in observing a phenomenon superficially (such as through reading this story), the mind does-not recognize the order and harmony of the workings of Nature's laws and God's plan. Yet, even if the **meaning** for these changes lies hidden, or if a **use** for an occurrence is not at first seen, it is not correct to question the **wisdom** of the **Cause** which **produced** the event; and the reason for this statement is because the harmony of the whole grand plan of God, which unites in one Structure a Univerccelum of Universes, this event can only be known and felt when is viewed within its general aspects. And no matter how plain an occurrence may at first appear to us, to be the result of a defect in any of the departments of the general plan, this false appearance does not prove that the plan is defect. Nor is it an adequate basis to investigate any theory, because a superficial vision gives superficial images.

Recall, that previous to the period of the earth changes and previous to the start of the alluvial deposits, the earth had given-off a different geological aspect, much more different then it did after the volcanic catastrophes had finished their venting after the event. Previous to the venting – the **north regions** of **England** and of **America** were entirely **submerged** by water, as also were the **Australian** regions under water. A great portion of the waters of the Pacific ocean which today divide Asia from America, **instead** then, formed the seas of the Arctic regions and also waters being frozen into mountains of ice. This Pacific water had also extending towards the south, flowing as a narrow strip of water in the form of a river, which joined the gulf of Mexico and the Caribbean sea.

The inhabitants of Asia could almost walk across the Pacific region by following the circuit of narrow strips of land, which they did. Occasionally using boats, these Asian explorers would finally reach the portion of the earth now known as **Yucatan**, being nation (2c-a). There was also an **isolated nation** (2c-b), which also had **extended** themselves across and along those same connected land strips and finally reached into **North America**, these would be the first American's to arrive on this continent. The east Asia tribe (2c-a) first crossing to America would at-first exist on land portions that are no longer existing, this land portion was west of California, within the Pacific region; and it would be during the pending earth upheavals, this land **sunk** to become the bottom of the Pacific ocean as it now exists. It was from these very early inhabitants which originated the **American Indians**.

Many of the **Islands** in the southern and western portions of the earth were completely submerged and **concealed** by the sea that passes between and divides the eastern and western hemispheres. Of those submerged lands, the Sandwich islands (Hawaii), the Friendly islands, and the island of New Holland, are the three prominent lands which were formed and have since become dry fertile land.

You may recall that the condition of the atmosphere at the time of the alluvial had already created a climate that was very conducive to a process of constantly creating and accumulating extensive icebergs and icesheets, creating them both in the waters and on land. As is known, these formations of ice were primarily existing in the northern and submerged northern-portions of earth. Also mentioned previously, was the fact that those massive ice formations and icebergs had really **only-begun** to form and intensified after the previous submersion of lands which was the catastrophic event occurring at the end of the **tertiary** period. And so, it was from the termination or close of the tertiary period and continuing up to the present time of the alluvial, no other major earth changing event had occurred yet.

The atmosphere at the start of the alluvial was in a condition or chemical state which constantly created and accumulated extensive mountains of ice. The changes in temperature were gradual though, and the great mountains of ice were as gradually melted as they were formed, occurring repeatedly. It was from this action the earth was preserved from another universal submersion **until** the present alluvial period, which, when revealed to the reader it will be clearly evident that this present inundation which will occur had more distinct and violent events than did any of the previous catastrophes.

From the completion of the cretaceous formation to the present period there have elapsed an almost incalculable number of ages – during which time the animal kingdom has changed its main Forms several times. And those **changes** were sometimes clearly shown, sometimes by a complete extinction of certain orders of animals, and then followed by a **production** and formation of new and more perfect organizations. These modifications would occur among the lower orders of the animal creation first and then from these lower ones there was a progression upward to the production of the quadrumana; and from these, again, evolving through many ascending Forms until finally to the evolution and the ushering-in of the lower bimana tribes of animals; and from these bimana, again changes occur, up to the creation of man at the close of the sixth day.

It is well to understand that – any one of these previous, essential changes, required nearly the time of a whole century to complete – and further realize, those changes were innumerable, and therefore countless ages elapsed during the ascension of the first Forms of man-like creatures of the fifth day up until the organizations of early man, whom exists in alluvial period now under consideration and occurring late in this sixth day of Creation.

During that long period of time between the tertiary and the present alluvial, the atmosphere and water had **gradually** became, as in previous instances, unequal in density - specifically in relation to the expansive force of the the igneous materials of the interior of the earth. This definitely **is-not** God punishing mankind for their sins because mankind was too stupid to be sinners. Instead, this pending event is purely an **effect** of the **universal law** of positive chemical ascension of particles. It is known that the water and atmosphere together compose the fluid and gaseous envelope of the whole earth. The action of one, determines the action and composition of the other. And further, it is the solid, external coating of the earth or the **crust**, that is the **medium** by which the two extreme compositions between the interior and exterior elements of earth are sustained in a state of equilibrium. If a density change in these external elements occurs, then, **it-must** have been caused by the chemical actions and ascension of rudimental particles which had now chemically arisen from earth's interior. These new and rising particles would then **enter-into** higher life Forms, or into a new strata formation, or even higher organic combinations. The atmosphere at the alluvial has also been chemically modified by the modifications of the water – but now, the external pressure of earth's envelop was diminished by the action of sublimation and recompostion occurring to each of the effected elements. And again, this process was already in action many ages before the whole mass of earth entirely lost its equilibrium.

It will be the present alluvial period when this **inequality** of forces upon earth's crust occurred, and here the balance was tipped. The result was inevitable: the mass in the interior soon became confused and universally disturbed, and the whole fiery ocean of the interior was in a state of inconceivable agitation. All the particles in this molten mass assumed random and impetuous motions as these particles **rushed** to different parts of the great hot interior mass, all being acted on and propelled by the expansive heat of the interior composition. This resulted in an unimaginable expansion of those particles joining the crust of the earth. The result was the mighty **catastrophe** of which the whole earth now bears evidence.

It was an **upheaval** of the entire upper portions of England and North America and including all the adjacent parts all being thrust upwards. Volcanoes that had before **given vent** to the expanding elements of the interior, were entirely **useless** against the great internal pressure. And the **explosions** and **earthquakes** which followed, shook the earth entirely to its center, breaking in some parts the whole combined strata. Some of this broken crust, then sank, while in others places the crust and strata were raised to an immense height. It is the results of this upheaval that geologists have noticed many prominence in which the upheaved strata seem upon one side to have been abruptly broken, while upon the other side they are gently inclined. These may be observed in the highlands of **Scotland** and in the Grampian mountains, and also in the upper portions of the European continent as was previously stated.

# Section 77

The changes of the face of the earth established **new positions** for the water. At first before the upheaval this great body of water **was** in general view one united body, extending through many valleys streams that joined this same body of water through other land portions. But when the **great change** occurred there were many catastrophic events taking-place on both sides of the equator; and by this action there was formed new islands chains, new lands masses, and new bodies of water. At this time the **Pacific** ocean **suddenly flowed** over land which minutes ago was an extended valley, next, this now submerged land, as it **sunk lower**, would give more room for even more water to rush in over the sinking land; and ever since those moments in time, this great ocean has divided the two continents. Also affected were the Mediterranean and Atlantic areas, which at this time had became more confirmed in their present form. And from that time until the present the earths geographical features in a general sense have not changed.

The enormous **icebergs** existing in the northern portions of the earth became **at-once dissolved** by the evolution of heat at those regions. This resulted in a general inundation and flooding of all the low, dry land of the earth, though in this present upheaval the water did not rise as far to the tops of ordinary mountains like it did in previous upheavals. There was so much melted water in such a short period of time that flooding in some low-lands it almost appeared to be a deluge or flood.

The inhabitants that were upon the continents before described were partially destroyed. The European inhabitants were almost entirely destroyed. The inhabitants of Asia and Africa were generally left undisturbed, although in some parts, for instance where now exists the Caspian sea, there had dwelt a multitude which were entirely swallowed up by the great convulsion; also a small nation upon the mouth of the Ganges and another group existing toward its upper extremity of that same region were completely destroyed. Actually this river had not formed and **did-not** exist to any great extent before this period and it was not until some portions of land near its then-existing borders sank, together with the inhabitants, and that is how the Ganges river was formed into its present condition.

Next is the inhabitants of Yucatan, whose land-mass had-then extended into the gulf of Mexico prior to this catastrophe, these groups of people were likewise partially destroyed. Both the Gulf and the Caribbean sea were formed into their present configurations by the sinking of inhabited land portions of Yucatan; while those that had fortunately dwelt entirely in central Yucatan were undisturbed and survived.

In total, about one half of the inhabitants of Asia and Africa **were buried** in the interior of the earth. And in all, about **two-thirds** of the total population of the earth was **destroyed** either by the great earthquakes, the volcanic activity, or the whole inundation. A few groups or tribes safely remained in Asia, and even more survive in Africa; and so these few tribes along with those that inhabited Yucatan were the only inhabitants remaining on the earth, with the exception of **three isolated tribes** in the west coast regions of North America.

This great catastrophic occurrence had produced a change in every department of animate and inanimate Nature. The water and atmosphere would-now soon became **permanently established**, and would-become composed of the same elements as are existing today, and also in nearly the same proportions. The atmosphere and the water together again, constituted a force which was able to balance the expansive interior substance and forces. Though catastrophic in the broad sense, the changes were good for the earth and its evolution, including all the plant and animal kingdoms.

Attention is directed to the condition of the inhabitants of the earth rather than to the plants and animals. This **new period** is represented in a **historical** sense, told by man in mythological tales using imagined descriptions, and these traditional stories were written in the various "primitive history's" of man who in error, believed this event to be the cleansing of the earth of all its impure and unrighteous sinful Forms. The early inhabitants would eventually described the utter-destruction and universal flood, along with the geographical and geological changes. However the **Flood** described in the Primitive History – was actually **not-as** extensive of a flood as they describe it, though the destruction was utterly horrendous and was nearly universal.

The **original** description of the Flood as a story, was told entirely in a spiritual context, and in doing so the survivors in error represented the great catastrophe in a imperfect manner, and has since been misinterpreted and modified. At the time of this event the survivor's had no language to describe these changes, plus the fact the early humans had no-means of knowing about the existence of other places of earth. So these ignorant, superstitious, and devastated persons whom had survived, and whom were existing at this post-catastrophe time-period, all began to believe in their minds they are the special-humans whom were saved from death by Deity and would repopulate the earth; because in their minds they were the only human inhabitants on the face of the earth to survive. And it is from this particular period on-ward which **marks** the date which **begins** the early recorded history of the human race – and this history now considers all the previous inhabitants as only lower mankind in the initial and developmental stages of this present and new condition of mankind; which truly does, now after the upheaval, represent man as we know ourselves.

The inhabitants which are represented in the historical tales and later writings as being saved, were those that had dwelt in the land of Yucatan, because all the others were generally destroyed. These people were as was mentioned, much more **advanced** in arts, sciences, as well as many other general intellectual developments. Recall that this **was not** the original and first land that was inhabited by mankind, but these people truly did originated from an original branch from east Asia, whom themselves were from the very earliest of original five nations of humans.

## Section 78

It was not long after the earth changes but still within the present alluvial period, the inhabitants of the various tribes and nations of the southern nation **began** to conceive of **substantial signs** and **symbolism** which they would use as either verbal or **written** forms of communicating. Using these signs or symbols as a means to represent their thoughts and surroundings.

These written signs became what is known as **hieroglyphs**. And over time, it would be from these earliest of signs and symbols which subsequent historians have all utilized as major **sources** of historical knowledge, which has given insight and understanding of many things concerning those early inhabitants existing, and in some writings a knowledge of the conditions of the earth is obtained. **But** keep in mind, that there is **no real** knowledge which should be taken or obtained-from the **very earliest** of those existing hieroglyphics, this is because these earliest-ones had no real significance in them, except maybe to those who made them.

Within this post-catastrophic period are the **beginnings** of mythological and theological impressions, and worthy hieroglyphs. It is the time of the first recorded imaginative impressions of early human history where man **incorrectly** dates and explains what they believe are their human origins.

It is within this period that the history of **language** begins. From here, language may be traced as it starts and then progresses through the various and successive nations, until languages are found in their present state in modern times. Language allows mankind to **Communicate** in a meaningful manor and this allows mankind to become a much-more social being.

**Man** in this period has become **perfected** both anatomically and physiologically, now progressing to a position in development where both physically and mentally man are now able to use all their latent powers and faculties, including early forms of language and writing. In a general sense it is from man's day-to-day living and daily encounters which prompted them to become more aware of themselves and allowed them to finally **acquire** a sprouting sense of an understanding of important **truths**. This improved sense of truth will be the demarcation and shift **inwards**, allowing mankind to actually become more concerned with the realm of interior and ultimate life which is their true destiny.

Man has begun to learn and understand that **ideas** do not flow from external to the internal because they finally have realize that thoughts **are-not** generated by external things, but instead, thoughts are evolved from the living principle within. And it is now being learned that these thoughts flow spontaneously from the interior, rising up through the organizational make-up of man and then into the external world. Man is beginning to **perceive** and **reason** upon the stupendous workings of Nature.

This is the time when we begin to learn that our **interior** conceptions **rule** more than what were previously thought. This one-step improvement will **eventually** become in the future, a universal **relief** to mankind from their past misconceptions, thus helping man to understand those important truths concerning our true nature.

External things, those things that are apparent to the five senses, are merely **shadowing** forth the interior and creative causes – those real and essential principles of the Divine Mind – also seen in this new light, all Forms are **merely receptacles** of the living active **principles** that generate within man motion, life, sensation, and intelligence. And as stated previous, the body is the vehicle of the soul to develop the Spirit.

It is known that plants receive nourishment from light and gain heat from the sun. The animal kingdom which man is a part, receive light and life from that **Light** which is the **Love** of the Divine Mind, which is directed by Wisdom. So Love is the Life and Wisdom is the organizer.

An organization is made of parts and qualities. The whole is composed of parts, and the parts are necessary to the whole. Yet these parts of themselves do not constitute a perfect organization, because the parts themselves could be disorganized, and if that were the case then the whole will be disorganized. In order to form a perfect organization it is **necessary to have** every part adapted to perform a **use** and fulfill a **purpose**. It is also necessary that these parts have life and motion and be connected in mutual relations with each other. This is because from combined unity comes the adaptation of the whole to and for the accomplishment of a use, all of which benefits its society.

The organization of man is of itself perfect in every department, because within man there is an equal adaptation – and an endless amount of uses –all which converge to just as many ends. And so when these are conjoined, they display one perfect use and end for which the whole was created! So, man is existing; they are composed of an infinite number of parts; and they are a microcosm and united whole within themselves. And so, it is very important to realize, that mankind would not be this way **unless** there were a **plan**, or an end and ultimate that is to be accomplished!

Mankind has therefore been created into a proper receptacle and vehicle for the spontaneous **breathing's** of the great Positive Mind, which has operated through Nature and by Wisdom, and has not only **formed** but has also **individualize** the immortal **Spirit**, to dwell in the world within!

Man definitely **is-not** an organization just composed of a mutual agreement of parts, nor just produced by some random and indefinite workings of some impetuous Nature; **but-rather**, man is the perfect Form, the **highest image**, the designed organization, of the Divine Mind that pervades immensity! And so it is, God made man in His image.

# Section 79

If there are any further matters concerning the general deluge, these matters will now be held idle from any further or immediate investigation. Any items concerning this flood and catastrophe **will-not** be discussed again **until** a hint of them comes into view as a consequence of the imaginary, unjust, false, and exaggerated, descriptions of the flood were given by the early historians of the "primitive history", a time when these early historians made **false claims** and used the story out of context – because these historians **had-intent** to show and claim **incorrectly** that those events of the catastrophe had special theological origins.

The purpose of the next discussion is to present a **concise overview** of the stream of mankind, **starting** from their origin, **then** following the flow through its many circuitous courses, **until** each nation as a branch of the original stream has contributed their part of the story, which will effect and established the general condition of the world as it is in our twenty-first century. This discussion **will-not** at this time present information concerning mankind's moral and intellectual developments, nor discuss any of man's theological opinions, because these items will-be spoken of and be dealt-with extensively, but only in a later discussion.

The following discussion, as stated, requires a **review** of information from previous sections, because all is **necessary** for a proper understanding of this **complex story**, which is the development, the unfolding, and rise of mankind. The beginning of this, is at the **birthplace** of the lowest types of **mankind** and then tracking them through their various developments until they form what may be termed a perfect man of the present period.

**Asia**, as all mythological traditions truly indicate, cradled the firstborn of the human species and nourished them from the lowest stages of infant innocence. They continued to exist there until the period of time that mankind began to **unfold** and develop some of their human powers and faculties, which eventually would led them to wander to other various potions of earth.

So the story goes: In the beginning, there was existing in the **interior** of **eastern Asia**, an **association** composed of the **first** human beings who dwelt upon the face of the earth. On a **parallel** line of development with this first family, there was subsequently located **another group** of a **similar type** of mankind beings, but these humans were of a weaker and more effeminate nature, and they were not as large, nor as numerous.

These two families congregated in **different places**, and each existed

**separately** in their particular regions, without the knowledge of each others existence.

Now then, **why** these two families were both mankind yet existing in two different and separate places is interesting. It will appear from research respecting the mammiferous species first approaching towards and evolving into man, that, **originally** there were **two distinct molds** or forms of these **mammal** types; both ascending towards man **nearly** at the same time and both progressing in their own environments to reach the human type organizations, both groups are human, just separately.

One mammiferous species **had existed** both in the **arctic** regions and in the upper portions of Asia for a good period of time, and these semi-humans were existing in these various regions ever-since the great revolution in evolution which occurred within the **types** of the animal kingdom, occurring at the finish and close of the fifth day of creation, as previously discussed. And, it was from that special period that these man-like creatures would progress and ascended to the **human** type, and then, these had migrated and were now existing in the interior of **eastern Asia**.

The second and other mammiferous type had already existed in the **interior** portion of **western Asia** for a period of time, and it was from that region that this second group would **evolve** and ascended to the **human** type. These creatures of the second group also had ascended and evolve by a very similar process and with the same corresponding modifications taking place physically and physiologically within the creature that would develop them into the lower class of mankind. This particular group of mankind developed into the more effeminate type previously described.

Both groups **did-not** discover each others locality **until** each group had increased in numbers and after they had became somewhat prosperous with basic needs of survival. It was from the security and comfort of living that each group was led to **explore** and investigate new areas and new lands. Mostly it would be the older or elder members of each separate family group that first started to do so. Surprisingly it would be the less developed and more-effeminate race that **originally discovered** the more mature eastern Asian inhabitants. It had taken nearly one and a half centuries to pass, from the time the two groups each were individually and separately formed as two families of man, until the time they met each-other and then **joined together** as **one family** of mankind. This is the original nation which has been spoken about and named tribe (#0).

After one more century had passed, two **branch** tribes sprang from the original combination, one branch flowed into lower portion of Asia now known as **Egypt**, and the other migrated into the interior of **Africa**.

Fifty years after this original division of the two branches, they had grown into two large tribes. One of these two would ultimately grow into a very powerful nation.

It was those mankind that were in Egypt whom had originally sprang from the rather more matured stock of the original primitive family combination, and because of this they had **retained** all the peculiar unrefined genetic characteristics of their more primitive state. These humans were powerful and energetic beings, and the great strength they had developed was the result of their strict efforts to maintain a healthy diet and other means of healthy living. They were un-diseased.

The other branch, the ones settling in Africa, also had many genetic characteristics from the original combination of the first family; however, much of their dominate genetics were carried-over from the more effeminate portion of the original combination of the two mankind groups. And so this weaker branch nation continued to possess all the imperfect and delicate characteristics of the more crude and undeveloped portions of that original family.

Another one hundred and fifty years after these two branches had become established was also the time when the inhabitants dwelling in Egypt **rose-up against** the other nation in Africa, attacking the weaker nation with all the vengeance of infuriated brutality; and warred with them until they **destroyed** nearly three fourths of their number, the rest being dispersed and soon the whole branch nation would eventually die-out and become **extinct**.

## Section 80

Now again, there are only **two nations existing** upon earth - the one in **Egypt** and the other which is the original combined family existing in **eastern Asia**.

One hundred years after the brutal war, the nation dwelling in Egypt would **relocated** to the southern portion of **Europe**. These were becoming somewhat more advanced as centuries past, and had progressed to a social level of civilized life. This nation was able to construction and built a beautiful city. This was built from **trees** not from stones, and a number of such structures were built, enough to house the entire nation. Already mature trees still standing were used as the rough frame. Other trees were cut and stacked next to these mature trees. The tops of the mature trees were bent or broken and then connected to each-other, and then thatched as a roof. This was the first concept of **architecture** in the uncultivated minds of the original human inhabitants. Growing wild in open areas of Europe were uncultivated low types of wild **grain** bearing plants, which had become a major food source and would helped sustain those existing inhabitants living near-by.

The southern European nation had multiplied excessively finally growing into a mass of **uncultivated** intellects. And because they were unguided and were **incapable** of directing themselves they would often become socially disunited and miserable. There was absolutely no harmony among them and they constantly struggled among themselves. After another one hundred years they began to divide into groups or smaller tribes and eventually split-from the central nation. **Branch nations** of these people moved and established settlements in **Central America** and **South America** which would eventually construct two more beautiful cities, but these would be of stone.

Meanwhile some of those that dwelt in **Asia** as part of the original family decided to explore so they separate from that eastern nation. This branch tribe set about on another journey of discovery, migrating in a southern and easterly direction. This was the time-period when the Pacific ocean was not yet formed as it is known today. Land masses and strips of land were pleasantly situated in the Pacific region which made it possible for a migration of people to pass from the eastern hemisphere to the western hemisphere. This small nation of mankind from Asia, would eventually travel the distance and safely **enter** into the upper portions of **America**. It was not by crossing the Behring's straits that America's aboriginal people crossed as some have imagined.

Within this story the names of places, countries, and especially names of cities, are used to give a perspective because at this early period none of these particular places spoken of had names which they could be referred to. So the use of the current and modern names are used simply because they are known and recognized, so these familiar names are used to designate localities and are used only for the sake of distinction.

The inhabitants whom had relocated to the southern portion of the western hemisphere, specifically those of Central and South America, contained an **advanced nation** of the original family. And the land portions of earth which this whole nation had divided into various **branches** tribes would became located in areas which are now known as **Spain** and **Yucatan**. A small branch of this nation occupied land which has since become the **gulf** of **Mexico**. Also branch nations went to land areas in **Brazil** and **Buenos Ares**. These southern nations became very skilled in the use of **stone** for the purpose of construction and had built their cities of stone and other durable material. Mostly they would build very low, yet extensive dwellings, with many of the buildings containing apartments for living.

Another five hundred year period lapsed since the division into branch nations, and during this time-period various portions of South America suffered from **two** catastrophic **volcanic** events, one of which would form the Mexican gulf, Caribbean sea, and Pacific ocean. During these appalling occurrences, nation after nation was destroyed and there was a depopulation of almost every portion of these South American regions. **Before** these volcanic eruptions occurred, this large and branched nation had made good progress for the general advancement of mankind. Beginning from the initial building of the cities of stone, down to the fifth century afterward, was a period of time when these rapidly advancing human inhabitants became comparatively more advanced in the sciences, farming, and hieroglyphical architecture; they enjoyed discovering new things, which helped them excel in the skills of gathering and understanding external information concerning their environment.

Using their advanced skills in science and architecture, it was at a later time the cities of **Herculaneum** and **Yucatan**, would be founded and built. There was also a primary city **near** the **site** of pre-**Pompeii**. But giving too many details concerning the social and physical conditions of the inhabitants of these cities would be unimportant at this time.

The following description concerns the time period of the building of Pompeii (#1) and of the permanent establishment of the **five nations** that arose upon the face of the earth during this period.

228 · *KNOWLTON*

The inhabitants of Yucatan extended their rights of possession almost to the islands now known as the **West Indies** and after a time a portion of that same nation migrated and established a city in Herculaneum.

Some people of the city of pre-Pompeii had developed settlements in various portions of land which existed southeast and north of this city, and also sending out a branch settlement which peopled Brazil, extending to its extreme boundaries. But pre-Pompeii as a great city, and her inhabitants as a great nation **yielded** all their beauty, grandeur, and magnificence – ignorance, pride, and arrogance – to the annihilating hand of volcanic action. All buried by the contents of a bursting crater.

This historic city is called Pompeii for the sake of distinction, but in **reality** a city that was later founded and settled **near** the same spot would for the first time use the name of **Pompeii**. The pre-Pompeii city now being discussed, can only be known to have existed, if some of its still-existing materials are discovered. This material may be found by seeking at a place a little north of the city that has subsequently been destroyed in a similar manner. This story has **not-yet** reached the time-line of the city of Pompeii which is known in the twenty-first century.

Yucatan was the portion of the earth where the inhabitants of earth had progressed and would develop **great ingenuity** and refinement in their artistic skills, using these skills to build ornamental and hieroglyphical architecture. These skilled craftsmen were the **most advanced** mankind on earth up to this period. Their vast conceptions and attainments continued to advance forward and they flourished for nearly seven centuries.

Advancing one more century leads to a discussion of a **new branch** of the original human family – specifically, the inhabitants that passed from Asia **toward** North America – **some** of these exploring and wandering people would settle fertile portions of the then, land-bound Pacific regions, forming small settlements here and there, or wherever suited their fancy and inclinations. And then **some** of these original Asian explorers had continued traveling eastward and would finally reached the west coast of the **North American** continent.

It was not long after the migration of the east Asia tribes across the pacific region land portions, that the catastrophe occurred that would change the face of earth, and this is the event when the Pacific ocean would finally became established in its present ocean Form; and a result of this event was the formation of various islands and island chains within the now formed Pacific Ocean. In this island forming process the islands known as the **Philippine** islands, Society islands, Sandwich islands (**Hawaii**), along with many others. The earthquakes, volcanoes, and upheaval caused the populations of these islands to be surrounded by water and **isolated**. There were no means of navigation to escape and besides there was nowhere to go; within the minds of those survivors it seemed like everything else had vanished. Some of these newly isolate island masses and island chains had already existed as fertile land and were adequate to sustained their new inhabitants.

After the great catastrophe mankind would again repopulate earth, spreading themselves into other land portions which became more inhabitable after the upheaval event. The remaining inhabitants of Europe, at this post-upheaval period whom had survived, would change their location, they migrated into portions of northern **France**. The movement of the Europeans into France would be extensive. Apart from the migrating Europeans most other surviving tribes and nations, such as the inhabitants of **Asia**, would **remain** in Asia and continue as before.

Another group of surviving humans were the distinguished and **powerful tribe** which had detaching themselves from the **southern nations** of Yucatan, Spain, South America, whom now emigrated and had proceeded along the European continent, then continuing along Africa and Asia, and parts of these would eventually settled **precisely** in the land where **previously** had **existed** the original **Indo-Europeans** of the first division of the original Family of Man. **And**, it was part of that same powerful southern tribe who also established themselves in the area now modernly known as **Egypt**.

## Section 81

Now passing in time to the close of another century, which can be characterized distinctly by the very **rapid** advancement of civilization. There was also an increase in man's intelligence in a manner which was noticeable and importantly, this progress was occurring among many of the newly formed nations. Egypt as stated, had become founded, settled, and in this present century is now confirmed as a organized, powerful, and great nation, the one which would be known to later and subsequent historians whom would write about them.

It would be from a **branch** nation or tribe that had later sprang-from that great nation of Egypt, which then migrated and settled in the regions of **Jerusalem** and **Jericho**. And later some inhabitants of Jerusalem and Jericho combined with another group from Egypt, and these would form a colony which then migrated and discovered the region of **Greece** and here they founded a settlement which would over time built a great city.

Some **explorers** from Greece migrated to other portions of Europe. There were areas permanently settled by a combination of tribes from Greek explores and many **others** coming-in from other parts of Europe. So then, Jerusalem, Jericho, Greece, and other new nations in Europe, all sprang **entirely** from the original settlers of Egypt. There would also be a stream of other families and groups of settlers coming-out of Europe which would finally settled the land-portion now known as Spain, which has now been **re-settled** again, after the original inhabitants were destroyed during the earth changes.

It would be during this passing century when, for the **first-time**, mankind would be able to represent their thoughts in a intelligent manner to each other by the use-of **hieroglyphs**. This significant event for man would be the first time in history that hieroglyphics had became sufficiently perfected and organized, so they could **shadow-forth** and express in an **intelligent** manner, written information. Man was now capable of expressing a particular thought, or explain a thing or substance. Man could now, with the use of proper hieroglyphical representations, express anything which the inhabitants **desired** to represent. And, it **was-not** before the close of this last century and extending into the start of the following century that the **keeping** of the **records** in a hieroglyphical form began, and from these earliest of records which have survived, the world has **received** a small portion of **correct** and definite information which concerns the primitive inhabitants of the earth and their early history. It is from these earliest of human written records, that people living in the present modern world depend on for historical information. It **will-be** these **various records** originating from different sources, which will be investigated further-on as this story progresses. There are **no-other** written records which give a correct impressions of the true beginnings of earth's inhabitants and their social and intellectual attainments previous to these earliest, of coherent hieroglyphical written records.

In regards to the **continuance** of God's plan of "successive progression" set in motion as a means to develop Man as a vehicle for the Spirit, there still remains that **complete chain** and an **unbroken connection** between the conditions of the earliest inhabitants and **now-tied** into this present period of hieroglyphic written history. Sadly because of man's ignorance, this is also the period when man would **combined** the **mythological traditions** of their earliest forefathers; and mankind would now **mistakenly** transfer and transcribe these imaginary beliefs into their written history **as-though** these myths were true, which they are not.

Well now, there will be given another **overview**. But this review is **intended** is to show more in-depth the migration and flow of humans **after** the great catastrophic events which are also known to some as the Biblical **Flood** or the Deluge.

Once upon a time, after the most recent catastrophic events of earth which had occurred during the termination of alluvial deposits and formations, was the period in-time when the only surviving groups of mankind set-about to re-establish themselves and continuing to exist, and to repopulate the face of earth, so to speak. First of all, it was **one** of the **original nations**, that fortunately had, **previous** to the earthquakes,emigrated by hopping across the land-laden Pacific region, whom began their journey from east Asia. These would remain living as an uncultivated and uncivilized tribe, all existing upon the western hemisphere or North American continent.

Next, are the survivors that have **two** large and flourishing cities are still existing in the southern portion of the same hemisphere or those in Central and South America, and this includes their dependent and branch tribes which had extended their domain eastward, reaching to West Indies, and it is upon these islands a few tribes were still existing.

Spain and Portugal were inhabited by a small tribe proceeding from the Grecians of the European continent. Also recall the region of Spain was previously inhabited.

Now also existing in regions of north France and Britain was a small and detached nation from the Grecians and these new lands are the land areas that were able to sustained them. Greece, Jerusalem, Jericho, and

Egypt, were inhabited as before stated and expanded upon. China, **Japan**, **Denmark**, **Sweden**, **Prussia**, **Russia**, **Norway**, and **Siberia**, each sustained detached communities from various portions of the earth. Eventually, as mankind flourished, multiplied, and subdued the earth, these various countries, cities, kingdoms, and empires, (which have been designated by their modern names), were in this order and this way, one after another, discovered, founded, and settled, all by the **various** and **heterogeneous tribes** that were then existing upon the face of the earth. The race of mankind at this period had become highly **diversified** in their appearances, habits, and generalize constitutions.

Beginning now in this period and still continuing with modern man, interesting **changes** began to occur within the physical and mental conditions of mankind. These changes were brought-about by the **effects** of the local climate, of food, in differences in modes of living, and any-other idiosyncratic tendencies that may have occurred. **Because** from these physical changes, there **inevitably** occurred, whole changes in the **classification** and reclassification of many of those different tribes of man. Environmental actions had caused specific changes within each area; these changes affected different individuals **according** to any modification which **had-already** occurred within an individual's genetic make-up, differing from the original type that first developed.

**Starting** from this point on-ward, this story will **blend-in** with the written histories of man, but not necessarily to summarize or state again what is already known to be true from this written history of mankind; but **instead**, to merely **present** to the reader only that **material** which is-not correctly obtained or copied from the "oriental traditions"; and **also** from this place, to distinctly **classify** the human species so that a proper conception of the **origin** of **language** can be known.

Next up, is the **origin** of **language** and its ties with the early development of **theology**. The **main topic** and point of this particular review, being the assumption and hope, that once the origin of language is understood correctly and its deviations made clear, then more easily will come to the mind of the reader, an understanding of the origin of the first **theological conceptions** of mankind and how those concepts gained their deep roots.

The **traditional records** of the primitive nations of Asia are **among** the **first** historical accounts that are in existence, at least in regards to those hieroglyphs where any information can be ascertained concerning the **original** nations of **mankind**. And it is known that **China** possess a written record of the world, which extends forty thousand years back from our twenty-first century.

There are various other parts of Asia which show evidence both of the long and steady development of science and civilization; yet at the same time, there other portions of Asia which indicate that mankind in these portions had continued to exist in a most uncultivated and barbarous condition.

There absolutely is no reliable historical information concerning the arts and refinements of the early and primitive nations, nor is there any history of their mechanical and architectural knowledge prior to the peopling of Egypt, which is now known to have occurred after the earth changes and great catastrophe. **But**, it is from this period of Egyptian hieroglyphics and **onward** that the marks of humans progress have been left by the distribution and civilization of earth by mankind. These records are **distinctly found** in many original and subsequent **history books** of **each nation**. Many of these separate books, actually tell the same story, but tell the story with some different characters and situations.

South America and **Mexico** were inhabited and established for many centuries before Spain became re-settled and again inhabited. And these southern inhabitants cultivated the **powers** of mechanical construction. Their acquired skills were past-down to future generations and improved upon, so when a **branch** tribe of these skilled and crafty inhabitants finally **emigrated** to Egypt, those skills help them to eventually construct a large and advanced nation. Then from the great nation of Egypt sprang another great nation, Greece. Recall that the art of stonework was one of southern nations greatest abilities.

It was the inhabitants of Greece from which many portions of Europe were settled, including places like **Rome**. And both Greece and Rome continued to flourish after being settled; and many of these groups and settlements began to development mechanical and architectural skills. **Sadly**, these craftsman **had-not** developed an inner awareness and so remained mentally uncultivated, lacking in any of those high and lofty faculties of the inner spirit; **none** of the inner truths, which are lying-still and undeveloped in the depths of man's soul, from-which **could-have** arisen the most sublime and truthful thoughts and sentiments which if properly applied, these abilities would-have totally redeemed the race of man. But, as we know, we remained mostly ignorant and crude.

## Section 82

It should not be necessary to go into details concerning the devastating wars that have occurred. Nor should it be necessary to mention the famines, fatal diseases and plaques, or even mention the desolating invasions, fraud, deception, scheming, and such, constantly occurring all throughout the **eastern hemisphere** at this time-period. There were barbarous and uncultivated dispositions prevailing within each and every nation, and each **would-elevate** a **potentate** or ruler to the highest degrees of arrogance and **selfishness**. Each nation, in each situation, choosing the **wrong path**, almost always heading in a false direction. Each nation as a whole, were possessed with unnatural envy, which then would develop into hatred, leading to wars – all this tragedy, **solely** resulting from the misdirection of human thought and judgment.

Some nations were winners, others losers. The losing nation would usually become **assimilated**, dispersed, or killed-off completely. And the identity of many tribes, and even physical types of the human species have become **entirely destroyed**.

Some of these ruthless invasions, usually coupled with persecutions, often continued relentlessly for nearly a century at a time. And they continued off and on for **thousands** of years, some have even continued into the twenty-first century. Beautiful cities had been built, mechanical inventions made, but-these were all **destroyed**.

An example can be given of the barbarous condition of mankind in this period, one which shows the results of the profoundly misdirected process of human judgment, this **example** is from a book containing historical writings of some of man's primitive history, and the story goes: "so, it was after Judea had become peopled, the inhabitants, not possessing judgment sufficient to govern themselves, chose a presuming and arrogant chieftain as their head, and placed him in their city to exert power and influence over the whole nation. After this chieftain had warred with parts of his own kingdom, and had incited hostility and bloodshed in many before-undisturbed portions, he died. And so likewise Saul ascended the throne of Judea; and he assumed the character of a tyrannical king, and warred with the Jebusites in Palestine, which, after being dispersed, these became mingled with other nations. And ultimately David seized the throne by force, gaining control of this nation, and changed the seat of government to Jerusalem. Here, assisted by others, warred with the Syrians, Chaldean, Amalekites, Edomites, Ammonites, and Persians, and succeeded in destroying the identity of some of these nations, and also warred with those tribes that were existing alone the borders of the Euphrates, and soon extended his kingdom from the Euphrates to the Mediterranean, and from the Phoenician territory to the Arabian gulf". This particular example gives a basic-overview of types of uncultivated and selfish dispositions, which all combine and exist together as the fabric and **framework** of man's complex mental condition. Man's ignorance appears to be **coupled-with** the dual nature of selfishness and arrogance, and all these combined appears to be the basis of a great portion of man's development.

As historical time passed, large portions of Asia **would-be** at any given time, either under the control of many different conquering nations such as the **Assyrians**, **Chaldeans**, **Persians**, **Mongols**, **Syrians**, **Tartars**, and **Turks**. And so, Asia, like many portions of earth, were subjected to the wars, conflicts, and struggles of each successive conquering nation. All nations were seeking ascendancy over each other; and all this conflict **was-fueled** by the outbreaks of **unnatural** and **unholy passions** which had been **excited** and enraged by these wars, occurring within the severely **misdirected minds** of the **youthful** generations. And so, over and over it can be stated that these most unhappy situations which mankind would experience were **entirely** the **result** of the ignorant, selfish, and undeveloped mankind, by all of **us**.

## Section 83

    The **western hemisphere** as a portion of earth existing within early periods of earth's evolution was a fertile area that was able to **develop** and **sustain** many of the lower types of the plant kingdom. The northern and southern portions of this ancient land mass had been the birth place of many huge and ferocious Forms of the animal kingdom, some of these creatures even stomping and moving about within the forests of the interior of North America.

    The **role** which the western hemisphere played in the manner of development of mankind had its beginnings from the **initial settlements** of emigrating humans, all originating from the small branch nations which originally separated from the first family (#0) whom themselves had migrated from and originated from, areas of the interior of Asia. These first North American people had arrived on this continent just about the **same** time-**period** that **another tribe** had also emigrated and descended into the southern portions of the same western hemisphere, migrating to both Central and South America; and in a historical time-line this appears to be a-little over nine thousand years before present day.

    These earliest inhabitants of North America were the sole inhabitants of this new land and would continue as the only inhabitants until the period of the **invasion** of the western hemisphere by various European nations in the middle of the second millennium CE. At the time of their arrival this small group of human inhabitants had basically **preserved** the general type and characteristics of the original human family (#0). It was very **soon** after arriving to their new home that these first North Americas would become **isolated** from all-other inhabitants of the earth, which including their neighbors in Central and South America, but these southern nations were unknown prior anyhow. It would be very **soon-after** the settlers arrived in the Americas that the **great catastrophe** of the earth would occur; this is the upheaval previously spoken of, where there was the **submersion** of land areas which would create the Pacific Ocean. Initially, the first settlements consisted of small tribes being located mostly on land portions of the continent which now no longer existed after the catastrophe. These land areas had extended west from the present California coastline, this land had **sunk** to become the bottom of the Pacific Ocean.

    Initially only **three tribes** survived the upheaval and existed in the post-catastrophic period; these small groups each were now occupying different portions of this North American land. There is no clear picture, as to the actual number of inhabitants composing the surviving population of these three small tribes; however it can be said, that they all **retained** the mental and physical characteristics of their **Asian** ancestors whom they had originally branched-off from.

After the earth-changes and after the passage of time, these tribes grew into many separate nations and scattered themselves across the whole of North America. However, because of their **isolation** from any of the other more advanced and more civilized nations of earth, not having any contact with those human genetics that had progressed somewhat in arts and sciences, these Americans would only **retain** the gross and **unrefined** traits which they had inherited from their early forefathers. These **American Indians** would eventually accumulate a great deal of useful knowledge which rose-up from the limited natural genius occurring among these peoples, and from the **keen awareness** of the environment that existed around them.

Instead of developing in the sciences, the Americans learned to **dwell** with Nature, encouraging a **truthful** and spontaneous **theology** much more refined than any other nations of the earth, ever. They saw beauty, harmony, grandness, and majesty, in all things in Nature. They would gaze in-awe and wonder, and would smile with radiant adoration at the environment around them. They loved Nature so much that they, in a way, became one with Nature; and it must be impressed upon the reader the fact, that these Nature-lovers came nearer to the development of a **truthful conception** concerning the higher spheres of "inner existence", and also of the Great Spirit, much more-so than has any others from that period, or since.

When finally the Europeans arrived, they would within a short period of time begin to **exercise force** against these peaceful aboriginal inhabitants, stealing their crops and other provisions of food. The Europeans then went further, rising-up and **attacking** the Indians, dispersing them to other portions of the land. And this hostility between the Europeans and aboriginals has continued.

AJ Davis, side-tracks from the story in this section - and gives a dissertation on the forming of America – gaining its freedom and independence, then he gives a report, on the topic of tyranny, which Davis reports, has occurred constantly through-out the history of mankind, and so he states: *Who can read with undisturbed feelings the records of the barbarous massacres, inhuman persecution, and unnatural and corrupt conditions, that are contained in the history of every nation upon the face of the earth? Who can contemplate the persecution of centuries past, with feelings of pleasure or complacency? Who, among all the inhabitants of the whole earth can, with feelings of pleasure, peruse the records of the destructive and immoral proceedings of chieftains, potentates, kings, popes, and emperors, who were uplifted in their own selfish minds and wielded the almost omnipotent influence of a superficial and chimerical theology?*

*Has not one chieftain after another proceed in the same manner, to carry out his misdirected and unnatural desires, at the absolute sacrifice of all morality, and all natural and divine principles? O Man, whom Nature by her immortal energies has created!, now, erect towering monuments from the materials of past history, only to remind subsequent generations of the results of the misdirection of man's faculties and the pollution of his internal possessions.*

# Section 84

Now, counting backward from the twenty-first century about nine or ten thousand years and arriving at this particular post-catastrophe time-period of the earth, just as the varied tribes of mankind are in the process of the re-populating of the earth. And in a general sense the whole earth is now peopled by **human beings** that are **diverse** in character and dispositions. Each tribe, nation, branch-nation, are separately **developing** what will be their peculiar habits, their local customs, and differing forms of government, each with its own laws. Each continent or region having its own peculiar foods and climates, and each area requiring different skills, implements, or tools which enable those groups to survive and further develop and adapt to their surroundings.

People existing in one region would display differing anatomical features and different physiological developments than another region, and these changes were all **dependent** upon **how** the local **environment** acted upon their original genetic characteristics which originated from the genetic developments of the first family (#0). Each region or even each nation would develop and speak different languages, using different dialects, possessing **altered** primitive traditions; then, as the populations grew, so did the differences in political and theological opinions; these topics became a large part of each one's daily existence, because everybody has to serve somebody. Difficulty and conflict would arise in many situation when two or more different nations or tribes interacted. Everyone was **motivated** by different conceptions of justice and different interpretations of what was good or evil.

As the beginnings of the **historical period** unfolded, mankind could now be properly and **correctly classified** into five distinct **varieties**; however, it is **not true** that there are five types of the human family. There is only one type of human, but there are five distinct varieties. And it should be distinctly clear to the reader, especially from all that has been presented concerning the development of the human race, that mankind, as they are now existing, and that means taking into account all the diversified conditions and developments which distinguish their five classifiable varieties, still can be seen in a clear manner that man has developed and has ascended from one original type! Man is man and variety is the spice of life.

The five varieties of mankind existing on the planet in this early historical period are as follows:

The white/pink in the **Caucasian** which extended from **India** into **north Africa** and into **Europe** and hence the name Indo-European.

The yellow in the **Mongolians** which exist in **eastern Asia**, and then, this variety also extending its presence towards Africa.

The brown in the **Malayans** which exist in **India**, **Africa**, and other portions of the **eastern hemisphere**, and extending into the **southern Islands** especially those of the Pacific regions

The black which initially existed in **Africa** only, after the great catastrophe, however recall, that the original Family of Mankind was black.

And the red which are the **American Indians**.

Very little debate is needed to establish the common origin of these dissimilar colors. The **original** inhabitants and first mankind were **black**; the subsequent nations were **brown**; the branches of these were **red**; and from the red comes the **yellow**, and from yellow the **white**.

White and Black then, it will be observed, are apparent opposites. There never was known an instance in which that, which was perfectly white brought forth its opposite black. There is known instances of the black bringing forth white, or a color approaching it, is another conformation of black being genetically dominate.

# Section 85

How and when did language develop within the earliest of mankind? And what were the necessary conditions which would spring-forth the first conception of a process of communicating ideas?

The word **language** is derived from the Latin lingua, which signifies the tongue. But, this word does not really convey the essential idea of mental or vocal communication.

When the original inhabitants first conceived thoughts, the methods these undeveloped creatures used to share those thoughts seem to naturally occur, and so those thoughts were **expressed naturally**, by using any combination of a facial expression or countenance, manual gestures, outward signs and symbols. Man could and did use any of these methods, and naturally chose and used a manner of expression - which **would-seem** to be **suggested** by the **character** of the **thoughts** they had conceived.

**Impressions** were made upon their **senses**, and then these impressions were **transferred** to the internal principle which evolves thought. Which is the action of the mind and any of its sensory principles and processes. But how are impressions **shared** with another person? A **thought**, - in order to be conveyed to the mind of another, **must** be in some way either distinctly expressed, or it must be shown by a **representation** or an example, which could be given of that particular thought. So then, by naturally using one's eyes, facial expressions, and gestures, or by using symbolical representations, a thought is able to be shared with another. And this is how the ignorant original inhabitants began to convey their crude, confused thoughts to one another. This action gives some explanation of the philosophy of vocal and physical expressions of the thoughts, feelings, sentiments, or affections, of the internal **living principle** found within man, and here it is occurring within these earliest of humans.

The very first humans did not converse because thought in man had not developed yet; but when it was time for mankind to first begin expressing their thoughts freely, it was done by configurations of their face and eyes, with their countenances and gestures. And man became skilled at this so that, when they had feelings of love, their countenances were shown with a bright illuminating smile approximating some type of pleasure. When feeling depression their gaze was downward, and if they had feelings of joy their gaze was more upward. By using facial expressions these early thinkers could show anger, fear, pleasure. Other times they might use their body-language or other gestures to show action, such as when showing speed they would run fast, if they needed food they would show weakness, if they wanted to play golf they would imitate putting; man was now able to share thoughts and converse with another by use of a **particular sign** which were naturally suggested or indicated by that thought.

When a particular thought has been excited internally within the principles of the mind, that thought was generated or caused by, **either** the action of exterior and outer objects upon the senses, or else the cause would be generated or influence by the internal consciousnesses.

During the time this manner and type of language and this type of communication remained in use the human inhabitants **were-able** to maintain social **unity** and a high level of peaceful coexistence and harmony as one family nation. These earliest forms of communication were used by mankind and remained unchanged for quite some time. **But** in the scheme of things, it was not really a long time before those once happy, open, and honest countenances and gestures, soon gave-way to and were being **replaced** by man's use of **artificial signs**, and it did not take long before these artificial signs would **gain dominance** over those earlier modes of expression. But man's shift in their preference from using gestures to now preferring to use artificial signs, soon became a turning-point and a downward spiral into **misery** and madness for earth's inhabitants. Man's once honest and open expressions had now became **deceptive** and **unreal** and their ability to coexist has become diminished.

The use of artificial signs had a significant affect on man's social interactions. The extreme deception that this style of communication facilitated would cause those once happy and unity interactions among individuals, tribes, and nations, to almost completely dissolve into chaos. Man was not yet intelligent enough to realize the real nature of their predicament and not able to see their own role in this confusion. And so in spite of this great difficulty in man's communication with each-other, it still must be noted that: - from this period of man's evolution onward, all the nations of earth began to **construct** artificial **objects** which would relate or correspond to the particular ideas or thoughts they intended to **represent** or express, and this is the beginning of the use of **symbols**.

Instead of facial expression man now had decided to **draw** or to form various figures, shapes, designs, and other symbolical representations and would use these as artificial forms in communication. At first these **representations** were mostly used to express or show, in a distinct manner, the general thoughts they had conceived. But there was no attempt yet to use vocal sounds with this new method of **symbolic** representation, and in doing this man **transitioned** from body language which was manual and physical, to now using **man-made** forms, objects, and shapes. Soon mankind began to experience an inconvenience and a great deal of frustration, - because they were not able to express minor thoughts. Man had reached another plateau in their ability to communicate effectively. It was apparent that any attempts at peaceful communication were now hindered by confusion. This misery came because man's primary means of expressing themselves had became **inadequate** and nearly useless.

Humans had reached another plateau in their ongoing development process, the root **cause** of this confusion seemed to be an **inability** to express the many **minor thoughts** that were constantly arising from their inner and outer worlds. This difficulty was especially evident in social settings. Not everyone understood a particular gesture or sign to indicate the same thing. Now a particular sign could be a **mixed signal**. The original meaning of the signs and symbols had now become so much more **complex** and in many situations the signs could have other meanings and different interpretations all depending on the specific place, person, or thing.

The primitive humans became perplexed and frustrated. So in order to remedy the situation and relieve this frustration mankind suddenly **begins using** certain **distinct vocal sounds** that seem to naturally occur and are stimulated from the thoughts in their minds. And in most instances these thoughts had originated from **internal** promptings.

The use of sounds for communication became useful at least for a short time; but it would not take long for mankind to learn that when using both gestures and sound **rules** are **needed** to assist them with this vocal babel; **rules** which would allow for a particular sound to **always-conveyed** the same meaning, whenever that particular sound was used. And this learning process and advancement in communication is where the rudimental conception of grammatical principles gets its beginnings. The new rules of **grammar** spread like a wild-fire among the early nations, because this new tool would allowed for the **return** of some **social unity** that had been lost. It is clearly evident that man is a very **social** creature and they sincerely gain great pleasure from vocal communication; man now having the ability to express not only major thoughts, but also minor thoughts was one giant leap for mankind.

As a result of exploring and wandering to the other various portions of the earth, man became more distributed and during this time-period man's vocal **sounds** started to be recognized as having a **symbol** or sign, and they began to **represent** those sounds by **hieroglyphical characters**, as tiny figures, and strokes. These hieroglyphical characters were first apparent in and around the settlements of people existing in **Yucatan** and its adjoining portions.

The symbolical or hieroglyphical methods of correspondence and language continued **unchanged** for many centuries without any perceivable advancement. Spain and Asia are the next advancing nations in which developments in human language occurred. **Spain** was **first** to **modify** the existing external representations of ideas into more perfect hieroglyphical forms using **mechanical skills** they had developed. They had perfected tools and devices, and the means to create beautifully crafted hieroglyphs.

The Spain inhabitants also were the **first** to draw figures on smooth surfaces, and here can be seen the first expressions of the art of painting. These artists had such a degree of perfection that their representations may be properly called picture-language.

The nation of **Asia** preferred to **preserve** the verbal and grammatical form of expression that already was popular. They made **improvements** which allowed this style to be perfected to their liking, and then it **become permanent** and so-well established, that there are remains of this language still in use today.

Those inhabitants dwelling in China became more confirmed in the **monosyllabic** language of the southern nations than did any other nation or peoples. And they enjoyed being able to **express** their thoughts in the language of representations, and they did this in the form of pictures and hieroglyphics. The Chinese have remained unchanged in the manner of vocal communication, while other languages were derived from branch nations splitting-of and relocating, existing in other portions of the eastern hemisphere.

# Section 86

It is probably impossible to trace the origins of each word in each tongue; because the varieties of dialects are overwhelming, plus, is not the intent to do that here. And aside from that, there is no accumulation of facts that would be useful. Nothing usable as a guide to any questions that may arise respecting the origin and primitive forms of a language. Each of those first languages all had their individual process by which they have assumed their present modifications.

The **first elements** of the rudimental **monosyllabic language** developed and originated from those earlier hieroglyphical representations which were given sounds to correspond with a particular hieroglyph.

Theses first elements of combining pictures with sounds which were used by the previous inhabitants as an advancement in communication was **adopted** by many nations, and it was from this **source** sprang the **Chinese language**. And as stated, this nation became settled and confirmed on this type of dialect derived from the original hieroglyphic sounds.

Other nations, also used and improved upon the original style of communicating with hieroglyphical sounds, soon progressed and adopted an entirely **new form** of grammatical, mechanical, and vocal communication. Here it can be noted that it is from the **impression** of **sounds** that the orthography or the formation of a system of combining letters of the **Greek language** would first become **established** – and this **language** was characterized by a form of **synthetical expression** completely unlike that of any other language at the time; and this new language was governed by entirely dissimilar grammatical rules. In later progressions and revisions of this language nouns, verbs, and adjectives, were formed by following the ascending grammatical rule of the Greeks and then these words were formed into syntax, and then these became established as distinct parts of speech.

It is easy to see that from the action of the Greeks developing their language, that the **classification** of **sounds** would now become the determining **factor** to the classification of nouns, verbs, adjectives, and prepositions, at least among the Greeks. What it was, is that **each sign** suggesting a vocal sound according to primitive usage, could now, by associating the individual sounds together, **according** to these grammatical forms and rules, **make them** convey to the minds of each other distinct ideas of any object, substance, qualities, actions, and even motives, concerning nearly anything in which they might have a desire to communicate their knowledge and their impressions.

Basically, the Greek language is nothing more than an **assemblage** of tiny symbols or distinct characters; and then, the combination of these would then "form" and constitute the word, and the word **associating** itself with the sound, and the sound calling-up in the mind the idea intended to be impressed.

Philosophically, it can be stated - the purpose of the sense of hearing is to **receive** an **impression** or mental picture which was derived from sounds. Hearing a sound creates a picture or impression upon the mind, which then, **correspond** or correlates to the impression which that particular sound gave, which had come from a word, object, or substance, or through the sense of vision.

There is another distinct nation who would **form** their own language, this was the **Hebrew**. They were somewhat like the Greeks and developed a distinct language or style of expression which had originated from their hereditary and local custom of verbal conversation. And then in succession and basically in a similar manner another language would have its origin and develop and promote the formation of a nation, and this is the **Latin**.

Attention is now turned to the aboriginal inhabitants of **America**. Their original form of expression had been absorbed into them from the early form of expressions of their Asian ancestors, but this form was imperfect, and had no system of grammatical rules to govern the sound, the gesture, or the representation, they desired to express. So in time they **formed** a class of **sounds** into **figures**, which figure they would mark upon trees, bark, stones, and other suitable materials.

At a later time these peculiar figure representations would become useless and the inhabitants subsequently abandoned the use of them – instead began the successful **invention** of more minute characters. And it would be from these characters, (which originated from an undeveloped intellect and imperfect faculties of individualization), they formed into compound expressions, and are illustrated and seen in the present **polysyllabic speech** of the American Indians.

The Indian tribes accumulate many of these minute figures into an **enormous** compound-expression just to convey a single thought to the mind – while at the same time, one of the **parts** of these compounds **would-not** convey any thought or represent anything to their own mind or any other mind.

In contrast to the language of these Americans, every character of the Chinese language is a substantial representative of a thought, and in this way the Chinese language is composed only of monosyllabic characters;

while the Greek, Hebrew, and Latin, all employ compound figures, letters, or characters, to write or to express a thought, which are different from those employed by either of the other nations.

All this information is to give proof that the **external expression** of thought, feelings, and sentiment, had first **originated** in the natural and basic combinations of gestures and sounds of the primitive inhabitants. And most important, it was those **primitives** who would **retain** within their **minds** the **mythological stories** that had originated from the ancestors. And in spite of early man being socially disunited and entirely separated from each other, they still were able to maintained that traditional early tribal **connection**, and it would be from them **originated** the various dissimilar modes of expression that now prevail in the earth.

Primitive history is **not-able** to give a reliable explanation of the development of language in any of the nations of primitive inhabitants existing on the earth **prior-to** the confirmation of those records of the inhabitants of **China**. Never-the-less, it was once **supposed** by some, that the Greek was the first tongue spoken, and this is because all the sacred writings originally being in possession of the Jews were all written in the Greek language. And then after this, there came the Jewish writings in Hebrew; then afterward, these were translated into Latin, and then in sequence, into the Indo-European and English and Spanish languages.

The evidence and conclusions made by modern philologists and linguists who have worked diligently and have searched profoundly into the subject of the origin of hieroglyphs, have stated that hieroglyphs were originally intended as alphabetical representations and were not used separately to convey thoughts. However this is not true. Instead, the best method to understand the use of hieroglyphs is, to know that hieroglyphics **did express** substantial thoughts in the earlier ages; **but**, afterward they assumed the form of alphabetical representations or letters, this occurred because at the later time they became more useful that way, and these writings or hieroglyphs are nothing more than an early form of synthetical or compound forms of expression.

In **review**, it has been made plain that **language** is an external and artificial **invention**, and is nothing more than a hieroglyphical mode of expressing sounds by using compound signs. And there was a fairly easy transformation from the first minute characters of hieroglyphic expressions, then turning them into letters or characters of an alphabet. The letters of an alphabet began to be used as letters of a word simply for their ability to convey distinct sounds or various dissimilar sounds. But before this event became rooted, letters at first were the words themselves; and so this basic use of letters to mean words **was-required** to first occur, before there was the progression to the formation of words from combining letters; but since then,whenever alphabetic letters are conjoined they constitute a syllable or word, and the word then can convey a single or compound idea by the particular sound which is associated in the mind with the thought.

Whether it is verbal language, physical signs, or hieroglyphical expressions, they all are man-made, external, superficial, devices which have basically become **deceptive** and are injurious to the human race. The various languages and multiple dialects of all the various nations of the earth at this historical period of mankind, have all arisen entirely as a consequence of the **misdirection** of man's faculties of perception and judgment, and in a tragic and sad manner have burdened the ignorant and undeveloped minds of the human species. However language is directly connected to thoughts and is totally inseparable from the origin of thoughts.

# Section 87

Thoughts need language, because without language it is extremely difficult to share one's thoughts. Language is especially useful and necessary whenever the subject matter involves the flow of complex thoughts, because these may require sentences to express. The mind needs and uses language as a means - to externally express its thoughts outward into the material world. So without verbal and written language there would not be much progress in mankind's development of their interior attributes.

From the beginning moments of man's first existence, mankind has **instinctively** and **inherently** progressed in their development as a special being, and so mankind is compelled to improve upon the **necessary** tools and methods of their development, and this this fact is the reason why man will always attempt to **refine** their manner of communication. **However**, even though language is inseparably connected with the origin of thoughts, language **did-not** develop first. Thoughts came first, and language followed as a consequence; language is only one of the tools necessary for communicating those thoughts.

It has been explained that those **earliest thoughts** originating from the undeveloped minds of ignorant mankind, have been **mistakenly** interpreted and then **assumed** to have meaningful information. This error in judgment has cause many problems to develop, all because those primitive thoughts and beliefs were believed as fact, **were-sustained** and given a **false identity**, and were improperly interpreted.

Future generations began to believe these **imagined myths** possessed some great significance, and a reverence was attached to them, and soon a huge mass of humanity believe that these imaginary thoughts coming from the minds of prehistoric man are sacred and holy. Yet it is **solely** from this activity and mis-interpretation that **misery** has plagued all societies and this continues in the present; billions of people have suffered during this time-period, - all **resulting** from the profound ignorance of man; then the continued use of these beliefs caused hatred, sectarianism, fanaticism, and sustain imbeciles in positions of power.

**Superstition** has inspired many chieftains with the spirit of tyranny and despotic behavior, and has sustained monarchs, elevated theological shepherds, and plunged the ignorant inhabitants of earth into the lowest depths of poverty, mental darkness, imbecility, and fanaticism.

The early humans **are-not** to be blamed in any manner for this misery, because it is **not-by** fault that myths were initially believed to be truth - there was no intent to do harm, no deviousness, and no conspiracy. Instead blame those humans **who-sustained** the mythological superstitions in a fanatical manner, and furthermore blame should be laid upon the shoulders of the silly, foolish, and **ignorant masses** of lost human beings who continue to sustain and to put their "faith" into mythological superstitions and imaginary events.

If the **only-source** of information concerning early human existence is from the "primitive history", and it has been discovered these teachings are known to be in **error** then **how** will man know of his history? And further, if this is the only source of early history, then, every theory pertaining to man's origin can **only-be** speculation.

Anyone trying to research man's origins will be **limited** and their research may seem entirely hopeless, and at times they have been left **wondering** whether truth will ever be known.

Men **have-only** been able to trace his origins using the **external** of the present order of creation of things and only those things which have existed in the interior of the world's history; therefore man's current history of the world, his ideas of the various sciences, and theology, are all understood **only** in the light of superficial evidence.

It is **impossible** for men to **descend** into the interior of his early history or into the history of the world to obtain the knowledge of things which are being revealed in this story. There are no time-machines.

AJ Davis, by the use of hypnosis **was-able** to descend into the interior of all things and arrive at the Germ or beginning of things, and was able to obtain a clear picture of things. Davis possessed a rare and special ability to "see" the past. This same ability has also been used by other men and women and instances of prophecy, dream interpretation, clairvoyance, visions, "seers", and more, have occurred **often-enough** throughout history, that further **investigation** is called for. A great deal of relevant information and data has already been obtained by clairvoyants. And a great deal of information concerning the origin and purpose of man is now available from multiple sources.

What is clairvoyance? Simply, clear-vision. Clear vision what! Clear vision **into** the **realm** of the interior of things and vision into the realm of mind; something akin to meditation. Meditation is the act of listening to God, where praying is the act of talking to God. Those special beings who have developed the ability for deep and spiritual meditation have revealed that man is a Spiritual Being.

The time for mankind's further awakening has finally arrived. Mankind are rapidly developing an awareness of their **inward-nature** and **real realities** which are becoming more evident; nearly the whole race of man is beginning to have a clear understanding and knowledge into the workings of Nature and the Universe. Clear vision is necessary to reveal mankind's potential. The development of clairvoyant abilities is an **indication** of the future abilities of man which are currently undeveloped and now sleeping. Realize that there is a **close-relationship** between a true **prophet** and a **clairvoyant**, and in some instance a true clairvoyant is the same as a true prophet, and both are used by mankind for spiritual development.

In review, it is learned that the visual **impressions** coming from clairvoyance are able to **lift** the veil of obscurity which **has-been** hiding the events of mankind's early beginnings; these clairvoyant impressions and images have also **exposed** man's downfall. These visual impressions give clear vision into the external, superficial, and mythical sheathings which are covering and hiding the real reality, the real truth of man's purpose, and now they are exposed for what they are.

The reader is encouraged to investigate the **source** from which clairvoyant impressions flow by reading the following. - It is first **necessary** to unfold, lay-out, and explain, the nature of the clairvoyant impressions. Clairvoyants have abilities both innate and natural, or they can be developed. And it is by the action of meditation with which they are able to descend to the **germ** of human existence. And then from this germ or this beginning, clairvoyants are then able to proceed an **explain** the "successive waves of development" which were being experienced in each age and generation. This is no joke, and these abilities have been tested, proven, and documented. One needs to realize, that when remarks are given through clairvoyant means, they may **differ** from those of **pre-established** doctrines of most systems of religion, sometimes they differ with present scientific knowledge; realize this occurs because theological investigators and scientists are **not-able** to descend to the germ of mankind's beginnings as clairvoyance can, they **can-not** descend into the interior of the early history of the world in order to obtain the knowledge of the things which can easily be obtained from clairvoyance. The works of theological investigators are **limited**, they are always ambiguous and indefinite in their nature. The **vagueness** of all theology occurs because, as was stated, the only source of knowledge which these investigators have, originates in error of the superstitious and mythological imaginations of an ignorant and undeveloped prehistorical mankind.

Superstition has inspired kings, chieftains, and it has sustained potentates, it has in error elevated theological shepherds while at the same time has plunged the ignorant and uninformed inhabitants of the earth into the lowest depths of poverty, mental darkness, imbecility, and fanaticism.

These men have gained their power by presenting to the ignorant masses a diverse mixture of about five parts error and three parts truth. However in some ways these men deserve great respect, because, in spite of their profoundly misdirected intellects, they were doing the best they knew how.

Understand, that the **spiritual elements** laying dormant **within man** have-not even yet unfolded their gentle teachings to the majority of human beings.

# Section 88

The Birth of Mythological Theology.

**Theology**: is the study of the nature of God, and usually the topic includes religious beliefs. It is a thing, that has been **systematically** developed into a set of religious theories. Modern theology still is based upon the **mythology** of primitive man. It is obvious that theology in general has been obscuring the path to any high and pure principles that may come from the internal nature of man. And theology is blocking mankind's spiritual development. This particular fact can be observed operating in modern man, whom has nearly lost completely the pure natural morality which dwells in the inner being. Most of mankind, are lost in senseless ambitions, separatism, and absolute fanaticism.

**A myth**: is a traditional story that generally concerns the early history of mankind; and usually within the context of this mythical story there may be found that the **intent** of the myth was to explain events which occurred or most-likely an **attempt** to convey something at a time when there was **no**-language.

The myth stories which did survive, were contained in the **memories** in earliest of man's undeveloped mind, were **passed-on** to succeeding generations by the action of **traditionally** story-telling, doing this by using vocal sounds and body gestures. This crude method was used during each new generation over the course of tens of thousands of years, **until** man's first forms of **writing** had surfaced, at which-time those mythical "tall-tales" were finally **recorded** in written form in the "primitive histories" of man, and now, **in error**, those modified traditionally stories are believed as factual. A traditional myth story was often **concerned** with some previous event or phenomenon, and the story **usually involves** tales of **strange beings**, or strange events, or strange animal. The whole myth story could-be an **entirely imaginary** thing and usually were; yet, these stories **somehow** continue to attract people's attention, and some people may still believed the story as true even though many others around them know for sure that it is false.

**Mythology**: which is the **collection** of myths relating to a topic, such as religious myths or even cultural myths. An important aspect of this collection of imaginary stories is that in many cases these myths were personal experiences and originally **only-meant** to be a particular individual's personal story, or possibly the myth story was an attempt to explain a circumstance which occurred, but then, the act or action of sharing the myth, had allowed it to be developed **mistakenly**. The act of sharing or transferring a opinion, a vision, or a thought, or an event, or dreams, or an idea, or anything, from one person to another person in a manual manner through gestures, or vocal sounds, or even words, is, as everyone knows, absolutely **impossible**.

It is absolutely **impossible** for a story to be passed-on from person to person this way without error. So it is fairly easy to understand what has happened, the fact is, when someone had only **intended** to describe an event or something to another person, the description was afterward **in-error collected** as a set of stories and were afterward **in-error** believed to be true. Then, to compound this error issue even more, these incidental stories were usually **altered** in some fashion afterward, sometimes by a **seemingly** innocent addition into the story of a new person, or a new thing, or some mystical being, and these modified additions **becoming combined** mistakenly into the text of the story, which then changed the meaning of the story. And now think about this, these same collections or combinations of mythical stories still can be **seen**, even **today**, and they are especially found as the foundation of nearly every religion. And just to reiterate the point, as has been stated repeatedly, - many of the mankind's mythological stories which had originated with primitive mankind, have been **perpetuated** into the twenty-first century.

Man's theology is based on error because of its **inability** to find truth which has been buried in mythology. Theology has lost its footings, and has in-turn actually become the **cause** of suffering, with theology being at the forefront of the **destruction** of nearly all elements of **truth** and natural morality within man. This **loss** of **morality** then, fuels the force driving men into bazaar natures of vice, folly, and a disunity of interests and separatism and has force mankind to live the consequence of absolute misery.

At some future time in mankind's development they will need to reap what was sown. So for the sake of humanity there is a dire need to get to the **root causes** of man's stumble-into misdirected morality. However, the process of rooting-out the cause is difficult, and the mind **must-be** open and **receptive** to be able to find truth, because one thing needs to be compared to another. Once the mind is open and ready, then the root causes can be inspected. The find the root cause of man's misfortune there is a need to understand and **define exactly** what theology teaches.

The Greek word Theos signifies the same thing that the Latin word Deus implies, and both these words were **intended** to represent the supreme moving Spirit that pervades the Universe, whom we call God.

The Greek Theos, and Latin Deus, are both words derived from **sounds** that the sounds themselves had no real meaning or significance. The origin of both of these "word forms" are **impure** and they have no value to modern understanding, so basically, they are useless. These two particular words are good examples of how words can have **injurious tendencies**, because they have been **mistakenly developed** from early man's vocal or written expression. Therefore, associate no lofty thoughts of an everlasting spirit, nor should any element of veneration be placed on the words Deus nor Theos. Truth is, there **never-was** a sound formed or a word uttered which could convey even the slightest conception of that all-pervading essence, that great spiritual principle, that Great Positive Omnipotent Mind of God.

Recall from a previous section, that initially, the early family of man dwelt peacefully with each other being in total harmony and united as a tribe. At that period, in social situations, they communicated with each other by observing the **natural language** of the principles within mankind. It was mostly by the use of motions, animated gestures, figures, and different configurations of their face and body or countenance, with-which early mankind were able to express their true feelings and thoughts in a non-verbal manner.

But as previously mentioned, it was when mankind began to **discover** their ability to produce vocal sounds and they were able have dialect; and later that evening, they were wooppin' and yellin' all through the night. Man took full advantage of this wonderful discovery and began communicating their thoughts by using these sounds exclusively, and **not using** their countenances as they previously did. It was because of the crudeness of those sounds, individuals **did-not** have the intelligence to understand these sounds. This caused a great deal of confusion and distrust, the inhabitants began to **wonder** what or who was **causing** such **evil**.

As is now known, the use of sounds for communication caused so much confusion, jealousy, anger, hatred, deception, cruelty, and frustration, that the disunity became so great among the inhabitants, they become **socially miserable**. No one was mentally advanced enough to find the cause of the misery, **except one**. And as this true story goes: so, once upon a time in mankind's distant past, there was **one** particular **individual** whose mind was more advanced and somehow **more intelligent** than the rest of his tribe. This self proclaimed intellect, had indicated and proclaimed to the tribe that **he-had** made a **discovery** of the **cause** of this **source** of **evil** effecting man, and he **convinced** his tribal relations, that **he-alone** had discovered this cause. This more intelligent man **did-not** reveal that his source was imaginary and fabricated within his own mind. And it would be from this period forward, **he-now** would be looked-upon and viewed by all his extensive relations and family as an "**inspired chieftain**".

What he had imagined and describe to his tribe, was that he had discovered that it was the "**breaths**' or winds, which came from above and which "had breathed among them a **malignant element**" which was **causing** all the confusion; and this act was the **first conception** of, and is the **origin** of **evil**.

At that period in time people were so ignorant, uneducated, idiotic, and fearful, that they would believe anything and everything that this **supposed** inspired chieftain communicated to them; and his word became their law. He gained control because he the inspired chieftain was the **most intelligent** among them, and so, his opinions were "kept" and **believed** among all the peoples existing, for many ages.

And at a later time, as mankind began to disperse to other lands, because of the disunity among them, these undeveloped, confused, and wandering, tribes went on their way exploring and emigrating to inhabit other lands, and **in-error** sustained **this belief** that the "breaths were evil". Believing the "breaths" or winds as evil is the belief the early inhabitants of earth **carried** with them in their minds. These people were completely unaware that the "winds" were just normal atmospheric mechanisms and other such disturbances that naturally occurred. They **did-not** have an inner awareness of themselves and **did-not** realize that the evil was in their minds. And instead, they believed the "evil" which was among them, must have come from something external, and so they **blamed** the "breaths" or winds to be the cause of this evil disunity.

Once the original family nation became divided and living separate, and after they had over time established **other settlements** in different lands and different continents, **some** individuals from those separated nations had **advanced** some within their intellects, and these more advanced minds started to **question** the reason for the "breaths" and they wanted more information concerning these evil winds.

These youthful and more advanced minds began to search further into their thoughts, and in their minds the question was to **inquired** for the **cause** of these "breaths". Some minds had **supposed** that there existed an "**unseen**" and undefinable **evil spirit** which was hovering over the landscape, and was living over this **disk** which man dwelt-upon, and now (still ignorant) they interpreted **incorrectly** that the **atmosphere** was an evil spirit. Well now, this definitely was an incorrect assumption, **but** it also **would-be** a progression and another **one step** advance forward in the overall intelligence of mankind. This forward-step would also be an advance in man's existing **theology**.

Next, in the generations that would follow, our early ancestors would continue advancing somewhat, but because of ignorance, most tribes were increasingly plagued with wars, envy, and deception. Yet in spite of the continued social disunity and selfish behaviors, this generation's more advanced thinking led them to finally **abandon** the original "impression" or belief system, given to them by their ancestors. Within a short time they had **stopped** blaming the atmosphere as the cause of evil, because it did not make sense to them anymore. And rising up out from the group a **philosopher** among them attempted to demonstrate his thoughts by drawing **hieroglyphical illustrations**, explaining that the **Sun** was the face of an angry, unholy, and evil-disseminating Being. And it was this **evil Being**, that had **caused** the atmosphere to breathe this evil into their minds.

So now, it would be this **philosopher** whom the inhabitants began to honor and respect, adorning him as the **inspired son** of previous generations. He was now viewed as a powerful man, and members of the tribe actually began to fear his presence, trembling at the images he "shadowed forth" and had expressed in **hieroglyphical characters**; so they fell before him with all the expressions of veneration, "for he had discovered their great enemy", he had discovered their fiery deus, their angry and consuming enemy. He **taught** his followers that this powerful Being, would consume their bodies and swallow up their spirits, pulling them into the invisible envelope that surrounded the globe on which they all lived. And he taught them this would all happen, except, were it not for his almost god-like **presence** among them!

His multitude of worshiper's built a large and massive edifice, with apartments constructed to his will, and elevated him to the highest seat in this temple. He became chieftain, prophet, emperor, and god, of all those nations and tribes within his circle of influence.

Somewhere in the historical writings of man, there is found a passage which **truly-applies** to these early and undeveloped inhabitants being discussed, and just as appropriately, this ancient passage applies to the people of our own modern times, saying, *"The priests bear rule, and the people love to have it so"*.

# Section 89

It is interesting how some tribes, individuals, or groups of man had mentally advance much further than the rest of earth's population. Actually, these same advanced nations were developing the ability of mechanical construction, and had invented simple tools to aid them with their work; and from the ingenuity of these inventions, the degree of progression their minds had been developing could be known. And so, it was those particular nations which existed in Central America and Pompeii (#1), that had become **united** socially, and advanced enough where they were able to construct large cities containing elegant mansions, majestic edifices, and lofty temples. It was by these southern nation's rapidly advancing minds, and from their mechanical abilities, combined with their primitive yet ingenious tools, which had allowed for such growth and progress. These nations had advanced enough that they **domesticated** some animal, and were using **camels** and other animals for assistance. What is amazing and significantly stands-out about these more advanced humans, is that their buildings and monuments would represent their thoughts.

After a passage of time, these craftsman had further developed their skills in building, now perfecting them to an even higher level, to where now, nearly all buildings and structures were **built** to **represent** a desire, and specifically, it would be a **desire** that their **supreme potentate** had disclosed to them; and which he further described to them, all represented various foods, animals, vegetables, birds, etc. So, one building would be built to represent the external form of a delicious fruit which was available to the them and which they admired; and so, when anyone desired this fruit, they would point to its representative, the building or structure.

Formal and complex buildings were constructed so that they represented the **precise** theological impressions of those people. And so their lofty and aspiring temples were constructed to correspond to, and also to represent, the inconceivable and "**consuming vengeance** of the **Sun**", which was the "Being" they feared and hated.

This was the **first hint** of hieroglyphical language, this is said because the cities themselves, including all of the cities buildings would represent their history. Not only their history, but the building and city was also their **system** and **creed**, and of course it was their language. Everything was constructed to represent some external object or some conception of the mind. And so, from all of this information which was just given, has **shown** some early **developments** in the areas of **theology** and **language** as it was originally developed with the original inhabitants of Central America and Pompeii (#1).

The high governor and chieftain of these southern people **contemplated** in his mind **secretly**, and had thoughts of a possible **plan**, which this chieftain had devised, for this reason - "to conceive of the resting-place of the sun, their deity", and in his mind he began to **improve** on the long-established **opinion**. He devised the plan first in his mind, then finally he expressed to his tribe, that he had made a **discovery** about their deity the sun. He explained his **new impression** and discovery, that now the Sun was **merely** a representative of an inconceivable "fountain of fire", which existed in the realms existing below the huge animal on whose back, he said they dwelt.

This new and more complex belief of the Sun - only being a representative of the fountain of fire would remain for ages. However it would be in succeeding ages, that the opinion and belief was now **confirmed** in the following hieroglyph form, saying: - *"That the sun arose after the spirit of darkness had passed away, and that the sun was a representative to them during many hours, of the great fountain of fire from which it sprang, and where into the depths of, - those inhabitants must inevitably descend, if they did not* **obey** *all the mandates and requirements of their potential governor".*

After having spoken to them in such fiery language, those crude ignorant masses of mankind believed his new story to be true, and now understood that the **Sun** descended into the **abyss** to become re-clothed with the fiery contents; **then**, on each succeeding day, the Sun rises and the evil contents will be able to be disperse among the inhabitants again; and so, now their new belief that the atmosphere, the heat, the invisible spirit or "breaths", would proclaimed to them with each appearance of the Sun – all the doom and inevitable destruction that would occur, forever, if they **dared** to even once, violate any commands which this cruel and oppressive potentate had given, they would be consumed.

In a general sense it can be understood that as intelligence within man advanced, also in general mankind knew more, it then **became-necessary** for the chieftain to **hide** the face of **evil** from view, in order for the potentate to **maintain power** and control over the ignorant masses.

It was in this particular period that the more advanced individuals of man within this Southern nation, had for the first time, questioned some aspects of the first beliefs, of the "breaths" and changed evil to now exist in the sun; so now that man had advance even more, it **became necessary** for the potentate/chieftain to remove the face of evil from the sun, and to now move the blame for evil to some hidden, remote, imaginary, and inconceivable **realm below**, - to a safe hiding place where human eyes and human knowledge could not possibly demonstrate or prove evil's non-existence. Besides, the Sun was too plain an object to continue solely as it had done, being the supposed originator of evil.

It was the ruling potentate, who was **sufficiently shrewd** and was educated in the art of **deception**, and who had reasoned within his mind, the possibility that someone would somehow discover the real truth, and this discovery would result in him losing control and power. So now he worried that he may lose his power, and his influence, and his empire ruined, his government overthrown, so he started **scheming** and planning, being impelled by a **desire** for power and control, so he thought of "that plan" where he would **move** the source of evil, shifting the source **down** to the "unseen" place below, to the **abyss**. In this act of selfishness can truly be observed, **the germ of error**, which has been **deposited** in the world by the early inhabitants and this still exists in modern times.

## Section 90

The characters in this story still do not have any names, neither are there names of cities, nor do any of the nations or tribes have names. This period is still the time-period of hieroglyph language and names were not invented yet.

But now the story diverts its attention to describe and give an **overview** of the **mental culture** of the inhabitants of the **interior** of **Asia**, and this includes those tribes existing upon the borders of the **African** continent. The intent is to show in more detail just how these tribes developed their own early belief systems, which was different than that one of Central America.

Recall that the first primitive family originally dwelt in Asia, and also it was from their crude, primitive undeveloped minds which sprang the original imaginary conception of the origin of evil in the "breaths" of the atmosphere. Their story progresses now, describing just how that original and **first mis-interpretation** of the very first mental impression had occurred among those eastern Asia tribes.

After the original primitive family had branched off, those who had **remained** in the interior Asia were not sufficiently developed in their mental faculties, and this lack continued for a very long time; and so because there was no mental growth these minds were not able to improve upon their basic beliefs and they continued to believe the original concepts of the "breaths" or winds were causing all manner of evil.

It was not until a much later generation of these Asian inhabitants would finally **produce** a special **individual** with **a mind** that was more intelligent and developed, who was **mentally capable** of contemplation. As he continued to mature and developed his intelligence, some of his thoughts and teachings concerned an **improved** understanding of the original hereditary impressions, especially concerning the evil spirits that were believed to exist around them. This advanced mind would **develop** a new belief system base upon **imaginary** and mythological beings and situations, which would propel this nation of eastern Asia in an **opposite direction** from that other mythology which was developed by the **European** nations.

Mostly, because of the different theologies between the interior Asians and European nations, and the fact that they each **not-knowing** the others doctrines, so, it would have been absolutely impossible for these nations to commune and exist together. Furthermore, each of these nations had no means of modifying or advancing their own theology. The eastern tribes continued with the doctrine they had originated, even though it was dissimilar and clashed with the subsequent branches of the primitive family.

**Tradition** was the method and **medium** of sharing previous information between each subsequent generation and it had originated by the action of individuals using gestures and sounds to relate their traditional stories (or myths as we know them). The first inhabitants communicated their opinions and experiences, continuing to tell these stories to each succeeding generation, **until** this period of the **individual** from Asia possessing the more advanced mind.

This enlightened mind contemplating, conceived of a **doctrine** or belief in his mind, and he taught these thoughts to the people of his nation. These concepts (he said) "were impressed upon his mind", by "some" **good**-influencing **Spirit**, that dwelt in one of those "breaths"; this new doctrine was in opposition to their forefathers ancient traditions, that had taught and believed that **all** the 'breaths" are of evil. So now with this new doctrine there are **good** and **evil** "breaths".

But a question is, why did a different theology spring-up within this eastern tribe? Simply, it was because of their different social conditions.

Recall, that the original family branch of the eastern Asia, divided itself into three tribes, well, as stated each tribe dwelt in eastern Asia initially. But these three tribes in order, emigrated and separately settled upon locations now occupied by the **Japanese**, **Malayans**, and **Indo-Persians**.

The first of these tribes **journeyed** in the **direction** of the **African** continent, and soon **discovered** a beautiful valley, (which has since been named **Shinar** – see Genesis xi. 2). This tribe of travelers sent messengers back to their kindred tribes, which resulted in those tribes migrating and also journeying to this valley of Shinar, where they soon united into one youthful nation, and dwelt together for many generations in peace and harmony.

A reason for this peace and harmony was that this portion of the earth was very fertile. Many trees yielded a kind of milk that the settlers made use of extensively. They also developed weaving, first by using any of the grass and wood fibers that were available to them. And they devised, constructed, and used hunting implements, and these skilled hunters would often succeeded in slaying certain species of animals, which composed a great portion of their diet. Having their basic needs meet, they now were able to begin to cultivate more of their craftsman faculties and eventually **became expert** in the construction of some very beautiful and delicate things; this craftsmanship can still be observed in the Chinese of today, who still display the perfection of all the delicate, eccentric, and fantastic inventions that were first developed by these Shinar valley peoples.

With improving social conditions there could develop a more perfected degree of mental tranquility, which apparent had become cultivated within these people of Shinar; and sprouting from the peace and tranquility, there resulted higher and **more refined** theological **impressions** among them. And it was under these conditions and was in this valley that, **the mind** of which was spoken put forth a new opinion, which-follows:

" The great waters", he said, "contained the spirit of which your forefathers have spoken. And at that time water alone was existing. The great spirit formed this ground, and also the many things existing about us, and the many gods above us and their grounds, and the grounds that extend further than the great spirit can see. This spirit was then, while existing in the waters, asleep. And they called him **Paramo**. But when he desired to have some living objects to worship him, he awoke from his repose, and **breathed forth** a spirit throughout all the waters, and the **waters moved** from their great depths. And this spirit which moved the waters was called **Narasayana**".

**Nar**, in the original Indian language, means water, and **sayana** signifies power to move; and thus the two joined together mean moving waters.

"In the depths of the waters, he taught them, was created a great egg. This, by the moving of the waters, finally expanded, unfolded its contents, and **formed instantaneously** the ground upon which they lived; thus, he taught them, the world was created".

"Together with the earth, he said the spirit **Vishnu** (which was the second spirit) **created** the human form – which he placed, as their forefathers taught, in a **beautiful garden** abounding with many delicious fruits, and from which went forth a **stream** that was divided into three, corresponding to the great spirits Parama, Narasayana, and Vishnu. He then said that the great spirit left the waters (for the waters had become land), and ascended into realms beyond the extent of their knowledge, and would only make his appearance to **him** (the inspired chieftain), whenever the people would consent to have one of their much-admired females **sacrificed** to his glory".

"The spirit which proceeded from Parama (which was Vishnu) still remained near the earth, and was **not** so **good** a spirit as the spirit who had sent him forth to create man. And the third spirit, or the spirit which dwelt in those "**breaths**" was the most-evil of them all, and was endeavoring to produce an **eternal separation** between the spirit that dwelt within man and the great spirit Parama". And, said he, "it is I who preserves you from the wrath of this spirit. And if you will consent to offer sacrifices, it will assist me to appease his wrath, and you will not sink into the bowels of the earth, were another egg still remains, and were the spirit that produces *these 'breaths', of whom we have been told by our forefathers, shall be compelled to live forever, among the spirits which he has persuaded and captured". Thus, he instructed them, they would live, according to the manner in which they had lived before, either near the throne of Parama, or in this great egg with the spirit which caused their forefathers to become evil by breathing evil into their minds.*

(the truthfulness of this story can be investigated by studying Hesiod, Thales, Pythagoras, and also study the Zend Avesta of Zoroaster, whom Homer quotes often. Read also, the sayings of Xenophon, Socrates, and Plato, and learn from these the demonology of the primitive inhabitants of earth. Also learn from these subsequent modifications of theological idealism, which occurred as a result of intellectual advancement).

# Section 91

Continuing this story, even though this next part will be jumping-ahead in advance of the chronology of the story, this jump is done because it is important to give a brief overview of "the system of **Zoroaster**", because in his story, one may perceive that the **same ideas** (concerning the origin of evil), make-up his story, with the only exception, Zoroaster's account being more thoroughly **systematized** and more clearly expressed.

So this story goes: The great spirit recognized by the eastern tribe under the name of Parama (subsequently termed **Brahma**), is named by Zoroaster, **Ormuzd**. This Being, he taught, was the one who existed in realms beyond the conception of man. This was a **good being** and, connected to him there-were Beings - **constantly** ascending up to and descending from his presence, these, described as **subordinate** good spirits or elohims. These good spirits occupied a sphere or station somewhat beneath Ormuzd. **Below** these elohims still existed another circle of angels or spirits that were still **less good** than those above them. These spirits were the first or lower **elohims**, and those higher and superior ones were **amshaspands**, or angels that were permitted on account of their being superior in goodness to the former ones, - to ascend to the presence of Ormuzd. The latter Being was considered a good spirit, and was "an eternal hater of evil".

In contradistinction to this Being (Ormuzd), Zoroaster in his story had **elevated** the Vishnu and Narasayana spirit of the eastern theologian to a position as lofty and commanding as Ormuzd. Him he named **Ahriman**. He was an **evil spirit**, and "an eternal hater of all goodness". In a sphere or circle beneath this spirit, Zoroaster also placed a legion of **subordinate spirits** – and **also another** sphere of evil spirits beneath these, all placed in groups according to their degree of wickedness.

By the power of Ormuzd, the earth and man were made.

By the power of Ahriman, the world and mankind were **made sinful** and disgusting in the sight of the good spirits: and he also **prevented** the "developing spirit" **within man** from being pure and good as was originally desired by the good Being.

Zoroaster also had **conceived** in his mind that these two beings, each with their mighty hosts, were engaged in a **mighty war**. And he **prophesied** that finally a time would arrive when the wicked spirit and his kingdom would be destroyed forever, and that the world and the race of mankind, would be saved and made good in the sight of Ormuzd, who would be very please that the whole race had become amshaspands or beings whom have overcome evil.

During the time of Zoroaster there was **not-much** advancement in the art of writing or the action of **impressing** their thoughts as hieroglyphs upon external objects, such as bark of trees, rocks, etc. And because of this, Zoroaster could only **teach** his thoughts and opinions **vocally** with sounds and gestures, and these **were-not** written down at this time. It would be later generations of Zoroaster's tribe, who would **confirmed** the truthfulness of Zoroaster's teaching's because they firmly **believed** that Zoroaster was better **skilled** at explaining things and putting forth his ideal conceptions to his brethren in a manner which made sense to them. For many generations after Zoroaster his doctrines would be an advancement for man, because the teachings derived from this oriental theologian's doctrines produced good consequences and more unity for those developing tribes.

So then, it **is-true**, that error **did-begin** with man – **error** began with man because of their **innocence**, their ignorance, and their **un-instructed** faculties. Mankind **did-not** have the necessary skills or mental faculties sufficiently developed to have a perception or even an awareness of the conditions which were necessary and required for their happiness; and because of their **lack** they cultivated **a deceptive**, artificial, and insincere behavior, instead of developing the interior purity and refinement which is **required** of man.

It was from a **small** stream of **error** which had **occurred** within man's **thought** process; then, this human error increased into a vast ocean and the many nations of earth being its tributaries. The **contamination** and sophistication of these **errors** flowed into the great stream of human iniquity. Mean-spirited ignorance, has covered the whole face of the earth, it has washed-away every blossom of peacefulness and then, left in its place only dregs of wretchedness and imbecility. This **small error** has prostrated, destroyed, and desolated nations; it has consumed and swallowed up the principles of morality and refinement that are part of man and which **belong** to man by nature.

From a **review** of the things being revealed and discussed, it can be **clearly-seen** that the **origin** of **evil** was truly seated in "the errors of human association", and **was-not** in those breaths, winds, spirits, gods, demons, or supreme potentates, whom man has been blaming and **falsely accusing** from the beginning, and continuing into our present time.

It was near the time-period of the middle of the **fourth** generation, this nation **became divided**, caused by their inability to socialize. One tribe journeyed to the east and located where **China** (#1) is now; a second tribe journeyed to the **east of Asia** (#2); and a third tribe proceeded to where **Egypt** (#3) is now located; and the **remainder** (#4) of that nation continued as before as the original family of Shinar.

It is noteworthy, that the **theology system** that was followed by the **southern European** nation and also followed by **these tribes**, continued for quite some time, remaining nearly the same until the period of time when, the **event** in the physical history of earth occurred, which is known as **the deluge**.

## Section 92

In this period of time of man's development, **the Deluge** or flood is about to occur; **but**, before describing the pending deluge, there should first be given some **recognition** and acknowledge to the **writer** of the book of **Genesis** and thanking him (or them), for expressing to all the many people that read it, a **distinct** and **truthful history** of all early traditional theology and any of mythological impressions which were given and sustained.

And so, at this particular place within our story, in the investigation into the origin of mankind, a significant **overview** concerning the **origin** of some of the sayings in the "**primitive history**" is necessary and these all will be reviewed, investigated, and then commented upon. As has been stated previously, **reviews** are given so that this complex and interwoven story may be properly revealed.

The book of Genesis was **written** by the **Jews** in Persia, however this period **was-not** the Babylonian captivity of the Jews, but **instead** this small tribe was a **prior existing** and smaller **branch** of a tribe of Jews, whom were **held** in **captivity** in Persia, but this event occurred a long time before the actual Babylonian captivity occurred.

Importantly concerning the book of Genesis, it is noticed that the written accounts contained in Genesis are exceedingly **truthful**, and they present a general reflection of the **theology** of the **Persians**, as it was received from their traditional history, which was by then arranged and made into a system by Zoroaster. **However**, there is no known record of these Jews in captivity in this period.

In order to show the **parallelism** which exists between the early conceptions of the chieftain of the eastern tribe (Shinar valley) Zoroaster, and the ultimate generalization of the same account which was written by the Jews and contained in the first chapter of Genesis. It is necessary to compare them side-by-side and topic by topic.

Now recall from previous section of our story, of the method-how that particular Shinar chieftain with the advance mind, had proclaimed to his people that the spirit of **Parama** dwelt in the great waters, and had, been reposed there for many ages. In **parallel** to that passage, corresponds the passage in the "primitive history" (Genesis), which reads as follows: *"and the earth was without form and void, and darkness was upon the face of the deep; and the Spirit of **God** moved upon the face of the waters"*.

Next, it would be the eastern philosopher that initially said *"**Brahma** breathed forth a spirit"*, which was Narasayanna which meaning moving waters. And then as a **parallel** in Genesis, the passage which reads, *"and darkness was upon the face of the deep",* was derived from the passage in the **Sanskrit** language, which reads, *"And Brahma was within the great waters and was asleep"* (the word asleep being rendered darkness in the other passage).

Next in the eastern mythology the account continues, *"and Brahma move off the waters, and the **egg** formed the grounds and the breaths"*; while in its **connection** with the primitive history it is related in this manner: *"In the beginning God (meaning Brahma) created the heaven and the earth."* - the word Heaven is in the Sanskrit language, rendered "breaths": in the **Hebrew**, "shemayim" - meaning the atmosphere.

And further, according to the Sanskrit version of the eastern myth, "the spirit" which was sleeping (meaning darkness) *"left, the waters, and then light appeared: and Brahma saw that it was good".*

Furthermore, this chieftain of the east, whom **had-retained** these early impressions and early thoughts of the race of man, which had come to him by **traditional stories** having been passed-on through the previous generations, and these stories **had-been** given in an imperfect manner, because of man's general ignorance and so these stories had been modified. So this chieftain, **having-lost** a part of the true original impression (concerning the condition of the early inhabitants), he instead, related and expressed his own modified account of his deity's creation, but doing so in a **modified form** and now expressing the story much **differently** than the story was originally received by Zoroaster.

And, as the chieftain is giving the story, **somehow** the following thoughts **came-to** his mind and he expanded the original traditional story, saying: - That after Parama had moved the waters, and the spirits had brought forth the world, by the development of the qualities of the egg; they, at the same time, **formed man** and located him in a beautiful and fertile place, according to the knowledge they had of their forefather's history: and then he **appealed** to the the **level** of knowledge then existing in the minds of that generation, and he spoke to them concerning their forefathers, which **confirmed** in their minds that this chieftain must be truthful.

And now the **same account** given within the "primitive history" merely **reveals** that the scribe or writer of Genesis had made an addition and had-written in a change, from the crude and particular manner in which the eastern chieftain had related his theory, - into that of a more general description he gave in Genesis – which is as follows: *"Let us make "man"* (us - meaning Brahma and Vishnu, the good and the subordinate spirit)".

*"So God made man, and breathed into his nostrils the breath of life, and man became a living soul".*

This same event is depicted from the eastern mythology into the Sanskrit language in the following manner: *"With the earth, man was formed; and the 'breaths' awoke him, and he was evil".*

Genesis, *"and God planted a garden, and placed in it the man whom he had created".* This then, is rendered in the Sanskrit language from the tradition of this eastern nation, *"and he* (meaning man) *was placed on a portion of the ground where grew trees, and flowers, and delicious fruits; which made our fathers happy and pleased the great spirit Brahma".*

Next, the "primitive history" tells and relates that, *"God saw that it was not good for man to be alone. So He caused a deep sleep to fall upon* **Adam***, and took one of his ribs, and closed up the flesh instead thereof. And of the rib made He, a woman, and gave her unto the man".* Well this same expression is described by the eastern chieftain, who had taught in the following manner, and also in this manner it is written in the Sanskrit: *"And while their fathers were pleased with the beauty of the good spirit about them, they felt lonely; and while they felt thus, Parama caused them to be asleep. And while they were "still" as the great waters, the good spirit sent them from his hand, a weaker number of mothers and other brethren. And the good spirit caused the fathers to awake: and they beheld each other, and our fathers loved them. And then they lived together, one with another: and the good spirit Parama was pleased".*

Returning now back on track with our story of the developing tribes of east Asia given in a previous description, which told the story concerning the very original human family and show how they were involved in the story of Genesis: - Recall, that there were two separate families of original humans, and these two tribes or families had develop in separate locations without knowledge or awareness of each others existence. The human people of one tribe being matured, strong, and gigantically constituted, these were **called** by the eastern chieftain *"their fathers"*. These were of the "original tribe" and these were in eastern Asia. And the other separate tribe was imperfectly-constructed and more effeminate species of first humans and was a weaker tribe; and they ultimately were the ones whom had discovered the more-matured tribe, and the two became **co-joined** as one family.

From that original combination of two tribes or first family, **sprang-all** the first human "impressions" and thoughts of traditional mythology and imaginary beliefs, which the eastern chieftain received; then, it was from these first impression, the chieftain **improved upon,** and established his theology, **until** it became established at a later time period into the

**Sanskrit** language, and then into **Prakrit** and **Magadhi**, the rudiments of these, then, enter into the **Indo-Chinese** language. Then, but also from the **same common source** as the Indo-Chinese came the rudiments of the **Greek**; and at which time the **Hebrew** was almost as perfectly established – and the **Latin** also was developing.

It becomes clear that these ancient traditional demonological thoughts and impressions, based upon mythologies, which then, had been preserved as "characters" or hieroglyphs, and which then, are directly connect and continue up to the establishment of the Sanskrit language – then these were translated into the Greek by some of the original tribes whom would become the **Germanic** nation – and these Greek Germanic translations **fell-into** the possession of the Jews – were compiled and transcribed into Hebrew – and these Hebrew copies **then-were** carried by a detached potion of a tribe into the Persian kingdom – remained there for several centuries, until Zoroaster finally systematizes the **crude theology** of the original manuscripts, and which was the **prevailing** theology among other nations as well as the Persians. And then it was by the Persian army besieging some parts of the Jewish nation, which terminated the Jews freedom, by the sacrifice of their liberty, and they **were-held** under the Persian government in captivity (not Babylonian captivity). At this time, the Jews re-transcribed the contents of these manuscripts into Hebrew, and carried these with them at the expiration of their term of bondage. Then the Greek **received** it from the Hebrew; and the Latin from the Greek; and the English from the Latin.

So the "primitive history" that is known in the modern world as the story of Creation, should be very deeply **respected** for the truthfulness it has preserved in its relationship with original oriental traditions, mythology, and theology, especially considering that, it has been transferred from one generation to another; that, some passages have been altered and others remove completely; that, there has been some imperfect compilation; and most important is the fact that, so **many** interested persons over the ages have been engaged in handing it down, in the manner described, to each subsequent generation up to the present! However both the original "primitive history" and the Biblical story of Creation are allegorical, mythological, and imaginary, traditional stories.

## Section 93

Having ascended up the rungs of hagiographical and archaeological ladders, concerning the history of the early tribes of mankind and now having **describe-how** mankind has formed their language, their writing, and finally their religious beliefs, the story **has-again** spiraled-around and has come to the time-period, when "the event" occurred. This is a major event in the physical history of the earth, commonly known as the **Flood** or Deluge was a great geological catastrophe.

At this present time, **just-before** the catastrophic occurrence of the deluge, there are existing the following **beliefs** among the inhabitants of earth: first of all there are the primitive ideas of the inhabitants of southern Europe and of South America with their progressive modifications of the original "breaths" being evil, then the Sun, then the Abyss. And then, the story of creation as given in a previous overview, pertaining to the conditions and progress of the early tribes of the Asiatic and African continents, which had established a different theology from that of other nations; however, no further important mythological opinions would develop from these nations after the acceptance and establishment of those opinions which were previously spoken. There also was that small nation which inhabited the North American continent, these explorers had only recently arrived upon this land portion just before the occurrence of the Deluge, these people had retained the beliefs of the original family branch from east Asia. So, these were the human inhabitants and their beliefs existing on the earth, **until** the occurrence of the Flood. This catastrophe was a **physical transformation** and for this reason many writers have termed this great earth upheaval as the deluge. The term deluge is taken from the Latin word: diluvio - to overflow, and diluvium - an inundation.

Since the time that this catastrophic event occurred, nearly all people who have learned about this event have then believed that it was a universal submersion of the whole face of earth. Most of these people have **base** their beliefs and opinions upon **superficial evidence**, and they have put a great deal of confidence in that superficial claim. The reason so many people believe this unreal superficial claim of devastation is because they **must-rely** or they do-rely, upon existing history for their knowledge.

And now this belief has been entrenched within the minds of nearly everyone; and because this event is believed by many to be a fact, - in response to this belief, there have been many people who have expended a great deal of their energy, using any powers, faculties, and resources, available to them, in **attempts** to **promote** and **expand** this **misconception**, because of the great expenditure these present people are acting as if it were of divine truth that was told them.

Heroically, there are other people, such as scientists, whose minds having become dissatisfied with the early mythological impressions, imaginary thoughts, and unreal philosophy of primitive man, and these scientific minds have **discarded** the superficial history, and have proceeded to investigate the **natural operations** of all physical laws and principles of the Universe. And these minds have discovered that a universal inundation was a physical impossibility: first-off, the atmospheric envelope **would-not** sustain watery vapor (rain) in sufficient quantity to cover the whole earth, and secondly, geological investigations have given great evidence, which is against such a possibility. Besides, there is no substantial reason why a universal deluge should occur in the first place. It would be **unreasonable** to suppose that Nature, has put forth her efforts to produce the highest type of physical organization, which is man. And why would Nature, after using her operations of unchanging laws, which include Her living and divine essences and her unchanging obedience to the great Positive Mind of God, first do all this creating – and then, after having created all things, sweep them out of existence?

Another topic is that some people have **claimed** that the purpose of the deluge was to punish man for his imperfections. **But** man like Nature, is **not-accountable** for his ignorance, at least not in a manner which would indicate he needs to be punished. These imperfections and errors of man, all had occurred as might be expected, and all **sprang** as a **necessity**, coming from mankind's uncultivated social and moral situation. And if these imperfections were viewed with God's plan of evolution in mind, then these imperfections of man are what **has-aided** mankind in their journey to perfection, doing this action, by **allowing** mankind to properly **know** and appreciate, purity and perfection. It is by trials and tribulations and it is **through** the imperfections of mankind that they **may-obtain** instruction and be induced to press-onward; to continue to unfold the organization of a more truthful physical condition; and to continue upward to the attainment of a higher spirituality and soul growth.

So now, moving forward in our investigation of the **cause** of the deluge, first **realize**, that there **are-no** physical and moral evidences, which point to mankind as being the cause of a deluge.

Make men love truth by causing their interest to correspond to truth, and then truth will be received by a natural influx from their superior situation. Men need not criticize each others thoughts, especially if they are using existing frivolous and superficial judgments. Instead, just present pure truth in all its native simplicity, and leave error and all its depressing influences existing in the physical and mental world to themselves. Because it is said, that the best antidote for error, is the presentation of the truth. And it is said that the truth sets us free.

# Section 94

Before continuing the discussion concerning the differing opinions of whether or whether-not the flood was a universal one, there first is a need to give a review of the flood itself then connecting this flood event to information already given concerning man's progress, which follows:

In previous sections, it had been explained how the **formation** of the Pacific ocean, Caribbean sea, Gulf of Mexico, and Guatemala occurred – then continuing and also discussing and confirming that at that particular period, the Atlantic and Mediterranean waters were also formed as they still are today. Also in previous remarks – there was made-mention of **the valley** that had existed within the pacific region and which now forms the bed of the Pacific ocean. And further, the story spoke of the inhabitants that remained after the catastrophe, who inhabited the Sandwich (Hawaii) and Philippine islands; and further discussing the fertile portions of land now known as the West-India islands, and spoke still more, of the portion of land which had sunk and now forms the Mexican gulf, and it was noted, to what extent those tribes had existed all throughout those fertile lands and islands.

Now, with all of the above conditions kept in mind, we will proceed with a discussion which concerns the phenomenon, cause, and result, of the **deluge** which was at this period of earth's history just about to occur.

The **primary** physical **causes** are based upon the chemical transformation of particles in the water and the atmosphere. What happens chemically, is that by evolutionary processes, "inferior substances" of elements and atoms are continually undergoing chemical changes, and then, as these changes in the watery element and atmosphere continue, eventually, it is by these changes which **cause** the **equilibrium** of pressures between the earth's interior forces of magma and the exterior water and atmosphere to **become unbalanced**.

Recall, there were stupendous icebergs that had formed in the Arctic regions. Also, parts of the eastern and western hemispheres were still concealed under water at that period and the land portions of those upper regions were actually in some cases almost sea-beds. Well, here is what occurs in this present catastrophe. The event was **activated** by the loss of equilibrium between the interior and exterior forces, and that, the molten contents of the center of the earth **became excited**, in an inconceivable manner, a similar manner which occurred in previous earth changes.

The Andes, Vesuvius, and the many other relieving vents **were inadequate** to restore the equilibrium. So the voice of the **earthquake** thundered through the bowels of the earth. It was mightier than the mightiest earthquake, and louder than the loudest thunder. It burst forth, and the earth trembled completely to its core. Fire, smoke, mist, and rain, would surround the whole earth.

Those tribes that were existing on the portion of lands intermediate between what are now called the eastern and western hemispheres were nearly all **destroyed**. Those few inhabitants that survived fell stupefied to the ground as if dead.

No words would sufficiently express or be able to describe all the sufferings and exclamations of the surviving remaining inhabitants. And about **three days** would elapse before the equilibrium was finally restored – and by the time the catastrophe had end, the northern land portions of earth had been elevated and other portions depressed and sunken. The water rushed from its former regions and filled valleys which had previously been dry land, and within those three days of devastation, the oceans, seas, lakes, gulfs, and rivers, of earth all became established as they are today.

In reviewing the conditions of the surviving inhabitants, by first noticing the effect which this great catastrophic event produced upon their minds. It is seen that those tribes which did not migrate away, and had remained up to the time of this flood in the Shinar valley, together with five small detached tribes that existed nearby, were all destroyed. However luckily, those people that had separated from the original Shinar tribe and had emigrated to China and Japan, remained unharmed; and it was these that had **retained** the **theology** and doctrines taught them by the **chieftain** of whom was previously spoken. Now those people remaining in China and Japan, sent messengers back to the Shinar valley to inspect and see if their elder brethren had survived. These messengers soon discovered that not only were there no surviving inhabitants, but startled, they also realized a river now existed exactly where the tribes had once lived. Upon returning, these messengers relayed their message to their governor exactly what was discovered and seen. Recall, as was stated, this tribe **did-not** known of any other nations on earth. Recall, that nearly all of the original nations and tribes had already previously separated because of disunity, so mostly, these inhabitants had always been isolated. So in conclusion these remaining inhabitants of Japan and China **assumed** that they were the **only survivors** on earth after this great catastrophe.

The governor-chieftain of these remaining peoples **responded quickly**, and instructed them, **saying** that the reason why all the other people had been killed was because they had **not** been **good**, and had not offered **sacrifices** to satisfy the demands of Brahma - *"Brahma seeing that the wick-*

*edness upon the earth was great, and the imaginations of the thoughts of their hearts were only evil, continually, began to repent that he had directed Vishnu to create their forefathers and them. And seeing that the earth was filled with wickedness and abomination in the sight of Brahma, he said, he would cause the great waters, of which he had made the ground and them, to sweep them off the face of the land".*

So the governor and prophet of this eastern tribe gave his selfish **impression** and explanation to these survivors stating and implying that the reason they were saved was because **himself** and his tribe were **better** than their forefathers and brethren that Brahma let them live. He **represented** these ideas by vocal **sounds** and **hieroglyphics**. He instructed them to **build** brazen images that would represent, as he said, the god of the **Sun**; and the head of this being was very much like that of the unicorn, and the body like that of a fish; and they placed it within a stone tent, and every year visited it and offered up sacrifices.

It would be from this time **onward** these inhabitants began to worship to sun, the moon, the stars, and the milky way, which they supposed were the habitations of spirits, being in number, thirty-three thousand spirits.

These mankind, as yet, did not designate each other by names, but merely by families or states of association. However the person who was their governor and prophet yet unnamed, he would be named in later generations by subsequent writers, and his name would be **Fohi**. This fact may be verified in the **Chinese** record of the present day. And furthermore, this person has been supposed by still more modern writers, to be the **Noah** spoken of in the "primitive history".

The Chaldeanic Persians or the **Japan** tribe of which was spoken, preserved in their mythology the same whole account with very little modification, except in their particular story, the father and head of the family whom Brahma had permitted to live, was named **Xisuthrus**. And this man has been supposed by modern historians to be the person Noah named in the Jewish account of the deluge.

The sects known as the **Buddhists** and **Jaina** preserved with great care the same traditional account, and this account ultimately **became** a portion of the Greek oriental history and theology: and in this ancient Greek version of the flood story, the surviving and remaining father's name being **Deucalion**.

So now ends this overview of the Asian survivors, having shown their progress after the event concerning the deluge, as the original account and version was given by the leader of that isolated eastern Asia tribe.

## Section 95

Attention is now turned to those survivors of the aboriginal inhabitants of **America** and to mention the psychological **effect** produced upon **their minds** by that same catastrophic event. And further, describe their original conceptions of the **Great Spirit**.

Again recall, that it was by the formation of the Pacific ocean during this last upheaval, and from this earth change, now these three small American tribes were **separated** from everyone else and had now lost all communication with the tribes of their ancestors and any other brethren whom they had previously knew, once had existed on the various island portions of the pacific region. These American Indians were totally unaware of those existing tribes living in Central American, nor were they aware of any other people anywhere else on earth.

There were very **few** Indians who had **escaped** the inundation, and the survivors **supposed** in their minds that this upheaval was a universal event. And these tribe were currently in great despair; one reason for their great despair, their thoughts of loneliness and great loss, was that the **majority** of their population had completely **disappeared**; they vanished because all of these brethren were killed because the land portions on which they were living disappeared. They had been dwelling on land portions **that-were** actually **west-of** the present California coastline, however during the upheaval, these lands sank into the Pacific ocean and all the inhabitants existing on those portions perished.

Now after the upheaval, these remaining three American tribes further reasoned, that they were the only people that were saved, and also, the **place** and the land portion where they are dwelling was the only land on the earth, supposing, that all other portions had sunk beneath the great waters.

The Americans had developed a completely **different** attitude concerning **social** affairs, when compared to any other nation or tribe which had separated from the original family. For example these American's developed within themselves truly **peace loving** dispositions. The Americans as time passed would become **very social** and united; and it was by a **well-directed affection** for Life, Nature, and each other, which not only allowed them to be able to exist in peace and happiness, but they also developed **social activities** and were able to experience **joy**. These inhabitants had developed to such a high degree of harmony that their particular life-style should be used as an example and seen as a very **noble** and **great development**, including a great progression of the "**interior principles**" of mankind.

Tribes here, lived life motivated by a unity and harmony in all their social functions, especially in their planning and decision-making, but also in nearly any events and activities they would have. **Formalities** were a very important aspects of their lifestyle and these formal activities aided them in developing **high moral** values. The Americans, **invented** tools and implements which allowed them to exist comfortable. They felt joy because they were living in a **garden**, which would cultivated in them the disposition to roam and hunt through the wilds of the forest. And they would pitch their bark tents "wherever they pleased"! They were exceedingly fond of hunting, and this employment they supposed **was-right**, because, why else would their forefathers have lived in such a beautiful garden. These are to be the earth's original conservationists.

The fact that they had cultivated a highly developed socially unity, led the way for the development of **honest relationships**, and developing a **trust** for "one's word"; and led to the development of **minds** that **did-not** conceive of crude and gross errors: for, it was to them, that errors **only-sprang** from social disunity and dis-organization and from having a mistaken or inappropriate conception of the **cause** of the existing **evil**.

At first these Americans had initially retained from their early forefathers the impression concerning the "breaths" as being the source of evil. **But** their ability to coexist in harmony, led them to **change** their understanding of the "breaths", leading them to a **new belief**, that all things around and above were all a part of **the Great Spirit**.

The Indians now saw the "breaths" as being good and were not evil as their forefathers had taught. The "breaths" to them proceeded from a good spirit, who desired to fan the sweat from their heated brow after they had toiled or they traveled great distances in the light of the good Spirit. So when fatigued and exhausted by the toilsome travels, they would joyously receive His refreshing breath, that came, as they supposed, from some of the good subordinate spirits. They saw that these "breaths" were generally good for them; and this belief filled their entire essence, and their goodness unfolded and developed all the tender dispositions of their nature, and they dwelt in **love** one with another. And as these **truthful conceptions** and their **tranquilizing influences** became established **immovably** in the minds and affections of each soul, these truthful insights would remain, and descended through all the succeeding generation of this great people down to the present time.

These Americans believed strongly, that the eye, the tongue – that plants and animals, including all the celestial orbs – **each** had spirits in attendance, so they believed that the power of speaking was communicated to them by the spirit of the tongue, and also the power of seeing by the spirit of the eye. They love, adore, and worshiped, the Sun: for it made their earth fertile in all the things which they cultivated. They worshiped the moon: for it was a good spirit to give them light while the warm and better spirit had gone to rest. They beheld the stars with awe and admiration: because they were little lights held out by the good spirits to give them light, and to make their earth look beautiful when the sun and the moon had retired to rest.

They believed that when they should lie down and die, the spirit of their eyes and tongue would convey the spirits that were within them to the beautiful habitations of the **spirit-land.** They felt conscious that the spirit-land was comparable in nature to the land upon which they dwelt. And believed that there would-be similar Forms and productions (plant, animals, water, etc), in the spirit-land where they may hunt, adore one-another, and adore the "good Spirits". The after-land was to them, a land of beauty and grandeur far beyond human experience.

**Finally**, it would be here in mankind's long history, that the **first instance** ever, from the moment the human Form first obtained an existence, to here now, this will be the first-time in which human-thought first took a proper truthful and **natural direction**. It was the spontaneous teachings of Nature which existed all around them, and the corresponding **prompting** of the **interior-principle** within, which had taught them of the Spirit-land. Disunity was not in their midst and therefore wickedness and abomination were to them unknown, Their thoughts were natural, true, spontaneous, and celestial. "The way's" of the American Indian were truthful, especially in relation to those thoughts and actions concerning their spiritual beliefs; it sure seems as though others could learn from them:

*Learn from this, ye theologians, philosophers, and metaphysicians, and let your now-ambitious thoughts sink so low that generations yet unborn will be unconscious of their existence. Learn from this, ye traditional historians, ye governors, chieftains, rulers, and potentates, and promptly discard all that has been; and begin, and travel the path of wisdom and virtue. Learn from this, ye classifiers, ye commentators, ye external and unnatural teachers, and let the ink which has been wasted in penning your thoughts be naught in comparison to the abundance of tears shed by you in the act of humiliation! Let external pride and consequent arrogance fall forever. Let high-mindedeness and pretended enlightenment cease to trammel your spiritual principle, and let this principle then seek true wisdom,* **derivable from** *the inexpressible beauties of a smiling* **Nature**.

Returning to the story: the Indians believing they-are the **only survivors** and that the great waters had swallowed up their brethren because of their wickedness, and had allowed them to live because they were good and favored in the sight of the good Spirit.

They **named** the surviving chief who was existing among them at the time of the catastrophic event is **Sottavarata**. The "tradition" of this person, with very little modification has descended through the minds of every subsequent generation. And this person has been supposed by some modern chronological and biblical writers to be the **Noah** of the "primitive history".

And **now**, attention is-turned to the collateral tribes of the Americas who had survived, these, which were **part-of** the nation that dwelt in regions of **Central America** and **southern Europe**. These are the people that are spoken of as being much more **advanced** in all the arts and sciences, and they certainly were more advanced than any other nation, at least then existing.

Their language and theology was of a more "inspired" tradition. A tradition which was full of beauty and grandeur and having more of a "fleeting nature", and much of their thinking always seemed as being directly connected with **unreal idealism**. Having not only an idealistic tradition, but also one full of grandeur, and so it was because of this nature that their beliefs have nearly vanished from existence. These southern people are those more advanced nations whom had **initially imagined** in their minds, many of those **more-progressed** thoughts that the "breaths" **originated** from the Sun. And **recall**, that about three generations prior to the flood catastrophe, these more advanced peoples had advanced even more in their belief system and now, had **removed** away from their theological system of beliefs, that peculiar belief of thinking the origin of evil came from the Sun; and then, having these more advanced thoughts, **moving** evil away-from inside the Sun itself, and **moving evil** to the hidden realm of the **abyss** below, where evil was now **hidden** and secretive, and now, the Sun was more of a **representative** of evil; and hence, these became lovers of darkness.

But now, because of the deluge-event occurring, it then became **necessary** for the **inspired chieftain** of this southern nation to now **interpret** the meaning for this tragedy, and it was necessary to give the people an account and reason for this catastrophe; he gave his answer by **using** the hieroglyphical traditions that had been handed down from generations past. This particular "inspired chief", had succeeded the chieftain who had moved the cause of evil, from the Sun to the abyss. This new chieftain spoke to the remaining inhabitants of the city that was destroyed, explaining to these terrified survivors his thoughts, so he said to them, that:

" *They the ones gathered together here, were the only ones known to be preserved; with the exception of three tribes that were know to be dwelling on the more inland portions. Saying also, that the angry Being who made that great fiery gulf, was infuriated and angry because of the short-comings and wicked transactions of their brethren, who perished"* - (those destroyed had dwelt upon land which now is bottom of the gulf of Mexico and including other land portions leading to and connecting the West-India islands). He continued, saying;

*"this angry Being had generations ago, conversed with their "previous governor", and because of that previous **covenant**, the angry being had previous, always watched over this tribe. And now, as He, was the **only good person** among all the tribes, and he was **permitted** to **converse** with the angry Spirit, who was opposed to the selfishness and wicked ways of most of the people of the earth.* He went on to say;

*"He had now entered into a new covenant with this angry Being, because this Being was grieved and lamented that he ever created so many tribes. The new covenant stated; the chief and his tribe were the only mankind that was allowed to live, because it was necessary that the earth should be peopled only by those who were, as good as he and his people were, and stating, that all wicked people were wiped from the face of the earth".*

One of their **vortical edifices** built after the earth upheaval and deluge, contains the hieroglyphical written promise or covenant made by the potentate whom existed three generations ago; but it is **only-now** in this post-upheaval period that the covenant is now finally being **confirmed** and re-presented by the new and present chieftain, and now being discussed by this post-deluge leader of this surviving Central American nation. This present chieftain, who is now using that previous myth promise, written in hieroglyphs, which he now claims demonstrates that their forefather actually did converse with the angry Being. For it is known, the theology of this South American nation, was not definitely confirmed or made widely known until the third generation after the occurrence of the flood.

This southern nation also believed they were the **only survivors** (not knowing other tribes), and they believed their god had repented for making so many tribes, because those tribes had developed wickedness, and so, their god destroyed those wicked ones on that account. The chieftain who had transcribed this traditional hieroglyphical account from the time of the deluge, was not named **until** many generations after him. And there is no trace of the name until these present ideas, views, and statements, are traced into the "primitive history" manuscripts which were spoken of, and that the **Jews** possessed, and in there this chieftain is named **Noah**.

Now next, this historical review will "place" these various separate nations and their current chieftains or governors, which had all survived the catastrophic flood-like event and were now each **existing alone**, and also to give a **review** of the past few sections.

First, the story as a review, has traced the **Chinese** mythology to the **Greek**, and also, has traced the mythology of these **southern** tribes of Yucatan, just spoken of, following them and ending up to the **Jews**, and the accounts are told in this manner:

The good that were saved and favored of the **Chinese** were **Fohi** an his family; those saved of the **Chaldeanic-Persians** (from Japan) were **Xisuthrus** and his family; and those survivors of the **Greeks** were **Deucalion** and his family. In the **American Indian** mythology the saved were **Sottavarata** and his family: and **each** family **believing** that the whole world had drown, with the exception of themselves. In the **Jew's** manuscripts, as was mentioned had originated from **Cent**ral **America**, is found that the saved were **Noah** and his family.

In the writings of modern commentators who, by studying oriental and heathen mythology, have **attempted** to established as a fact, that each of these story's and traditions all come from one account, and believing all originating from one source. Such a supposition in **not-justifiable**, because all the traditions that are in possession by the different nations **cannot** be traced to one source.

In reviewing the "primitive history" it can be stated, that the description of the deluge or flood is a well preserved account of the story, especially when considering the numerous events and future problems which govern all circumstantial things, and namely things akin to traditional stories. Basically though, and in a true sense, the account of the flood is an **exaggerated** and **poetical representation** of that one particular catastrophic event, which is substantially, a true event; and for its truthfulness this **history lesson** demands the highest respect.

# Section 96

And now the story will proceed to another **category** of ideas, or a new topic which will be reveal and then discuss, which is the **origin** and successive **modification** of these various "primitive history's", until they appear in their present forms, being written in modern text. The "primitive history" is the **separate** accounts from each nation, generally **compiled** and existing within the story of Creation.

These following ideas are the particular "**sayings**" which are written in various histories of various nations; each, which are written according to the existing religious theologies of each belief system.

The first of these may be found in the early manuscripts of the "primitive history", clothed with the following words: *"And God said, Let us make man in our own image and likeness"*. Well now, many a noble and highly-cultivated intellects have spent time, talent, and wealth, engaged in the task of establishing a **superficial interpretation** of this subject, the action of the creation of mankind. And there have been just as many intellects having been employed in spreading and dispersing these superficial opinions, and without doubt, sufficient energies have already been spent wastefully, when all of their energy could have been used to properly instruct and cultivate the moral and intellectual powers of many a nation.

The desires and prejudices of men have waged **war-against** the promptings of the interior spiritual judgment, and have **restricted** and limited the range of their own and others **reasoning powers** and restricting it to the limited circle of knowledge of a sectarian and hereditary belief. Many of these highly-cultivated intellects, with differing opinions, and most likely good intentions, have endeavored to **establish** preconceived opinions. But, in doing this, they have established a deep-seated stance and steadfast opinions, that now, only breaths **sectarian contention** and local hostilities among so many groups and individuals. So, men have **severed** the affectionate ties of congeniality, yes, cutting those ties which should unite mankind as one vast brotherhood of man of earth.

The many theories and opinions regarding the nature and creation of mankind,which are **forced into** the world, are all **external**, interruptive, and unholy **invasions** upon human affections and judgment. In time, volume after volume has been written concerning God's creation of mankind and the Universe, all without producing the least bit of relief to the depressed and ignorant world.

All those teachings are **unprofitable** and injurious to the race; they are **local**, isolated, **sectarian**, and entirely opposed to the highest good of every living creature. They are entirely unreal, impure, and wicked. They are corrupting, spoiled, impaired, and insufficient - to all the pure affections of man's true nature. These imagined beliefs and mythological stories are the **corrupt foundation** of all universal sectarian hostility and superstition. Those men and women that are sectarian, are at war with all the pure, social, and moral interests of mankind; and when it becomes possible for mankind to exist in peace, **they-would** if left undisturbed, join in one - as the **whole-race** of intelligent beings.

The situation of mankind's climb to perfection is radical and treacherous journey. Mankind as a whole needs a trustworthy method which could be use as a guide for a seeker of truth, something which would give good indications whether an opinion or set of values "be made by man" or "be made by Divine". So then, let the mind be open, search into the internal realities, find the qualities and principles that are good, divine, and indestructible.

Now continuing with the investigation concerning the origin and modifications of the various "primitive history's, all modified following the catastrophic flood-like event. The post-flood tribes which had now become co-associated and **co-joined** as one family initially in the valley of Shinar, recall, these people had received the early impression of their forefathers, concerning the creation, and also those improvements that were made upon it this by their supposed "inspired chieftain". In this **inspired chieftain's story** of mankind's beginnings, he called to his assistance from the depths of the water, the deity of whom has been spoken of, subsequently named **Parama**, **Vishnu**, and **Siva**. This chieftain first conceived of an original spirit Parama. Yet this conception, suggested the idea of a second spirit; and this conception of the second, brought on that development of a third spirit.

The first deity, he supposed to be the great good spirit which had paused and reposed from the remotest period of eternity, back to the time of the creation resting in the bosom of the great waters. And, the chieftain conceived that as this Spirit awoke to activity, he breathed forth another spirit to do the work which he (**Parama**) had designed.

**Vishnu** was the subordinate spirit that was created. And Vishnu was (according to the chieftain), a part of Parama's soul. He move the waters and continued to do so until he created, from the superior materials of the **egg**, the earth and man. Then the chieftain supposed the spirit **Siva** was the **cause** of those "breaths" which inspired the bosoms of this tribe and their elder brethren with envy, hatred, and deception. Here, in these earliest of historical comments had **originated** the thought, which has clothed itself in the word **trinity**.

There is essentially no change in this part of the **oriental mythology** and this version continued for many centuries; it ultimately fell into the possession of the **Persian tribes**, who preserved it until **Zoroaster** who would **systematize** it, along with other existing traditions, into his **Zend Avesta**.

What Zoroaster actually did, was he **changed** the deities into the **characters** of **Ormuzd, Amshaspands,** and **inferior spirits**. And by doing this he formed from the three, a **trinity** of good, celestial, and holy spirits, among whom **Ormuzd** was supreme. And seeing so-much evil among the inhabitants of the earth, and seeing war, persecution, and tyranny, all existing "He" (Ormuzd) began to reason upon their causes. And by thinking this, the thought came to Ormuzd's mind concerning a corresponding trinity of "infernal fiery spirits". The greatest of these spirits was **Ahriman**; and he was attended by spirit-beings of inferior rank and subordinate, and also millions of deevs.

It was Zoroaster, who presented the **trinity** in a new form; and from this it was **transplanted** into the **Jewish manuscripts**, and can be verified, as seen in the brief, yet comprehensive expression which reads, *"And God said, Let us make man in our own image".* It was subsequently stated in another form in other references, *"Father, Son, and Spirit".*

And then there is the expression that everybody seems to know, *"Let us make man".* Well this peculiar phrase is **derived** from the early myth in which the "us" means Brahma, Vishnu (or Narasayana), and Siva. And the trinity also corresponds with the similar phrase, the greater, the lesser, and the least; or Father, Son, and Spirit; or as stated in Zoroaster's story of creation - Ormuzd, Amshaspands, and superior subordinate spirits.

An item which is most important to understand, is that in the **original conception** and impression within the original inspired chieftain's mind, the characters were distinct and **singular**; but then, these single characters are later classified and divided by Zoroaster into **plurals.** And finally they were ultimately and comprehensively expressed in the primitive Jewish transcript, according to the original conception.

# Section 97

It was through the ability, "of obtaining a clairvoyant impression", that Davis reports; that the biblical expression, *"in our image and likeness"* as is stated in the "primitive history" **really does** give a **glimpse** of a substantial and **truthful idea**. However, this claim can only be verified by possessing a complete understanding of the natural environment. Yet this idea can also be seen in the spiritual environments. **But**, if by chance someone is studying and investigating only the **external meaning** of biblical phrase " in our image and likeness", it **reveals nothing** and truly it has no spiritual meaning, especially for the level of progression that mankind has obtained at is period of history.

One of Davis's objectives was to reveal the true value of historical writings and traditions. Also to reveal just how much credibility our more advanced society should give to the historical writings of the early tribes of mankind. The first objective was to show that, if the outer and **external meaning** of the "primitive history", gives **evidence** of the **interior meaning** of those writings, then those writings are simply, primitive history. **So why** would someone endeavor to give more meaning, or give a different meaning, to any particular passage or phase, and then **veering** from the meaning which the external view had already clearly shown?

The answer to Davis's inquiry is simple, yet requires a knowledge of the **particulars** which were surrounding this earlier time-period in which these manuscript were written. Those particulars were a multitude of common everyday local events. Some of which could be incidental; - for instance, a particular could be the language at that period; or a particular could be the level of intelligence that mankind had obtained at that time; possibly, it was the particular popular phrases of that period; or the politics; or the weather; or the ignorance that prevailed, and on and on.

So in truth, the only things which the "primitive history" **professes** to be, is a **truthful** and **comprehensive history** of **opinions** concerning creation before the flood. And it also tells of the customs, manners, dispositions, and movements of the successive nations that were known; it tells of the re-population of the earth after the flood, and the distribution of the early tribes; and it also discusses the lives of their leaders, chieftains, prophets, kings, holy men and women, and emperors. These primitive histories profess to give the history of war; of the subjugation and captivity of tribes; of the up-building and downfall of kingdoms and empires; of the vice, misery, and imaginations, trials and tribulations of many nations of the earth. The "primitive history" professes to be this, and professes no more than that. The book in its **external meaning**, truly proves its claimed profession, as a collection of the history and movements of early mankind. And so, any of its interior meaning, **has-its** own interpreter, which is the exterior profession of a history book.

And so, if someone professes that there is some hidden meaning in the "primitive histories", then they are mistaken. Because, if some other theologian or preacher thought differently and from them a different interpretation were to come-along, then, that different opinion and any of its professing, would have been devised and arisen from those promoters **who profit** from it, and then the opinion is out of context and is not in accordance with its own stated intentions.

The primitive histories of mankind are a set one of a kind manuscripts, and any reader should be **deeply impressed**, and "give due respect" to it, and especially to the **truthfulness** of those historical traditions. **But**, at the same time, there is a need-to **expose** and **discard** all untrue theological interpretations, and shed all unreal and unholy claims and statements; all those things, that have-been added and **applied** to those writings should be ignored and deleted.

Now the **next category** of ideas of which the real origin needs to be traced, is the traditional story and opinion concerning **Cain** and **Abel**.

Recall from a previous discussion concerning the **original branch tribes**, describing them as the offspring of the earliest and first family of man, and it was related in that story, that one tribe conquered and destroyed the other - the triumphant nation, afterwards journeying to the **European** continent.

The history of this event, written as the story of Cain and Abel, as it is found in the Old Testament of the Jews, was initially **transferred** along with other and similar original primitive impressions, **passed-on** down-through successive generations and centuries by tradition using sounds, gestures, and hieroglyphs; and those early inhabitants **relied** upon "correspondence" or obvious-representations of their thought impressions, until it the story appears and is **first expressed** by a writer among the **early Egyptians** written in hieroglyphs. And to truly understand the story of Cain and Abel, the event must to be understood in a similar fashion, language, mind-set, as did the early inhabitants know things, which was by their **obvious** and **connecting correspondences** and **representations**, and this is the only method that will reveal exactly what this story represents and exactly what is this stories true purpose and meaning. The following will reveal that true meaning and its representation:

*The younger and weaker tribe which was* **Abel** *corresponded to light, purity, and innocence.* **Cain** *which was the Stronger and grosser nation corresponded to darkness, wickedness, and abomination.*

*For it was known, according to the early theology,* **darkness** *was the* **first principle** *in Being, and therefore was the oldest and most powerful; while* **light** *was subsequently created and was consequently weak and* **unmatured**.

And now in **comparison**, there is the following which was originally written among the **Egyptians** as follows:

*And from the forefathers sprang two children, whose names were* **Osiris** *and* **Typhon**. *Osiris was a good and gentle brother, and was loved by Brahma. Typhon was a strong brother, and cultivated the things of the earth, For Typhon is the child of darkness which was over all, and forever.*

*But Osiris was a child of light, because light was permitted by Vishnu the good spirit". But Typhon, which is darkness, was represented as attacking and overpowering Osiris, which is light and innocence.*

This ancient Egyptian recollection of the story, is the **first** written (hieroglyph) **correspondential account** of this story and primitive tradition, which, as stated, was later passed-on from generations to generation using vocal sounds and by using gestures and signs.

**This story** was admitted or added into **other manuscripts** after the Egyptian version, and appeared among the Chaldeanic writings. Then afterward the story was transcribed into Greek, and ultimately into the Hebrew oracles and manuscripts; and then through the medium of writing, it was conveyed to all following generations who then admitted it into the "primitive history", and in this particular version of the story in the "primitive history" the characters are named Cain and Abel.

## Section 98

The **next topic** or idea to be analyzed and traced all the way back to its origin, is **the seven days** that are represented as having been elapsed, during the formation of the earth and all the "things" on it. And also, then discussing the seventh day, that particular day smiling upon the completion of the grand work, and giving rest to Brahma, who blessed It.

The story here flows like this: - Many centuries would elapse before the early inhabitants first began to make **astronomical observations**. They lived outside in the open and would stare into the nighttime sky; they soon began seeing relationships between the phenomenons occurring around them, and what they **learned** from these observations of the winds, the atmosphere, heat, light, the sun, moon, and stars, and also all other visible objects, all which **they supposed** were **gods**. From that development the primitives began to use **numbers**, and it was with the use of numbers, early mankind were able to determine the **seasons**. Knowing when seasons would occur was a great step forward for mankind, **allowed** people to communicate about a topic, and also it allow man to know when-to visit one another.

With man's use of numbers, the first inhabitants learned when to expect darkness, by the periodic recession of the sun behind the western lands. And when to expect light, by the display of light coming from the eastern hills. After learning that this cycle seems to repeat, in time, they **eventually** became convinced, and then **confirmed** in the **opinion** that "these cycles would always continue". The sun continued in an unvarying appearance and disappearance, almost as if it were alive.

As the original first family multiplied, growing so much larger, this action of population growth led the early inhabitants to begin forming separate tribes or branch nations, which in time would **completely separate** themselves from each-other, actually moving to different areas or regions, and some of these explorers ultimately emigrated to a different portion of earth.

So it was in this time-period, two branch nations separated from the original family, one tribe was named in hieroglyphical form, being represented as **darkness**; and then, naming another tribe, by hieroglyphical representation to be a representation of **light**. And because the early humans **could-only** perceive general relationships and correspondences between things, then their interpretation of and their design of these hieroglyphs was also in general **corresponding** relationships. And so, these general relationships were at first passed-on by vocal sounds and gestures, and then they were later recorded as **hieroglyphical** characters.

Astronomy was one of the first scientific advancements mankind was able to teach himself, and man still looks-up into the sky. Man's progressive ability to **reason** concerning the world around them, and especially learning about "cycles" led to gaining knowledge regarding the **periodicity** of days and nights.

Early mankind at their first stages, had difficulty communicating much beyond their own minds and **barely** could perceive general-relationships between one-another or correspond, and also, they could take-notice of any similarities which existed between each other; and in this **present-period** man had advanced greatly, and now they had the use of a formal type of writing; and so of course, this is the special period when mankind first becomes able to **record** their thoughts, mark actual events, and would mistakenly in some of those recorded items or events, give a description which might even have been an imaginary **hallucinations**. So irregardless of whether it was an actual event or if these were imaginary hallucination, all these **could-now** be represented in hieroglyphical characters.

These various tribes of mankind continued on for several centuries using their newly discovered capabilities of communication, using them now in conjunction with those scientific discoveries of the use of numbers and astronomy made in earlier time-periods; until there was **a new valuable truth** discovered; that the **moon** was **created** and **destroyed** twelve times, while the **sun** was passing just-once through the circle of the **zodiac**. And this event was a natural occurrence for man to establish in their minds; and in a further sense, the establishment of the cycles of the moon led to the first idea in their minds of the concept of a **year** cycle.

The inhabitants were developing an **adequate** and much more peaceful ability to communicate. And in addition, by using **hieroglyphs**, there now would be an improved method which will enable different tribes to write and to show correspondence of things to each-other, or **symbolism**.

The twelve periods of the moon's destruction and then its anticipate reconstruction, equaling, what would be later known as a month. Next discovering the phases of the moon at regular periods, and those divisions equaling seven days and nine hours, with this leading to the conception of weeks.

So, it is from numbers, establishing periods of time, that the **Egyptian**, **Chinese**, **Persians**, and **Jews**, developed the conception of the **divisions of time**. But, it was not until following generations, who would finally divide the week and reduce it into days. Days themselves, would of course become classified into hours, and this event occurred by the genus of someone whom noticed, that by watching a changing shadow, that was given-off by an immovable object, situated in the light of the sun.

Names of days came later: Sunday instituted by the **Danes**, adopted by the **Saxons** originally meant, "day of the Sun", which makes-sense, other names for other days followed next.

In a similar fashion as the Danes, the division of days became introduced into the **Jewish** historical writings – and this is where the days were only designated by the phrase, "the evening and the morning". And then, **because** the seventh day was the last or the great sun-day, it was looked upon by the Jews as being of divine origin. And as they "absorbed" the already-existing impression, that the light on that day was peculiarly pure and serene. This early system of **numbering** was adopted by all nations and tribes on earth and each system has nearly the same rules for enumerating; and still remains the same.

And now time is on our side. Six days were observed as times for labor, and the seventh was appropriated to rest. And this is doing, as the good spirit Parama did, after he had finished the creation of the world and man, according to **oriental mythology**.

Mankind in astonishment has always looked to the stars and planets and space, and in that period it was part of mankind's education, their entertainment; it was their **field of observation**, and from it they received **unfailing** instruction and wisdom. This is why there should be no-wondering why, man loves space so much and exploring space is man's **duty**.

# Section 99

The **next topic** or idea to discuss is still within the same class of ideas before mentioned, this idea is of the **origin** of **language**, as it was suggested in the mythological tradition, which was also contained in the "primitive history" that reads; *"the whole earth was of one language and of one speech"*.

Recall, it was when the early human family initially **perceived** that they possessed the **power** of **vocal communication**, and began to convey their thoughts to one another through that medium of sound. Man first believed this power came from the "breaths", and therefore they believed that this power should be used and cultivated. However, after only a few generations had passed, new opinions were formed and it was discovered, that this faculty of vocalizing was the cause of the **disunion** which had been experienced by their forefathers; so then, that particular enlightened generation finally modified the original tradition, changing it, and now believing those "breaths" to be the **source** of the **evil**.

This **tradition**, passed down from previous brethren, implying that the "breaths" were **evil spirits**, along with another thought they had **imagined** and **supposed**, thinking that these evil spirits **gave** one speech and one language to mankind, so that mankind would **deceive** and dislike one another. This **opinion** of the evil "breaths" creating one language, continued for many ages, both before and after the deluge event. This was the **single belief** among all nations on earth. And it is important to know, that all early nations have most of this story or at least a part of this story admitted in their sacred theology, and the reason these myths are sustained, **is-entirely** from the simple fact, that these stories were **handed-down** and told by their forefathers through tradition, and because of tradition, holy sacredness has been placed upon these beliefs and were confirmed in their minds **because** they associated its sacredness with its old age. If it's old, it must be good.

From the **action** of each generation now being able to pass-along their traditions in hieroglyphic form, a great deal of knowledge was accumulated and gained; now, one generation could accurately passed-on to the next generations, and each could add to their own general knowledge. And this all adds up quickly. And in this **present generation** it continued gaining knowledge from terrestrial and astronomical observations which they made of their surroundings. All had multiplied the combined knowledge man now possessed, and this is what **eventually** gave them sufficient instruction enabling them to **construct** a **language**, which turns-out to be the parent of the subsequent **Sanskrit**.

The early **hieroglyphs** were impressed upon the soft **bark** of trees and palm leaves, and it was in this method of artful language their thoughts were recorded. This framework of early writing would continue for a long period, and these manuscript mostly remaining in the possession of governors, chieftains, and lawgivers. These are the individuals whom sincerely believed and taught that their language was of a **divine origin**.

This **next development** of the present topic, the origin of language is **strictly** a **mythological** one, and it is one which is found among the Chinese, Chaldeans, Brahmans, and other Hindustani tribes. Their belief was this, that the **Vedas** (scripture) and the **Brahmanas** (commentary), held in their possession, are sacred oracles, written by celestial Beings in divine language: - and these collectively are known as the **Shaster**.

The Vedas are those writings of what composes the first part of the Shaster – which signifies and represents life, light, truth, fire, wit, law, ordinance, and celestial knowledge. The Brahmanas then, composed the second part and themselves are composed of Orphic hymns, which the followers **believe** to be heavenly. In many ways, these are much-the-same as the **poetical songs** of the early Egyptian tribes, praising the great and good Being whom, formed the **Sanskrit** language. And the Psalms and book of Job are **imitations** of the Orphic hymns of the Shaster, which, **were-in** manuscript form among the Egyptians and Chaldeanic-Persians.

For many continuous ages the Sanskrit was the most perfect language known among mankind. Over the period of many generations this language was revised, improved, and cultivated, by later writers who used it until it was finally perfected by **Brama** the lawgiver and holy prophet of the Hindustani tribes, whom was **supposed** to be able to communicate with the deities. After the perfection by Brama many more centuries passed before there was a further development of this same topic, the origin of one language, and reveals that this **same theological** tradition is also found among the Persians.

Many more centuries passed, during which time other tribes began to **migrate** from the southern portions of the earth moving into Asia and Africa, and **bringing** with them a **different mode** of **expression**. This new mode of expression is connected with the formation of the Chaldean or Persian language, this said, because the Persian language is from a root consisting of a different form of speech than the original Sanskrit. Afterwards this new dialect became perfected and finally established by the process of **uniting** with its rudimental form,- a dialect of the Sanskrit.

After the Sanskrit language became established and confirmed as the official tongue, those people who used it would develop a **belief** that it must have had a spiritual origin, **because** they cited that this belief was according to the sacred tradition of their forefathers.

Moving-on, now is the time-period that Zoroaster lived and when he was the Persian lawgiver. He wrote the Zend Avesta and stated it was a **gift** from the gods, and he was **convincing** enough that his people believed that this was given to Zoroaster, just as the **Brahmin** believe the Shaster was given by a communication with the Deity. And, the Persians also **supposed** that their language originated in the same way.

The Jews also **believed** that the knowledge, instructions, and direction, received by **Moses**, their lawgiver, was directly from the Deity. And likewise, the followers of **Mohammed** supposed that the **Koran** was written in celestial spheres by God, and was **given** to Mohammed while in a cave.

So, to give an opinion concerning the original state of language, it is said that:

*"the whole world was of one language and of one speech. And it came to pass that as they journeyed from the east, they discovered a plain in the valley of Shinar, where they dwelt".*

It is appropriate to remark here and reveal that the above verse is from a particular manuscript, and know, that the substance and content of this manuscript was **transferred** and now can also be found in the "primitive history" of the Jews, placed in a position after telling of the flood, and it sustains that particular position in their book. **But** the account **should not** be placed there, because, in truth this phrase relates to a circumstance that occurred many ages **be fore** the flood event.

Many people from the past and also continuing into our present day, are **still believing** that language was communicated to the forefathers by the deity himself. These people have this belief even though they are educated and enlighten in some regards, and these people still find it **difficult** to correctly understand how the law of natural and progressive development operates. They **do-not** realize that language is also part of progressive development. **But** all should now-know, that this law of progressive development is a Divine and unchangeable Principle of the Universe, and continues on whether mankind understands it or not!

Said again in the name of truth, **discard** all further belief in the mythological idea of direct instruction from the Deity. Language has unfolded itself step by step, as a law of natural progression and developed. Language had its beginning in a rudimentary form in the animal kingdom with vocal sounds, and then this early use of sounds being advanced greatly and then perfectly developed by man. In truth and with pure reasoning know, that if language was an effect of a celestial cause, and if language's origin is truly divine, then, **should-not** language be pure, celestial, and undeceptive?

Know that **there-are** things which are divine. The nature of the mental and physical constitution of mankind is divine, perfect, and harmonious. This will **never-deceive**. It is perfectly good and represents the true divineness of its great Origin and Cause. **Deception** however, **does-exist** in the world and exhibits plainly all the descriptions of concealment and disguise. The things of deception really **do-not** flow from the interior of man's nature, but instead they arise **merely** as a **consequence** of man's unholy, imperfect, and **impaired situation**, and this situation is specifically in reference to his relations with fellow-beings. *Unholy situations produce unholy effects.* Therefore, it is best to **realize** that the **interior principle** which is purely of Divine Origin, and can not be made evil, nor can it be contaminated. And therefore, all evil is simply of **external** and **superficial** origin, and is felt by all as external; and so, in order to banish evil from the earth, a **change** must-occur in the social condition of the whole world.

Language is one thing which exists among superficial things that is still existing; and so, as the **effects** of language are shown to be imperfect, so then, from having that knowledge, it is **evident** that language **must-have** originated from a source which in a similar way is **imperfect**, such as has been revealed concerning the early developments of mankind, which are now known, - the thoughts and actions of early man were of a uneducated and superstitious origin.

# Section 100

Now moving on again to the **next topic** in the series, and a very interesting topic it is, because this discussion concerns the **mythological** theory of the **origin of evil**.

The general and natural cause of evil has been given, but, the particular information and particular source for evil which has been given in this story, does not agree to the popular and social accepted conceptions which are popularly believed by today's mankind, by us. So because of this difference, it is **necessary** to **review** the early conceptions that **were-discussed** prior, and then, to follow their developments so that the **truth** may be revealed.

So we know that the first human inhabitants believed that the "breaths" or winds, inspired them with **evil thoughts**; which suggested in their minds and confirmed to them, the existence of a malignant deity who was opposed to them, and who destroyed their social love and breathed among them a spirit of envy, hatred, and deception. Later this superstitious conception was **modified** by the southern tribes of Central and South America by **transferring** the origin of **evil** to the light and warmth of the atmosphere, and then, even blaming the Sun itself – and then also, by further conceiving that the Sun was the representative of a corresponding Fountain of undiminishing fire as the Abyss. At first this idea remained solely among these southern nations.

**But** separately, the eastern tribes conceived, that it was a **type** of a **spirit** who existed **between** them and the good deity who **prevented** their having divine commerce. It was this particular belief which would still **exist** in a similar form among all the tribes of the east up to the time of **Zoroaster**, who would re-arrange this belief and **established** in the world, the beginnings of a belief system in-which there are **two antagonistic**, eternal, unconquerable **deities**. *"One was the god of evil, and the other was the god of goodness".*

The throne of **each** of these Beings was surrounded by subordinate spirits, of a character and disposition which would **correspond** to and represent the deity to which they were each attached.

Zoroaster had imagined and conceived of a numerous amount of **deevs**, which he claimed were joined and associated with each evil deity, and he further stated that these were the deity's **agents** to distribute evil imaginations and unrighteous thoughts and desires into the minds of all mankind.

The Jewish rabbinical writers **are-not** any more free-from these mythological imaginations: for one, they had **adopted** the Persianic opinion and transferred it into their writings. And then from this writing comes the origin of the passage in the "primitive history" which speaks of: - the appearance of an **evil spirit** in the form of a serpent in the garden of **Eden**, and asserts that the woman, being gentle and unsophisticated, became deceived thereby, and was induced to partake of the fruit of the tree of evil; that she transmitted the forbidden fruit to her associate Adam, who, being equally delighted and enchanted, partook thereof – and they were both made sinful, whereas before, they were pure and unpolluted.

The early rabbins used this idea as the origin of evil, and within this the Jews also have expressed the idea that God planted the garden of Eden, and made man and placed him there, and then directed him not to eat of the fruit of the tree of evil; and God did all this without once telling Adam the full consequences that would result from man eating from this fruit. Here, for some reason, the rabbi's have presented an occurrence of the Deity placing before the youthful minds of the first pair of humans, a irresistible temptation, without giving them constitutional strength to resist its captivating influence. Instead they have represented the Deity as saying, *"in the day thou eatest thereof, thou shalt surely die"*. **Well**, it is interesting, because **this-idea** is also represented by Persian's belief that one of the evil deevs of Zoroaster's version of the infernal deity, as speaking and contradicting the words of the Divine Being, by saying to them, *"ye shall not surely die"*.

And more, because then the rabbins show Adam and Eve as not opposing the promises of this evil spirit and shows them performing the action of eating the forbidden fruit, they then are represented as **falling** from a state of innocence to the depths of evil, and **supposedly** from that time up to our present day the world has not yet, been saved from or have experienced a resurrection, and so nearly all souls remain locked in those depths.

The first human pair are also shown as being **driven out**, from the beautiful garden and away from the Deity's presence, only to roam uncared for throughout the wilds of an uncultivated earth.

So in reality, this peculiar Adam and Eve story that is told in the "primitive history", is really nothing more than an expanded and a much more comprehensive description of the original **mythology**. The content of the "primitive history" plainly **does-follow** closely to the contents of the Zend Avesta of Zoroaster, however, it does not progress much, nor transcend the mythology of the first oriental and heathen tribes from which this story is copied.

The word **diabolos** is only another name for Zoroaster's imaginary deevs; and **deevs** is another name for "breaths". In the English version the same idea is expressed using a multitude of words, such as darhiess, death, sin, devil, Satan, and evil; and then progressing to the modern American version of this same phenomenon, evil is expressed as being part of Murphy's law and also in the Star Trek television series this evil deev is known as Q.

Here is an interesting question, **how** is it possible for the simple and profoundly primitive history of the oriental **mythology** able to **become** the foundation and driving-force for such a vast amount of deceit, improper-interpretation, immoral, dishonest, **theological speculation**? This question is asked because it is apparent that nearly all of mankind, have been **led-by** these theological speculations, and they all seem to follow.

Mankind have **not-investigated** the origin of these ideas, such as *"ye shall surely die"*, nor has man bothered to even investigated the internal meaning and significance of those words. But instead have spent their energies and have descended into the study of foreign languages in an **attempt** to search, to discover, and decipher the original application of the mere words. And so by taking this **detour** man became lost and have-now developed **in-error,** the **ideas** of temporal death, moral death, and spiritual death; and these have now been erroneously recognized in all **theological speculations.** All growing out of that simple verse of the traditional story, which says, "ye shall not surely die" - and its opposite declaration by the Deity.

There is no such thing as **natural death**. Because by a law governing all organized substances, which includes every particle composing these substances, these all **must** out of necessity, **undergo** a specific change and decomposition. And when matter **forms** an organization in any particular department of Nature, this organization then, is completely supported and perpetuated by the **law of association** or by a **reciprocal** change of particles with other substances. Therefore the **particles** which are flowing into a new organization,well, these substances which the new organization receives, **must-have** been extracted and taken-away from some other organization of which these particles previously were a part. And some may view this action of Nature, this natural chemical law in action as it applies to Matter, as a death or resurrection.

However, when these substances enter into any new organization, they receive **new life** according to the development processes contained in the body of which those particle had become a part. **Therefore** it is a fact, that bodies or organizations are constantly being produced, sustained, and developed, and are nobly perpetuated in every department of the Universe. **Therefore** there is no such thing in existence as natural death: - because, in a chemical exchange of particles, from one form of life to another is in

**essence**, nothing more than what is an absolutely **necessary requirement** of each and every organized substance in being. So what is called natural death, is not death, but instead is mere a **change** of organization. Know that, such a thing as natural death **never** has **occurred** in any of the recesses of the great Universe.

The notion of **moral death** has no teeth and no real substance, and it has sadly arisen from ignorance and a completely **superficial view** of social disunity in general, and this includes the superficial view of individual disunity of a person's thoughts and actions. This notion of disunity of actions, only **shifts** the **blame** for mankind's misery to some myth or superstition. So instead, realize and know, that there is an **innate divineness** of the Spirit of man, which **prohibits** any possibility of spiritual wickedness or unrighteousness. The desires and affections of the **Spirit** proceed from within and from without.

**Desires** spring-up from the **material relation** which man sustains to his brother and to the Universe.

These desires proceed from sensation, which creates inclination, which **demands gratification**. And realize this **process** is part of material life, and the material world; however, man is **destined** to gain knowledge and develop wisdom, so that these desires are purified.

Now then, there is another class of desires which are **affections**; these types of desires are also originating and springing-up from within an individual, and these are **directing** and **controlling** the outer material being. These affections are the parts and elements of the **Spirit** which ultimately desires **purity** and **perfection**. And so, it is the **principle within** that illuminates the external, and this occurs whenever any pure and divine thought or principle is presented into the mind for meditation and contemplation. And when this specific action occurs during meditation, then there might be seen a **glowing aura** surrounding that being.

Affections are the elements that recognize goodness, gentleness, and purity. It is the element of **Love**, which is the **immortal principle**. Its workings and effects are the morals and affections of man, and they are immortal and cannot die. **Morality**, then, is a consequence of the unchanging divinity of the **S**pirit, and is something that is as undying, as the immutable laws which govern all subordinate organization. Moral death, is therefore a manufactured expression, meaning nothing.

**Spiritual death** is only another form of the expression "moral death", and they are both meaningless: and be assured, these words spiritual death never has had and never can have the least particle of meaning, in other words it has no meaning.

If the word **death** is used in a sentence and in a place where the word's use, is only to describe darkness or even something which corresponds-to the conventional idea of darkness, **then** in this sentence the word is well use and in this manner its meaning is good. **But** natural, moral, or spiritual darkness is **impossible**: because darkness is an expression that **implies** the existence of light. And man **has-not** retrograded from perfection of his spiritual and natural organization, toward the lowest point of imperfection, because this action, said again, would be an absolute impossibility.

**Retrogression** is a another word like the word death, having no meaning. And this fact is stated because everything in existence is unfolding life and beauty, and furthermore, all this action and activity of unfolding and developing, is according to "the law of progressive and eternal development".

Let Nature be **heeded** as She proclaims her divine instructions, and then continue heeding Her, even though that might mean that an individual will be required to relinquish all artificiality – which will be sacrificed by Nature's omnipotent authority. **Love** that which is lovely, and deal gently with all which has been misdirected or imperfectly developed. And then, at the same time love, adore, and express the truth, because Truth is a principle which unites and harmonizes an entire Universe.

## Section 101

The **next topic** to review is the **origin** of the **manuscripts** written by, or concerning, the **prophets** and **oracles** whom were spoken of in the "**Primitive History**" of mankind. And in the process of this review, give enough explanation and insight into the **conditions** surrounding these sayings, so as to show how these writings were later understood by theological writers. And another thing to explain is, exactly where do the early manuscripts of the Primitive History originate from?

As stated, the reasoning faculties of early man's mind were uncultivated, undisciplined, and undeveloped; yet, man's powers of imagination and their love of the marvelous effect and cause their minds and imaginations to be very **susceptible** to external **influence** and impressions. All of the various external, physical events which were occurring around them were mysterious and strange, and all these events were believed to be either **good** or **bad**. Earliest of mankind totally lacked the ability of proper reasoning.

A process occurred by circumstance, and this was where man's great imaginative powers became **combined** with their nearly perfected powers of memory; and then, because of man's limited and undeveloped judgment faculties, primitive mankind became quite capable and prolific at **imagining** in their minds almost any description of things. Early man was only mentally capable of thinking and **believing** that all external appearances and events **were-produced** by the invisible and great multitude of spirits and deities which existed around them.

So, in order to properly discuss the prophets of the Primitive History or Old Testament, our story must now turn back again to **reveal** and further describe **one specific person** whom existed among the primitive family. This particular person (discussed previously) was **organized** mentally in such a way, which **qualified** him for the office of a **governor** of his people, as well having the duty and position of a person who **warns** of impending events, he often gives advice, and sometimes to discipline members of his nation. Recall that, this is the particular person who is **first** to have conceived a thought and was able to have an opinion, giving the **reason** or the cause of all the disunity and contention existing among them as a tribe. He had determined that it was the influences of the evil spirits of the "breaths". And he further stated, that he **received** this information through the medium of an **impressive dream**.

This governor, believing that his dream was made known to him because he was better and wiser than any other, decided he would explain his dream and make it known to everybody, claiming that he himself was the chosen one. And he was immediately **declared** the **prophet**, and was elevated by the people around him. The ignorant masses thought and exclaimed that "this person must have superior holiness", because he was able to communicate with the deities.

Primitive mankind at this time has just begun to realize that the thoughts which came into their minds when they slept might have significance, so the act of **dreaming** was at first, believed to be the **medium** of **celestial conversation.** And so, **whoever** dreamed an important dream was called upon to relate that dream to all, and once the dream was declared, then it was the governor who would **interpret** the dream, because that was his place and his right.

Now besides dream interpretation there are **other sources** of mythological impressions which came to early man, and some of these indications came as **omens** or as **signs**. Omens were usually based upon or centered around something originating from either the animal or plant kingdoms, and these were considered either a good or a bad omen. The **character** of the omen was always determined by the governor. So here, the profound ignorance that had already captivated mankind many times, is now again plainly seen within the process of having beliefs in an omen or sign, **because** here again the inhabitants were making **no-attempts** in the use of their **reasoning** capabilities, and instead, they continually absorbed into their dull minds, precisely what their leader was explaining to them. This time-period for mankind could certainly have been called, the age of imagination and ignorance. The minds of the general population of early man were so profoundly undeveloped that everything to them was a correspondence or representation; and it was solely by means of correspondences and representations, that they became aware of the thoughts and intentions of each-other.

And now begins the period of history where kings and rulers were in the habit of having **persons** who professed to **interpret dreams** as their **counselors**. Many of these persons had developed and improved their intelligence and **were-now** elevated to a high social positions, this new social position was because they **were-believed** to be in communication with celestial beings; and by this action of **supposedly** speaking with those celestial beings, had enabled them to **foretell** events and **interpret** all occurrences. This was a much more common and prevalent custom among eastern tribes and families than with others. Dream interpretation and the "reading" of signs and omens, were intellectual advances for mankind in one way, but mankind also had still **retained** and held-tightly to all those **traditional** impressions of early generations, **not-realizing** that these were mythological and imaginary.

It could be said, that most of those dream counselors of the eastern hemisphere which are the ones who **claimed** to be in possession of these peculiar powers of dream interpretations, **were** as **serious** as could be, and truly were **not deceiving** others intentionally, but **were-deceived** themselves; not only deceived by their own ignorance, but also were deceived by the overwhelming ignorance of the minds of mankind existing around them. These first-existing and developing dream-readers **were-not** yet, self-aware of the extent, degree, and range, of their own knowledge, and also, unaware of the **reliability** of their interpretations; so they mistakenly and unknowingly made **erroneous exaggerations** concerning their impressions and dreams. As it turned out, each king had counselors who would **prophesy favorably** in regard to the prosperity and perpetuation of his particular kingdom, and they would also interpret favorably concerning the peace and happiness of the king's dominions. And especially, if there were strong indication of war and hostility looming, they nearly always prophesied there would be success in battle.

When any of the kings, themselves dreamed, then,these dream-counselors or **prophets** were called to reveal the meaning of his dream and **were-always** very **indefinite**, unspecified, and very **vague**, but would give general remarks and only state or establish a **probability** of the event to occur.

In those generations of eastern Asia tribe which would follow this period, many prophets arose among the Persians, Chinese, Chaldeans, and Egyptians, nations who all **recorded** their impressions and their **pretended communications** with the deities, done by **imprinting** their marks and hieroglyphs upon soft impressible substances, and then of course these were safely preserved for the sake of their divine and celestial contents.

This state of things concerning dreams, dream interpretation, and prophecy, continued on for many ages, mankind is advancing as a whole race, even-though they are generally ignorant imbeciles; and in relation to the origin of manuscripts, this particular time may properly be termed, the **era** of **oracles**.

# Section 102

It is known, that with the passage of time the world would progress somewhat and in general was now becoming more enlightened, and many improvements and advancements have taken place; this general progress and improvement is universal and is occurring all throughout the world of living things. Even Nature has **confirmed** her truthfulness, by a consistent progression and development of **increasingly complex** productions. And as Nature plainly shows her beauty, mankind's intellect also becomes more stimulated and more **intrigued** by those wonderful things they saw; in this way, Nature actually **prompted** man to become more **introspective** of the world around them. The expanding intelligence of mankind, a result of further developments of their **reasoning faculties**, led them to begin discarding many of the original superstitious conceptions of their forefathers. This action of freeing the mind of some of its burdens, would allowed man to develop a more truthful and exalted conception of the **Great Spirit**, which some minds **had-finally** started to believe had created and who controls the Universe.

The developing mind of man had become aware of **apparent errors** in their beliefs and finally had come to question the imagined beliefs, also they began to **question** themselves concerning the "breaths" being the cause of the evil around them as their forefathers had taught. There must have been some spark ignited inside the undeveloped Soul of mankind which led to the opening of their minds and **motivating** their reasoning thoughts. What else would have prompted men to question the traditions formed by their forefathers?

This present time-period had produced some very noble and **expanded minds** all which began to emerge among the differing nations of earth. And in time it would be some of these more advanced thinkers whom developed the **skills** that were-necessary and which would enabling them to use improved **tools** and methods in the art of **writing** hieroglyphs. And as it turns out these genius of their time, not only reasoned profoundly, but now they were also able to **record** their thoughts and their productions . And it is the action of thinking and writing, which gives the first indication of a **mental resurrection** for mankind.

Among those gifted individuals whose minds were expanding rapidly were many Chinese, Egyptian, Persian, and Greek philosophers, whose advanced minds conceived thoughts of **pure principles** of **morality**, these principles they promoted and would put into effect by the example in their daily living patterns. And it was some of these great thinkers that had developed high and truthful **conceptions** concerning the great first and **essential Cause** of the Universe. From their fast developing awareness of the world around them, they began to developed a belief in the doctrine of **immortality**, which eventually became a part of their teachings.

The east Asia nations were developing quickly, however the mental progression of men and women existing on other land portions of earth were developing at a **slower** pace. These less intelligent groups continued to say and perform **pretend** prophesy. These prophets would **fake** truth, and pretend and fabricate prophecies which they falsely claimed were divinely instructed. Around this time-period the **Egyptians** and other eastern tribes **discovered** the power and art of **inducing abnormality** by various gestures and manipulations. What was discovered was that there existed peculiar persons who were very **susceptible** of being **influenced** in this manner and were easily induced into an abnormal state of consciousness; these special individuals were selected and brought into the presence of the king's counselors, who would **affect them** physically , and make them appear as if they were dead – inducing the sleep which they supposed was necessary in order that they might have direct communication with the deities and be able to receive advice from the them.

The procedure of inducing an **altered state** was a necessary development because they could-not always dream when they chose to. So, in order that a dream might be had, when desired, they would throw these persons into a state, similar to death, and would receive from their lips, the **vague** expression of their dreams; which then, would be interpreted by the counselors or prophets present, and then would send forth to the king the interpretations as being true and divine.

The use of this power or technique of placing someone in an altered state, continued for some time until it was finally discovered that in most situations, these dreams and visions were unreal and unreliable. **However**, - the real reason those dreams and visions were incorrect was because these techniques were **improperly used**. So the **power** and **sympathy** of an altered state was in themselves real and useful, however these undeveloped skills were used incorrectly and were instead, made to be the agents of perpetual deception. And so, here is an example of how dreams, visions, and prophecies, being used unwittingly as the **agents** and **causes** of an immense amount of disunity, deception, and wickedness, pounding down among the families and nations of the earth.

It is surely impressive, but at the same time it is also ridiculous, that some of these early oriental prophecies, especially the ones that were derived from erroneous dreams and visions, have somehow become tangled and immersed into the mythical writings which **now-form** a part of the Primitive History of man. This tangled mess was perpetuated and sustained, and continues into our modern times. And so, it is right and proper to set straight the fact that the **urim** and **thummim** among the Egyptians, are nothing more than a modified medium and means of obtaining knowledge of the future and used as a means of **sustaining** the jobs and professions of those men and women whose lives and talents were spent in the occupation of prophesy.

Nearly all physical manifestations occurring in Nature were **incorrectly understood** by these various primitive nations as they all attempted to gain an insight into the future. And nearly all these future predictions of events and actions, were imagined or fabricated entirely from **assumptions** made according to the prophesies of each nation. For example: an occasion might arise that would need an interpretation because someone had noticed a rainbow appeared in the sky shortly after a terrible event, and being ignorant of science, the interpreter **did-not** understanding the phenomenon of light refraction and its various colors; so whenever a rainbow appeared, they conceived the **rainbow** was an **omen** or an expression by the Deity, who supposedly gave a promise, that the land should not again be overflown with water. In our modern times, from modern scientific knowledge it is clearly seen that it was their ignorance which allowed them to conceive of such fantastic and imaginative conceptions.

There are other types of prophesy besides prophesying war, even though some of these other prophecies are ones actually derived from the same sources: for example, in the saying: *"summer and winter, seed time and harvest, shall never fail"*. This phrase for the most part is a true prophesy, and is a perfectly natural statement, because it is based upon the decision of a learned and convinced judgment, whom is just simply stating the fact: "that which is now, and has been from the beginning, will be perpetuated". In addition there are several other types of prophecy which early man used to explain the world around them; some of these other early impressions are loyally represented in the Primitive History, but beware, because they are complete **exaggerations** made by some of the authors of this history; and their reason for doing this was sometimes just to bring praise and **profit** to themselves. Prophets were actually employed and engaged in protecting kings and kingdoms from the invasions which were constantly expected to come from other nations. Which is why each nation would have prophets who would prophesy against an opposing nation, yet at the same time also have ready a positive prophecy for their own nation.

Prophecies and stories where told of marvelous works, of prosperity, of being assisted by deities and special beings, of triumphs and of pending doom. Other prophecy would lead families and nations on tedious and protracted expeditions; and in some cases the prophecies were used by a particular king or ruler for **maintaining** power and used simply for the end result of governing and **controlling** those ignorant and superstitious people. The assortment of words such as sheol, hades, tartars, and gehenna, were originally used by the prophets to express death, darkness, the grave, pain, wretchedness, and sepulchrous abodes, and on occasions they were all used in describing their enemies. In our modern time the meanings of these words have been misinterpreted, or used deceptively, and have now taken-on a whole new meaning. As these words now stand in the Primitive History, they represent and express merely and only those things which they were applied to by the Jews and Greeks, who would represent them as dark and loathsome valley, or some impassible and dreadful gulfs, maybe signifying a dark and gloomy grave. Prophets would assign words such as these to any unbelieving, stubborn, or resistant persons, condemning them to the hideous and dreadful valley of gehenna, or to the pit, sepulcher, or hades.

Some prophets continued to speak of the gulf or abyss that had been imagined and taught by that powerful potentate/chieftain/governor of the southern tribes of Central America. And the reason for this continued tradition, was that it was from those southern tribes, whose branch nations settled in Egypt, and which were the **origin** of the **Jews**.

# Section 103

All the particular **prophecies** that are contained in the **Primitive History** are the ones that have been retained from the collection of numerous **manuscripts** of the ancient prophets. And those ones that have been retained **seem** to have a connection with one another, and a connection with the doctrines which the Jews felt very anxious to sustain. This was done with a **purpose**, so that the gentiles might be entirely overwhelmed by the influence of their preconceived mythology.

More writings and manuscripts were **rejected** as useless and irrelevant by the Jews, than are now contained in the Primitive History. This process occurred at a time before the manuscripts which now form the **record** were even collected for arrangement.

The second part of the Bible in a similar fashion, is also a compilation composed of a **selection** of **manuscripts** made into the New Testament by the councils of bishops convened at **Nice** and **Laodicea**. And some of these manuscripts have absolutely no connection whatever with the primitive records.

The number of **sacred writings** which had been composed by each nation during the "era of oracles" were many. And it would be after the "age of prophecy" that various nations made **selections** from all these materials; and so, each nation would form its **own** sacred records. And from all of those original writings the **Jews copied extensively**; but they eventually would only preserved and used those particular writings that were in **perfect unity** with their own **preconceived mythological theology**. And any of those peculiar manuscripts and writings which were-not united with their philosophy, these were then, methodically reviewed three times, then rejected and thrown into the fire.

One reasonable reason why those unused manuscripts were destroyed, simply had to do with the fact that nearly all of those that were burned did not have a name and date, and many did not show a connection at all to any circumstances which would indicate are reveal their origin, so they were not useful and no retained. Now in speaking and dealing with those writings which were kept, most of these sacred writings had been physically stamped upon, impressed upon, or written upon, some type of adequate materials such as the soft bark of trees, or clay, and these were written in **hieroglyphical** and pictorial characters.

The Jewish rabbis are well informed concerning the origin of the Talmud; the Mohammedans are well aware of the origin of the Koran; the Brahmins know of the origin of the Shaster; the Persians know the origin of the Zend Avesta: But modern theological speculators do not know of the origin of the particular history which they have often defended by the pen, the stake, and flame, and most powerfully and effectually by the potency of the **sword**.

For many centuries the Primitive History was uncondensed and was not in a book form like it is seen in modern times and was mostly consisting of a collection of manuscripts. The initial number of manuscripts which were first collected and maintained would be enough pages to fill at least three full books. All the writings were without names, but it was evident that nearly all those manuscripts were written by different persons. The historical periods at which the manuscripts were written, vary from six thousand to fifteen hundred years before the present time.

The **original manuscripts** in possession of the Jews were written in the **Greek** language. In addition to these original writings, the Jews also collected other manuscripts from other nations and writers, and in a similar manner their contents were also transcribed into the Greek by them. And it was at this period that many portions of the Primitive History were transported into Persia by the Jews; and the Jews along with the manuscripts were retained in Persia for several centuries, until the Jews were taken into captivity, at which time they transcribed some of them, and the remainder they brought with them when they returned to their own country.

Moving ahead in time, this now, is the period of which was just spoken of, this is that time when many of the original writings, namely those writings which turned out to be **opposed** to the Jew's peculiar opinions, and so they were **rejected**. And now, those writings that were **saved** were **combined**, and these saved manuscript would then constitute the last will and testament of the Deity as recognized by the Jewish rabbinical writers.

This collection remained unchanged for nearly one and a half centuries after they were compiled – and then a new revision occurred, one which resulted in a further rejection of some of the manuscripts then-existing, and it was here where also occurred the **division** of all those manuscripts retained, grouping them into books. These were subsequently divided into chapters, each book being **named according** to the person who was **supposed** to have written the manuscript. Chapters were subsequently divided into verses; but all these divisions are the work of recent date.

There are some passages in the Old Testament which seem to be prophetical and they appear to relate to events which actually did occur; however, in some cases the compilers occasionally had changed the tense, and doing this to make the prophecy appear more definite. And there are many instances that could be pointed-out which would reveal places were the present tense has been changed to the past tense, and then in other place where the future tense is used instead-of both the past and present tense.

When peering into this particular period of mankind's history, and specifically with reference to the development of **religious dogma**, it could be correctly termed a time or an age of diverse theology with many beliefs and systems of beliefs were in existence, and then add the fact that all these various systems are **interspersed** with folly, ignorance, prejudice, fanaticism and trivial pursuits.

Now in **review** of the preceding information given, there was the explanation of the **origin** of the oracles and prophets, which hopefully has been made plain to understand. Realize, that those writings are **merely** historical writings originating from the minds of undeveloped man that **can-not** be depended upon for being truthful or realistic. They are merely indications and **examples** of the effect of **ignorance**, effects of uncultivated judgment and imagination, which fell upon primitive man's mind and are now shown in man's historical writings. Basically this collection of manuscripts are **unimportant** in respect to the great end which these sayings are designed to accomplish.

# Section 104

Well the question may be asked, is there the possibility or even the probability of truthful prophesy?

The **method** used in oriental prophecy was to **interpret** signs and omens to be indications of future events which would unfold and occur. But this method was not reliable and the events seldom occurred as anticipated; because a sign **must always** show the particular event which the prophesy was made to indicate, or else it is not a sign.

Prophets and dreamers were in the habit of producing simple, **vague**, and meaningless, signs to represent some great and glorious events or even appalling catastrophes. And so, it was because of their meaningless simplicity and vagueness, that these prophesies were unreal, and then because of this fact, finding any connection between the prophecies and the occurrences is **impossible**.

Many prophesies apparently were actually fulfilled, and this fulfillment was done in a substantial manner; but these are **incidental** occurrences and did not follow the prophesies true form of fulfillment.

Things or events prophesied according to existing **probabilities** did sometimes occur, because it was a trend that was taking place which the prophesy foretold; but there is no evidence of the actual fulfillment of all those ambiguous prophetic claims which were given by many of these prophesies which are contained in the Primitive History.

Irregardless of the prophets particular mode of prophesy, many of their prophecies were impure and unholy to begin with. They were very **destructive** to the morals and happiness of the prophet's own nation and **always tended** to excite hostility, envy, and sectarian vengeance, in the minds and hearts of those to whom their prophecies were against. Many of these prophecies were certainly not celestial pure or of a refined nature; this is known because all the prophet's deeds and expressions were always blackened by **sectarian fanaticism**. Again, those prophets were not deceiving but deceived.

Is there true prophesy? In the first place, in order to prophesy or foretell accurately and truly an event, the person **must-be** in communion with the **original design** of the **Divine Creator**, and know of the **laws** at work which are developing that design. The mind, when it correctly understands these things, is then able to foretell occurrences throughout eternity. **Therefore**, there can be no truthful prophecy **unless** the laws fulfilling those designs, are completely understood. And yet still, it is **impossible** to foretell an occurrence absolutely and **with-certainty**, by any signs or indications of any external event or circumstance. It is a thing, which never has been done, and can not be done by any Being in the Universe.

Prophecies are truly made concerning the movements of the planetary system and concerning eclipses that are to occur; but there can be no sign or indication which would demonstrate the occurrence of an eclipse before it actually takes place. And when the eclipse does occur, well then, that is the sign. So then, whenever any prophecy which was made is being governed by unvarying laws, then it will be for this reason alone that it is infallibly true.

Besides, it is **impossible** for any mind to be enlightened from the higher realms concerning **incidental** external circumstances. Because all incidental and external circumstances are **soon-fading** from memory, these things are temporary and are forever changeable, are not connected with any design, nor are they produced by any interior-cause, nor are they governed by any general principles. And it does not matter how advance a mind becomes, whether existing in higher realms or just the simple-minded and uninformed minds of man's present state of existence. So to definitely foretell of war, or an accident, or some other incidental circumstance, is positively an impossibility; because it is not in the power of any internal and general principle to foresee, foreshadow, and foretell, to someone's mind, some merely **incidental circumstance**.

It is upon **interior principles** alone, that a prophecy can be made with an absolute certainty of its accomplishment; and therefore, if it were possible for these to see and foreshadow external and incidental circumstances, then a prophecy concerning such things, might be relied upon. But, as this is not in the nature of general principles, and is beyond the power of individual influence, then it is said again, it is **impossible** for any Being, either in this or even higher spheres and states of mind, to foretell any particular circumstances of an event, with the absolute **certainty** of their occurrence.

## Section 105

Before discussing true prophets and truthful prophesies, it is necessary to give the following: - realize that there are **immutable** unchanging **laws** governing the entire Universe of Creation. By immutable **means** that there is a universal tendency of all things, which can not by any possible means, be interrupted, changed, or frustrated; yet the effects of these laws are plainly seen as those unvarying manifestations and developments of Nature and the Universe. Another item which requires attention concerns those **artificial causes** which are continually producing **unreal effects**, which later are the fleeting and quickly fading and disappearing, circumstances connected with social and physical existence. The best process by which mankind may become **acquainted** with these immutable laws, is by analyzing external, physical events and actions, and then by seeking to know and discovering their **interior cause** and the governing principle of those things.

No one should base their conclusions or their opinions only upon what they see from the external and visible effects of things or events, these really **can-not** be depended upon to give an true indication or show clear picture of what is the interior cause of those things; because, in order to become properly acquainted with the cause of things, well then, the effects or Form of that thing or event **must-be** thoroughly analyzed. So then, by becoming **acquainted** with the **interior** and moving **principles** of Nature, we humans will become acquainted with the elements of the Divine Mind of God, and may also become acquainted with the universal designs. These designs can be seen as the **effects** of creation and the **developments** of evolution which constantly are manifested throughout Nature.

A **true prophet** is someone who becomes acquainted with the **interior cause** of things and events; and from that action they can become correspondingly familiar and acquainted with the effect of things or events; and so, if a prophet's mind **relies upon** these interior laws for their foundation, then any effects and external manifestations, including future effects, **may-be** prophesied the utmost certainty many millions of years in advance.

It is without dispute that all physical effects which occur, are all governed by **Laws** and **Principles** which are the real producers and the real driving-force of the **causes** of all those physical effects; and all physical effects which are seen, all developments, and all manifestations, are simply the real and **inevitable consequences** of the interior, divine, and creative, **First Cause**.

The very first thing which occurred in the beginning, a **Cause** produced an **Effect** and that first effect became the cause of another situation of cause and its effect; and so, cause and effect became universal and eternal, according to the **promptings** of the interior essence or divine Cause, which will produce one general, external, and celestial, effect.

So these rules which have been just given, dictate what is termed prophecy, and are the only basis upon which rests all **truthful** and infallible **prophecy**.

Now, speaking in a general sense about mankind's development, it has been shown that the **conditions** and circumstances which **surrounded** the first types of mankind as they began their upward development were **very unfavorable** to the proper unfolding and development of their sprouting mental faculties, and man's mind was a blank-slate. The **consequences** and effects of these unfavorable circumstances, was the **unfortunate development** of an **improper tendency** of these faculties and inclinations of man to make wrong choices, and man continually **misinterpreted** the meaning of things, events, communication, and even misinterpreted their own imaginary beliefs.

So the **first misdirection** of man sprang from unfavorable conditions, and this first misdirection of mankind **was-not** connected with any law, design, or principle, which governs the Universe. Man mind was blank except for animal instincts and the beginnings of the development of reasoning skills and so **was-not** previously pure and **did-not** fall from grace, nor are mankind being punished because they ate from the tree of knowledge. Instead, the **first error** was merely from the youthful tenderness and innocence of man's undeveloped mental faculties, and from there is where **sprang** all the crude and **imaginative impressions** which still are wrongly instilled within the minds mankind and at the present modern day, still cover and clothe the minds of man with a most unreal and unfortunate garment or error.

Man's ignorance is the cause of their first misdirection yet it is the these particular circumstance which they now have the **power** and ability to **remove**. Man can redeem themselves and all those first errors and misdirection of our early ancestors can be changed and corrected. It is us mankind who have the power to create new and improved circumstances, and to correct, control, and even annihilate, those first errors.

Now as related to prophesy, **realize** that the unfavorable circumstances which mankind has created for themselves **are-not** events that can be **prophesied**. These circumstance which surround everything, including us mankind, only can occur as thousands of other and various events and possibilities occur and these circumstances are **absolutely impossible** to foretell with certainty. However many of the early prophets did, **pretend** to prophecy and foretell of wars, famines, and pestilences, and the prophets would **produce** simple **signs** which **they thought** corresponded to the event and claimed they foresaw the coming of the occurrence prophesied. Other prophets, would in a similar manner **attempt** to predict the destruction of cities and downfall of nations, and would speak of many things that were supposed to occur in the future, and would **say almost anything** that would **bring them profit** or advance in their own position or advance those for whom they prophesied.

Many of these pretend prophesies are **still-contained** in the Primitive History. Some of them were actually fulfilled; but this action of fulfillment of some, gives absolutely no evidence of any divine instruction which was supposedly given to their authors: - and this is because, all these **external circumstances**, which **are dependent** upon favorable possibilities, are entirely beyond the reach of all prophetical minded or divinely-instructed persons, because these things are **not-destined**, but instead, flow from the **corrupted** and fleeting circumstances which mankind has situated themselves, and so, are simply the ever-changing tendencies of human society and the circumstances of physical existence.

# Section 106

In review, the **main objective** contained within the preceding two sections, was to **make-plain** and to **establish** without bias, the **probability** of truthful prophesy occurring, and also, to rightfully **defend** the Primitive History or Old Testament, against the many false and imaginative interpretations that have been **imposed** upon this collection of primitive stories by later interpretations especially in reference to the more modern theological **speculators**.

The Primitive History gives a very simple and detailed description of the prophecies of men who lived at a time-period which was **before** the time when the manuscripts were actually compiled into the Old Testament; and many of these men made no claims to prophecy beyond the limits of their own era.

There is another objective - in making these facts about prophecy plain and clear, which is, to establish a **division** between **real** and **unreal** prophecy, because then, a comparison can be made. Realize that **there-are** prophecies contained in the Primitive History that are true, divine, and righteous; and so then, it will clearly be noticed, noted, and revealed, that those who had prophesied in an enlightened manner **were-instructed** or became instructed, concerning the **interior workings** and tendencies of Nature. And these **glorious prophesies** proclaimed-upon the unchanging principles of cause and effect, many grand and holy truths – and proclaimed many occurrences which will transpire – and foresaw and explained all the effects that will be occur and be accomplished.

The prophets were generally more advanced and more educated, ant these more advanced men had their **internal** thinking principles so **expanded**, that they were able to **recognize** the interior workings of all divine law, and thus, could with certainty, prophesy and proclaim great and glorious truths. But on the other side, which brings up the truth and **awareness** that modern theologians have **misused** and twisted the original meaning of these prophecies and have repeatedly **misrepresented** them. This **tragedy** for the most part is due to their **misdirected** religious **education** and its lack of honest and truthful instruction.

One extremely important revelation to know, is that **there-are** many words, phrases, and sentences, that have **been-inserted** into the Old Testament. And even though in truth these **were-not** inserted or introduced with any evil intentions or mall intent, but instead, know that the additions and insertions only occurred **because** the compilers seriously **assumed** that those additions should be made, in order that the whole history give a good story and they might present a useful, and connected and comprehensive account, of the things to which it contained allusions to. So yes it can be difficult to know what is truth.

There is still another objective in making the point about true prophecy clear, is so that the mind may now be **freed** from **unnatural affection** and **sectarian prejudice**. Spiritual freedom which undoubtedly is the first necessary step toward a re-organization of society and the world; and then we will be **inspired** with the love of truth and truth only and then be able to focus on our future growth.

An important point to review concerning bible prophesy is to realize that many local prophecies, that can be found in the Primitive History, concerning events or circumstances, which in some of the prophesies were actually fulfilled, **do-not** necessarily give any true evidence of the celestial instruction of their authors, nor do they indicate or even hint to having a superior theology; and so, any belief in having a superiority is an **imaginary** belief. And because those local prophecies are **external** and **superficial** in their nature, they should be shredded and disregarded by any higher-minded, peaceful, joyful, beings who are pressing forward to the attainment of a higher order of things. And taking it a step further, it is profitable to **understand**, that many prophecies of this external nature, which are found to be true, well, these have their **own proof** and so any further **erroneous** interpretation or "stretching" the intent of these prophecies any-further than they truly are expressed, is completely and positively **useless**.

Now then, on the other hand it is well and good to report, that **those** special and pure prophecies which **are-founded** upon the principles of Nature, and which will **of-course** be fulfilled, - these should be highly regarded as important and **substantial evidence** of an enlightened judgment and high and lofty **spirituality** on the part of their authors, and these special instructions should be admired and appreciated. And more, because it **is-proper** that these prophecies should be **proclaimed** to the world: - but, not only as a means in which mankind are finally brought to a truthful comprehension of the causes of things, but also, to bring about the event predicted and prophesied.

So when those noble and enlightened intellects and prophets proclaimed that, *"an end shall be made of sin and transgression, and then everlasting righteousness shall be brought in"*, they **were inspired** with the grand and brilliant truth of a universal resurrection from all immorality and relief from all unnatural social conditions, and that gives a view of mankind's future.

And more good news, because **the mind** which foresaw that *"death would be destroyed, and He that hath power over death, which is the evil"*, **was-inspired** with a high and truthful conviction, of those truths which Nature everywhere proclaims and contributes evidence. And that particular mind had also **conceived** the notion that this temporary, mortal, and often-changing, corruption which mars and stains the happiness and peace of our society, **would-be** in time, finally exchanged for the **genuine principles** of Nature and at that time mankind would be made incorruptible. This special mind who had this vision and had thought this belief, was because **he-saw** that there would be a time when those corrupting and impaired influences, which have long shrouded the whole mental and social world, would be ended and then society and the world would be clothed with happiness and immorality.

Ever since the miserable world of social disunity began mankind has cried-out in mental suffering, and also since that time all the **good** that is to come to mankind and into the world **have-been** proclaimed by all the pure and **inspired prophets**. Prophets **peering internally** into the real reality, and even proclaiming, the **final restitution** of all intelligent Beings to primitive innocence and universal harmony. And those true prophets plainly saw, that when this occurred, there would be no more sorrow nor pain, because the old and corrupted things which have destroyed the peace of society would have passed away and all things would have become new.

The true prophets saw that this pending and eventual great renovation would constitute *"a new heaven and a new earth, wherein would dwell righteousness"*. They saw the evils of society – the immoral and corrupt situations of mankind – and **proclaimed** according to the unchangeable law of progressive development, that *"evil would ultimately be banished from the earth"*, that *"the sun of righteousness would rise with healing in his wings"*, and that *"goodness and brotherly kindness would reign universally"*.

These prophets with expanded and opened minds, contemplated and associated with all things presented before them, to see and received divine impressions of eternal truths which originate from the depths of the inner reality. They **did-not** speak of higher spheres, **because** the world was **not-yet** sufficiently enlightened to receive the truth concerning these things. But they did speak in a most profound manner concerning present evils and mortality, and they spoke concerning future goodness and the permanent restitution of the whole race to peace and harmony.

The true prophets **foresaw** that a **great Exemplifier** of the true moral and spiritual qualities of man **would** ultimately **appear**. They saw that **He** would plainly be known because of His superior qualifications, which would be shown by all that purity and gentleness of disposition, and by all the loving kindness, and the con-sociality that would develop and ultimately reveal to the world a type of social harmony and spiritual perfection never before seen or known.

They saw that this Exemplifier would **possess** all the natural abilities and superior endowments to become and to be the First, the Light, and the Way, become one which the whole race would ultimately progress. The prophets saw that it would be in **Him** would be developed all that high moral purity and spirituality which every human being possesses undeveloped and which is only waiting to be unfolded. **He** was to be a **simple-type** of spiritual goodness and having a perfect social qualification.

This coming of a future truth and unfolding of a brilliant society which the prophets had proclaimed wholehearted and joyously to the world was because they-were **impressed** and **compelled** to do so by the teachings of their **internal principles** which are able to communed with the Divine Principles that sustain and control the Universe, and these principles emanate from the inexpressible Vortex of celestial Love and Wisdom.

With relation to prophesy, all in all it can be seen that these truth-telling prophecies brought light to the weary minds and hearts of mankind. They also show that their authors had a **truthful knowledge** of the principles of **Nature**, and also knowledge of the divine design which those principles are constantly exhibiting. These great prophets **justly-prove**, that their minds were **maturely-developed** and were proper and fit receptacles for the **influx** of wisdom and knowledge. They foresaw, - that which has been already fulfilled, and sometimes saw, that which shall be in future. So their prophecies in particular, are able to be scrutinized and are able to be demonstrated true, because they are **based-upon** those unerring laws **that-must** of necessity, ultimately **progress** in the effects predicted. The prophets saw that **truth** is a positive principle, and that **error** is negative and superficial; **they-saw** that Truth and Love which are positive and eternal must transcend and subdue anything which is merely fleeting and superficial.

# Section 107

In the next **topic** in the series, will be a discussion of the **birth** and **use** of **that Being** (Jesus) who was the **highest** personification of Virtue, Purity and Goodness.

Before proceeding straight to investigate of the special Being and **noble personage** and before discussing any of the prophesies concerning **Him**, which are joyfully found written in the Primitive History; first, a concept must be brought to the surface within the context of this discussion, by inserting, some **highly-important** thoughts and reflections in reference to "the Divine origin" of **Truth**, and to show its unchangeableness and omnipotence.

First to ensure that it be clearly understood within every mind that man **did-not** create himself, nor did man create anything in the plant and animal kingdoms. And mankind **did-not** plan and execute the creation of the earth, or the solar system. Also, man is not in any way connected with the production and the establishment of the harmony of the Universe. Further, man is not engaged in developing a new divine principle, or able of unfolding from the Vortex of the Divine Mind any laws or principles which never before existed.

Mankind can not with all his pride and presumption, annihilate or change one feature or quality of a single particle that enters into the composition of an harmonious Universe: nor is man competent to alter truth by resting-in confidence in its opposite, which is agony.

And while mankind **is-capable** of believing or disbelieving, and they can **choose** to have an affection for some preconceive impressions or so ideas which they consider truth, yes they can, if they so choose, but, Truth itself remains the same and is not affected either favorably or unfavorable by the fleeting opinions of man.

**Truth** is an element of the Divine Mind and is developed by the principles of wisdom, uniformity, and harmony; and these are qualities **which-are** what characterizes and makes perfect all that is created. Truth is therefore of **Divine** and celestial **origin**, and is a **necessary** and unchangeable **principle**, and it is **eternal**. So it will be known, that because Truth is divine in its origin, eternal and unchangeable in its nature, and omnipotent in its constitution; then, if a prophecy has truth, then it is Divine.

You may recall, the early inhabitants of the earth **conceived** the notion in their primitive minds, that they lived upon a flattened sphere, supported by as many huge living monsters as an imagination could imagine. Mankind instinctively made attempts to understand the world around them, just as the human mind is compelled to do, and they attempted to understand the causes of things created because they had the innate **inherent characteristic**, which is Reason. **But** when the undeveloped mind of mankind **failed** to reason correctly, they instead formed within their imaginations many conceptions of strange and mythical beasts. Sadly they lacked sufficient intelligence and enlightenment to comprehend the truth, nor were mankind aware or able to understand the principles upon which they and the Universe existed. Instead, ignorant early man chose the wrong path.

Early mankind sustained a universal belief that the earth was entirely motionless, because these primitives **could-not** believe that such a sphere could possibly revolve and still remain in the same position, sustained by nothing. Now **realize** that many of the writers of the books contained within the Primitive History still **believed** this same conception to be true, and it makes sense that those prophets would occasionally express those opinion in poetical descriptions and verses and then entered them into their sacred compositions, **simply because** that is what their beliefs were at that time.

The false opinion concerning the flat earth was held onto for many thousands of years, and would have continued, however finally a **Grecian** and an **Egyptian** philosopher both would express their conviction publicly that the earth revolved. This opinion gained advocates and supporters, **but** sadly, they were few in number in comparison to those who still sacredly believed in all the imagined and superstitious traditions of their ignorant forefathers. And so once again, in error, the flat-earth theory continued again for many more thousands of years. Now then, that exact-same flat-earth impression and belief continued universally until a well-known **philosopher** of modern times discovered those "interior moving principles". These new thoughts continued to overwhelm his mind and were long reasoned within his mind - to be an incontestable demonstration that the earth and all kindred bodies **revolved** unceasingly, and in harmony around the Sun their parent. He is the philosopher who discovered the truth; but the **truth** had **always-existed** in the same manner, from all eternity! However, it is a historically known fact that the nations of the earth which existed during Galileo's time, **opposed** our philosopher with all their might, **because** for many ages prior mankind had their supposed **sacred oracles** and prophets who had always taught a different doctrine; and because the traditional oracles were old, they must be true. And so, all the various steadfast priests and rulers of the land who wanted to maintain the old traditions, whom were **incited** by an unreal and **superficial** abhorrence and hatred of this philosopher's heresy, well, they opposed this learned man's efforts of advancement and **come-near** to sentencing him to flames and burning him at the stake. It was still those **false impressions** that had clothed their minds with **fanatical hostility** against all new theories and discoveries; especially any opinion or idea which might in any way attract the attention of mankind and drawing it away from those **controlling things** which these king, rulers, and priests were so firmly defending.

In the upcoming and anticipated review of the Primitive History, the writings themselves will be spoken-of in a manner which is aimed at revealing the History's truths; and this overview will be done with caution and gentleness, because this book is deserving of that treatment. However, this book deserves **no-more** veneration **than-do** the teachings of **many-other** good minds that have lived and written many inspiring verses throughout our historical period. And while there is-discovered within those pages some **interior** and immortal **truth** which is clearly being revealed in many of the expressions, precepts, and examples, which are written and recorded there; **realize** that these pages should be loved and admired **only-for** their reality and usefulness – not merely because those pages are found in this particular book or printed pages. A book is a book, but Truth always was, and always will be!

# Section 108

There is a negative side-effect which has arisen from the time this History was first compiled into its present form, and this effect has continued and prevailed into modern-times. This History book has **generated** superstitious beliefs, **enabled** ignorance, and **led** to establishing a number of mistaken beliefs systems. And there has been more hatred developed from this book than it has developed love; mostly because it has produced **selfish** and **arrogant attitudes**, all which originate and stem from the book's mistaken identity. It is for those reasons that a **review** of this book is called-for. It needs to be revealed that some parts of this History are merely collections of writings coming from **other-sources** of knowledge or originating from **compendiums** from a multitude of various early oriental **mythology** - Jewish, Egyptian, and Persian, poetry. Then, to complicate things even more, not only did the Jewish scribes include the early mythologies into their book, but also included in this history book are other beautiful written stories and suppositions coming from the brilliant **imaginations** of many **uninformed** minds of these **historians**.

Yet, also found in this same book are many **noble** and **enlightened** persons whom are represented within those written pages, good men and women whose powers of thought and capabilities of imagination **justly-demand** the deepest esteem and admiration. And honestly, that is a nice relief, because there are so many allegorical and symbolical representations contained in this History that are exceedingly beautiful, are **capable-of** being interpreted in a most brilliant, up-lifting, and magnificent manner.

But, see how **gloomy** does the world clothe this history: - by their action of **falsely spreading** upon this book, much more divinity than the Book even claims for itself. And because people do this harmful activity, it shrouds the truth, by hiding-it in a garment of **gloom** and **impenetrable mysticism**. These grossly ignorant minds make false claims that have had serious detrimental effects to the welfare of mankind. Because the action of hiding truth ultimately does violence to the judgment faculties of man's mind by keeping their minds away from a natural condition and mode of action; and then above all, these false claims **distort** the original true meaning of the writings taking them far away-from their original purpose.

Here is some advise to contemplate, know that when good and enlightened men and women finally do put forth their thoughts to the world, and when they put their noble works forward in an appeal to mankind for respect and praise of their thoughts; the reader, needs to make a clear **distinction** about what is written. Because a choice must-be made between those particular thoughts and ideas which are correct and righteous, or to chose those thoughts and ideas that are unrighteous. The advice given implies that everyone eventually will need to pay-attention to that distinction of things righteous and unrighteous, because all will eventually be required to chose exactly what it is they serve.

By the process of scrutinizing the "Primitive History", this action gives the investigator an **opportunity** to become **acquainted** with some of the **former class** of mankind, which were a much less-developed class of humans and their teachings were somewhat primitive. The pages within this compilation of writings represent some of the thought processes of these rapidly developing tribes of man. But keep fresh within one's mind that these worded pages should only be admired according any information which is found to be useful, and if this action is accomplished, then the history is **naturally-worthy** of praise and adoration.

Good men and good deeds should be praised, **but** no members of classes, races, or nations, of any of the human family, should have some **superficial-distinction** of their characters or have a belief which would set-apart one sect better than another. It is a **violation** of the plainest laws of equity and balance; and furthermore this type of thinking and these actions, may cause one to abandon the divine principles of harmony. Anyone who is on the spiritual path should be aware that the are in existence spiritual writings which have originated from many other spiritual minds which are **as-good** as the spiritual writers of the "Primitive History".

In **reviewing** what has been given concerning prophesy, it was determined that **many** of the early writings of the Jewish historians, prophets, poets, have truthful prophecies and they **are-profitable**, meaning that they promote peace and harmony. But it was also mentioned that some prophecies from these same sources **are-not** profitable, and the reader must determine their value.

So then, it will be in this following important **investigation** of the **origin** of those allegorical and **mythological theologies** of mankind, that **an-attempt** will be made to be conscious of the feelings, affections, and judgments of those many men and women whom are deeply involved in the written material found in the "Primitive History"and who have given their love and admiration to this book; even-though in some instances, they love it more than even their bodies – and love it more than the divine elements of God. Because many zealots, simply are **anxious** to have their present opinions and convictions prevail.

If the Primitive History is an oracle of Truth as is claimed, - then it will still stand, so fear not. If this historical and spiritual book is revealing truth, then no assistance from man is necessary to make it better. However, no matter what these writings may-claim, all still need to be researched, because this action firmly **enforces** the necessity of investigating all things unbiased and without entertaining the least doubt that there is an incorruptibility and immortality of Truth. Remember it is Truth which will set you free.

Trust and cherish the fact that truth will always continue to live, whether it is believed or disbelieved, and it will still be truth whether looked upon by the educated or uneducated classes of mankind. Truth itself **illuminates** its own features with a smile of undying beauty! Let Nature, the Universe, and the Divine Mind, then, be the source of your instruction. The mind of mankind in its true state, is free to think and act – free from all sectarian bondage and superstition.

**Mythology** is the results of **prior ignorance** and **misconception** and from superstitions; and then from effects of mythology all the miserable attributes of sectarian affections and prejudices within the race of mankind have arisen. The many prejudices that exist have profound effects which severely affect the ignorant uninformed minds the most; these in many instances even establishing cruel walls of distinction between husband and wife, parents and children, brothers and sisters, nation-vs-nation. Learn from these unholy situations which can only bring separation and hatred. Instead, apply reasoning and not seasoning to **modify** any of your early affections and clearing your heart and mind in preparation for peace and truth, so that this **mindful reasoning** which is gained from quiet spiritual meditation may bring forth good and truthful sentiments.

# Section 109

Now the story proceeds into a discussion concerning **prophesies** and **opinions** found in the Primitive History, and at the same time, **searching** within the contents of this "History" in order to discover any indication or **find** all, that **relates** to or might even have a **connection** with that special, particularly **significant** and **notable personality**, whom is **the-first** with an **elevated character**, that glorious and special personage **Jesus**.

Jesus's birth and life have been clothed and colored with so many **unjust descriptions**, that the whole world of the twenty first century are in a tizzy, – erroneous and unjust descriptions have been expressed about his great man's life, which simply are **not-true**. So what will be revealed in this search for Jesus, is that many of those historical writers whom provide commentary on the life of Jesus and who repeatedly used words and phrases which were **imagined**, it will be discovered that the **only-use** of their exaggerations was to **embellish** the details of Jesus's life.

Before beginning the investigation of the Old Testament of the Bible, **in-search** of Jesus, it is important to first express clearly the facts which the various historians, chronologists, poets, whom have written these famed stories and historical accounts, all wrote in a style and manner that **normally** would occur and wrote or taught by using the **common language** of their **particular** time-period, and by **using** words and phrases which would **naturally** and normally be used in day to day conversations. Those historians, writers, prophets of that era and situation were **attempting** to address a particular audience, an audience of uneducated, undeveloped, and ignorant people, and so therefore, **had-to** speak and write in a manner and style which was **necessary**, so that the people who were existing at those times, would **understand** what was being said or written. It should be well-understood in the reader's mind, that any average literate person existing in those times, **understood** all the **descriptive exaggerations** which may have been a part of their languages of that period.

Another important fact to acknowledge, and one which may-not be completely realized, is that the prophets, poets, and writers, in general, were all merely human beings and without-doubt those writers may have had previously formed **opinions** and convictions, however that fact arises from what would have been a normal-result of their surrounding environment from birth onward through their individual life and which surely **affected** their writings.

So, now finally, the first thing to be said in relation to finding **Jesus** within the Old Testament, is the reader needs to be aware that there are many accounts and statements given about Jesus which contain in their content, plain outright **contradictions** of the fundamental laws and principles of Nature.

Jesus, **undoubtedly** is The One with the superior purity and majestic greatness. There has not been another human being like Jesus yet, at least none are known. Buddha was not really like Jesus, nor was Moses, not Zoroaster, not Mohammad, or any-other prophet; no Dali Lama; no Pope; and surely no mythological speculator. It was only **Him**, whom came to **light-up** the world. And yes, **Jesus** is the one who **became the Christ** by His development of the Christ Consciousness.

What is the **origin** of the doctrines found in the Old Testament which relates to Jesus? Plainly it can be know, that these doctrines concern the coming of the Christ, **are-derived** from the teachings of men who have been called prophets. So, the prophets will be the starting-point on this necessary search and investigation, which is to properly **understand exactly** what the prophets were attempting to teach, and also, to **discover** where-did the notion of a Savior first come from. So to find the answer to these, it is necessary to begin with some considerations and investigation concerning the **five books** attributed to **Moses**. And then along with the writings of Moses, our search then will continue full-steam, and also considered any other writings which may be connected to the subject of our search.

The first book of the Bible, called **Genesis**, was not written by Moses and this fact is known because the first part of Genesis consists of typical traditional allegories of primitive ages, which **all-had** existed in the world long, long, before Moses lived.

In Genesis, there is the description of the formation of the world, of the creation of Adam, of the garden of Eden, and there is, the tree of knowledge. All of these stories were existing in hieroglyphical written form, and these stories were represented in **figures** and **characters** which **were-known**, understood, and used, by the previously existing **eastern nations**. It is clear that this book - Genesis, already bears enough external evidence to verify its own origin. But theologians have **assumed** that Moses must have at least been instructed in the knowledge of these things many ages after they transpired, which is most-likely true; anyhow, **that-is** the reasoning theologians have given for attributing the writing of Genesis to Moses. Moses was old but he is not that old.

In a strange peculiar manner, some theologians have erroneously **assumed** that the earth is no older than what date is indicated by the chronology of the Primitive History. Some theologians, also have believed and have **endeavored** to prove, that the allegories recorded in the book of Genesis were actual, literal truths. Furthermore, it is well to realize and keep in mind this all important fact, that it is on these **vague assumptions**, all Christian writers for thousands of years, have endeavored **to-form** a connection between the fall of man in the garden of Eden, and this is all based upon their interpretation of various passages which are found in Genesis which relate to the birth, life, and office of Jesus the great **Moral Reformer**. These Christian interpretations have also included the notion of an eventual restitution of mankind whom has fallen from grace, which they **assume** was to be accomplished by the ultimate triumph of the divine principles taught by Jesus of Nazareth.

To anyone with a clear and truthful mind it is distinctly evident that this idea of mankind once being pure and who now is fallen from God's grace, **could-not** have been entertained in the minds of any of the prophets, who wrote any of the books and that includes either the Old or New Testaments. The **apostles** of Jesus, in giving their account of the birth, life, and preaching of Jesus **did-not**, in all their writings, even once indicated any such idea. They **do-not** speak of the original purity of man and of his fall, - especially in connection with the-use of the birth, life, and preaching, of the one they loved so much.

The Apostles themselves **do-not** claim or even indicate that Jesus was a means by which the whole race of mankind would somehow be restored to any level of refinement, which they once possessed. The apostles **say-nothing** of the garden of Eden, nor do they mention the fall of man, nor mention any of the allegorical sayings contained in the book of Genesis. Another fact should be made-clear, is that those who would write about Jesus concerning his birth and preaching, there were men of intelligence, they could read and write and **would-have** surely known of any biblical writings, if they were in exist in the first place, which they were-not. Therefore if the plan of redemption **manufactured-up** by theologians were true, and if those writings had been known by any of the apostles, then surely, those things would have been known about and written about.

Now looking at the first book of the Old Testament, it is clear from many expressions in Genesis, that this first book **could-not** have originated with Moses. But instead, it was written by a man who sacredly compiled the traditional mythology of the ancient forefathers. **Moses** did however, truly write the other books attributed to him. The wonderful stories of history contained in those four books of Moses are **generally-true**. So, it is for the truthfulness which can be found in them, that the books should be inspected, respected, admired, and appreciated.

There is a historical account of the birth of Moses, but the circumstances surrounding his birth, really have no bearing on anything under investigation involving these first five books, though, the birth story of Moses is probably true. And so, **because** the story itself was astonishing to the inhabitants of that region of Moses birth, they interestingly wrote their stories of Moses in such a marvelous manner and with such fantastic descriptions, these stories **lead** to Moses's youth standing-out and being noticed by other people and he became a **distinguish** young man. **Notoriety** followed Moses, and he actually influenced many people in a very positive manner, just by the stories they had heard about him; then, as these stories spread, they were further **altered** and improved upon by many other tribes, especially the **Egyptians**. These fantastic stories in fact would later help **compel him** to succeed, and live up-to the hype. Moses formed a **studious** habit which helped develop, unfolded, and greatly improved, his mind, which proves the notion that if you tell someone they are great and give them helpful praise, they may turn out that way.

Moses was indeed in a happy situation and everyone around him truly believed he was destined for some high and sacred office, and certainly, Moses played-along, enjoying his fame. All this praise, most likely operated upon his self-love, because he pressed forward, he did the work, and he walked the walk, and attained wisdom and knowledge which **transcended** the wisdom of any other man living in those times.

During this period when Moses lived, it **was-common** to use expressions that were prevalent among the eastern nations, such as *"the Lord directed"* - *"the Lord spake"*, *"the Lord showed me"*. Recall how the early inhabitants thought it was the "breaths" that spoke to them; so here in Moses's time there is seen the evolution or higher development of **that-style** of speaking, an evolution of thought had occurred, where **first**, early man would say *"the Breaths directed"*, *"the breaths spoke to them"* and then-next advancing to Moses's style and manner of expression. These "cant" phrase were used **improperly** because they were **used** as some type of moral statement; some "cant" phrases were soon found in many writings, and these became a **means** of expression among the prophetical writers.

Moses as a young man would grow and prosper, and ascended to manhood with a healthy and athletic constitution, and he was in possession of many **superior intellectual** endowments. Moses soon became a learned teacher, **always attributing** his impressions and his thoughts to the influence of the Lord's invisible spirit; and as just stated, this type of "cant" expression was part of the customs and convictions of Moses's time. These customs were in existence to Moses as a child, it was one of the earliest impressions instilled in his mind. Moses truly would be considered far more intellectual than almost any other person of those times.

# Section 110

Moses's long extended **expedition** as the head of the Israelites through the desert, is well known. And, it needs not be asked, as-to whether Moses was designed to be a leader and governor of the Israelites, because this fact is obviously not in question. Moses is Moses.

So now, in the following discussion, the main objective is to show and give an account or description of the **theological opinions** that have been **derived** from Moses's extensive writings, and also to give some historical information that is found in the Old Testament which relates-to those miraculous performances which Moses was said to have performed.

First of all there are many erroneous impressions and beliefs taken from the **supposed miracles** which Moses is said to have accomplished while journeying about with the Israelites. These errored opinions have sustained a place with mankind for millennium, and therefore need **clarification**.

The account told of Moses **passing** with his followers **through** the **Red sea** on dry land, is very truthful. **Except**, the method of how they crossed on that dry land, which was just prior a sea, and what caused the separation of the waters **is-not** told truthfully. How the actual event occurred has been written in entirely a **figuratively** speaking style, and this style of expressing this event was simply used to **enhance** the story. Moses simply "spoke-out" or recited a **procedure**, which he was always accustom to performing. So then the way the story was told, the writer was **only expressing** in an external form, and telling the account of the event **by-giving** a description of a procedure. Moses being a believer in God's might, and firmly had the belief that God worked this way, was **trained** and was observant of this procedure and used it frequently. Moses **was-only** giving praise to the Origin of his thoughts, which Moses believing as he did, that the Lord was the suggester of the idea for him to cross the sea at this point.

But, the crossing and passage across the Red Sea on dry land, with the waters being separated to the sides of the sea, had occurred previous to Moses's crossing, and this same action **has-occurred** since. The simple truth is that at the time of the event, well, the water had **merely receded** from the shallow and elevated portion of the sea-bottom, over which they crossed; a sand-bar, which has since shifted. The tide had ebbed and they crossed a sand-bar.

And another point, it was customary to wave a rod over, or to kiss, or to smite (hit-hard) anything and everything, and by doing this maneuver as a way of **urging-on** a progression of some-sort. Then there is the account of Moses and his tribe being chased and followed by the Pharaoh, which is also true, and just as true is the account of Egyptian army's **destruction**. As the story goes, Pharaohs army, in attempting to cross at the similar place that Moses did, had great difficulty. The army was large, having many men and equipment, and because of the great numbers of soldiers and equipment, the whole army was **delayed** in crossing the sea, and then, as the army did try to pass, the **tide** returned and they were drowned. And so Moses, in error, truly believed in the event of him being saved from his enemy were from and by a direct action of God.

Here are some other remarkable things related in the stories of Moses, such as, smiting a rock for water, or another such as his rod being changed into several forms, - for example a snake; also there is the story of the wandering Israelites being feed with manna from the sky. To explain whether these are true or not, is irrelevant, and investigating them would be a waste of time and effort for they are useless bits of information that do not give moral or physical relief to the human race.

Moses speaks of receiving some divine commandments while upon Mount Sinai, and of receiving instructions from the Lord from a dark and immovable cloud. Saying that a voice came from out of the cloud and gave the stern commandments, which constitute the law to govern the Israelites. In a sense this event is true, but the **actual story** goes like this: Moses, after having been with the Israelites for many years and discovering that many of them were desiring for a change in their situation and their government. But Moses himself had come to his own **conclusion** and belief, thinking that his people **needed** strict laws. Moses had realized that it was **impossible** to inspire the minds of his followers with true and substantial moral principles because they lack intelligence. And like many people, these Israelites seemed to enjoyed fantasy and science-fiction more than truth.

So in his mind, Moses has a conviction and in his mind he believes strongly that it is best if he **retains power** over these extremely fanatical and superstitious groups. Moses had **decided** he was divinely inspired and went on a trip to the mountains, leaving the people behind because he need some peace and solitude and need to meditate and listen for God's voice. He meditate on things what he believed would be required to guide those wandering peoples, whom he saw spread over the plains below. And during his meditations many important thoughts were suggested to his mind. So he began to write upon stones, writing statements he believed would impress those masses below him. Moses doing this action just as he had believed as a youth, that his thoughts were caused by an influx from invisible, celestial beings; Moses on the mountain this time, had **supposed** that the Lord had impressed upon his mind these instructions. Moses was of himself capable of writing those commandments, because of his intelligence and because he was aware of his peoples needs and desires.

# Section 111

There is a particular opinion concerning Moses which is based upon an assumption. Many writers have **supposed** that the laws of Moses were established and then set in motion to govern the world **until** the great Moral Reformer (Jesus) should make his appearance. As it turns out, this particular assumption is somewhat **true**; – However, the two systems of moral government are **not-quite** so intimately connected as so many are led to believe, and especially as they are being taught through the teachings of modern Christianity. In order for that connection between Jesus and Moses to be true, at least in the sense which was intended by theologian's, it would have had to be by the **preconceived intention** of the Divine Mind. Otherwise, if it was-not preconceived, then it would be necessary for God to have "called into being", a purer spirit for the purpose of doing away with the old law, and then, to establish a new law, why; well in answer, it would-have been because God must have made a mistake with His first law and now needed a new law.

But instead, the truth concerning the **two** separate laws was **this fact** that, - in-between the time of Moses up-until the time of Jesus, this new law that **supposedly** Jesus brought, was now really new but in reality was just "one more step" in the progress of **intellectual development** of mankind, and the teachings of Jesus was an **improvement** in the mode of government which had been in use before Jesus's period, which was only those imperfect commandments of Moses. And so, it was by mankind's progressive development, **refinement**, and intellectual attainment, of one more progressive step which was the method and reason of how the **new reformation** by Jesus was determined. Jesus was **more progressed** than any thing before him.

So in this case and situation just described, concerning the two laws, it was not necessary for God to have a higher or more refined principles to govern the Israelites any more than those instituted by Moses. So, the crude yet efficient laws of Moses were **correct** and timely; **because**, if Moses's commandments had been mild, gentle, and highly refined, as was Jesus's, then, if that had occurred, it would have been tragic, because then, those gross, crude, and imperfectly-develop intellects of man existing in Moses's times, would have surely **disregarded** the teachings. And furthermore, what would have followed would be disunity and disorganization as consequences.

But as the case truly was, Moses's principle requiring *"an eye for an eye, and a tooth for a tooth"*, was something that equaled the mind-set and was appropriate for the mentality of those tribes, and these laws were something which they could readily understand and obey, without misunderstanding their meaning. So in Moses's time-period, the commandments of Moses were themselves an advancement and "one more step higher" in the progress of man's intellectual development, and this progress was a huge improvement in the mode of government which before that period was grossly imperfect and even more crude.

The laws of Moses were actually high moral laws compared to those that mankind used in previous generations and governments. But the laws of Moses have no true connection with any other theological system, except, that they can be used to **indicate** and mark a steady moral, intellectual, and social, progression in the condition of mankind. Therefore the writings of Moses are still useful to the world at the present day, though only as a means of enlightening the uninformed, and also these commandments help prevent the establishment of arbitrary moral laws and government.

Recall, the ancients were in the habit of relating to their environment and were able to understanding all things by the action of how things correspond, relate, are equivalent, similarities, and allegories; and those undeveloped minds needed to show the relationship between things in order to **interpret** a meaning. This action then, became a basic **pattern** which was always used in the manner which they communicated. With this **method** mankind could **relate** accounts of things and events, tell their stories, express thoughts. This method soon had become such an **ingrained habit** within the learned knowledge of man, that they would **often-speak** as if their correspondents and allegorical representations were themselves true. Importantly this learned method and habit pattern was a part of them, and actually, it was them; and so it came to be, that this method is exactly how the many stories and prophecies were related and written traditionally, starting from the very first action of writing; and this method or style **was-continuing** into this period with Moses, as can be learned from Moses's writings.

The **method** of language and communication used during Moses's time, this **custom** of speaking allegorically, is evident and widely **used-by** the writers of the ancient primitive history, and particularly by the writer of the book of Genesis. And these customs were also in the writings of the Old Testament, which are often characterized by the allegorical and highly-figurative descriptions of things and events, and it was in this manner the characters being related to in the various historical stories are explained, **as-though** they themselves were true, doing this action **instead** of the description being said in a proper way which would represent things according to the **intention** of their writers.

So to set things straight; the following narrative is what a clairvoyance's impression of some things concerning Moses: *Moses, that Being discovered as he was among the rushes; being believed by all to be **destined** to some high office, and growing up in the knowledge of these things, and in order to make good, the opinions that were entertained of him, and which he himself believed, he studied much, and obtained great intellectual acquirement's. His natural faculties being thus highly developed, he was capable of conceiving more truths than others, and so, became the chieftain and governor of the tribes of **Abraham**. These he lead out of **Egypt**, crossing the pass of the Red sea into the wilderness, where one generation passed away; and the subsequent generation, absorbing all the knowledge and all the opinions of their fathers, **became fanatical** and enthusiastic. Moses being inspired with more brilliant and truthful thoughts than others, owing to his natural capabilities, produced the law and ten commandments, **supposing** himself, that he was **assisted** by a divine influx.*

*Moses was also **capable** of **foretelling** some occurrences, (this capacity was surprising to his brethren). His ability arose because he was sufficiently enlightened to **reason** by observing the tendencies of existing circumstances. He could accurately make conclusions relating to occurrences and situations. He also would receive information from his assistant **Joshua**, on whom he would, by **manipulation**, produce **abnormal-ness**, so that he might **dream** and relate his visions. (Recall, the Egyptians also performed these manipulations).*

*In general Moses's prophecies were true, and he did those things which he seriously felt to be his duty; **although** many of his wars, persecutions, and invasions, are repulsive to more refined feelings of an enlightened mind. He **wrote** the four books in a language and style suited to the customs of that age, and intended no forgery or imposition; but **believed** he was **inspired** with divine teachings emanating from the fire, smoke, and thunder, on Mount Sinai.*

*In judgment of Moses's historical and prophetical relations, he should be approved, admired, and appreciated, simply because his observations are **substantially true**. But, any further than this, Moses's writings are disconnected from any theological system that has been subsequently **invented**. Moses wrote and spoke using the popular and customary forms of expression and the singular modes of allegorical representation, which also were customary among the Egyptians and other Eastern tribes, whom are all a part of Moses's life. These writings with **respect** to the search for*

Jesus, then, so far, have **no-use** in common with the birth and teachings of the Great Reformer, of whom will be spoken-of more and more. Moses as a contemporary expressed himself in a similar fashion as did other writers within his time-period; many writers usually would use the **third person**, which would naturally give the impression that it was not Moses who wrote, but instead some other person. Also, there are many instances in the book of Deuteronomy were sentence structure such as the pronoun, first person singular, has been stricken out by compilers, and instead the third person singular inserted.

In other place of Moses's writings there is the use of present tense, which has in some instances been changed to the future tense. And as it turns out, when reading Moses from the present English version, it is impossible, according to our grammatical rules, to decide whether Moses was the writer, or whether the books were originally anonymous and then subsequently named by compilers. And most-likely if investigated and viewed properly, the last chapter of Deuteronomy was written by another person, who intended to relate the traditions concerning Moses's discovery of the promised land, his divine instructions, and his death and burial. All in all the general information given of this account are true history, and need no qualification. **Aaron**, who was a contemporary and assistant of Moses, was, according to the relation they had, nearly as useful an official as Moses himself, and aided in leading and governing the children of Israel.

But the account of the story given by Moses (as written by himself), displays much more of a generous and forgiving nature than was possessed by any other person then living; and he was **declared** to be the greatest prophet that ever arose in Israel, and that the Lord knew him face to face (Deut. xxxiv. 10). However this declaration concerning him is an **exaggerated description** of his powers of mental conception and also of Moses's openness and susceptibility to be in-tune with his internal promptings or intuition. He was the most enlightened person then existing, either among the Egyptians or Israelites. So Moses led the children of Israel through numerous difficulties and deep painful suffering, until they came near to the land of their contemplated future abode, there dying. It would be Joshua, who was pre-qualified to advance to Moses's position as prophet and governor.

# Section 112

**J**oshua was naturally well qualified in both his physical and spiritual manner. His mind was fertile and receptive to "correct" instruction, as a result of his being influenced by the manipulation of Moses, as spoken of previously.

From Deuteronomy, ninth verse (concerning Joshua): *Joshua, son of Nun, as being "full of the spirit of wisdom, because Moses had laid his hands upon him".*

Joshua was therefore capable of performing the duties of his new station with as much enthusiasm and the same exactness and efficiency as was characterized by the leadership of his predecessor Moses. So **Joshua** now became the chieftain and governor of that expedition of Israelites.

Under Joshua's command the Israelites **attack** the inhabitants of the "promised land". They are **motivated** by the unholy belief that the Lord would sustain them and that the Lord sanctioned them. This spirit of righteousness which characterized the attitude of the Israelites as they fought desperately, and apparently at the sacrifice of all natural sensibilities, brotherly kindness, and affection. An then in a similar manner, there are some theologians whom have made **similar claims** stating nearly the same peculiar belief, that somehow God the Divine Intelligence approved of and sanctioned those bloody and inhuman invasions by the Israelites.

Joshua being **rendered** or caused to be **susceptible** to **interior impressions,** by **being subjected** to **abnormal-ness** (? hypnosis), could with ease and precision, prophesy many things that would and did occur, both for and against the children of Israel. As to the question whether Joshua wrote the book that is ascribed to him is not clear; but know, that the things written in the book of Joshua pertaining to Joshua and the Israelites are true, and no comments are necessary.

In those early days the Israel nation had no king. So after Joshua died this nation would be governed by a number of Judges; and hence the **Book** of **Judges**, follows Joshua.

There were great hostilities among the Canaanites (from Palestine), Ammonites, Edomites, and others, all toward the children of Israel. This was the cause of frequent wars which would occur between them. The tribes of Israel were not able to defend themselves and suffered great afflictions.

The Israelites at this period **occasionally** worshiped false gods and spirits, but **generally** believed in one God whom they called the God of Abraham, Isaac, and Jacob. During the period of the Judges, the Israelites became idolatrous and extremely enthusiastic, this zealousness led to a **fanatical hostility** raging between the governors and various portions of the Israeli nation.

Recall now, that Moses **had-taught** the Israelites that it was by the **supposed assistance** of the Deity, that turned the waters to blood, and Moses claims this assistance also as well in all the other "wonders" performed by Moses. He also taught that he talked to God, face to face. **Aaron** would continued to give the same kind of instruction. And in a **continued** sequence of rulers, these teachings were handed down and advanced by Joshua, and became just as cherished and believed by the Judges and all the children of Israel.

The Jews and Israelites of this period **believed** that both **good** and **evil** originate from the same Divine source. This same general belief can also be seen in all their writings, and it was conveyed to others through the expressions which they would use such as, *"the Lord commanded", "the Lord deceived us"*. One day the Lord was with them, the next day the Lord had turn against them. And they carried this belief even further, and now would claim that all their weaknesses, afflictions, persecution, along with their unhappy situations, were all from the Lord, thus believing that all evil proceeded from the same fountain as does all goodness flow. They also believed that the Lord was the originator of all thoughts, feelings, and sentiments, whether those thoughts were good or evil, pure or impure; for, as stated, they **could-not** account for the evolution of thought, especially with the undeveloped mental-state of mankind's progression existing within their time-period.

It was very **natural** for Moses, Joshua, and the Judges, to have written the history of the afflictions, the expeditions, and proceedings, of the Jews **interspersed** with descriptions containing allegorical language, contained along with more conventional forms of expressions.

So now, other than what has been given, no further instruction could be derived from the theology and movements of the Jews or children of Israel and their governors which could be of value to our present age.

# Section 113

The book which follows Judges (Ruth) appears to have been **written** by the **same person** who wrote both Judges and Joshua: this implication is noted, because the connection is clear, and the book's composition is uniform and historical, as are the others.

The Book of **Ruth** is useful, mostly because it contains some very beautiful writings, many of these describing acts of devotion, kindness, and refined affections. These instruction give descriptions of the peculiar customs of how matrimonial engagements occur. And these customs were upheld universally and were at first widespread, yet in time these customs would be modified, and then as time presses into the following generations, these customs will be completely reformed. The real objective of this particular book appears to not only illustrate these customs of those Eastern nations, but it also had a historical purpose for the Jews, which was to establish the genealogy of **David** and his successors, down to the Babylonian captivity.

The stream of genealogy from Ruth is continued in the first book of Chronicles. However, it is clear that the compilers misplaced those books, along with their chronology, this is stated because the book of Ruth is nothing more that an introduction to the book of Chronicles and it seems as though the intention of it was meant to be an introduction or beginning section to a concise history record, which was then being **compiled**, of the Jews, from David to when Nebuchadnezzar invaded and overpowered Jerusalem and then led the Jews captive into Babylon, known as the Babylonian captivity.

After Ruth, is the book attributed to **Samuel**. Now this man Samuel, a child of Jewish birth, was loved because he was **supposed** to be the chosen of the Lord. It was during his lifetime that the governing Judges would finally give-way to the establishment of a kingdom, having kings much like those who reigned in various potions of the eastern hemisphere.

The transition of Samuel from infancy to youth appeared surprising; and because of this he was soon elevated to a high degree of honor, and his position not only brought him pleasure, but also it brought him great monetary profit. This led Samuel to become a refined person, possessing high morals within his character, and also allowed him to develop noteworthy social qualities. He **supposedly** belonged to a perpetuated line of prophets and that was very important to some, however this fact is unimportant.

The book of Samuel can be viewed in a similar manner as was described in that relationship of the book of Ruth as it related to the book of Chronicles, and to now, with the book of Samuel where the same relationship can be seen, and viewed as a mere **introduction** to the book of Kings, including the continuation of historical information and closely following the book of Judges.

The Book of **Kings** is indeed an index, that **describes** all human governors as being from the fountain of terrible misfortune and misery, because of the **tyranny** and oppression they have caused, where instead they should have given the pure and silvery streams of a well-ordered social government, and a pure and refined morality which should-have existed. The book of Kings bears some evidence of being a **compilation** from abundant written materials and other manuscripts, and among them must have existed the book of **Isaiah**. This notion is stated **because**, the thirty-seventh chapter of Isaiah is identical with the nineteenth chapter of the second book of Kings which appears to **have-been** copied from Isaiah, who must have written previously and whose writings must have been associated with some of those writings that had precede his book. Probably the thirty-seventh chapter of Isaiah is not derived from Kings, but actually inserted as the nineteenth chapter of second Kings, and done so from a serious conviction held by the book's compiler, who thought that verse belonged there.

It can be noticed within the verses of the book of Kings that, even though the writer shows some confusion, he ultimately gives a concise description of the movements and jurisdictions of the kings of the Israelities and Jews. Interestingly, it appears that the book of Kings was written by the same person who wrote Joshua and Judges. So apparently, the book of Kings was originally compiled at the time the Jews were under Babylonian slavery. There are no prophesies found in the books of Samuel and Kings which would apply to our present time, which is unique, because here is an instance where all the prophecies of the writer, apply specifically to the period in which they were made. All the prophesies found in these books applied to the movements of kings and nations, wars, famines devastation, and pestilences.

All the prophesies in Samuel and Kings were true, - because of the **author's superior power of interior perception** and his overall understanding. These remarkable prophesies give good indications of mankind's progressive development, showing a step-forward in mental progression for man. The teachings of Samuel were a major advancement away-from those gross, rough, and imperfect prophesies which originated from the more primitive and superficial teachings which were usual and common with the eastern nations.

The Books of **Chronicles** are next, and these books explain themselves, needing only this remark. It appears as though the last verses of the second book of Chronicles may have an intimate connection with the book of Ezra, the book which follows Chronicles.

Within the writings of **Ezra** can be found some very valuable instructions, this said because this book contains an abundance of devotional material, which describes many events connected with the return of the Jews from Babylon and then continues by describing the rebuilding of their city and temple.

# Section 114

Next in the compilation of the Old Testament is the Book of **Nehemiah**. This is a continuation of Ezraite history that further describes the rebuilding of the temple, as well as various descriptions of other national occurrences. It is interesting that the style of this book is able to **sustain** the character of both secular writings and ecclesiastical history.

Nehemiah was a good and friendly man, loved by his people. He also was a man that had become **interiorly enlightened**, especially dealing-with events and occurrences of his time-period. This book when viewed from a comparison between the original manuscript and what is now available, showing clearly that it is manuscript which has been altered by inserting non-original text. And it was this addition which enabled the writings in this book to remain in circulation and use, other-wise it would have been trashed.

The Book of **Ester** is another book that does not give any prophesies of the future events or things, but is primarily focused upon the immediate concerns of national history, and therefore only relates to those times it was written. This book is not connected to any theological system, and needs no further review.

Next in succession comes the Book of **Job**. This book reveals many clear examples of hope, praise, and worship, together with describing topics such as distrust and oppressive and painful suffering. The book bears external evidence of being from **Egyptian** origins; this is know because in this book there is a **distinction** made between the evil spirit or tempter, and the Lord. This particular distinction between good and evil **is-not** recognized in any of the books preceding the book of Job. Also a very similar story already in existence was according to the traditional Egyptian theology - **Osiris** being the spirit or Lord of light, goodness, and prosperity, and **Typhon** the spirit of darkness, evil, and adversity.

Also in the book of Job, there is **presented** a character suffering inexpressible afflictions. Then, along with this suffering, many other characters are introduced, who play respectively the parts of consolers, tempters, and persecutors, with some of these characters endeavoring to add more pain and create more distress, while others would act as moderators, by showing sympathy and spiritual affection, and some of these kind characters endeavoring to console the sufferer.

The book of Job was **obtained** from the **original manuscript**, but the story was transcribed incorrectly; **yet**, it answers the purpose for which it was intended, which was to represent **allegorically** the great afflictions and oppression to which man was liable, and describes how man must look to the Good Spirit or the Divine Mind for assistance and comfort. It teaches submission, purity, and humiliation. It also advises that a person obtain affectionate **devotion** to **truth** and virtue, and develop immovable confidence in the Divine Mind who breathed into being the earth, plants, and animals, as well as man and the starry heavens. It teaches that there are **evil consequences** to impaired and unholy situations; the horribleness of unrighteous thoughts; and shows the slavery and imprisonment of any particular mind and conscience which continually show no-good thoughts. Meanwhile, Job also teaches a devotional resignation to the Divine Love and Wisdom that is universally prevailing, and to the Divine Design or laws and principles that create, govern, and control, all things. It teaches that meekness, charity, patience, perseverance, and virtue should characterize the disposition and actions of every being who is susceptible to those pains and pleasures ordinarily connected with human life.

The book of Job contains a good deal of inspirational advice and aides in developing an awareness of self and self's action and thoughts, which is the intention of the book of Job. Its heartfelt instructions are pure and good. There is one thing however which is confusing, which is, that the book of Job introduces some characters into the reader's awareness that are later neglected and forgotten; while many other characters and thoughts are retained and their part continued throughout the whole historical and **allegorical relation** within the story. So when view in this light, the intentions of the book of Job can be made useful. But this book is somewhat **confusing** and incoherent when this book is put in **relation** with every other part or books of the Old Testament.

In the books of Nehemiah, Esther, and Job, there are not found even the slightest reference or slightest indication concerning the coming of a Savior.

## Section 115

It is now necessary to **review** some previous sayings and primitive customs which were previously discussed. The intention is to show in more depth the **migrations** of some of the inhabitants of earth, shortly after the last great catastrophe. These migrations in particular relate to the **formation** of the **Jewish** and **Egyptian** nations. So it is **necessary** that the **origin** of early religious beliefs be reviewed and be understood, other-wise the matter would be left in some obscurity.

Recall, that in a previous discussion, specifically one relating to the issue of the nations that were existing upon the earth about the time of the deluge, and especially concerning those that dwelt in **Central** and **South America**, it was stated that they **conceived** that the **Sun** to be the face of a deity who **spread** among them evil, because of their abominations. They **believed** the Sun to be the great vortex of central power and around it the whole Universe revolved, and this imagined belief constituted their peculiar **conception** of the great Creative Cause. At this time it is **not-necessary** to speak in detail concerning the various movements of this Southern nation, nor speak concerning their division into tribes and families – but **instead** directly state, that after this Southern nation's discovery of the art of **navigation**, they emigrated to the eastern hemisphere, where they formed settlements in **Egypt** and also near **ancient Jerusalem**.

The Bible **does-not** give a connected account of the **origin** of the **Jewish nation** after the flood, but simply speaks of **Abraham** being instructed by the Lord in a dream, to journey with his wife to another portion of the land, whence sprang the various tribes of the Israelitish nation. This account is generally **correct**: for, it speaks of one of those tribes which came from the South, and settled in the east near Egypt, the same tribe of which Abraham was a distinguished member. From him forward the history is correct in all its essential particulars.

The first account of **building** and architecture after the flood, when the earth had become dry, was that story concerning the building of the tower of **Babel**. This particular account, represented the descendants of **Noah** as congregating upon a beautiful plain, a place where all materials for building and establishing a city were abundant and accessible. Retaining the terrible memory of their experience concerning the flood and all its horrors, they **conceived** the idea of building a **tower** so high, that if another possible flood would occur, that no waters could rise and ascend to their new exalted habitation. It **seems evident** from this story, that the people **were -not** altogether **convinced** of the unchangeableness of the

**promise** which Noah believed and **interpreted**, and had come from the Deity which Noah proclaimed was indicated by *"the bow in the heavens"*.

At that time of the building of the tower, the world was represented as being of one language and of one speech; and so it is clearly seen, that among these tribes, there was a **unity** of intention, and this was **easily** communicated vocally to each other. They are represented as saying, *"Go to, let us build a tower whose top may reach unto heaven"*, and it is **assumed** that the object of this tower was to protect them from being again destroyed. This descriptive account continued on, and represents that the Lord **agreed** and sanctioned this movement, by promising that whatsoever they desired and undertook should not be prohibited, and that there should be no interference in the accomplishment of their intentions. The building of the tower then progressed, and **massive stones** were conveyed to the spot, and were adjusted with a uniformity characterizing a superior order of architecture. And while they were pleased and elated with their progress, and exulted in the probability of the fulfillment of their anticipations, the account represents the Lord to say, *" Go to, let us **confuse** their language"*!

The descriptive account of the tower of Babel reveals that the Lord **first agrees** to approve their proceedings and the Lord promises that the builders would not receive from him the least interruption; and **then later**, represents him as repealing his promise, and sending forth his power to **destroy** their means of vocal communication!

Bringing that same description now into modern times and terms, this story is understood and **believed** by theologians and their followers, to be the origin of the great variety of tongues and languages among mankind. **Yet** for those who have studied the theological writings of **Zoroaster**, are aware that six thousand years are spoken of in his Zend Avesta in connection with his story of creation, and he tells the story in such a manner, as to show plainly, the visible **similarity** between his account and the account of the six days of creation spoken of in the book of Genesis.

Among the **writings** of the Grecian, the Persian magi, and the Egyptian priest of the sun, may be found **allegorical** allusions to an oriental tradition, concerning the building of a Jaina temple, and how it was constructed in order that the inhabitants might escape another inundation. With all the evidence it seems to be **very convincing** that the account of the building of this tower is **derived** from an oriental **allegory**; this is because, there **does-not** appear to be a single instance in writings or mythology to give any indication that this event actually took place, other than in someone's mind.

The next objective in relationship to the origin of the Jews and Egyptians, is to show the **origin** of the sect called the **Zends** or the fire and sun worshipers.

Recall, that after the **earliest** of the southern nations of South and Central America first became settled in that portion of earth, it was the theology of those nations who **believed** that the Sun, was not only the center of the whole Universe, but also it was the **throne** and habitation of the omnipotent governor of all things. And this was the **same theology** of the Egyptians, Jews, Chaldeans, and some of the Persians, verified by reading **Herodotus.**

Because of their long standing differences in opinions, there was generally a **deep-seated** opposition or **aversion** existing **between** the **Israelities** and the **Egyptians**, and this was mainly because of the dissimilarity of their beliefs: one believing that the Lord resided in one place, and the other existed in another place; while the Zends and other sects were still worshiping the sun, and paying homage to the various celestial bodies.

There was also a sect of **Druids** who were similar to the Druids of the Germanic tribes, which were originally called **Teutons**. This sect had grand formality in their mode of worship; for they wore badges, and were appareled with clothing bearing representations of the sun, moon, and stars, together with the signs and characters of the zodiac. These would secretly worship the sun in their temples or any of the sequestered sanctuaries in which they would congregate. Their form of **compact** (code) and mode of **recognition** were made up entirely of **allegorical representations** of the tower of Babel, of the various materials employed in the towers construction, and of the various **degrees** of mechanical and masonic labor. So each member of the sect or association, was made to correspond to the men who were engaged in building the temple (or tower) and their institution, corresponded to the temple itself.

And **after** the **building** of **Solomon's** temple, the **associations** of this sect, **changed** their institution to a representation of the temple built by Solomon. This sect, then, arose upon a foundation entirely allegorical. But as **time** will sacredize any institution, they were finally led to **assume** that their origin was of a divine nature. See how this **assumption** has progressed into error, within the minds of man.

It may be seen specifically in the fifth chapter of the first book of Kings, that the Jews were not of themselves capable of building the temple according to the desire of Solomon; and that, the king was obliged to send to **Hiram** king of Tyre, for some of the **Sidonians** to come, because they were skilled in masonry and built the temple. **Solomon declares** that the

Jews were not skilled in the art of architecture, and were unfit to construct the temple as he desired. So it was by the assistance of the Sidonians that Solomon had his temple built. The interior of this temple displayed all the grandeur and magnificence which the art of man could possibly produce, from those earliest of sublime conceptions of architecture; for instance, in the dome or center was a spectacular **sun**, glittering with the finest gold, and throwing out radiations of the most exquisite beauty. The interior **represented** the moon and stars, and the signs and constellations of the **zodiac**. Together with this, there was a general representation of the most gigantic and pusile animals that were then known and worshiped; and also represented in the temple were many portions of the plant and floral kingdoms that were most esteemed by the forefathers of Solomon and to those who built the temple.

So it may-be said, according to the account of Herodotus, that the temple was a **complex representative** of the whole creation, and of the Sun as the central power of the Universe.

In the twenty-third chapter of second Kings, it may be read that **Josiah** commanded that all the abominations of the temple and its builders, and of those who worshiped the sun and moon, should be destroyed and abolished. He did all this destruction **because** he had no sympathy with the sects of the Druids and Zends or with any other heathen abominations.

The objective to be gained by the above description, by-relating to things in the Primitive History, - is to explain clearly, the **affinity** and similarities existing between the **opinions** of those Southern tribes whose origin has been revealed, and those modifications of the same opinions as existing among the Jews and Egyptians. And furthermore, this same connection between the three nations is **also-revealed** in the Old Testament, if looked for.

# Section 116

As **Josiah** ruled, the law of Moses is-said to have been discovered, and his rules adopted and applied as the Law over this nation which he was King.

Following the time period of Moses's actual writing of the laws, up until the rule of Josiah, a **main task** of the initial **believers** of Moses's laws, was **to-convince** the entire Jewish nation in **adopting** those laws. For instance, **Hilkiah** and others had been thoroughly engaged in promoting those laws and commandments of Moses. It will be noticed in the book of Kings, that there is frequently mentioned, the heathen worship and abominations that were prevailing. And again it can be noticed, in the worshiping of the Sun, as mentioned in the book of Job (the star Pleiades).

All the differing sects that existed in that period, had in their possession **many** written **allegorical representations**, and numerous written correspondences. These were all existing, long before **Homer** or any other **Grecian** poet wrote any of those representations into **verse**. However, there is **Hesiod**, whom was a contemporary of Homer, Hesiod **was-able** to explain some of these stories, including many of those with demonic personages which were supposedly speaking to the mind and imagination of Homer. And then, in the writings of Homer there is scatter throughout, demonology and allegory expressions. In another historical account, given by the Jewish historian **Josephus**, who writes concerning the magnificence of the exterior and interior of Solomon's temple. So it is clear by all this recorded **documentation** that many of the things related in the books of the Primitive History or Old Testament which have been examined so far, **must-have** been derived from **oriental traditions** and **demonology**, which had at the time those books were written, **formed** the **foundation** and **theology** of many early sects. As a consequence of those oriental myths being available, they were alluded-to by Moses, Joshua, Solomon, Hezekiah, Josiah, and others whom were aware of those early manuscripts.

So then, in order to **confirm** what has been said upon this subject, especially to those great minds whom are exploring the labyrinths of antiquity for their information; well, those great minds are referred to the **images** and **hieroglyphics** of Egypt, including their primitive records. Because, these ancient representations, are almost as old as the hills, and they descend into the interior of time, going many ages back in time much-previous to the chronology of the Primitive History. And in addition there are those manuscripts that are also, as old as the hills, and these suggestions refer to the traditions and writings of the **Chinese** and to their records, which extend in an unbroken manner, thirty-four thousand (34,000) years beyond the chronology of the Bible.

Furthermore, by making **close observations** of the written matter contained in the Old Testament, and noticing the style of the writings found in those books, they will be found to exhibit, **undeniable indications** of allegorical and figurative conceptions; which as a fact, accounts for the presences of many vague and ambiguous expressions which occur among the writings found in those books. It is also clear from various external evidences, which all point to the same conclusion, and that is, that the accounts contained in those books are generally **founded-upon** actual historical facts and this is in spite of the vast amount of skepticism which has arisen from the ambiguous style in which these books are written.

But, it is **no-wonder** that skepticism has existed in reference to such a combination of impossibilities and fantastic occurrences, as a literal view of these writings would present; and for those who are attempting to interpret them literal, now its known why your so confused. And it would be equally **natural** to **expect** that an immense amount of superstition and **theological speculation** would grow out of a **superficial view** of such marvelous revelation. And so it is natural that skepticism has arisen concerning these myths, it is because some minds are superiorly **enlightened**, and these enlightened minds cannot place any confidence in those things which neither addresses their judgment nor their affections.

And now, because of the negativity surrounding these biblical writings, the enlightened mind is being led to discard these teachings. And as a consequence of their distaste and negativity they **have** also **become** unable or **unwilling** to believe anything concerning the great truth of **immortality**. However this unnecessary disbelief of something that is of truth, arises from many situations, but all of these **barriers** stem from **lack-of** knowledge and understanding. The **closed minds** now believe in the divinity and sacredness of every word recorded in the ancient writings which now compose the Bible.

For an example of confusing biblical writing: when passages occur in the Old Testament which make the Lord say one thing and do another; or when, as in the cause of **Saul**, - an evil spirit is represented as proceeding from the Divine Mind; and when, many expressions of "similar character" occur, some of which are found in **Jeremiah**; realize this, that these have their explanation in the fact that, initially the different tribes and nations had first **envisioned** and then **assumed** the notion, that the evolution of thoughts proceeded from what **they-believed** was an influence and an effect of the spirit of the Lord. Therefore they would in their writings use the expressions, *"The Lord spoke" - "The Lord directed"*, etc, saying these things in-order to **justify** that particular **opinion** they had, and further, they would always write in a style or manner to **imply**, as if they actually believed in this manner of receiving instruction and knowledge themselves. So when Saul desired the presence of the witch of Endor, he was merely desiring to have an experiment performed. One that would surprise and terrify those who would hear of or witness the occurrence.

It should be clear to every reflecting mind, that **neither** Samuel **nor** any other physical being or any organic organization, **after** it had died and had **given-up** its interior moving principle or spiritual essence at the moment of death, could then resurrect itself, and actually experience a resurrection, including a recharge and return of those vital powers and mental faculties which before had characterized the living organization of the body.

It may be inquired, " How does anyone know from their **limited** acquaintance with natural laws, that such an occurrence never took place" ?

In answer to this, I would mention that the Laws of Nature and the Universe are the **mediums** by which God's designs are accomplished - and that **each law** which exists at the present time, **must have always existed**: for otherwise, the unity of plans and designs would not have been completed.

Therefore, if such an event **ever-did** occur, it **must-have** been designed, and therefore was a result of an eternal law. And if that peculiar law, in that particular instance, accomplished an eternal design, then it would make sense that other instances of like nature **would-have** subsequently been apparent and numerous.

# Section 117

Proceeding in our story, and now, to the book titled **The Psalms** of **David**. This book follows after the book of Job.

Soon after the decline of King Saul, **David** became the chosen of the people, and was generally beloved. David possessed many superior **social** and **moral** qualifications. And he was a man generally inclined to have ideal and grand thoughts, these thoughts originating from his **high moral** and spiritual goodness, and his truthful social affections and friendships.

David's deep **meditations** were facilitated entirely from his moral influences that naturally flowed outward. Along with this highly inspired ability, he possessed a great sense and spirit, and an **attitude** for **obtaining wisdom** and understanding. His **interior faculties** were **very expanded**, mostly by his frequent meditations, and it was from this action of turning his mind inward and listening, that he developed into a **suitable receptacle** of pure expressions, of not only feelings and sentiments, but also gaining prophetical knowledge.

He loved the silent and undisturbed groves of trees existing near him because this is where he could retire and commune with those more interior and truthful streams of his thoughts and feelings. He, in his thoughts would breath praise to the Divine Intelligence. He felt it was a great privilege to be alone.

The peaceful times he had alone, allowed King David to compose and contemplate his **psalms** of praise to the Divine Mind. He loved mankind, and adored and worshiped Nature, the Universe, and the Creator. He was a good man, and he gave a example by his good and proper deeds. And so, these descriptions are examples of a very spiritual being who lived the type of living, that is worthy-of and profitable to imitate.

David as a prophet spoke many truthful **prophecies**, and among them were some concerning the prosperity of **Zion** also known as the city on a hill, and he also spoke of a **great Reformer** who would possess in-combination all the physical and spiritual perfections which are contained in this rudimental sphere of material existence on earth.

An example of David's **insight** can be read in a prophesy from Palms 2 verses,7,8,9, -- a prophesy like this one which will soon follow, concerning the birth, preaching, and spiritual kingdom of **Jesus**, and which was made before the chronological period of Creation as it is set forth in the book of Genesis, and consequently more than Four Thousand (4,000) Years before **Jesus** was born. So more on David and Jesus, in a bit.

First, it is necessary to explain, that many portions of David's Psalms are somewhat **flawed** and imperfect, and some being irrelevant, and others simply not worthwhile to retain. Also know that the present book of Psalms is not complete and contains only a small portion of those **Orphic hymns** that were originally composed by David.

The Egyptian Orphic praises are very similar to those written by David, but the Egyptian ones are not as grand. In addition, David had also composed poetry and other Orphic praises, which can be found by researching among primitive manuscripts. Actually many of David's sayings were not collected or obtained by the Jews, and others that were in the Jew's possession were voted uncanonical and burned.

There are some things related in the books of Kings and also found in Chronicles which, concern the life, government , and deeds of David; and those descriptions of him found in these writings, does not appear to be consistent with how superior he is described elsewhere. However, these other books do show him at times being unfortunately situated, leading to a development of a "sensuality" which normally would not have occurred.

David **alludes** to the birth and kingdom of **Christ** more than any previous writer in the Old Testament, and therefore he demands more attention. King David's allusion to Christ is distinct and obvious, and it could not have had reference to any king who arose after him in Israel.

When David, in the seventh verse of the second psalm, declared the decree, he himself impersonates the **Son** that was to be born (speaking in language supposed to be uttered by the Divine Mind). And he goes on, stating that his kingdom would include even the heathen, who would come into his possession, and that he would inherit the uttermost parts of the earth.

David narrates this prophesy in an ambiguous manner, but the language is sufficiently clear to apply only to the spiritual kingdom of **Jesus**, which was peace and righteousness. He also alludes to this period of Jesus in later chapters, although with a little less clarity. Yet his allusions show crystal clear evidence of his own spiritual love and wisdom.

King David was a man given to devout meditation and in particular, his meditations in the last three chapters of the Psalms are a message describing the praise that should flow-out from every heart to **Him** who rules with a divine majesty, the whole Universe. And when he spoke concerning the mercy of the Lord enduring forever, it was from a natural conviction that dwelt upon his mind, unfolding righteousness and mercy from his serious and truthful contemplation of Nature around him.

David, like others, had-been **led** to **suppose** that the apparent **evil** existing in the world, which was constantly disseminated by an evil spirit proceeding from the Divine Mind - the result of an obedience to this evil would banish the transgressor from the presence of the Divine forever. But he was cautious and constrained, and did not really acknowledge this early belief because his inner awareness cried-out from the ten thousand voices arising from every department of Nature; these indications were telling his inner soul the truth, indicating that this traditional opinion **could-not** be entirely true: so he frequently **proclaimed** with a great passionate display of emotions that *"the mercy of the Lord endureth forever"*.

The book of Psalms contains many blemishes and imperfections, but in a general sense its teachings have useful applications and prophetic instructions. And when the writings are viewed this way, then the book of Psalms can give profit to the reader. But it is a book **void-of** any of those **needed** general principles which could aid mankind in better understanding the unchangeableness of Nature, of her laws, and of their Creator.

## Section 118

Next after the Book of Psalms comes the very useful and wise **Proverbs** of **Solomon**. The writer had the opportunity early in his life to be instructed in the most diversified manner, these, which when he reflected upon them created within him great knowledge, and rendered him a wise person.

**Solomon** was a man of superior abilities having a perfect physical organization or body, which was characterized by good health and robust physical energy. However he **did-not** naturally possess those same refined and elevated qualities which were characterized by his father David, at least not to any high degree to make note of. But some of his other faculties were greatly developed and he was able to **unfold** and further develop these other attributes to his benefit, giving him great powers of **discernment**. These powers were the attributes that then led him to a disposition for **meditation**, much like his father had done.

He understood construction and building practices, and these were qualities enabling him to plan and direct the **building** of the **temple**. There is another trait which was developed in him which was very beneficial and this trait would be seen as having strong **moral principles**; these special abilities could be seen displayed in the exceeding grandeur, perfections, and magnificence, which characterized the temple from the base to the dome.

King Solomon experience quite a lot in his lifetime and in hindsight it may be seen that all of these experiences were necessary to unfold the wisdom and understanding which he truly possessed and which exceeded any other king existing either before or since he lived. Thus, the wisdom of Solomon.

Taking into consideration his peculiar temperament and body organization - also the fact of his being born into wealth, and being in a elevated and spoiled situation, - the numerous physical influences with which he was surrounded and the vast experiences which he possessed - he should be considered truly an enlightened man in social and general affair. Solomon, much like his father, saw God in Nature. His proverbs gave good advice and spoke of the attainment of wisdom, and also spoke of a **future** time when mankind would organize their lifestyles and would live by the principles which govern Nature. He also advised on the advantages of sobriety, both in early and advanced life.

When speaking of the wisdom of Solomon, know that it is **almost impossible** for anyone to obtain the same wisdom and understanding as he possessed; because it would **require** the same situation, influences, and physical constitution which had surrounded and characterized him. All men are differently constituted, and their external experiences are exceedingly dissimilar; but all experience the **promptings** of their **internal principle** alike, and all would cheerfully obey its teachings if it were possible.

Ask not then, why all are not righteous, but instead search for the reason, among the millions of poor, unhappy, and unfortunate situations, that the human family endures. Then know, that in order to remove these destructive influences and obstacles - learn from Solomon to be wise; so that the world may become **sensible**.

The book of Proverbs is one that is full of very good and tangible ideas, thoughts, and various statements, all having resulted from Solomon's life and experiences. The writings themselves are a collection and give an abundance of detailed information concerning correct living. This book is useful to read by almost anyone because it gives teachings that should be applied to the human race.

The next text of the Old Testament which follows Proverbs is **Ecclesiastes**, or the Preacher and this book appears to be a continuation of the book of Proverbs. Ecclesiastes is a book which displays a great deal of knowledge and instruction, and in a sense the book could stand-alone because the knowledge found in these writings discusses **valuable principles** and ultimate realities and so, may be read with profit and pleasure; the scraps of truthful expression which it contains are worthy of consideration. This book has **no-mention** of the coming of the Reformer (Christ) nor do they mention anything of his spiritual kingdom.

The book following next in the succession of the Primitive History is the **songs of Solomon** which consists of poetical meditations similar to those contained in the book of Psalms, with the exception, that these poems are of a more crude nature and having a more sensual character. The Songs of Solomon are **supposed** to be referring to a beauty and harmony from the establishment of His spiritual kingdom. But these **could-not** be prophesies of the coming "Reformer", because Solomon **did-not** possess the spirit of prophesy. Besides, there are many ambiguous and inflated expressions contained in the book all which do-not give any useful information of truth or morality. And therefore this book is somewhat **useless** because it is void of any exalted principles that are needed to instruct the race of mankind.

# Section 119

Next, following the writings of Solomon is the book of **Isaiah**. Isaiah possessed a warm temperament and affectionate social feelings; and all his moral and intellectual faculties were highly developed. He was gifted physically, mentally, morally, and spiritually; and these characteristics prepared him to become a fit **receptacle** of the spirit of **prophesy**. His mind was so well formed that not only was he able to receive knowledge of a divine nature, but also had a keen sense and was able to **associate** with the principles of the Divine Mind existing throughout Nature. These are the principles, which are the **agents** and **mediums** through which eternal design is accomplished.

Isaiah, by being in tune with Nature and being spiritually-qualified, could and did prophesy often, and these were those **special prophesies** which would became fulfilled only when the **Messiah** came to breathe purity, social unity, and then consequently righteousness. Isaiah did-not prophesy concerning the day and hour of, or even the circumstances that would be connected with the birth of Jesus and the anticipated establishment of the spiritual reign of this noble personage.

Furthermore, Isaiah **did-not** prophesy concerning any contingent, external, and circumstantial events, that would serve as an indication of this coming occurrence; because, it would have been **impossible** for him or any other human being to speak with certainty concerning these events. But he could prophesy and speak with the utmost confidence concerning any event that would result from the work and manifestations of divine intention, especially respecting the nature of those things which he had became enlightened.

Isaiah much like all other prophets seemed to be perfectly fitted for the use for which he was intended. And it **was-not** necessarily or particularly a special quality that was within him, or in any other person, to be at times in possession of the spirit of prophecy; **but** it was more of an **influx** of Divine **intention** which came to this prophet as a result of a superior organization of a Being; and this was not made so by the person himself, but by the **superior influences** both internal and external that have governed and developed him from birth.

And now comes an interesting topic, is there the possibility of free-will? - considering that there is the **inseparable connection** which is sustained between the Universe and the Deity, the whole forming one grand system; so it is impossible for any rational mind to conceive of such a thing as **free will** or independent power or faculty. Because if such a thing existed, the result then, would be a Universe that is disunited and then the Divine Mind would be incapable of communicating life and animation to its various recesses and labyrinths. The **chain** of cause and effect and the bond of unity, harmony, and reciprocation, would be broken; and the Universe would no longer be an organized system of beauty and grandeur, but instead only an incomprehensible ocean of chaos and confusion. So what does free-will mean?

The Universe **must-be** animated by a living **Spirit**, to form as a whole One Grand Man. That Spirit is the **Cause** of man's present organized form, it is a co-eternal principle **and-is** the disseminator of motion, life, sensation, and intelligence, throughout all the complexities and consequences of this one Grand Man. That spirit is the spirit of Truth, of Love, and Wisdom, and a Spirit of inexpressible Knowledge; and this is the great Positive Mind.

Then in addition, this interior Spirit **must-have** a **Form** through which its attributes may be developed, in order that it may be called a perfect organization; and that Form is the expanded Universe. Therefore, there are only **two principles** existing: one the **Body**, the other the **Soul**; one the Divine Positive Mind, the other the Universe. Man is a part of this great Body of the Divine Mind. He is a gland, or minute organ, which performs specific functions, and receives life and animation from the interior moving Divine Principle.

Here then, is the result of these considerations just given: namely, that man is an organ produced and developed by a law which is pervading the whole organization of the Divine Mind, this law will therefore continue to govern man throughout eternity. And, the question arises, if it were possible to envision a particular organ or gland of the human Form **existing independently** of the other parts, then, it would be possible to conceive of the necessary details of the word **independence** as applied to man, viewing him in connection with the vast organization of the Divine Mind, as part of its body. So, if the event could possibly be proved true, that there are organs within the human Form that could exist independent from the body, then, and only then, might it be proved that man is truly an independent Being possessing and exercising what has been termed **free will**; and since this is a bazaar and unlikely-idea that will **never-occur**, then it can be stated that there is **no-absolute** free will.

Isaiah was in possession of many high and noble qualities which had rendered his mind suitable for the influx of prophetic knowledge. And he, in a clear and concise manner proclaimed these to the world. Isaiah did not prophesy just simply because it was a merit or ability that he had, but the occurrence of prophesy with Isaiah was more of a **natural consequence** of the relations he sustained to those laws which he felt would develop the event he was compelled to prophesy.

# Section 120

It has been stated that Isaiah was a very enlightened Being and he possessed superior knowledge and was keen on **meditation**. Some of his inner thoughts led him to prophecise; and he could speak-out with confidence and certainty. He was convinced that new beauties **will-rise** from a social and **spiritual elevation** of mankind which will come-about by the **triumph** of moral and natural principles.

From his prophetical **meditations** Isaiah saw that the world of mankind **would undergo** such a grand and significant change, so-as unity, peace, and righteousness, would spread over the whole earth. And his thoughts were not restricted by any religious or sectarian dogma, nor did he encourage any outward form of worship. The thoughts which would flow from his inward connections were as expansive as Nature herself. He spoke of the **unfolding heavens**; and spoke of the mountain of the house of the Lord, and continued, by further speaking of the holy magnificence that will characterize the great temple of mankind. These very compelling and uplifting prophesies are **to-occur** after goodness and virtue shall **have-become** fully developed within the hearts and minds of mankind.

Isaiah saw that the **germ** of **righteousness** was **deposited** in Nature, and is also existing in man. He saw that this germ, this **seed**, would ultimately **unfold** its divine qualities into roots, and that these roots would produce a body, which would **ascend** and put forth branches throughout the world, which would come to bud and blossom on the mount of the Lord on the hill of Zion. From this would be unfolded the beauty of the **tree** of **righteousness** whose everlasting branches would ascend through all the celestial heavens.

Isaiah saw in his mind a future when **one would come**, who would "judge among many nations", and who **would-deposit** a **germ** whose growth would produce a social and **moral resurrection** of all the world; and this resurrection would be a world where there exists harmony and righteousness. He saw that one would come who would rebuke and scold many people, by **unfolding** and revealing the **proper principles** that **belong** to the nature of man which are to occur, when this successful achievement of these developed principles is finally complete and at which time, all error and false instruction would be forever annihilated.

Isaiah saw that this development would cause all nations to *"beat their swords into plowshares, and their spears into pruning-hooks"*, and that then would be peace on earth and universal industry. He saw that when this event would be accomplished, *"nation would not again rise up against nation, and that they would learn war no more"*.

Isaiah saw that error and ignorance, which are sometimes the **causes** of the various systems that exist, would ultimately be banished from the earth, and that all **sectarian** and local hostility would be **annihilated**. He saw that when this **unity of intention** and action become universal, *"wilderness and solitary places would be made glad, and that the deserts would be made to blossom as the rose"*.

He saw that the world would be no longer be dreary, abused, and neglected, place caused from the worldwide existence of sectarian artificiality, but would be converted into an **Eden** whose fragrance would diffuse universal happiness.

He saw that this would be accomplish as an **inevitable** result of the moral and spiritual teachings of those **principles,** which **have-existed** in Nature ever since the Universe had a being.

He saw that social unity would unfold spiritual righteousness, which would become as a great mountain, a sanctuary in which the whole world might congregate, and where the **true worshiper** might worship the Divine Mind in spirit and in truth.

Isaiah spoke kindly of the kings and kingdoms that existed, and spoke of the kingdoms that **would exist** upon the earth, but also at the same time warned, scolded, urged, and advised, them to be wise with all gentleness, meekness, and humiliation. For Isaiah **saw**, that the **One** who would come into the world, would be one who would neither fail nor be discouraged, but would instead exercise **judgment** among the nations, and that the isles would wait for the fulfillment of this law.

He saw that this great **Moral Reformer** would see the laborious effort of his own soul which is the **completion** of that unique and holy development of his social and **spiritual government** and then, would be satisfied. And Isaiah saw that the time would come when, unto these Divine principles every knee should bow, and every tongue shall confess, that in them they had righteousness and strength.

Isaiah also exerted his influence to console kings, because many nations at that time anticipated invasion and destruction. He was considered by all as a general consoler, and would endeavor in his writings attempting to convince and console their minds by **using** many external **representations** and **comparisons** in his verses, even though these comparisons had **no connection** with the event or occurrence being prophesied; but his comforting word did satisfy them by the truthfulness of his consolatory assurances.

Isaiah **knew** the signs or prophesy he gave were merely external representations and knew well, that those **were-not** confirmations of the event

PRINCIPLES · 363

or occurrence foretold. But, Isaiah also knew the level-of his ability and spirit to prophesy, and because of the **influx** of **divine principles**, he was sure that many of the events which he foretold would inevitably be accomplished.

Isaiah, **foresaw** the birth, the life, and the preaching of **Christ**, and the ultimate triumph of the Principles which he had been and would persistently teach. He was unable to speak of the specific time or place or of any particular incident or circumstance that would be connected with the coming events of the things he **absolutely foresaw** and revealed that these would absolutely occur.

## Section 121

Respectful thanks, is given to Isaiah. Because, **even-though** he lived on earth in the material world he still **was-able** to develop into a highly enlightened Spirit. His mind, his disposition, and character, being so highly **developed** was the source which enabled him **to-see** through all the sectarian hostility, hatred, and anger, which prevailed. Through his inward spiritual connection and his inner impressions he could see mankind in a future sense, and knew that man will **ultimately succeed**, and that all this madness would be destroyed forever. And, it would be at that time, when the earth and the Universe will be the great worshiping Temple. A temple, in which there would be but one Eternal Preacher and Admonisher, which is He - the Divine Mind!

Isaiah could see that this great and unfailing **Shepherd** would **spread** his righteous influence throughout the world, by his teachings - which will be those principles of love, unity, and kindly reciprocation. This shepherd of the world, will make every silent stream eloquent; every flower inviting; every grove a sanctuary of prayer and devotion; and the whole earth a "fold" of peace and safety; doing this so-that all might be **gathered** in happiness and love; and from this fold of His, none would go astray.

Nature breathes-out her immortal and interior teachings because She is a child of the great Divinity. She **communicates** these teachings to man, who feels these breaths as the inexpressible promptings of his internal Being. And, mankind is able to feel these **because** man are children of Nature, just as Nature is of the Divine Mind. The **Spirit**, the "developing principle", - in this way **receives** the **truth**, because the Spirit has the ability to be **influenced** by divine influx, and **yet**, dwelling in the world, the Spirit **has-become** encompassed, **encased**, **hardened**, with every species of gross **materiality**. The true Spirit of mankind, therefore has **not** as yet **unfolded** its deep internal qualities, not in the glorious manner which it ultimately will unfold to. And this will occur when new and superior influences are unfolded in the social world.

Nature, according to the prophecies of Isaiah, is performing the **ultimate design** of the Divine Mind through Her eternal laws, the accomplishment of which, will conspicuously display the infinite perfection of the Divine attributes.

There is an overwhelming compulsion to speak more of the prophecies of Isaiah, to keep them fresh, because his is a great example of someone on the right path: remember that those prophecies are **true** and **steadfast**, and if the people of the world happily receive the wisdom they contain, then they will all be skilled and accomplished, and all possessing a **higher level** of understanding.

"Abandon all sectarian affection and impure high mindedness. Seek to become enlightened, and strive to banish all ignorance, superstition, and hostility, from the earth. Desire to become suitable receptacles for the influx of Divine intention, unfold your interior nature, enabling you to associate with the knowledge of higher spheres. Discard the unholy influences now connecting your social relations. Go forth into the world and preach the doctrine of the Divine Theologian, and become a useful instrument accomplishing the designs of the Creator that can be seen manifested in his unchangeable laws"

# Section 122

The book following Isaiah is **Jeremiah's** prophecies and historical records. Jeremiah was not like Isaiah in either his physical or mental organization; not possessing much of that spiritual refinement nor devotion to truth and knowledge as did Isaiah. Yet, Jeremiah's **social qualities** were very active and his **affections** were exceedingly strong. His affections were for the whole race but his prophecies referred mostly to events of that era he existed in and contain **almost-no** allusion to the great and glorious period of which Isaiah prophesied with strong-feelings.

Jeremiah's moral powers **were-not** as developed and his attributes would remain unfolded because he **did-not** possess the abilities to prophesy, and especially concerning an event such as the coming of the Moral Reformer; but, he did possess good powers of **observation** which were developed to an adequate degree to where he was able to fulfill the office he sustained as prophet.

His time and talents were spent chiefly scolding, instructing, and consoling the Jews, whose bondage he had correctly foretold. He was compelled to prophesy of the invasion, conquest, slavery, and suffering of the Jews under the severe and powerful administration of **Nebuchadnezzar** (586 BC). Jeremiah was living during the time-period that this awful event occurred. And during this time he was greatly involved in the trials and sufferings of the Jews, and so his prophesies were limited by this event, which of-course did occupy his mind on a daily basis.

Jeremiah **does-make** one **allusion** to the great **Moral Reformer** and His social and spiritual kingdom, yet this is very brief. Yet in this particular prophesy, there is sufficient prophetic knowledge being demonstrated by Jeremiah which was combined with a power of spiritual perception, to make this prophesy **seemingly definite** and true. And this is found in the 23 chapter, 5$^{th}$ and 6$^{th}$ verses. This allusion was not perceived, even by the apostle Matthew or any of the other historians of Jesus, though Matthew did suppose and think that another passage in Jeremiah - 31 chap.15$^{th}$ verse, was prophetic, but it was not.

Jeremiah speaks plainly about false prophets and prophetesses, occurring within Judaism as well as among various other tribes and nations. Many of the passages within this book are **expressions** of deep sadness and sorrow because of the **afflictions** imposed upon the Jews or upon any other nations.

In the book of Jeremiah as a whole, there **is-no** discovery of useful or expansive principles which the world seeks and needs to guide them, nor are there found any absolute prophecies concerning the coming of the new era which is so anxiously **anticipated** by humanity, and already being envisioned by previous prophets. Many parts of this book were **revised** by subsequent writers and the future tense was **exchanged** for the past tense, which would seem to **convey** the **impression** that many events and things in this book were written after the Jews were set-free.

The next Old Testament book following Jeremiah is, **Lamentations of Jeremiah** – this book contains Jeremiah's deep contemplation of things that would bring relief to the Jews in captivity. And these writings are Jeremiah's **feelings** and social **sympathies** towards the sufferings and afflictions that were being experienced by his brethren during that degrading event. Jeremiah was so depressed by the situation of the Jews he exerted himself to prophesy concerning Hope, which could be used to chase-away the sorrow.

All in all, the books by Jeremiah are-not useful or important in respect to the coming of the great Reformer. The books mainly relate to the wars, suffering of the Jews, their captivity in Babylon and then, the downfall of Babylon. Jeremiah had also recorded into writing as history the **many** socking **catastrophes** that happen to various kingdoms and nations of the east, though, these are written in a figurative and indefinite style and are not connected to a theological system, - so these are of no importance to the world at the present day.

## Section 123

The next book is that of **Ezekiel**. This writer was in a similar situation from youth to manhood as was Jeremiah, possessing similar physical and spiritual qualities.

Ezekiel **would-not** be considered a true prophet, and only occasionally, - busting-out from the excitement of his spiritual elevation during **meditation**, and then, sometimes **uttering** many vague, yet **truthful sayings**. Some of these sayings concerned the heavenly city of the Lord, Zion. Other written verses of his sayings, spoke of the **tree** of **righteousness** whose **germ** would be deposited by **Jesus** – who was the **fair-example** of purity and refinement – whose qualities and principles **would-be** unfolded by generations to come.

The majority of the book of Ezekiel contains writings which mostly relate to that time-period in which it was written, although, there were a number of writings of Ezekiel's which pertained more to, and describe more, the previous generation. Many phrases and sayings of this book are somewhat crude and offensive and they **do-not** give to the mind any good "food" to promote spiritual thought.

Ezekiel did nearly the same as many of the prophets preceding him did, they would **falsely prophesy** and **claim** the Lord had spoke through them, and making the Lord say what they themselves had said and wrote, **then**, making matters worse, they would **attribute false** and **deceptive prophecy** to the influence of the Divine Mind, which of-course was not true. For instance, there is a particular prophesy in his book where Ezekiel writes as though the Lord instructed him concerning the method of baking of bread – or again, giving the instructions of how they should purchase, boil, and eat a lamb – how they should choose the color, how to cut the cloth and make garments, etc; this is unprofitable writing and petty.

It helps to know that Ezekiel's written expressions were nothing-more than him using the **common words** and phrases normally used in everyday encounters of life. There are no hidden meanings in the writings of Ezekiel, instead they were merely his own mentality, combined with his own habits, which are shown in his thoughts; and justly, Ezekiel's writings and book **do-not** make claims to be anything more. It is a **collection** of **figurative descriptions** with some prophetic allusions, along with historical records of the Jews both in Babylon and in Jerusalem.

The book of **Daniel** comes next following Ezekiel, and it contains more historical, allegorical, and mythological, representations and prophetical visions than the previous book.

Daniel was eccentric and he possessed good social skills and qualities but, would be characterized more by his **perceptive** and moral faculties which were highly developed within him. He would not be someone that could be considered intelligent. And he only possessed a mental development slightly beyond a rudimentary level. Because of this limited elementary education Daniel was only able to **perceive** things, and mostly from and external and materialistic view, and so, this is how he spoke and taught.

The **visions** coming from Daniel's mind were of a type and character that would be most-likely viewed or considered as being **ambiguous** and unconventional, and perhaps being slightly **strange**. There were some visions of his which were both definite and defined enough that a reader would know the topic being revealed did not occur, but then in other visions, Daniel was so **vague** and indefinite that the vision could have applied to almost any material catastrophe. Yet, these vague and strange visions **are-now** in our modern time **use-often** by biblical **commentators** and they can be interpreted to fit almost any fancy of the commentator. And then, from those forked-tongue theological speculators and commentators had spun some of Daniel's visions and now had connected them to the apocalypse.

Daniel's powers of analogy and his **ability** to form comparisons was a strong characteristic he had developed and possessed, with these abilities he prophesied about the rise and downfall of kings and kingdoms, and Daniel would represent or **compare** these events and the people involved in those events by referring to them as strange and unique animals.

Some of Daniel's **metaphorical beasts** had more horns than any animal that ever existed upon the earth. Nevertheless, his comparisons were **true**, though symbolic. He symbolized some kingdoms by describing or giving a mental image of various **metals** which would **signify** the character of the kings and the different ages in which they would reign. His prophesies all related to kings that were to rise and pass away and about new ones that would rise-up in their place. These prophecies are **true** and they have been in-fact **fulfilled**, seen in all the successive tyrannical governments that subsequently existed on earth. But even-so, these prophecies are so ambiguous and superficial that they **don't-fit** the interpretation given them by many biblical commentators. Absolutely, these visions of Daniel are capable of being **misinterpreted** to represent almost anything that would suit the commentators bias. And it is embarrassing to realize how many false and imaginative interpretations man has read-into and misinterpreted, falsely rising out of the allegorical images and descriptions given by Daniel.

It is **quite astonishing** and nearly unbelievable for the mind to **grasp** how these non-scientific writings, which were written by unscientific men, and then being interpreted by theologians who also are not versed in scientific fact, **could influence** so many people. The answer seems to lie in the deep seated ignorance of mankind. Of all Daniel's prophesies he makes no allusion to the Sun of Righteousness which had been so brilliantly spoken of in **Malachi**, and so perfectly exemplified in the life and teachings of **Jesus**.

# Section 124

The book titled **Hosea** follows Daniel and this book starts by relating in her story a description and account of the **Lord** speaking, and giving a command to Hosea on how to choose a spouse, and it continues with the Lord giving directions on how Hosea should marry, and how his children should be named. This is useless and it is doubtful that it has any truth.

Hosea makes no claim that he is able to prophecy, but instead was a general observer, contemplator, instructor, and admonisher of the Jewish nation. His writings reveal the extreme depression being experience by many tribes and nations within his circumference of living and knowledge. He saw the gloomy apprehensions the Jews were experiencing in anticipation of attacks and vengeance from the Medes (Iranian), Persians, and Babylonians. So because of this, Hosea's time was spent mostly consoling the Jewish nation rather than developing his inner qualities.

The book of **Joel** follows Hosea, and is mainly a summary of the writings contained in Hosea with the exception of the introduction of new figures, and also the author has a different way of speaking and different writing skills.

Joel encouraged the Israelities to **reform** their hedonistic ways or else they would experience the dreadful judgment of the Lord, for *"He, would rain down on them with consuming vengeance"*.

Joel also presents descriptions of some very terrible actions and events of divine judgment which would come swiftly, which are meant to **play-upon** the sentiments of **fear** and superstition of his listeners. So in strong words he spoke of a day which would come when: *"The Lord would pour out his Spirit upon them, and their sons and daughters should have visions, and their aged men should dream dreams; when the sun would cease to give its light, and the moon be darkened and changed into blood, and the stars would refuse to shine, and the earth shake to its center, and darkness reign universally".*

This broad statement by Joel, is a **vague** yet powerful representation that bears all the appearance of a literal prophecy, yet to be fulfilled in a future time. **But**, it should be seen by anyone with an enlightened understanding and inner awareness, that all these physical transformations **are-opposed** to all **natural-laws** and opposed to the harmony of the Universe. Therefore, if this is read in a literal sense then the figures are false and insignificant. But recall, - this was a **mode** of expression that was **used** during that particular period of mankind's progression and

Joel **only-intended** to awaken the apprehensions of the Jewish nation and to impress upon their minds terribleness.

Joel also says, *"The Lord will show forth wonders in the heavens and in the earth - blood, and fire, and pillars of smoke"*. It is totally unprofitable, to consider these sayings were ever spoken by or had ever proceeded-from the Divine Mind; and so it is infinitely beneath his supreme dignity and divine majesty to **condescend** and to present to man such terrifying and grand panoramas.

The prophet Joel **does-not** speak of the new coming age, and there is nothing to be found in this book which relates-to or foretells the coming of the great Moral Reformer Jesus.

The next book in the line of prophets is that of **Amos**, and his writing is truly a **prophetic document** containing prophecies which concern the various kingdoms and cities which had previously been prophesied about or against in the book of Daniel. The book of Amos may also be considered as a **collection** of private **meditations** and reflections **based-upon** historical events, all that had been revealed in previous books which were existing at the time-period of Amos. These writings have a connection with other prophecies and various records which would come later. There is **nothing** in the book of Amos relating to the Great Reformer.

Now proceeding to the book entitled **Obadiah** which contains the **thought impressions** and prophecies of a **herdsman** who evidently, by being **excited** by the then-existing circumstances, **could-not**, because of his peculiar mental constitution, refrain from uttering his opinions and contemplation. Obadiah also **spoke symbolically** but that was very briefly, yet comprehensively, concerning things referred to in previous books. There exist no apparent use in these sayings nor are they capable of being of profit.

# Section 125

The succeeding book is titled **Jonah**. This book starts in an abrupt and broken manner and does this peculiar action by the writer speaking of Jonah as someone being commanded by the Lord, told to go to Nineveh and preach **against** it and the announcing of the city's destruction, and more. The book displays the Divine Mind as repenting - and as cursing the people who, as He afterward acknowledged, *"knew not the right hand from the left"*. It represents God's incompetency to be able to pick the right person to fulfill his commands.

Its doubtful that such a being as Jonah ever existed. The origin of the book of Jonah is not revealed.

However, *Mankind, still, at the present day are very much like the citizens of Nineveh. They are ignorant, not knowing the interior of things from the outward nor knowing their right hand form their left. They also have a love and admiration for superstition, and have distorted imaginations. People of today exist among grand and beautiful external things. There are some beautiful and well constructed cities. And there are temples for the worship of imaginary beings, not transcending much beyond those of Zoroaster. There are idols and images that convey to the mind, superstitions and mythological thoughts, not much above the worship of the Ganges or of the Juggernaut. And because of ignorance and a disorganization, dens of disgusting and repulsive behavior, of hatred and anger, causing nearly the whole race to become dangerously diseased – like the inhabitants of Nineveh.*

By reading from the book of Jonah the impression and images given to the mind are an almost perfect representation of what the mental condition of the people living in our twenty-first century, in today's world, like those of Nineveh, people of today are still basing their beliefs on superstition and mythology. **But**, the book of Jonah is also full-of **good instruction** and there is so much that can be learned, which would give aid to the diseased mental conditions that exist.

# Section 126

Next are the writings found in the book of **Micah** which is devoted to thoughts and meditations similar to those contained in previous books by the prophets, along with the fact that many of Micah's thoughts concerned the immense and overwhelming afflictions that were being imposed upon the Jews and Israelities who had been **contaminated** by frequent acts of **idol worship**.

This book is written in a style which is full of expressions of sadness, sorrow, and regret; the book sometimes uses **figurative** descriptions and it contains very little prophesy. It makes quite a few references to the vast amount of evil and wretchedness, both surrounding and influencing the Jews and the house of Israel. There is no principle contained within this book of Micah that would make or give a useful application.

Moving on to the next book, which is titled **Nahum**. It is found that this book seems to be focused upon explaining the evils which fell upon Nineveh coming from a direct curse by a revengeful God.

The book of **Habakkuk** comes next. This writer mostly spoke concerning past and present hatred that has spread throughout the Jewish nation. And within the writings of this prophet there are no allusions made which applies to our search for Jesus and our search to determine a period of time when the great Reformer would be born and live. Instead the contents of this prophet's book are confined to only giving allusions to events and circumstances that were occurring within that particular era.

Now follows the book of **Zephaniah**. The style and writing of this book are symbolical and expresses severe reprimands against those prophets and priests who prophesy falsely, and who had defiled their sanctuaries of devotion by those false predictions.

Zephaniah has visions which really are allusions in reference to a period when happiness would again bless the Jew and to a time when the house of Israel and the Lords house would be cleansed. But, there are no allusions or indications as to the period when the kingdom of **Christ** should be established on earth, or when the tree of righteousness should bloom. But, this book is worth reading mainly the reason that there are many beautifully-expressed sentences written within this book, though they only are referring to the then-existing circumstances.

The book that follows Zephaniah is **Haggai** which is a book composed of some warnings and advice concerning the rebuilding of the temple after the return of the Jews from their bondage in Babylon.

# Section 127

The book titled **Zechariah** is next in sequence, and in the process of giving the over-view of this prophet and writer much more caution and gentleness will be given to him, because, this author has a very truthful and beautiful vision which is in addition to his writings, and it concerns Him who is to come (Christ).

The time-period in which Zechariah lived and wrote were times of turmoil, so it will be seen that most of the history which he recorded was concerning the sufferings of the Jewish nation. He records his prophetical reflections with a style which is often reflecting the warmth of his inner feelings, but at the same-time these writings show that he believed strongly in the message of his prophesies, and because of that conviction, he would often use forceful expressions to convey his message.

Zechariah appears to have written under the influence (of a joyful optimism), because these writings are characterized by positiveness and determination which both show forth his kind, generous, and very affectionate, disposition. In his text Zachariah describes a variety of visions, and these are mostly of a "local" nature, even though the character and style in which they were composed, makes them seem as though they can be applied to other situations and occurrences, and were **susceptible** to being misinterpreted or someone could even twist the meaning to apply to other time-periods. It appears that in general Zechariah was very popular and well loved among his countryman. His character was pleasant and friendly and he possessed a superior sense of judgment and decision-making.

Approximately one third of the book of Zechariah is closely connected with the topics and subjects written in previous books; and then, the other two thirds are devoted to expressing his meditations, including his prophetical allusion concerning the birth of **Jesus**. Here in this par, Zechariah speaks of a pure and **perfect person** who will ultimately rise among the Jewish nation but, whose teachings would be applied and **fulfilled** only in some **future generation** and even our present time-period could be that special time. This prophesy can be seen written in 6$^{th}$ chapter, 12$^{th}$ verse. Then also, a prophecy found in the 9$^{th}$ chapter, 9$^{th}$ and 10$^{th}$ verses, in-which Zechariah reveals in a strong stern manner that there will come the **ultimate relief** of the Jews, Gentiles, and all the inhabitants of the earth from ignorance, mental slavery and any physical conflicts or disagreements.

Zechariah gives stern warnings and advisory **caution** to all those who have made **speculations** concerning this subject of Jesus's life, stating in his peculiar manner that any investigator should read very cautiously and then reflect upon the expressions used by Zechariah to represent Jesus and his social and spiritual government. Jesus here is called **the branch** - which is indeed one of the **most-perfect** and truthful expressions contained in the Primitive History.

Sadly for multitudes of people, many theologians have already made wrong assumptions from just reading these passages from Zechariah in a superficial manner, comparing or connecting them frivolously with other isolated passages in the Bible, then **believing** that Jesus was a Being expressly destined and created for the purpose of redeeming the race from a fallen and degenerate condition. Others have **supposed** that Jesus came merely to establish a connection between the spiritual nature of man and the Divine Mind, believing that, this will serve as a medium through which spirits from this rudimental sphere might approach the presence of **Him** who made the Universe. Then there are others, who have **supposed** that Jesus was a material Being and organization, that would be capable of receiving the Divine Mind itself, and that by existing as-such a being, He came to reconcile and elevate the spiritual nature of man to a degree were then, a perpetual communion with holiness and righteousness might be established.

A question can be asked, do any of these theological speculations which were made by this prophet have any truth or merit?

The first of the assumed opinions from Zechariah may have some measure of truth, in that Jesus actually was a **destined medium** and was an agent to unfold a higher level of perfection in mankind so much more than has ever been possessed by man before. So yes, Jesus was created for this purpose, **however**, Jesus **was-created** just as all men and women of the human family are created, and all are created for the same purpose, and all are created by the workings of the laws and elements of Nature. And all are a part of God's laws and God's Nature. And all are children of God.

The **assumption** that Jesus came to redeem the world of mankind from a "fallen condition", **is-not** in accordance with God's laws of Nature, nor is this notion found in any of these teachings under review from the Primitive History of the Old Testament. So anyone whom is believing this fabricated notion, is **disrespectful** to the Divine Essence which has breathed life and animation throughout space. The word redemption instantly brings to mind the thought that something has been lost or forfeited. But rest reassured that nothing pertaining to the spiritual nature of man has been forfeited even to the least degree, that would then, somehow require supernatural restoration in order to put mankind back to a position that they had once occupied.

It would seem logical that if mankind **had-once** in the distant past been socially united because all had understood God's laws and all understanding perfectly the laws which breath unity, harmony, and happiness into creation, that these ancestors would have initiated new laws and social decrees which would have corrected those mistakes and these new laws would have been passed-down these great and wonderful laws, so that by now all would have been living in that higher society before.

Therefore in **review**, the **first** opinion has no foundation, because the belief that at one-time mankind was pure, perfect, and united, and that they afterward degenerated, and this occurred because man ate a little of the fruit of the tree of knowledge is false and bazaar. Reality says, that mankind **did-not** at any time in the history of the earth, exist and live in a higher state of unity, harmony, nor happiness. **Instead** mankind's development **has-been** merely misdirected, commencing from its primitive early stages, and **now** only **needs** gentleness of instruction, with a pure and useful knowledge, to effect its elevation to the **next level**.

Nor is the **second** opinion true, that a Being was **expressly designed** and adapted in order to destroy the harmful and damaging effects of this transgression and then to restore mankind to the position they once sustained. This second opinion, is implying that a spiritual being, namely Jesus, was the **medium** through which, mankind may ultimately receive **forgiveness**; and then after being forgiven for our sins mankind would then, be admitted to higher spheres of existence, dwelling with God. Well, this does not seem like a very profitable belief to entertain, nor to cherish and hold onto; because, **nowhere** will there be found any **evidence** that Divine Love and Wisdom could be so incomplete as to **lose** all connection with Its own **law** of **progressive development** and then need to reestablish that connection.

And the **third** opinion shows great **disrespect** to the character of God and his **Divine Mind**; because, it implies that when God was creating the Universe He had a fore-knowledge and predetermination. This assumption, hints that God instituted laws which are the very elements of His will and utterly unchangeable, But then afterward, found himself **incompetent** to carry them out, and now being God being **unable** to perfect the grand system He had erected. Well most-assuredly, this supposition is directly opposed to God's celestial dignity.

Zechariah has spoken the truth because he calls **Christ** a Branch – of the Great Tree, whose Body is composed of the whole world of mankind. He is a branch of the great creation and is **the example** of creation putting-forth and developing its interior qualities, just as Jesus did. Jesus **became** the Christ. So, what this world should be thankful for and delighted in, is that this **Branch** has **produced** such **delicious fruit**.

It **does-not** make sense then, that this Branch **would-have** originated and controlled the great tree of human existence, but **instead** what makes sense, is that mankind was produce from the qualities contained in the **germ** of the world, which were absorbed by the roots of this great tree, and so the tree became developed through all the successive stages of its growth; until, it **became prepared** to unfold a **Branch** which would bloom with the immortal fragrance of interior purity and exterior gentleness. And this Branch is Jesus, the elements of whose soul breathed peace on earth and good-will to men.

Jesus then is the Branch alluded to with so much feeling and elevation of thought in the book of Zechariah. And this should be considered the **most truthful** and significant expression that can be applied to the great **Moral Reformer**.

# Section 128

Succeeding Zechariah is the book of **Malachi**. And in this is contained **superior prophecy** concerning the Branch. This **Branch**, which was unfolded **upon** the **Tree** of **mankind**, whose roots extend through all lower creations down to the incomprehensible Vortex of the beginning and from which Love and Wisdom perpetually flow.

This great Branch is described by Malachi and called "The Sun of Righteousness"; and truly might have been called the "Flower of material and spiritual **perfection**", that would bloom with healing qualities, that would elevate and make happy the whole body of mankind.

The writer of Malachi uses expressions, such as *"The day cometh that shall burn as an oven"* or, *"the consuming fire of the Lord"* or, *"the day of the Lord",* and others, these are simply expressions that were used only as **ambiguous comparisons**, and are designed to represent a calamity that was ultimately to occur against the Jewish nation at the time of the destruction of Jerusalem. These are severe and vague denunciations found in the Old Testament that **have-now** been **misinterpreted** and have expressed to the world the **wrong message**, and have given the world many harmful and useless impressions, all used by twisted minds to twist their theological theories and speculations further. And sadly, those misdirected minds have incorrectly interpreted many phrases in the Primitive History of man in a most wicked manner. Those phrases such as - *"the visitation of the Lord"* - *"the day of judgment"* - *" the vengeance",* and the *"consuming fire of the Lord",* and many similarly worded expressions, all were words and forms of speech along with other common phrases used by the writers of the manuscripts now composing the Bible. The prophets and many other biblical writers spoke and wrote in a very **unguarded** and vague manner, **not-knowing** that their thoughts would be misinterpreted in later generations.

During Malachi's time the Jews recently had been slaves held in a long period of bondage and they had experienced so many devastating invasions, that it naturally makes-sense they were **unable** to have confidence in their own power of ever obtaining relief from their suffering. So they fled for **refuge** to the **God** of Abraham, Isaac, and Jacob, whom, they believed "possessed sufficient power and spirit of retaliation to revenge them of their enemies". This scenario gives an indication why those expressions are frequently found in written form dispersed throughout the Old Testament, and now as proof these strong expressions are especially seen in various passages in Malachi.

It is Malachi then who **implies** that "one being" was to be created who would be king over all the nations with the **purpose** of giving comfort which would give **relief** to those then-enslaved inhabitants, from their extreme suffering and unfortunate situation. That one-being to be created, Malachi calls him **Elijah** who is the one which has been **supposed** to represent the great Reformer spoken of. **However**, this phrase of Malachi's **has-no** interior meaning.

Here, completes the review of the sequential books of the prophets of the Old Testament. During the review of these books, particular attention was given to all those prophetical **allusions** which were written and may have **pertained** to or were concerned with the birth and teachings of **Jesus**. In general most of these allusions pertaining to the Christ were very vague, and certainly did not focus on anything specific; and so most writings of these prophets **merely** seem to anticipate a coming event and **had-not** in any particular way given isolated or circumstantial evidence pointing directly at or in a convincing way to Jesus. Anyway, it is **impossible** for prophecies to-give specific information concerning the particulars of Jesus's birth and life.

All of those hints and allusions to the coming of the Messiah, **were-merely** hope-filled suggestions that had been **developed** among the prophets in response to the harsh circumstances which were surrounding their very depressed situation, which the various nations of the earth were experiencing, especially during that era. And, as has now been learned, those prophesies which were implying the coming of a Messiah were-merely **alluded-to** for the purpose of **consoling** those minds laboring under the prevailing affliction that this event was generally appealed to. It was the **possibility** of some measure of **relief** and restoring a sense of confidence and energy, that had inspired the minds of not only the prophets, but also inspired the downtrodden nations of mankind with hope and brilliant anticipations. And so, aside from this fact the writers of the Old Testament **professed** mostly "to relate mere historical truths"; and many of their expressions and illustrations are strictly mythological and allegorical, being derived and formed from prior and early-ingrained mythological and theological opinions.

In **review**, within some books of Old Testament there are many beautiful conceptions – things that give a literal meaning or show a spiritual connection. However these thoughts that are contained in this Primitive History are written in a **language style** very similar to modes of communication used by our ancient ancestors, which were full of allegorical phrases, mythology, and imaginary illusions. We have learn that many books in the Old Testament **are-not** suited to the needs which are required for the progression and improvement of modern mankind; **because**, they promote and spread immoral and unrighteous principles. They spread far more hatred than they spread any purity and celestial refinement which would naturally be expected to come from the Divine Mind, which is what these writings are **claimed** to be.

Any **spiritual interpretation** of these Old Testament sayings would be positively **useless**, because they would be incapable of having a profitable spiritual application. Besides, if the Bible were clothed in this manner of spiritual interpretation, then, the book **could-not** have supplied the physical requirements of the human race, and neither would it have soothe the afflictions of the suffering, nor could it have been food for the widow or the fatherless. Nor would it have been able to reform the arbitrary and unholy governments that now exist in many parts of the world. It could not have wipe tears, from off all faces, nor banish pain and sorrow from the earth; nor could it produce a social resurrection, in-which the superior results would be seen in mankind's spiritual happiness and exaltation.

Furthermore, a **literal interpretation** of the sayings of the Old Testament, for the purpose of collecting written materials to sustain unrighteous theology, would itself not have any positive tendency to produce the good results that are direly needed. Especially if those written materials were collected from every department and sub-department of the civilized and uncivilized world, such as these writings from the Old Testament.

Yet the voices asking humbly of Nature can not be hushed until the things called for are given in abundance. And Nature, dwelling within living Forms, speaks-out and loudly calls for amelioration from ignorance, vice, imbecility, and every other species of social iniquity, transgression, and disorganization.

Nature has unfolded her choicest qualities in **some** noble Forms of the **human** family which breath the very elements of charity and philanthropy. They exercise a benevolence that is without limits – they possess an affection and sympathy which truly **understands** the many requirements of all who suffer in pain and poverty.

As the Old Testament then, **only claims** to be a history of circumstances and events concerning only the ages in which it was written, and then as the men called prophets **only claim** to have provided nothing more than **expressing hope** and anticipation of relief for the nations that are suffering, then the Book **fulfills** its requirements. And most important, it has been **discovered** that there are some expressions from the Old Testament that can be distinctly applied to the life and character of Jesus.

The books contained in the Primitive History have been collected and arranged by the agency of interested compilers; and as to the events of "the fixing of the chronology", the positions of the books, and the division of those same books into chapters and verses, have all been merely the work of those who were **commanded** by rulers to collect and arrange them; and even though much of this material is generally true, these **can-not** in any essential manner benefit the race; it would be well to consider the Primitive History only in terms of the namesakes meaning, and thus let it sleep.

Mankind immediately at this moment should forsake all dogmatism – all sectarianism – all mythology – all unrighteousness – and become at-once **associated branches** of the great Tree of Righteousness. Then, the **whole world** of mankind may fully experience the ennobling consequences which would arise from a good and proper development of their inherent qualities. Then indeed, will the earth develop her choicest beauties, and then will man be **competent** to appreciate the excellency of Nature's productions and become happy.

# Section 129

Among the **Hindu** and other eastern tribes, the **Shaster** is **supposed** to be of divine origin. And because of this, they consequently adore its contents, they strictly adhere to its teachings, and endeavor by all kinds of persuasion to inspire faith in the minds of those who disbelieve, and their intent is to spread widely its doctrines and rules.

The Hindu entertains the highest respect for the writers of their religious book, and believe firmly those writers were inspired by good spirits to communicate such a divine revelation. And they **assume** that the world refuses to accept it because the world is alienated from the favor of their deities. So therefore a non-believer is not permitted to enter into the enjoyment of their holy religion which they venerate with the highest devotion.

Much the same description is observed in the situation with the **Persians** with reference to their religious book; with the Mohammedans (**Muslims**), and with the portions of the civilized world who have received and put confidence in the **superficial** interpretation of their Primitive History.

All **sects** that base their religious origin upon things contained in their particular history, believe that the reason why all others are not as they are, is because they **have-not** ascended to a higher degree of knowledge, and therefore all those other non-believers are groping in darkness, being weak and outcast and unassisted by that Mind who created them and the Universe, while true believers are permitted to enjoy His divine teachings exclusively.

All sects see only the **superiority** of their own religious possessions and **assume** that their **light** transcends the light of all others, as to render the others in absolute darkness. Separatism with superiority has become fanatically believed, defended, and promoted, by the believers of **every sect** and every system of religion. Each group of believers, boasting and growling hysterically, "that all others are not as they are", claiming their superiority, is because all other sects besides themselves are under the banner of contempt by the divine mind who had instituted their own peculiar sect or religion.

However in truth, it really does not make a difference which belief system is cherished because they are **all-alike**. Whether it is the Shaster, Koran, Zend-Avesta, Primitive History, or anything else that someone is fanatically **attached-to** - In truth, just about every religious person on earth are all devoted to the peculiar faith that was **impressed** on their mind early into their life, and therefore are all alike and are **merely** subjects of a peculiar customs, education, and misdirection.

Moving on, because now that the Primitive History is in **repose**, our story shall proceed into an **investigation** of many principles and sayings recorded in the **New Testament** which have been **unjustly** interpreted; and in giving this investigative account, also reveal the **harm** those erroneous **interpretations** have produced as they are sowing the seeds of error and sectarian dissension throughout the civilized and uncivilized portions of earth.

The first **opinion** that needs investigation is the **belief** that the New Testament was suggested by the Old Testament. There exist a specific **claim** that the prophets from the Old Testament foresaw and prophesied about the coming of the New Testament. And then this opinion goes further, by claiming and stating that the New Testament Scripture came to do away with the old law, and to establish a new law in its place. However, in searching among the writings of the Old Testament there **will-not** be found one slight hint concerning this idea of the "new testament". The prophets of the Primitive History **nowhere** speak of a new law that will be written and which will be given to the world to give direction to mankind. And absolutely **nowhere** do the prophets imply that such was ever intended. When the prophets alluded to the dawning of a new era and the establishment of the spiritual Zion, the Zion upon whose summit would **bloom** the tree of righteousness, those prophets were in no way hinting that these related to any written record such as the New Testament.

And further, it is **incorrect** for mankind to belief that the Divine Mind ever instituted laws that he subsequently repealed.

There exists **no-evidence** to convince the wise and discerning mind that a single law which once controlled and actuated Nature, has ever been repealed or has in any way changed: but instead, there exists universal and unequivocal testimony, both in the general manifestations of Nature and in the united experience of all mankind, that no established law either physical or mental has ever change in the least possible particular. Because thinking with this manner of reasoning would be similar and just as righteous to believe that the Divine Mind had-created physical laws to govern those earlier generations of past, and that He afterward, discovered these laws to be incapable of operating as He first intended, and so, He therefore annihilated them and created new ones in their place to govern the same Beings. With that bizarre manner of reasoning it would be as correct to assume that the physiological laws actuating and governing man's physical constitution, are somehow now entirely different from those controlling the body Forms of previous generations. Because if these things had ever happened they would surely present a unequivocal demonstration that a law that was once created and instituted by the Divine Mind can be changed and a new and different one occupy its position to perform the same office.

So therefore, for those who believe that the law given by Moses to govern the Israelities was of divine origin and was considered by them to be a constant and unfailing code of government, and believe afterward this old law was repealed and annihilated to give place to a new and different combination of principles – is a belief in something which is **contradictory** of the celestial purity of that Divine Creator, who, like His laws is unchangeable.

## Section 130

Many of mankind have a **belief** that the Primitive History is of divine origin and is the center of all moral and righteous truth; and by choosing that belief are **implying** that Reason, – pure promptings of judgment – Nature, - and all other things should be considered as a subordinate to this old history book. And there is a further implication that the truth this book contains is-not yet universally believed because the majority of the whole world is still in ignorance. When in truth, the assumption of the Bible's divine origin is founded upon a **desire** or **need** to have confidence in the potency of its truth.

God's laws always were and always will be. And so, remember the fact that the earth revolved even though the whole world of mankind, whom were existing before the fourteenth century, all were ignorant of the fact that the world was a sphere and instead believing the world was flat. The earth has revolved as it does from its beginning, and yet, it wasn't until man "ascended" to a proper degree of **mental refinement** and knowledge to finally uncover and receive this truth; and so, in the very same way as that, many other truths have been concealed; hidden in that same way for a want, or need, and a lack of mental capacity to receive them.

For example: the natural productions of the plant and animal kingdoms are constant and unfailing, and these are **not-affected** by the mental convictions of man in the least way. Nor has there ever been one physiological law that has been stopped or arrested in its operation, because of mankind's lack of awareness and universal ignorance of that particular law's nature or the law's mode of action.

Some of those things which have always been in action, are those laws governing the solar system, and developing the plant and animal kingdoms, and perpetuating physiological operations in the human genetic constitution; these are all Divine and Eternal and these are **not-affected** either by belief or disbelief. And so, it is these laws which proclaim the wonders of universal and immutable principles which are always emanating from the bosom of the unchangeable **Creator**.

Now if any system of religion has the **same origin** with these laws of the Creator, then, will its **effects** be as pure, as unfailing and as universal as the laws of the Creator.

All **arbitrary** and whimsical **laws** which are in existence upon the earth have **originated** in the **human mind**. And these arbitrary laws, which includes the laws of the Hindus, derived from the Shaster; the laws of the Muslim, derived from the Koran; the laws of the Medes and Persians, derived from the Zend-Avesta; or the laws of Moses, derived from the Primitive History. And add to that group, to include any of the diversified modifications of these laws made by man which may be existing in any other portions of the earth. **All-these** arbitrary law are local and **limited**, their influence is partial and localized, and their **tendency** is to **restrict** the teachings of the real **universal law** as seen displayed in Nature and in man; **therefore**, any man made or arbitrary laws are unholy, imperfect, and positively **unprofitable** to the advancement of the whole race of mankind whom are all **created-equally** by the same Divine Mind, God.

So then in **review** of these things stated, it has become **equally justifiable** to suppose that all religions and various superficial systems of worship have **originated in the human mind.** And this observation takes into account and includes those beliefs of the systems of the Chinese, of the Hindu, of the Muslims, of the Persians, of the Jews, or of any other system, **who-derive** all their distinctive impressions from the teachings of the Primitive History. Because any belief that has a **tendency** to destroy the natural benevolence of a noble mind or to restrict its movements and limit its sympathies, its feelings, understandings, and affections, **is-not** divine. Any system of belief which infringes on the high moral susceptibilities of mankind and instead compels man to forsake the purer and truly divine promptings of Nature, is operating in plain site and is retarding any mental and spiritual progress, and this selfish action only tends to generate sectarianism and unrighteousness.

So, to answer the initial question of **whether** those who have **speculated** on some **imaginary relation** which the teachings of the Old Testament **supposedly** sustain to those of the New Testament - should think seriously and reflect upon all those man-made justifications which this speculation is founded. And it is suggested that everyone should **reconsider** the fact that, **if-the** Bible is truly of celestial origin, then, its effects would have been pure and celestial. And if the Bible is of human origin, then, its effects must have been, as would be expected, from the ignorant and unrefined mental development of those early historians.

Let these mental reflections **always** be a part of the process of reasoning and the steps to be taken before one's affections are given to any particular or peculiar religious system, and this specifically is applicable to use before one's judgment approves whether there is truth or falseness in any of these systems.

From past investigations it has been noticed that the Old Testament **does not** contain a single reference concerning the production of the the New Testament. And the prophets **never-implied** that such a book would be written, nor once was there mentioned the name of **Jesus**; and furthermore, these prophets made no reference to an account of Jesus which afterward in a later time, would be given to the world in the New Testament. Nor is there any allusion in the Old Testament pointing to the proposition which has been claimed by theologians, - saying, that the law of Moses given by the Lord of Abraham, Isaac, and Jacob, was to govern the children of Israel only until a new law and a different set of principles were given to take its place. So our search for Jesus within the Old Testament has not yielded much.

This here, **therefore** is the inevitable and legitimate **conclusion** of these investigations: that the Divine Mind **never** institutes a law in one age, to be superseded in another age and by a different law, that Nature everywhere proclaims and demonstrates this truth, and furthermore, not even the Bible itself makes any pretensions to the contrary. And so, those **erroneous** prevailing opinions must have arisen from a **misdirection** of the human mind, and these assumptions are based upon the early impressions and education gained by those theologians, and so, from both misinterpretations and falsifications of the Primitive History.

# Section 131

The first book of the **New Testament** claims to be according to **Matthew** even though there are no claims that it was written by him. This fact however involves no useful inquiries; though, a statement can be made in reference to this claim, simply, that the sayings of Matthew were afterwards **transposed** and then its contents were **modified** materially by revisers and compilers.

The book according to Matthew starts-off with a genealogical history of the succeeding generations of Jewish ancestry, starting with **Abraham** and ending with the birth of **Jesus**. The Gospel then proceeds in a serious manner to describe the birth of Jesus.

In the investigation of this manuscript it is not necessary to delve into all the specifics and particulars of each passage, but instead the main focus is on those items which are most important, which is, the **internal meanings** of these passages. And then, determine **whether** those instances and verses in Matthew where truth is expressed in relationship with the birth of Jesus have meaning.

Matthew describes and relates the event of **Joseph** and his **dream**. Joseph is said to have received instruction while in a dream from an **angel** concerning the holy and **immaculate conception** – which surprised Joseph because it was opposed to his experience. And he was also directed by the angel of the dream and shown where his future path and movements would take him.

Now whether this information is of truth, is somewhat questionable. Maybe, if by chance Joseph had also **presented** his own testimony in this matter, and if he had personally stated that he had received Divine instructions, well maybe then, some confidence could be placed on that description given in Matthew. **But**, the book of Matthew **was-not** written **until** long after this alleged occurrence took place, and that was long after the death of Jesus. Besides, it is **not-realistic** to believe that a dream would have been the only medium used by the Deity to make a declaration of such a wonderful and truly incomprehensible event. It would seem that, if God, the Divine Mind had intended to "declare to the world" that this child was of His spirit, then some grand and noble event would have occurred instead of this **vague instance**, which was put before mankind in the New Testament.

This idea of an immaculate conception is an interesting phenomena **because** it presents a story of an event were only a **portion** of the **world** is led to believe that a violation of physiological law must have occurred and that somehow the reproductive principle which has been established in Nature, were entirely **set-aside**. And furthermore, this small portion of people **are-led** to believe that the conception was produced and determined by an **invisible** and **unknown cause**. And then the rest of the world those other ninety nine percent of mankind, **are-not** included in this stupendous one-time miracle of God's creation but only those chosen few.

This occurrence is called a **miracle** because of the **strange** and unbelievable causes and **violations** of physiological laws used by God to accomplish the occurrence. Mankind believes this event actually took place, **because** it is related in the first book of the New Testament, and also, **because** it has been believed by their ancestors and confirmed by Biblical commentators. And so now in the modern times this story's truth is **accepted because** it is immersed into the "hereditary affections" of men. However, it **is-not** in the least degree sanctioned by a sound and well developed judgment. At most, it is a speculative hypothesis, however it is one story that **is-not** a well-grounded conviction.

In contrast, the great philosophical and scientific researchers do not just believe in the existence of the laws of Nature, and the laws governing the planetary system, and laws of the Universe, only because their ancestors told them, but because their judgments are **convinced** by knowledge; they are convinced because Nature is constantly demonstrating the truth of these laws.

So from here, it is not necessary to make a public appeal in order to **prove** that a **unnatural conception** is just **not-probable**. Instead it is really only necessary to **think-upon** the celestial majesty of the Divine Mind, and from that awareness know His unchangeable laws and understand that God would not be engaged in such a obvious transgression of his own nature and dignity, nor would God condescend to produce such **trivial evidence** of his Divine purpose.

The common and prevailing ideas concerning this miraculous conception of Mary **can-not** possibly be received and believed by every mind: and it must be plain to all who possess any high degree of spiritual discernment, who should know, that whenever a opinion **can-not** be understood or believed by the **universal mind** and also, can-not be sanctioned by the sublime faculty of **reason**, then it must be an **un-truth** and be in error.

The human **mind** will open-up and admit all things that-agree with its nature and which are connected and friendly to the mind's requirements. But most-likely no man ever really believed the miraculous conception story, especially as it was told in the first book of the New Testament. But mankind have instead really just cherished the opinion; yet this cherished belief is not from a conviction of their judgment, but instead it is **merely** from an affection for "hereditary impressions" and old manuscripts.

It can be stated in all honesty, that to have a faith in this peculiar idea of an immaculate conception, **has-never** climbed high on the ladder of reason: because when the reasoning faculties turn their attention to - the faith of the affections, they inevitably **discover** a totally unreal and imaginary belief, and will speedily **retreat** from that unreal view quickly, as by a positive repulsion.

Man's faculty of Reason is a flower of the Spirit: and it blooms and its fragrance is of liberty and knowledge. **But**, the affections flow **merely** from sensation, upon-which, there has-been impressed and formed a hereditary faith, which is a faith arising from mankind's ignorance. This faith exists only as an **unreal** direction of the **desires** and affections; then from the working of these affections and desires, some are led to believe that their judgments are convinced. This is only supporting faith with faith, and endeavoring to **deceive** the judgment. This false and hereditary faith is standing in awe and it is **fearing** that **Reason** may break her fetters, discover the deception, and discard all imaginary, hereditary and superstitious beliefs forever.

The mind of man is constantly being developed further and the mechanism which drives this development is man's ability to Reason. And the fact of the matter, is that the **reasoning faculty** is first unfolded and developed as a **result** of an immutable law, which is a law that is pure and Divine. And because of this law being Divine then consequently, the judgment – the reasoning – the intellect of man – **must-be** in the same way Divine; so therefore whatever that it can-not sanction, the Divine Mind never created.

The written account given of the birth of Jesus by Matthew **does-not** indicate any intention on the part of Joseph and Mary to have the pregnancy be understood and believed that he was the legitimate Son of the Deity which was deposited and developed in a material Form as is claimed by theologians. If this account of the birth was true and was to be the basis upon which all evidence should rest of the divine incarnation, then would not Joseph have proclaimed these facts in a tangible form to the world, and Mary would also have done the same and any mother would; because if this occurred, then, it would have established the truth in minds throughout the neighborhood at least. This knowledge **would-not** be secret and undoubtedly there would have been many, many testimonies and other writings.

# Section 132

Matthew next, after having relayed the account of the birth of Jesus as he received it **traditionally**, closes the chapter by saying - *"And all this was done that the prophecy of Isaiah might be fulfilled"*, further saying, *"a virgin shall conceive and bear a son"*. In answer, this particular passage is **entirely disconnected** from the subject on which Matthew was speaking, and **can-not** possibly be made to represent a intention on the part of Isaiah to give a prophecy concerning this circumstance; and neither are these verses in any way affirming that the prophesy is true. This quotation which was used by Matthew is entirely **derived** from the (7th Chap. 14th verse of Isaiah), and is used by the writer of Matthew **in-error** for a purpose for which it **was-not** designed.

Think about this, - if such a Divine creation and manifestation as an immaculate conception were possible and if this action were really from God and this immaculate conception were truly a part of the original design, then it **does-not** make sense that such a grand event would have been only proclaimed in such a simply manner and only taught by giving such **superficial evidence** attempting to prove there was a foreknowledge of the event's occurrence, **only-by** this supposed event being prophesied.

Here is a good experiment concerning the quote in Matthew concerning Isaiah: - the best way to understand the origin of this expression in Isaiah, is to read the passage while at the same time keeping in mind the information which has just been given, and thus, see how utterly disconnected the passage is with the circumstance related by Matthew.

*After the death of Solomon, the Jewish nation became divided into two (2) kingdoms or monarchies. The kingdom of **Juda** possessed Jerusalem as its center and capital, and during the time that this passage was written, **Ahaz** was their king. The other nation was called the kingdom of **Israel**, whose capital was in **Samaria**, and **Pekah**, was at this time their king. The nation of Juda followed the line of **David**, but the nation of Israel followed that of **Saul**. Also, **Resin** was the king of **Syria**. Pekah and Resin fought many battles against each other, each, meanwhile, entertaining hostile intentions toward Ahaz and his kingdom which was then at peace.*

*Subsequently, Resin, king of Syria, and Pekah, king of Israel, **joined** their armies and marched into the kingdom of Juda, against Ahaz. **Isaiah** was generally beloved because of his strong social affections, and for the abundant sympathy which he always showed toward those were under trials and afflictions, of whom he was a **general consoler**.*

*Isaiah - was **requested**, by king Ahaz to come and **prophesy** to them concerning what **would-be** the outcome, if the two kingdoms were to wage war – king Ahaz needed a sign from Isaiah of its truthfulness. Isaiah states; "Behold a virgin is with child, and beareth a son. Butter and honey shall he eat, and before he shall know to refuse the evil and choose the good, these kingdoms shall be relieved of both their kings".*

According to biblical chronology it was over seven hundred years **after** this prophecy that the birth of Christ related by Matthew took place. When Isaiah did prophesy concerning the establishment of the kingdom of peace and the growth of the Tree of Righteousness, he used general and unlimited words and expressions, and many of those expressions are open-ended. But still, he presented no sign, this was because the only thing he did was that he expressed the "tendency of things", and did so in the nature of his **interior promptings** and **intuitions**.

Matthew continues the dialogue by relating an account about a **star** that was seen in the east by the **wise men** who came from the east of Jerusalem; and these wise men were instructed by **Herod** to go and search out the residence of the child, so that he, along with the wise men, might go and **worship** him. And Matthew further relates that those men had **followed** the star as a silent guide and indicator.

First of all it is **not-easy** to see a star in the daytime, and secondly it is quite impossible for a star to perform the task of office messenger or tour guide. Anyhow, the wise men go alone in search of the child and when they finally get to the site they dropped-off their **gifts** and departed in another direction, because of their **inner promptings** and intuition which told them to not discuss with Herod, the whereabouts of Jesus's location.

Next in Matthew, Joseph has another dream which indicates for Joseph to depart from Nazareth with wife and child, and flee into **Egypt** remaining there until the death of Herod. Well, Matthew in this record **contradicts** entirely the record given of this same circumstance found in the book of **Luke**. Because in Luke in the the third chapter, twenty-third verse, says, that **Jesus** began to be about thirty years of age before he began to preach. In the thirteenth chap, thirty-first verse, he relates that, "one came to **Jesus** and said get thee out and depart hence, for Herod will kill thee". While in Matthew it relates the story that Herod died before **Jesus** returned from Egypt. This peculiar **discrepancy** has been ignored or "wiggled-around" by Biblical commentators by reporting that Luke's account is referring to a different king who succeeded Herod, but with the same name. However, there **does-not** exist any evidence of these being of independent origin, and this independent - two different stories theory - is surely not derived from any reliable sacred text or Christian ecclesiastical history; the **fact** that these Gospel manuscripts **were-not** even combined into one book, instead these two manuscripts would remain uncollected and **uncompiled** for more that three hundred years after the birth and life of **Jesus**.

# Section 133

Matthew continues by speaking of the prophecy in the book of Hosea, eleventh chap, first verse, which says, *"out of Egypt have I called my Son"*. Plainly this passage has no significance except with the verse's connection with the verses preceding it and following it within the same book of Hosea, which then, the verse is in context with itself.

Then Matthew, in another account, again in connection with the account of Herod's putting to death all the male children, Matthew quotes from the thirty-first chap., fifteenth verse of Jeremiah, which says: *"In Rama a voice was heard, weeping and lamentation, Rachel weeping for her children, and would not be comforted, because they were not"*. Well, this passage is **derived** from one of Jeremiah's **pathetic** attempts to meditate on all the pain and suffering occurring all around him, and this was his heartfelt attempt to describe suffering in general. And so this passage also cannot sustain a connection with Herod's call for the destruction of the children.

Then again, Matthew speaks in connection with the return of Joseph from Egypt and his going to the city of Nazareth, saying that this was done *"that it might be fulfilled which was spoken by the prophet, He shall be called a Nazarene"*. (Matt. ii. 23). However in the historical time-period in which this passage was recorded, this expression had **already existed** in one book of the Psalms, **but** this one book was voted uncanonical previously and had not made it into the Book and that is why it is not found in the Bible to show as proof.

Further, Matthew in (chap. viii, 16-17) gives a quotation of prophecies of Isaiah, fifty-third chap., fourth-verse, the way this prophesy is used by Matthew is that he tries to make a connection with Jesus's healing of the sick and casting out of devils, saying that *"himself took our infirmities and bore our sicknesses"*, yet this is not in reference to Jesus but instead this is in direct reference to and concerns only Jeremiah, and not Jesus. Jeremiah himself during his lifetime did suffer many personal persecutions and afflictions, and so it is Jeremiah who Isaiah is referring to, because they actually were true-life **friends**.

Matthew also quotes a prophecy referring to Christ's dwelling in Capernaum. But this is quite a questionable quote if ever there was one and it does not appear to be connected with Matthew's intent.

Again in another account, Matthew describes the event in the garden in which Peter drew his sword and cut off an ear of someone, and further states, that this act was supposed to fulfill another prophecy. What, Peter with a sword? Why would Peter have had a sword? Peter, one of the most active of the Apostles of the Great Reformer; Peter, who possessed purity, charity, and righteousness, should not be connected with swords.

In all total, Matthew makes twelve quotations from the prophecies of the Old Testament, each of which is disconnected and out of context from the subject he is attempting to explain and make clear. Instead these twelve passages are merely collateral and **abstract sentences** contained in various books and writings of the Old Testament, and from which, if these phrases are disconnected from their original context, then, they have no significance. Because, these strange occurrences recorded by Matthew were minor and isolated circumstances, really having no connection with general law, and could not have been truthfully foretold by any person receiving interior or divine instruction.

# Section 134

Having briefly spoken concerning those superficial evidences which had been accumulated by Matthew and used by the writer of that book to verify his **traditional** history; the next investigation will be to proceed an speak of the **origin** of many **important doctrines** and principles, and especially those doctrines most admired and deemed worthy by theologians, as they are taken from the book of **Matthew**.

First of all the book of Matthew **truly-does** contain many sayings that are **worthy** of close analysis and deserve to be further explained, and this is because these special doctrines which hold a **close relation** to **real** transpiring facts. It is from these true events that the writers had gathered the materials of Matthew's record which they had all superficially collected. Matthew proceeds in a indiscriminate manner to give a historical account of the **process** of Jesus **selecting** the **apostles**, with Jesus picking those twelve who would assist him with his workings, and whom would eventually aid in the spread of his teachings. Matthew goes on to give an account of the **sermon** that was preached upon the mount, and speaks of the influence it had on the gathering of listeners, and further describes the message and principles Jesus is trying to instill in the minds of the multitude; and along with this, Matthew describes the prophecy of Jesus concerning the destruction of Jerusalem. The purpose in listing these accounts from Matthew, **is-not** to determine the validity of these occurrences but **instead**, the objective is to **analyze how** - some of the most prominent theological speculations that exist in the world – can possible be **based solely** upon the historical narrative of Matthew? This is a dilemma.

The first doctrine to review, concerns the **use** and **intention** of the birth and teachings of Christ. It has been **supposed** by theological speculation, **claiming** Jesus was a **designed instrument** possessing in spirit, the divine qualities of the Creator, and his mission was to **redeem** the race from a extreme degree of physical suffering and spiritual death, and Jesus would do this so that they might then be **restored** to a position that they had once occupied, and would again become subjects of the favor and goodness of the Divine Mind and they would exist in heaven.

And then in a similar manner comes another doctrine which **supposed** that Jesus came to **inform** the race of new principles, new ones which had never been taught before; and in this manner Jesus would be giving to the world of man, "the way", by which mankind might be restored to primitive innocence and spiritual perfection.

Again, in another passage, it is **supposed** that Jesus came to be and act as the **mediator** between the Divine Mind and his children. Meaning Jesus was to be a creator of a mutual affinity, a connection, as one who might join-together the universal creations of earth and their Creator! This doctrine is believing that Jesus came to form a connection between cause and effect, so that a new relation and new understanding might now-exist between God and his children which had never before existed!

The belief that Christ was to be a medium through which man might ultimately ascend to higher realms, is a **false assumption**, and only creates hostility, exclusive sectarianism, and presumptive arrogance; so **plainly** this belief **is-not** something from God. If this hierarchy of beings were to occur, it would elevate one person above another, and would tend to establish exclusive privileges. It would form a deep and harmful impression upon the uninformed masses of mankind, telling them that **they-are**, "by their born nature", to always be exceedingly sinful beings, who are depraved and whom are **despised** by their own Creator.

These **assumptions** concerning the birth of Jesus breath envy, bigotry, and superstition, into every heart. It is a type of belief which actually depreciates Nature's constitution, and so these assumptions should be banished from the world forever.

# Section 135

It has been speculated and **supposed** that Jesus came to bring knowledge of life and immortality into mankind's awareness; and it was supposed that it will be Jesus who brings to light these principles, so that these may be revealed to man as being new principles. And in addition, it is **supposedly** the **action** of Jesus performing and completing all the processes and tribulations he is to undergo, which culminates at the resurrection; meaning that by the time of the resurrection, Jesus will have taught the entire race of mankind concerning the new truths of spiritual life and of immortal existence.

However, in response to this: first, this is a crude speculation and assumption of Jesus's purpose, and was **incorrectly** placed upon Jesus's shoulders. When in reality, this is only an invention, devised by theologians. Second, the doctrine of life and immortality **is-not** expressed clearly in either the Old or New Testaments. To know and completely understand the real-origin of the principles of life and immortality is to have **core knowledge** of the nature and composition of Matter; and also, knowledge of the Divine Essence which animates Matter and all its Forms in being. Third, the doctrine of immortality, as well as a belief in spiritual life **had-existed** in the world a long time before either the New or Old Testaments were written. And fourth, this quote from Matthew stands-alone as a incidental remark which **does-not** appear to represent any important feature of Christ's mission on earth.

And then: it might be argued that Jesus came to confirm and further develop that essence which had already been implanted in the human mind. This **can-not** be true because nowhere in the Bible does Jesus confirm the prior theology of early mankind nor does he enhance or develop those early beliefs.

Again: it is **supposed** that **Christ** was designed as a medium, by and through whom man might escape eternal condemnation and be saved. Sorry to say, but this is one of the most ridiculous concepts that have been imagined by mankind. This type of thinking has its roots in primitive mankind, and had been used successfully to frighten and to prevent hysteria in early mankind; but, it is no longer of any use or need by man; yet, somehow this concept still flourishes and is **mostly-believed** in those same places where ignorance, superstitions, and folly are found. This belief originated in darkness and so it can only develop darkness.

Mankind has been led to believe in an existence of an ocean of never-ending fire and heat; a place where one wave of fire succeeds another, all sustained by the fuel of rejected souls and condemned human spirits. And there is **supposed** by some that Christ came to pay a debt that mankind had fallen into. This is a popular and imaginative belief which had originated in the very bosom of darkness, ignorance, and imbecility, it is not worthwhile even to mention its hideousness and absurdity, because soon it will die in the place where it had its birth, darkness, and soon it will be sacrificed on the altar of pure Reason and Intelligence.

According to the written record of Matthew, **Christ**, in the process of foretelling the destruction of Jerusalem, used many **metaphorical** illustrations and **expressions** so that he could **make-clear** his point, and because Jesus knew these phrases were **already** in use and were able to be comprehended by his listeners. These metaphors really **only-illustrate** the mentality of the general public in Jesus's era. This is apparent because He uses these heathen parables and frightening illustrations to help them understand the message.

Many theological speculators and theologians have encouraged the belief in hell, and they do this mostly because of its age of origin. Their thinking is that because of the old age of this belief in hell, gives proof of the belief's sacredness and truth; however these speculators should pause one moment and reflect, because with **further research** into the depths of antiquity, the deeper and darker grows the folly, ignorance, superstition, and imbecility, of the human mind as it was **then-existing**. So, just because it is old does not mean its true, it only shows how far back stupidity goes.

The teachings of the **Christ** then, are **used-inappropriately**, because Christ, in dealing so extensively in oriental allegories and the customary expressions of those days, as He needed to do to convey his message, He has instead been misunderstood as though He were teaching this doctrine; and it is supposed that because of His persistent instruction of this teaching, that I constituted a part of his peculiar mission to mankind, yet this claim is rubbish and nothing more than a theological proposition based upon mere imagination, for which there is absolutely no rational foundation.

# Section 136

Theologians have a habit of manufacturing ingenious and cunningly-devised **creeds**, claiming those creeds are based upon doctrines and principles which have their origin in the Bible. These creeds are put forth to the world, accompanied by severe and urgent **demands** for their belief. And to enforce these demands, theologians will quote a passage from the bible such as, *"He that believeth and is baptized, shall be saved; and he that believeth not, shall be damned"*. This policy of quoting from various passages or statements of a holy book, is also the method used by Matthew, who had tried desperately to confirm the truthfulness of his gospel by quoting randomly from the prophets of the Old Testament. And this same policy is used by every religion and sect and has propelled itself into the twenty-first century, and furthermore this policy is especially useful where ignorance, fanaticism, and foolishness exists all-around, and up and down. And so, as it has ended up, our modern world is chock-full of superficial theology.

Up to this point in the investigation into the New Testament, in response to the information from the preceding discussions and from the foregoing considerations, hopefully the answer has now been made clear that **not-even** one of those theological propositions, which Christian speculators had used in an attempt to determine the mission of Christ on earth has any merit nor can possibly have the least foundation in truth.

Again further speculation: it is **claimed** that Christ had a Divine authority, to prove and establish miracles, and with that authority he supposedly performed many hard to believe miracles. Matthew relates in his writings concerning some miracles that were performed by Christ after He had descend from the mount, and continues by explaining how Jesus also performed various miracles while He traveled through various portions of the land. Now if the scripture is read properly, it appears as though Christ only performed those miracles when He had been earnestly solicited, by those that were desiring relief from their afflictions, being those who pull on his clothing, those who stop Him along the way. It was only then, that Christ is represented as **rewarding** their faith and confidence in him, by causing some miracle to happen and complying with their desires. But, He does not perform these miracles out of random sympathy, but only when prompted.

Now again more theological speculation: it **is-said** by some that **no-system** of religion is **sustained** by miracles, with the **exception** of that system found in the **Bible**. But this is **not-true**. Because, **Mohammed**, who wrote the **Koran**, appeals to the authority of miracles to establish a belief in his revelation – miracles too, which he says he himself performed. He says that he was transfigured, and thus, was able to pass through ninety heavens in one night – had a long conversation with the **Deity**, and returned again to the earth early on the subsequent morning.

**Zoroaster** also constantly appealed to the marvelous faculty of the human mind for credibility in relation to his very strange and miraculous conversation with the gods.

Again speculation: it is said that miracles were not only intended to demonstrate and establish the Divine authority of **Jesus**, but also to establish an undisputed Christian system of theology, and that His mission and the Bible were established by supernatural evidences and manifestations. And so here, the miracles are considered works accomplished by supernatural potency.

What should be clear by now is that nothing is, and nothing can be, but the Divine Mind, which is the First Cause, and it is Creation and the Universe which is the Effect. Cause and Effect uniting into one and only one united System. And it makes-sense that whatever occurs in the Universe, **must-occur** because it is **caused-by** a natural action or instigation. Nothing, therefore can occur which is opposed to the principles of Nature. All things therefore, whether organized or unorganized, developed or undeveloped, **must-be** natural.

# Section 137

Again more speculation: it is **alleged** that the apostles were **selected** to witness these miraculous displays given by Jesus and then to communicate the facts to the world. And further, it is **supposed** that during the apostle's journeyman-ship, it is assumed that the apostles will do this task truthfully, because they were of good character and are men who would not be influenced easily.

Well to answer that, if the purpose of choosing those apostles were because they were truly chosen to communicate the knowledge of the miracles and the teachings of Christ to the world, **why-then** did they not write voluminous accounts of the miracles performed, writing more so they may be dispensed throughout the Christian system? And then, would not this written material be available in our modern world as a monument of **evidence** of a Divine intention, and as a display of the absolute truth of the Christian religion? **Instead**, in the gospels there is no announcement of any such intention of Christ, nor is there any convictions claimed in the apostles own minds. The **miracles** are reported by the apostles as being **merely incidental** acts which occurred on their journeys, and were not regarded by any of the apostles nor by Christ himself as being anything else in any other manner.

Matthew certainly was **not-capable** of being an eye-witness to those miraculous works of Jesus which he writes about, because he was an officer under the **Roman empire** many years after the death of Jesus, and did not become an apostle until he was older and advanced in years. There is no historian of Matthew's time which had wrote about him because he had **deserted** the Jewish beliefs and adopted the Christian religion. He then only wrote a few accounts, and at last died a martyr in **Persia**.

So then, the alleged proposition under review of whether Christ was preordained with a mission to accomplish **can-not** be proved true, by either a review of Christian tenets, or even common world history. Besides, this alleged belief was not even taught by **Jesus**, and scarcely hinted at by the apostles and entirely disbelieved by the whole Jewish nation, who were obviously in a place and condition to be eye-witnesses to all the occurrences; and if these events had been convincing they would have been convinced and the events which occurred would have been recorded.

Again there was more speculation: it is **said** that the **miracles** were **designed** to confirm and to establish the Christian religion. And as Christian authority now **claims** these miracles truly were performed and actually witnessed two thousand years ago; and they further state that it is inappropriate and even immoral for any true Christian believer to entertain any thoughts that these miracles did not occur. Well now in reply to this and to be completely fair, any belief in miracles **should-cease**, when the **evidence** for them is **lacking**. Because, if the miracle has **no-proof** of its truthfulness, then these beliefs are founded in the imagination. Faith in them may exist, but only as a fleeting conviction of the affections.

# Section 138

The **miracles** as they are recorded in the New Testament are of such a nature that they **create-fear** and wonderment in the minds of anyone who may have witness them, heard-about them, or read, these accounts. In the first place, the miracle stories are really not presented well and they do not represent the objective for which they are supposedly intended. The intention was to verify Jesus as the Christ. However, as these supposed miracle events are represented and reported in the Bible, they signify **nothing** and are basically **void** of any great and celestial dignity for-which they would naturally be **expected** to possess; well that is, if they truly are of a celestial nature and are Divine in their origin.

Matthew and the other writers of the **Gospels**, have **unintentionally** done a dis-service to all of mankind, by giving the **wrong impressions** of the events which occur during Jesus's ministry. The Gospels fail to represent properly the events of Christ's ministry because they **divert** one's attention to some **far-fetched** description of an anomaly. Jesus, was a man who became the Christ. Jesus, was the first man that had developed the "Christ Consciousness" and with that consciousness Jesus **became** the Christ. Jesus said, brothers and sisters, "I am the Light and the Way". He said "be as I am, and you shall do as I do". But, because the Gospels have been written improperly, and have given **improper representations** these writings have since, been misinterpreted, and then, the teachings of Jesus were misinterpreted a **second-time**.

Within the Gospels, the disciples described the events of Christ's ministry, using a **type** of **expression** which actually are **contrary** and very **destructive** to what-would or should promote harmony and be in harmony with everything else occurring in Nature and within the Universe.

What is a miracle, anyhow? Miracles are what happens to imaginary beliefs. Miracles **always-seem** to **defy** God's laws of Nature, defy all Divine law of anatomy and physiology, defy chemistry and all its attached sciences, and also defy the successive development of Matter. Miracles, most-likely **do-not-exist** in God's Universe, and instead, they exist in the minds of mankind. God's way's exist in Nature, and these Divine ways are clearly seen occurring in Nature every second, of every hour, of every day, forever. It is that simple. If it is not in Nature, then it is not of God. So, do spacemen exist? Yes, assuredly. Did Jesus change water into wine? It is doubtful to have occurred instantaneously, though the process where water which was utilized by the grapevine during its growth to produce grape juice, can eventually be made-into wine.

So the **disciples** and Gospel writers were using expressions such as, *"He laid his hands upon him, and he was healed"*; or *"we sowed the seed, and we gathered the harvest"*, or *"one applied the medicine, and was cured"*, or *"the sun retired behind the western hills, and all was involved in darkness"*. In this **style**, writers use shorten phrases where there is **no-mention** of **the intermediate period** between cause and effect, which goes entirely unnoticed by Gospel writers. And Matthew **only-recorded** the events in **general terms**, basic, and short 'n sweet; but, attempted to write in a complete and comprehensive manner, but did this by only writing just the beginning and the end. This same-style of narrative is **frequently used** in the writings of all the apostles.

**Jesus** was the real deal, he did exist and he **did-become** the **Christ**. Christ is the ultimate mind-set, the ultimate **connection** of a created Spirit - with its Creator. Jesus taught mankind to be Christ-like. Be as I am, do as I do. Jesus said, feed the hungry, heal the ill, love your neighbor as yourself, and love God. And all that is being Christ-like. Jesus lived his life in such a "way", that he became the Christ. He walked the walk and he talked the talk. He traveled about, teaching, preaching, and healing, and promoting the advancement of mankind, and did all that without needing to perform some miracle; his **mission** was the advancement of mankind. Jesus came, He saw, and He conquered evil, because he was the Truth and the Light. Jesus shows that it is truth that God created man to be his companions. Jesus showed us the way.

So in conclusion concerning biblical miracles, those **unjust interpretations** of the actual events found in the New Testament should be **reviewed** using the insight which has just been given as well as using the faculties of Reason and Wisdom to guide the way. **Eventually** it must be said, that those things related in the New Testament which are concerning the life and purpose of Jesus, really **do-not** have any important bearing upon the questions relating to the truth or falsity of Christ's Messiah-ship. The miracle stories **do-not** contain within their pages any grand and elevated principles; there is no natural beauty or excellency which would have any beneficial tendencies that would reorganize mankind.

Even if thousands of such "miracle experiments" were performed, such as, the casting out of devils or transforming water into wine, or maybe destroying of a number of undeserving swine, or cause the withering of a vibrant fig-tree, what would have been accomplished? What possible use – what grand design – what **celestial** result would be accomplished by performing these miracles? Has the belief in miracles rooted-out evil from the earth, destroying it completely? Surely not. Yet, have not the very existence of those interpretations caused war, persecution, martyrdom, and death? And, have they not divided nation from nation, by establishing an antagonism in those persons with personal and national interests, which instead, should unite them as a brotherhood?

What has been taught and learned is that the theological propositions which have been and are founded upon the "supposed supernatural miracles", are so completely transparent, that the discerning mind can easily see through to their utter nothingness.

# Section 139

Proceeding now to an investigation of those fundamental and essential principles that are **claimed** to be a pure and celestial theology, or rather, proceeding now into an investigation of the **four pillars** upon which the **theological superstructure** is sustained. Paying particular attention to the possibility that this **attack** upon those four pillars, might-be, what will demolish the whole system, and leave nothing of it but a mass of disgusting rubbish.

The first point to investigate is "**Original Sin**", the second "**The Atonement**", the third "**Faith**", and the fourth "**Regeneration**".

First. - **Original Sin**. If a complete analysis were given to this unlikely-idea, in all its numerous forms and modifications, it would be a waste of time and would have given-credit to something which is not capable of meaning anything. This concept is unworthy because of its unsoundness and lack of credibility. And, know that there is one principle involved in this subject of original sin in-which the human mind has been immorally **perverted**, and so, this particular principle demands a brief notice of attention.

In this one particular principle, it **represents** man as being originally pure in his physical and spiritual nature, *"even as a flower from the bud of the divine creation"*, and that the **original man** possessed nearly all the characteristics of a **celestial being** as pure, spotless, unsophisticated; and then at Creation man was formed coming right-out of the earth below our feet. **And-then**, while man was existing as a pure being, **temptations** were placed before him that were of such a captivating nature, that man was **unable** to resist them. From here, this idea is nuts, and gives the notion the Divine Mind is confused, and then, this thought charges **God** with the act of **creating** man and endowing him with all the grand attributes of purity and goodness, but at the same time **withholding** from man a competency and abilities to resist that temptation!

So then, the whole idea of original sin, is based upon this grand but unjust treatment of the Wisdom and Love of the Creator, and questioning the integrity of God. It **assumes** that man was tempted, that man then failed and finally, yielded, and that mankind's spiritual death then followed. This hysterical imaginative belief, **disconnects** the whole world of humanity from any spiritual communication with the Holy Essence which had breathed mankind into being. It incorrectly teaches mankind that millions upon millions of humans are **in-debt** and owing to the divine curse, destined only to writhe in the waves of darkness – and live in the bosom of a burning abyss, whose dissolving fires were blown into a flame by the very breathe of - Divine Love!

And think about the implication of it, according to this doctrine of original sin, an innocent man who has-had no negative experiences – who was totally pure and undefiled – suddenly came under the wrath and curse "**of that Being**" whose very **essence** is Love, Wisdom, and celestial Perfection. This is a corrupt proposition, violating the very sensibilities of men, and this impossible notion is destructive; it has originated in darkness and still exists in the darkest recess of a distorted imagination. This is a great debt which was caused by man's fall from grace and spiritual death and which now the whole race of mankind is said to owe to Him who had spoke the word, and they lived!

The Divine Mind is said to have **assumed** the human form, in which he calls himself "the Son", for the **purpose** of **relieving** the race of this debt, which he himself created – and then, by living on earth, suffering all descriptions of persecution, and then at last dying in public disgrace. He himself suffers innocently in-order to remove effects that must have originated in his own Infinite Wisdom. And this action, is called the **Atonement** or **second** pillar. This statement is equivalent to saying, that the Creator instituted a celestial plan to deceive and implicate mankind, of which he later repented, and then, could not stop its awful consequences without his Son - even himself – dying the death of a persecuted martyr.

The **third** essential element and pillar in "the received theology", is called **Faith**. This, like many other **alleged** Christian virtues is **not-capable** of showing evidence of itself, nor is it even known to be existing **until** the person verbally makes the fact known to the world, exactly what it is they now have a faith in. It is similar to many Christian principles, so called, that are **never-able** show itself manifested by deeds or correct actions, but these are only known to exist when the world is told of them by someone. Having faith that the sun will rise tomorrow which is based on past history of the sun rising makes perfect sense. But, having faith that Jesus is coming to save you is ridiculous.

The **fourth** point and pillar of theology is **Regeneration** such as Jesus being resurrected. This principle is founded on the **assumption** of regeneration being an actual spiritual event, and therefore this doctrine is fleeting, fading, and an unreal effect, which is proceeding from a cause (faith) which is equally unreal and unsubstantial. Regeneration is considered as an effect resulting from faith. And the idea of faith has resulted from who-knows-what, because it is impossible to tell what or where. So then, this idea is entirely useless to dwell on, especially a term containing no interior meaning. And furthermore, such a word, has generated fear and confusion, and will continue to do the same, unless abandoned, along with every species of superstition and unrighteous thoughts.

Just given, are the **supposed** four substantial elements which constitute and sustain the great theological superstructure of Christianity. Their qualities are impure, their composition is decayed, they are unwittingly performing the work of their own destruction; and behold the temple falls; and who shall stand, only future generations will testify.

## Section 140

There are probably no verbal expressions that have made the feeble mind of man tremble with fear and dread, more than those words that had been used by Christ, while preaching and prophesying.

Sometimes Jesus used hateful words in his teachings and these harsh isolated phrases have been a source of wonder and extreme perplexity, because, **how** could He this particular exalted Being who is represented as someone who possessed great spiritual refinement and brotherly kindness, have used such violent and unkind terms, when He was only speaking about of those who were **merely opposed** to the doctrines he taught? It would have been very plain to every pure, benevolent, and philanthropic, mind who is hearing or reading Jesus's statements, saying that the **mental state** of that person must be impure and **unjust**. Any person, who could look upon the face of Nature and point out the weakness of erring humanity, and then say to his own brethren - *"ye serpents, ye generation of vipers"* or, - *"Ye scribes and Pharisees – Ye hypocrites"*, was himself a hypocrite. So then, could Jesus have condemned these men who were merely his uneducated and misdirected brethren, whose opinions and mental condition **was-not** caused by themselves, no, the cause was by being born and raised in the inferior, unfavorable, and unsuccessful circumstances that existed around those individuals.

It is best to **realize** that the well-informed mind would-be personally aware, that the causes of evil lie not in man, but around him. And this knowledge at once creates a universal forgiveness, and forbids the application of any harsh terms to a brother, and even more to a brotherhood of man. However, any persons who are **not-familiar** with the cause of **moral evil**, are usually in the habit of accusing each other falsely, and are often applying to each other, terms no less unjust than those like "ye serpents", "ye vipers".

Now some theologians have **supposed** and expressed that those harsh words used by Christ had an **interior meaning**, which **they-say**, is not discovered on the surface. Well then, if an expression has a meaning that is not discoverable, or is not perceptible, then, should not the words be discarded, because at this point they are entirely useless?

Probably there are **not-many** terms which have oppressed the minds of mankind more and piled-on more gloom and dread than terms like - *"hell-fire"* or - *"everlasting fire, prepared for the devil and his angels"* or - *"weeping, wailing, and gnashing of teeth"*. Remember now, it is the expression and not the meaning which terrifies the weak and undeveloped mind:

for example, **sheol** being a Hebrew word, has no specific application, but instead was a **widely-used** term, plus, it was used by the early inhabitants to describe almost anything. And **hades**, a Greek word, is used in a similar fashion.

And speaking of hell, this brings up a most remarkable and conspicuous personage, who may be considered as an **inmate** of this man-made theological temple, and this being who is alluded to is called the **devil**. This potent being, has been as active in establishing his portion of the kingdom as any good or bad influence which has been discussed so far. And now because of his popularity, it may-be best to analyze the term "devil", so that the reader may become more familiar with his **origin** and the disposition of this allusion.

This term devil is synonymous with satan, which was derived from shaitan (Arabic). This term originally meant almost nothing, but it was generally used in a loose and unguarded manner, and then, depending how the word was used or phrased, it could mean, full of energy, or lively, godly man, deified spirit, disease, an evil-doer, and many others. In the Bible, devil means evil, wickedness, hatred. And so, when this evil deity is represented as *"going up and down the earth"*, or *"going about like a roaring lion seeking whom he may devour"*, the word "devil" is nothing more than putting human personalities or characteristics to evil. And so, any person with good judgment can easily see that the devil causes the most turmoil, in places where **ignorance** and **superstition** exist.

Anyone who may have researched the **early** application of these various terms, has probably learned that the ancient **magicians** deified an Evil Principle; the beliefs and theology of the magicians was at a later time systematized by **Zoroaster**, who **possessed** all the recorded materials existing prior to his life; and it was from these early materials which Zoroaster erected his **supernatural revelation**.

The terms "hell" "devil" "satan", and any other of a similar type, have created fear and have developed a type of superstitious apprehension throughout the world. However when these terms were initially used they were **only-intended** to express that-particular meaning which the ignorant and uncultivated inhabitants of the earth had **created** by their false and **imaginary conceptions** and **impressions** of the mysterious and unknown world around them; and then sometimes these words were used to indicate the character and attributes of man. In some ways these mere words should be **regarded** with at least as much respect as any oriental, poetical mythos, because they can be used as an **indication** of mental development and show the early workings of our ancient human mind, simply for the fact, that these show some of the imaginative and marvelous conceptions which those mind used to **cope** with their mysterious and majestic world.

Now it has been **supposed** by the majority of mankind, and especially by those acquainted with the teachings of the Old and New Testaments, that the **resurrection** and general judgment were never presented to the world before the life and disclosures of Jesus; and that the "golden rule" was then supposedly for the first time promote and made widely known by Jesus, and was never conceived of or expressed by any previous mind. That is **not-true**. It is well known by many, who have explored the pages of antiquity, that **Confucius**, the **Chinese** philosopher, expressed the "golden rule" nearly six hundred years before Christ lived – and this is just about the time **Zoroaster** also flourished, who **succeeded** in establishing throughout the whole eastern world the doctrine of a physical **resurrection** and general judgment. Zoroaster even prophesied, with a great deal of ingenuity, truthfulness, and it was easily understood.

Zoroaster's conceptions of a general resurrection and judgment were themselves **derived** from the many hieroglyphical writings of those conceptions, of earlier ages, which had been traditionally handed-down from generation to generation, and then, with Zoroaster, they are presented in a more systematic and rational form than those which are contained in the New Testaments, which the apostles endeavored to spread as teachings on the authority of the teachings and martyrdom of Christ, even-though those teachings and ideas had existed for centuries prior.

# Section 141

Matthew, after having related the prophesy of Jesus concerning the destruction of Jerusalem, and after he supposedly had made many other indiscriminate and casual sayings, then closes his Gospel by giving a description of the trials, sufferings, condemnation, and crucifixion of Christ, who truly was a person of **remarkable excellence** in all his physical and spiritual possessions.

Matthew made some remarks about this very unjust crucifixion. He relates that Christ was extremely disliked by the Jewish nation, and that he was accused, arrested, and transported to the presence of **Pontius Pilate** – who was not seeking to condemn Jesus but was compelled by the loud, angry, and unrestrained crowd, to yield and give his approval, and in doing so seal the condemnation. After this event - a cross was prepared, which Jesus was forced to carry, and which he did with gentleness and humiliation, until he arrived at the spot where He would be sacrificed. They placed a crown of thorns on his head, and gave him impure and bitter drink for his thirst; and then nailed him to the cross, perforated him with spears to increase His suffering. He is represented as having few or no followers, and those who did come, wept beneath his body.

After dying he was taken from the cross and placed in a sepulcher, then moving the stone to close off the opening. He was guarded three days, and after this he appeared to three of his disciples. And then after that he was seen by nearly five hundred souls; then he ascended into the clouds and disappeared to occupy a position as Judge on high. Remember, this event **is-recorded** by Matthew, Mark, Luke, and John. The apostles writing this record, were pure and honest men, whose testaments are worthy of the highest respect. **However** this account written about Jesus **was-not** a demonstration of this events actual occurrence. **So-then**, exactly how was this opinion created and what were the causes that were involved in producing the well known story, and especially, why these persons wrote with so much pure simplicity? The answer will be reviewed soon, but it will be after first discussing all the various **theological speculations** which have been **assumed**, based entirely on these records.

This martyrdom of Jesus is called the "Vicarious Atonement", which supposedly means, that Jesus's suffering and death were for the purpose of removing the sins of the world – and he suffered an innocent and humiliating death, which the Divine Creator is represented as having instituted and sanctioned. If that is true, then why should the Jews be persecuted for crucifying Jesus? Because if indeed the persecution was originally designed by God, and that

Jesus the Christ should in this way suffer for the redemption of mankind, then it is a justifiable persecution. Because, he would not have been persecuted nor put to death had it not been for the Jews who performed that service. Then why not say that the Jews were an **essential** means employed by God, in the accomplishment of this vicarious atonement?

But the death of Christ really had no possible connection with the sins of the world, nor is his death connected with the cause of sin. **Sin**, first of all, in the common accepted use of that term, does not really exist; but what is called sin is merely a **misdirection** of man's physical and spiritual powers, which generates unhappy consequences.

It can be **assured** that the death of no being will root-out and completely destroy the evil consequences which mankind suffers. The **only-process** which will root out evil is by **education**. And it is through gaining a general knowledge of the causes of these evils, **plus** the general progression of the capabilities of mankind, these will restore permanent harmony and happiness to the race.

Further: concerning a **resurrection** there are no laws governing Matter, which indicate that a resurrection of a body is possible, and especially as the **supposed** ascension process of Christ occurred and as is explained by the writers of the New Testament. The original term is **anastasis** and was **rendered** resurrection in the New Testament. The original meaning of anastasis implied a rising up, an elevation, a progressive reform, a resurrection, a gradual and steady improvement. And it should be added that the general-resurrection is founded upon an **assumption** that the Bible teaches this, which it does not.

**Paul** was one who philosophized upon the subject of the resurrection, and he truly believed in a general, tangible resurrection. Still, all his expressions, as well as those of the other writers, would confess to having more than one meaning, such as the ones suggested above; and besides that fact that they could be misinterpreted, those same words and phrases used now, have become greatly modified, especially since language has become so extensive and diverse; and so therefore, what words mean now, may not always be what they had meant originally.

Adding to this confusion over the word resurrection, Matthew, then relates in his account of the resurrection, a most marvelous phenomenon concerning the temple being "rent", the earth quaking, graves opening, and their tenants being quickened into life, and this appearing in many cities. (Matt, xxxvii. 51-53.). People really believe this occurred as stated **because** it was related in the Bible; **however**, if the same description were told in the Zend Avesta it would not have been believed.

And lastly, a comment on the possibility of a day of **Judgment** will be sparse because not much comment is required; this is **not-taught** in the scripture of the Bible, nor is it believed by any enlightened biblical investigators.

# Section 142

The writings of Matthew **have-all** of the material that is contained in the successive books of the Bible, **however** the **collateral** information which is contained in the other three Gospels writings **which-will** either **confirm** the events Matthew had previous revealed, or they will **differ** with Matthew's account. So with that in mind, the material in the other books of the New Testament will be **reviewed** and given notice; doing this so that the **origin** of these manuscripts and the prominent principles can be established. **But**, before doing that, a few facts need to be given that relate to the history of Matthew which are of importance to this story.

**Matthew** became an officer under the Roman government some time previous to the death of Christ, and he remained in this occupation a long time, straight-through until old age. While Matthew's life went in this direction, **Paul, Dionysius**, and others, were preaching the important doctrines of Christ. Matthew had deserted the Jewish faith and embraced the Christian religion, this occurring not very long after Paul's conversion, and **that-is** when he began to write concerning the things he had **heard** and seen pertaining to Christ and his teachings. In Matthew's writings, it is **apparent** that he had **grouped-together** the sayings of Christ just as they flowed out of his thoughts, **but-not** in the order of their actual occurrences. And further, in many places he **compacts** into one sentence, what had taken place over a period of months.

Matthew's manuscripts have **never** been **known** to the world. The **only remains** of them are contained in a Greek manuscript. But they were originally written in Hebrew, and were originally for the express use of some Jewish converts.

After Matthew had written a few manuscripts, he was **captured** by two officers of the Persian customs, and carried to the governor, there he was pronounced guilty of heterodoxy, and was condemned and died a martyr. The writings of Matthew **were-not** intended to be placed in the Bible. The Christ did not direct Matthew to write this for the world.

The book of **Mark** contains many things that are in **discrepancy** with the contents of the book of Matthew. But there is no evidence that they intended to place an imposition upon the world. And the discrepancy does not effect the moral purity and correct behavior of either of the historical writings, but instead, it rather shows a more pure design, because **they-give** to the world something that those spiritual men seriously believed to be true, and which was also believed by others.

Actually the discrepancy absolutely **proves** that there was no designing plot – no collusion, where someone could point to and say all occurrences and things in those books were fictional and were made-up to relate to each other and so the books would confirm each-other. And it also **proves** that they wrote **merely** based on **external impressions**; and it also **proves**, that they each wrote **separately**, not being acquainted with each others private opinions and views; and shows that they wrote free from any intention, except that of presenting a pure and truthful account.

# Section 143

The book of **Mark** begins differently than did that of Matthew, for instance, Mark does not begin by introducing a genealogy, he instead starts-off by quoting from the book of Malachi, third chapter, first verse, with the prophesy concerning **One** who would come to prepare **the-way** for the introduction of the teachings of **Christ** to the world. But, Malachi's quote is written in the first person context, and has no connection to the future-tense, and no connection with **John the Baptist**. However, the expression which Malachi makes **does-apply** to the **fact** that John preached and prepared the way for the introduction of the gospel, but it just **was-not** a prophesy.

The book of Mark contains no distinct doctrines that are not contained in Matthew. It is written in a more condensed manner and it is clear and easily understood. In a few instances Mark's descriptions of a particular event differs slightly from Matthew who is relating the same event.

The writer closes the book of Mark by telling a command that was given to the apostles to go forth into all the world and preach the Gospel, and then the writer, stating in a harsh and severe manner, such as, *"He that believeth not shall be damned"*. Well, it is statements and words like these that **do-not** seem possible to have come from the thoughts and expressions of any-being who is possessing a high degree of spiritual knowledge.

It is **understandable**, that the meager **fact** of the apostles preaching **could-not** alone have been sufficient to produce the faith in Christ's teachings, **so-some** exaggerated statements **were-needed** and were-made in a manner that would produce that belief in faith through salvation. However, **how** is it possible for faith, by any process, to be able to produce salvation from anything? The only effect of faith is merely a tranquility of the mind. And then, out of a tranquil mind flows bright hopes and anticipations. Faith however, **can-not** save someone from sin, or pain, nor from a miserable life. And faith can not save one from moral or spiritual death. **Faith** is simply an involuntary expression of agreement or approval of the judgment of the mind, producing a calm mind, which is then counted as happiness. However, this expression of happiness is **confined** to that particular mind, whose judgment made the decision, and faith **is-not** something that can be communicated to another, nor can faith give to its owner any physical or spiritual requirements. So how can faith give salvation?

A man **can-not** just believe or disbelieve at will. He can-not control the convictions of his own judgment, - but instead here under Mark's statement man is obliged to submit to be controlled. Man can not have faith on any subject "at will", anymore than he can by the exercise of his will have a warm or cold feeling, or have a love or hatred, or even have a delight or displeasure. So it is quite unfair to demand that a man do something that is so **entirely beyond** his power. It is extremely **doubtful** that Christ ever gave that command to Mark, or anyone else.

# Section 144

The next passage in Mark **reveals** evidences of the existence of **methods** that can be used which will enable those persons who truly believe, to now be able to see signs. *"And these signs shall follow them that believe: - In my name shall they cast out devils; - they shall speak with new tongues; - they shall take up serpents without harm; - and if they drink any deadly thing, it shall not hurt them; - they shall lay hands on the sick, and they shall recover"*. This is a **senseless** run of words, which is one of the most inappropriate passages that could possibly occur, especially for theologians and any of the followers of this philosophy and teachings. It **does-not** appear as though anyone has cast out evil from the world, nor does it appear that anyone possesses the power of casting out devils, at least in the sense with-which the phrase is used in Mark's statements.

It **does** appear though, that some theologians have discovered a new tongue or language, because they use words and phrases which **no-other** person can discover even the smallest particle of meaning or significance, or even understand clearly what is being stated. In the New Testament here are many statements that are **incapable** of being applied to any real principle, or any phenomenon, or development, in any department of Nature. So in this particular statement of Mark's he is not trying to deceive anyone and it does really seem like he is describing something, **however**, as it turns-out it is just another twisted phrase which theologians have manipulated.

**Here** seems to be a **place** of **opportunity** in our story, to take time and make a **review** of some of the later and more **modern** developments among followers of **new faiths** or new religions. These new belief systems or faiths which have all occurred within the last couple of centuries. These new forms of religion under review, really do not need to be investigate in an in-depth manner because they are known, and therefore no particular details are required, and only a review is necessary.

First to be mentioned is the performances of the sect known as the **Mormons**. The founder of this sect presented to the world, not only his own testimony, but also that of many others, in relation to his and their religious faith and miraculous performances. They **profess** to **heal** the sick by the *"laying on of hands"*, to cast out devils, and to **converse** in unknown tongues. They can produce evidence of an **artificial character** of these things and of their actual occurrence. There exists no interior evidence, no probability, or no use, in any such performances, and so therefore, they should not receive the credence of any rational mind. One thing however they claim, and that is, that they report they have evidence of them being in possession of the right faith, and this evidence is something they could produce in abundance; which is, **they-claim** they could converse in **unknown tongues**. This peculiar statement and claim, is in one sense true, because some of the **dissenters** from that faith do not hesitate to acknowledge that they could and did "converse in a language unknown either to themselves or to anybody else"!

The followers of **Ann Lee**, whose history is also well known, also make the same claims as did the Mormons, and their faith produced the same evidence; and the **dissenters** of this sect make, without hesitation, precisely the same acknowledgment.

**Therefore**, what is best, is to **beware** of superficial testimony, external appearances, visible, tangible, sensual evidences; because these things are invariably in every case, answer in a **deceptive manner**, and in many instances are directly attempting to **deceive**. Beware of phenomenon, or marvelous circumstance, - beware of any miraculous developments either occurring in Nature or in man, because there exists a strong **probability** that there are **latent intentions** connected with these types of claims and evidences that seem to **constitute** the very elements of deception.

# Section 145

The ancients of mankind, yes those earliest of thinkers, thought the elephant was a **miraculous conception** of Nature, **believing** the animal possessed a spirit and also had reasoning abilities. The early race of man also thought that spirits communed with elephants, and also believing that the **spirits** instigated the elephants thoughts; and more, they were also believing that spirits, ghosts, witches, angels, devils, including many similar mysterious personages, all existed in great abundance.

There are persons **who-believe** that man is in **constant** communication with spirits, and those spirits are either of a good or evil character; and so they claim, the first spirit is that thing which causes all the **good** thoughts, and the other causes all **evil** thoughts. Those same persons **also-believe** that men possess the power to either move toward the pit and gulf of evil, or they can move toward the throne of goodness. And they say this power is termed "free-will".

Those people who claim this belief in "free-will", make man as a powerful, independent, and self-existent creature, and they fiercely **endeavor** to influence and impress upon man's mind their **peculiar reasoning**, claiming that if mankind is sinful it is merely the result of their will or a result of their affection for evil; and this peculiar reasoning **further claims** that this sinful quality which man possesses can be overcome and can halt, but **only-if** that person **desires** to be free from it by "faith". And furthermore, they claim and say that man can approach the throne or sphere of celestial goodness by the same process of simply exercising his own will-power to chose.

Well now, if mankind possessed such a "free will" as that, it **would-give** man unlimited control over the laws, forces, and actuating principles, of the Universe. Man would possess the power to resist all temptation, and be able to disregard all influences of eternal laws. It would give him power to command, and then, that action would teach him that he existed uncommanded. It would give him power to control, while at the same time, he would not be capable of being controlled, influenced, or actuated!

Some people have made **adjustments** in their **claim** of man possessing free-will by stating that man has "free-will" but it is only in a **qualified sense**. Those people say this because, the very moment an example is needed to prove their claim that man has free-will, well, all of a sudden this doctrine and this idea of free will is instantly proved to be **unsound** and somewhat **useless**, and in truth it shows that man's power is limited. **Because**, if man cannot under all circumstances and conditions resist being influenced or actuated by something, then the truth is known and it is clearly seen that the philosophy of man's "free will" is **not true**; because the fact is, that if man is **even-once** being influenced, then that action establishes the real truth, that man is **actuated** and motivated by **adequate forces** and governed throughout eternity by immutable laws.

There are other people, who say and **believe** that man may produce in himself the **power** of working miracles, and those people say that they have succeeded in presenting a demonstration. Still others, at the present day, **believe** that man does-not possess an inner spiritual principle which will retain its identity after the physical dissolution of the body or death occurs. Well, these minds do seem to reason by deductive reasoning, **but-not** analytically; and so, the conclusion is illegitimate and basically **unsound thinking**. Because man does posses an inner spiritual principle, yet it is still undeveloped.

It is best to know that there are existing numerous sects, entertaining as many different opinions; and know that each sect is **anxious** to sustain its own particular creed.

The followers of Ann Lee seriously **believe** and still to this day teach that, **select persons** among them commune with the spirits that inhabit celestial spheres. They frequently **induce**, by excitement, a cataleptic or trance condition of the body, and then **are-said** to be in heaven, walking among and talking with the angels. And when they return to their outward consciousness, they are able to relate these marvelous excursions to others, and doing it with all the seriousness and solemnity of truth – **because** they believe them.

If so many believe in miracles then surely miracles must exist in our midst somewhere, and are probably of the same character as those miracles mentioned in the book of Mark, which **he-claims**, are the things which should be believed and followed by all true believers. If this is true, then, is it **just-as** reasonable to admire and respect heathen, ancient, Chinese, Persianic, or Mohammedan, eagerness and give those believers the same respect and admiration which is given to those who eagerly believe and teach the doctrines of the Primitive History's Judea-Christian miracles? Should not a true believer also regard the Mormon and Shaker claims and evidences as reasonable and give that system of belief the exact same degree of veneration as is given to the things which are merely related in the books of the New Testament. Certainly **modern eagerness** is as much to be respected as ancient eagerness is respected.

Now progressing onward, to a further discussion of the writer of the Gospel of **Mark** personally: His name was John Mark. He was born, raised, and residing through his life in the city of Jerusalem. He lived at the time

John the Baptist and Jesus were preaching, He was a believer, and felt anxious to have the new faith spread, and so he sincerely made attempts for Christ's teachings it to be believed by all people; but he **can-not** be properly termed an apostle. He had a small family, and was pleasantly situated, prosperous in both the capacity of his residence and his financial affairs. He was accustomed to keeping-open his house as a place of entertainment and resort for Jesus and the apostles; and this action of Mark's continued during the whole public life of Jesus.

After the crucifixion and death of Jesus, John Mark **compiled** some of the remarks of Jesus, and also made some impressions concerning Jesus, from a few **official notes** which he had kept, **gathering** them into the form of a manuscript which he designed and **intended-only** for those new converts coming from paganism. But it should be remembered that most of the manuscripts written in those days, mostly upon bark or some similar substance, were **never-copied** as writings are now copied in modern days. So he alone possessed this record, and it was scarcely read or even known to be existing by any other persons other than those for whom it was immediately designed; and his manuscript remained unknown until a long period after his death. And exactly, **what-right** did Constantine and the bishops whom were assembled at the councils of **Nice** and **Laodicea**, have **to-vote** the book of Mark as canonical, and this action by the church is not very easily explained, especially for the fact that many similar manuscripts and epistle were easily rejected and were burned according to the decision that was made of those particular writings having similar misdirected judgments?

Mark **never-suggested** that he had desired or had intended that the world would read his historical impressions and thoughts, or for his writings to still be continued into the twenty-first century. So the question is, **why** is there such a superstitious worship of Mark's personal diary, which has been believed and sanctified by later generations who know nothing about him?

## Section 146

Now next, a brief review of the book of **Luke**, which follows: - Luke was a candid and worthy author. His writings show a good amount of candor, and he writes in a manner that is easy to understand. Luke approached his subject with seriousness, and he always intended truthfulness. His writings are based upon his own beliefs, and in the teachings of the Christ. Luke did not add any inspirational remarks into his knowledge, and does not give special favor to anyone. His writing style gives hints to the reader that he **wrote exactly** what was on his mind and wrote what he and many others around him most surely believed, shrugging-off any claims that have referenced his writings as being special or supernaturally inspired.

It is Bible **interpreters**, who sometimes have made **exaggerate claims**, stating **falsely** that the book is pure, and further stating that the Bible may contain a holy purity. **But**, the Bible **does-not** make this claim for itself. The Bible makes no claims of purity which are claimed and demand of it. There are some biblical commentators who have even accused Luke and some of the writings contained in Luke's Gospel, to be very critical and at times disrespectful to the book's holy purity which those particular interpreters have attach to the book; but instead they **should-defend** the Bible writers against claims of superstitious falsification.

The New Testament like all other books, should be respected for the natural worth and truthfulness which may characterize it, but for no other reason. **No-book**, or any other superficial production of man, can legitimately and truthfully **claim** to be inspired by the Divine Mind. It is best to realize, that nothing can be of divine origin **except** those things which are **completely connected** with the laws, qualities, and principles, **contained** in the great Tree of universal causation, which is God's Will. And **realize**, that many books may contain truth, yet no book is worthy of the veneration which the Mohammedan pays to the Koran, the Brahmin to the Shaster, the Persian to the Zend Avesta, the Jew to the Torah, or the Christian to the Bible.

The book of **Luke** does not quote prophecies, and the comments Luke does make are similar to the previous gospels. This book does not try to promote any new doctrines that would need to be explained. However, Luke does describe and use new **parabolical illustrations** with his writings.

Luke was of Jewish birth – was educated in the Jewish religion, who's teachings he continued to follow nearly to the time of Paul's conversion from the Jewish to the Christian religion. Luke in his early life learned a trade, which was the **custom** among the Jewish people whether the parents of the young were or were not wealthy. He was a successful artist and for this he was well respected in his profession. He is said to have painted the first portrait of Christ, which is to be seen at the present day in the Roman Academy of Design.

After Luke embraced the Christian religion he became very involved in its early works; he was reliable and a constant co-worker with many of the apostles and believers, spending most of his time in various portions of the eastern world. Luke personally **did-not** have his own first hand accounts, but instead, **relied upon** others for the information relating to Jesus, these accounts written by Luke came from his communications with eye-witnesses of those events. One of Luke's particular friends was Theophilus, whom Luke felt very anxious to convince of the truth of Christianity. It was to Theophilus that **Luke wrote** his gospel and the **Acts** of the Apostles; and interestingly, these books were written for **no-other** purpose than to produce a conviction in the mind of his close friend.

One special thing about Luke is that he absolutely **did-not** pretend to aspire to become seen as a gospel writer, nor would he want to become portrayed within the standard cyclopedia of theology. Anyhow there are some other writings of Luke's which are interesting: for instance, he wrote concerning the **origin** of the Ephesian church, explaining how it was established, what teachings and ceremonies were adopted, and he explained the process of how he and the brethren of the church celebrated each others initiation into the new faith. In general Luke's books are full of some good information and have purpose and they deserve respect.

## Section 147

Proceeding-on next to the book of **John**. This book displays warm-feelings, affection, and promotes a social and religious attachment. The book shows a good deal of respect towards others; it talks of aspirations, and it readily displays noble sentiments; and all these writings show the true character of the author as he lived his life. In the book of John, there are a few references to the prophets and prophesies of the Old Testament, but in general John's book **does-not** offer any new propositions that differ much from the preceding books. John does make one casual and unguarded statement, writing *"if all the things which Christ performed were written, even the world itself could not contain the books that would be written"*, and from the character of this statement it should be easy to see this sentence is meaningless.

John was born and resided most of his life in Ephesus. His early religious impressions were few, which led him to have an open mind, so when these things were presented to his mind, he would exercised a great deal of judgment and reflection about their merits before accepting any new doctrines.

His manuscripts, in a similar manner as Mark's were for a long time **hidden** from public observation, but were later translated into the Hebrew language. Later, they were sanctioned by the council of Nice, and finally sealed as canonical by the emperor Constantine, and were then presented to the world as constituting the fourth book of the New Testament.

The fifth book of the New Testament which follows John's Gospel, is entitled **Acts of the Apostles**. This book is a **historical commentary** and registral production of **Luke**. The book of Acts basically contains only a record of circumstances, experiences, travels, discussions, and the unpleasant circumstances that the Apostles endured. The book of Acts **only-claims** to be a book of historical information. It gives a description of the formation and **establishment** of the **church**. There are many descriptions of the unity and peace which prevailed among the early believers. However, there are no new doctrines or principles, requiring explanation.

# Section 148

And at this place, now brings our story to reflect on the birth, life, preaching, experience, disposition, and death, of a very highly-educated and much-loved writer. He contained purity of soul. He wrote many friendly epistles to his brethren and to their churches. Ecclesiastical historians have collected some very truthful information relating to the birth and life of **Paul**; and so the utmost **respect** is given to those historical accounts.

**Paul** was born in Tarsus. His early life he spent in Rome, and was much admired as a **well-respected** citizen of this Roman city. After receiving a superior education, he subjected himself to a long and protracted course of guidance and instruction of the teacher **Gamaliel** in Jerusalem.

Gamaliel was a professor of ancient literature, natural philosophy, and traditional science, and in addition he was recognized as a superior teacher of languages. He was a Jewish rabbin. From him, Paul received many doctrines and religious hypotheses, which afterward to a certain degree, gave Paul direction to his religious meditations and writings.

Paul was fond of the Grecian poets and philosophers, and it was from them that he received much of his inspirational thoughts along with methods of rational thinking and reasoning. Some traces of this early education can be seen, in the similarities of his writings in the New Testament, and also seen in many of those moral views of the Grecian poets.

After Paul had completed his education, he was truly a very **enlightened** man, at least according to the information that was available to him at the time. Peering into Paul's social life, would give the impression of a person whom could be said, was of a **very complex** character, which was the result of Paul's various experiences, those experiences both of a pleasing nature and disappointing nature, all leading to his social complexity which tended to modify and develop within him new traits of mental principles.

Paul, much like Luke, learned a useful trade, which was that of tentmaking, this skill Paul would later discover was useful and became a great advantage and had great importance to him. Being a Roman citizen for most of his life, his religion, his character, and his philosophy were much like any other Roman citizen. He was a pure, worthy, benevolent, and devotional, man, characterized by his superior qualifications all which constitute a truly great and good mind.

During the time that **Jesus** lived, and while Jesus's doctrines were being disseminated, **Paul** was a most **violent opposer**, both despising and rejecting those doctrines he would later embrace. This opposition continued for many years after the death of Christ. It was during this period

Paul embraced the **Pharisaical** philosophy. And soon after he joined this sect, he assumed the position of commander at the head of a group of men or army composed of the same sect, and with his army marched against and **persecuted** the Christian believers unjustly and without warrant. He actually was the **cause** of a great deal of violence and bloodshed against the Christians. He was both stern and arrogant with his opinions and principles.

There is a particular story that has been told for ages, which relates to Paul traveling to Damascus, where he experienced a sudden change in his motivations and intentions; and later, this occurrence has been related and described in such a manner as to imply and convey the **impression** that it proceeded from a miraculous or supernatural interference of the Divine Mind of God; which it did not.

However, it is only necessary to give the **true explanation** which will dispel and completely **dissipate** all superstitious ideas of a miraculous interposition by God. The true story is very basic and proceeds as follows: - "it was from this period in Paul's life when he was traveling, that, the inherent mental faculties of Paul **suddenly** took a different direction, and he became devoted to the Christian religion; the consequence of which was a violent denouncement of the doctrines and persecutions of his past life". Paul then rejected the Pharisaical doctrines, and now **devoted** the remaining thirty years of his life and talents to spread the Christian gospel. His **epistles** were generally **directed-to** the prominent members of the churches, and were also addressed indirectly to the whole congregation. Hence, some of those epistles were preserved, collected, compiled, and immersed into the New testament in the following order: - 1. Paul's Epistle to the Romans – 2. Paul's Epistles to the Corinthians – 3. Paul's Epistle to the Galatians – 4. Paul's Epistle to the Ephesians – 5. Paul's Epistle to the Philippians – 6. Paul's Epistle to the Colossians – 7. Paul writes two of many epistles to the Thessalonians – 8. Paul's epistles to his friend Timothy – 9. Paul's epistle to Titus – 10. Paul's Epistle to the Hebrews.

# Section 149

Paul's letters make-up a large portion of the a New Testament, and on investigation of these letters it appears plain that Paul **never-intended** or expected these writings to be universally read. These literary compositions to his friends and the churches, were mostly written for those persons whom those correspondences were addressed. Not only is the internal evidence of these letters sufficient to warrant this conclusion, but the historical evidence also entirely demonstrates this truth.

Some have **supposed** that an interior meaning is discoverable in every expression in the Bible, **but**, these people also believe that these interior meanings can-only be perceived by those who have a high degree of spiritual discernment – while others, whose knowledge is confined to the sensuous and earthy impressions are constantly interpreting the contents of the Bible in a more crude and literal manner.

The action of someone having a belief in hidden meanings within the Apostle's writings is attempting to clothe the Bible only in a spiritual garment, and this is only covering or concealing those crude expressions, which are sometimes loose, unguarded, and even insignificant,statements and concealing them so well, they are now **sugar-coated** with a brilliant external, superficial, and ornamental garment.

Another important point to make about the Bible itself, is that **language** has **changed**. Recall, the early inhabitants had used terms such as Venus, Mars, Juno, etc, to describe their gods, who supposedly were existing in the invisible world; also recall, that their history they preserved in hieroglyphs. **But-now** those same terms today are names of planets. And so the **issue** is that language has in its varied applications become extremely changed from the time-period the New Testament books were written. Therefore, **whatever** it was that the writers of Matthew, Mark, Luke, John, Christ, Paul, or any of the writers of the Bible, had previously written may have meant something different than it does now.

There is an important **distinction** between the **interior meaning** of a term or expression, as opposed to the use of the phrase within a **spiritual application** (which has also been called an **interior meaning**). In must be distinctly understood, that **no-mind** can search-into and analyze the interior meaning or **origin** of **words** or expressions, without arriving irresistibly at the conclusion which has been now attained – which is to know that the contents of the Bible, like those **words** of all other books, have most-likely originated among a number of causes; and then, all of these producing factors **must-be** taken into consideration before any validity or importance can be attached to the records of the Old or New Testaments, as well as any others of this type of book.

This much may be said to console those minds in need of comfort, know that Reason and Wisdom, like the sun, will shine and bring forth all desirable and congenial results, when the clouds of obstruction and misconception are dissipated for ever!

# Section 150

Within the ten books or epistles of **Paul** there has been no discovery of a different or distinct set of beliefs beyond what has been already given in the review of those book.

**Paul** was a good man – worthy of the greatest respect and confidence, the **new religion** coming into being he sincerely embraced. He was convinced that this "new faith" ought to be spread far and wide.

Paul is the **only writer** in the whole Bible who attempts to prove his faith by an appeal to Nature. His philosophy was evidently instilled upon his mind prior the him embracing Christianity: and in his Reasoning he would appealed to both external and visible events and actions occurring in Nature, and many times during discussions he would speak of Nature, just in order to illustrate and demonstrate his doctrines. He shared these thoughts with his brethren, but **never wrote** a system of moral philosophy to be taught and believed by further generations. At least not intentionally.

The doctrine of **the resurrection** – is a literal rising of the natural body - is believed literally by some, and those same people also believe Paul clearly and positively taught this doctrine. This, however, is a belief that is **not-true**; though sometimes, whenever this form of expression is used, someone may mistakenly believe this is evidence that there may be a belief in such a doctrine. He says, *"We are sown in a natural body, and raised in a spiritual body; we are sown in dishonor, and raised in glory"*, (1 Cor. xv). It is clear from these expressions, that Paul uses the terms natural and spiritual, dishonor and glory, by contrasting each with the other, and in doing-so what is noticed is that the superior item would be made more beautiful, by being place with an inferior item. And plus, realize, that Paul's thoughts were elevated by a high degree of hope and anticipations.

Paul was inclined to great internal meditation, this occurred because his peculiar temperament and disposition would admit to it. There were times that his contemplation and deep thinking were very instructive and beneficial, **but**, he sometimes became **confused** with the **dilemma** of the two opposing forces, or intrusions of the outer world upon the senses, affections, and passions, in contrast with the promptings and warnings of the internal sense of purity, justice, refinement, and righteousness.

**Somehow**, from some of Paul's expressions, theological speculators have derived, "a smoothly-woven theory" that is **claimed** to exist, and this theory believes that a pervading **evil spirit**, or his agents, are incessantly affecting man's internal purity through the outer world of materialism and sensuality; and that the good is preserved by the Divine Mind. And then continuing with this hypothesis, Paul's writings say, that man should distinguish the good from the evil – distinguish the broad road which leads to a burning abyss of everlasting destruction - from the narrow and straight path leading as far away-from that dreadful abode, even going as far away from one extremity of the Universe as can be from another. With that type of hypothesis, those **theological theorists** throw the responsibility on man, and accuse him of being immoral. And then, at the same time teach man that ten thousand influences are harping upon him and even trying to control him, either for good or for evil. It is plain that such a **peculiar thought process** not only shows a **complete misunderstanding** of the writings and teachings of Paul, but also, it shows those speculators **do-not** correctly know the nature, constitution or characteristics of mankind.

Paul, after having preached for thirty years he found peace knowing that he had "declared" the whole gospel without reservation. It was at this time he was captured, and brought before a Roman consul, and then he soon came before **Festus**; whom absolve Paul of the charge. Paul, however, had already also appealed to **Caesar**, so he was sent to Rome, where he finally died, a martyr to Christianity.

Following the epistles of Paul, are the similar letters of **James, Peter, John,** and **Jude.** The contents of these are very similar to the letters of Paul, pertaining to the same general principles. These letters do not have any new principles, and their teachings have no important bearing on what had already been written in the preceding books of the New Testament.

# Section 151

After the epistles, follows the **Apocalypse** or **Revelation of St John**. The contents of this book have appeared to everyone as being difficult to interpret, hard to understand, and mysterious, and are beyond the possibility of giving any use or having any application. To some Revelation is so obscure, as to defy any attempts of analysis.

The book **seemingly** does bear every mark of truly being a revelation. And even after careful reading and study, it continues to have the illusion of a true revelation. **However**, what is most featured in this book are obscurity, ambiguity, and to giving descriptions of fantastic and figurative expressions. There probably is nothing more **obscure** than this revelation, because its contents **defy interpretation**, though at the same time there is the demand of the most and unreserved faith. And then, in addition to the fact that to read and understand this book requires a great deal of faith, the book forbids the erasure or insertion of a single sentence; this is a demand which is **more-likely** to be **man-made**. It **does-not** make the least bit of sense that God would state this kind of demand, and such a demand in-itself surely removes any celestial purity which would be expected. This book ends the New Testament.

There is a great deal of doubt in the minds of investigators as to the authenticity of the books of James and Jude. Actually, these books, together with the Revelation of St John, were not voted upon and received into the New Testament as being pure and canonical, **until** nearly three hundred years after the council of Nice. The Apocalypse and the books of James and Jude, together with the second chapter of the second epistle of Peter, were voted pure and canonical in the year 633 AD, at the **council of Toledo**. In this particular year in the council's seventeenth canon, it had been decided unanimously that the Revelation was written by John, and that the books of James and John should be compiled and written into the New Testament, and should be stamped with the holy seal, and considered the Word of God!

If the council at Toledo had simply followed suit and **had-rejected** these books as did the council of Nice, and also as did the council of Laodicea, then a great amount of suffering by mankind would have been prevented. However simply for the fact that the Apocalypse was accepted into the Testament, it is worthy of some review.

This is the end of the old and the beginning of the new.